Proceedings of the 1988 International Conference
of Services Marketing

Developments in Marketing Science: Proceedings of the Academy of Marketing Science

More information about this series at http://www.springer.com/series/13409

Edward G. Thomas and S.R. Rao *Editors*

Proceedings of the 1988 International Conference of Services Marketing

Cleveland, Ohio

October 26-28, 1988

Editors
Edward G. Thomas
Cleveland State University
Cleveland, OH, USA

S.R. Rao
Cleveland State University
Cleveland, OH, USA

Reprint from Original edition
International Conference on Services Marketing: Special Conference Series, Volume V edited by
Edward G. Thomas and S.R. Rao
Copyright © Academy of Marketing Science 1988
All rights reserved.

Developments in Marketing Science: Proceedings of the Academy of Marketing Science
ISBN 978-3-319-17316-0   ISBN 978-3-319-17317-7   (eBook)
DOI 10.1007/978-3-319-17317-7

Library of Congress Control Number: 2015938798

Springer Cham Heidelberg New York Dordrecht London
© Academy of Marketing Science 2015

Printed on acid-free paper

Springer International Publishing AG Switzerland is part of Springer Science+Business Media (www.springer.com)

SPECIAL ACKNOWLEDGMENTS

SPONSORING AND COOPERATING ORGANIZATIONS

Department of Marketing, Cleveland State University
Academy of Marketing Science
Association of Travel Marketing Executives

SESSION CHAIRPERSONS

Sheila J. Backman, University of Illinois
V. V. Bellur, California State University, Bakersfield
James M. Daley, John Carroll University
Linda Delene, Western Michigan University
Peter Everett, Pennsylvania State University
Terrence J. Kearney, Marquette University
Paul M. Lane, Western Michigan University
Pavlos Michaels, Marshall University
Joseph L. Orsini, California State University, Sacramento
V. Kanti Prasad, University of Wisconsin-Milwaukee
Duane R. Prokop, Gannon University
Wolfgang Schmidt, Canadian Travel Press
Edward G. Thomas, Cleveland State University

PANELISTS

James J. Carroll, Pepperdine University
Lance P. Jarvis, University of Central Florida
Edward J. Mayo, Western Michigan University
C. P. Rao, University of Arkansas
JanHendrik A. Vroom, California State University, San Bernardino
Thomas W. Whipple, Cleveland State University

DISCUSSANTS

John T. Bowen, University of Houston
James J. Carroll, Pepperdine University
Tim R.V. Davis, Cleveland State University
Gideon Falk, Purdue University Calumet
Jeffery M. Ferguson, University of Colorado at Colorado Springs
David C. Gilbert, University of Surrey
Rajshekhar G. Javalgi, Cleveland State University
W. Benoy Joseph, Cleveland State University
Lance A. Masters, California State University, San Bernardino
John Walsh, Wilfrid Laurier University
Ronald Zallocco, The University of Toledo

CONFERENCE PAPER REVIEWERS

Sheila J. Backman, University of Illinois at Urbana-Champaign
V. V. Bellur, California State University, Bakersfield
Barry Berman, Hofstra University
John T. Bowen, University of Houston
Tom A. Buckles, California State University, Fullerton
David J. Burns, Purdue University
David P. Campbell, University of Alabama at Huntsville
James J. Carroll, Pepperdine University
James M. Daley, John Carroll University
Tim R.V. Davis, Cleveland State University
Linda Delene, Western Michigan University
Jeffery M. Ferguson, University of Colorado at Colorado Springs
Jon Hawes, The University of Akron
Tony L. Henthorne, University of Southern Mississippi
Lance P. Jarvis, University of Central Florida
Rajshekhar G. Javalgi, Cleveland State University
W. Benoy Joseph, Cleveland State University
M. Sami Kassem, The University of Toledo
Terrence J. Kearney, Marquette University
Paul M. Lane, Western Michigan University
Lance A. Masters, California State University, San Bernardino
Edward J. Mayo, Western Michigan University
Pavlos Michaels, Marshall University
Joseph L. Orsini, California State University, Sacramento
V. Kanti Prasad, University of Wisconsin-Milwaukee
Duane R. Prokop, Gannon University
C. P. Rao, University of Arkansas
Benjamin Sackmary, Buffalo State College
Margery Steinberg, University of Hartford
Sharon V. Thach, Cleveland State University
Mark B. Traylor, Cleveland State University
Muzaffer Uysal, Clemson University
Thomas W. Whipple, Cleveland State University

REVIEWERS FOR "BEST CONFERENCE PAPER" AWARD

Raj Aggarwal, John Carroll University
Barry Berman, Hofstra University
Naresh Malhotra, Georgia Institute of Technology

TABLE OF CONTENTS

Papers From Opening Competitive Paper Session

Paper From Services Marketing Curriculum Workshop

Papers From Competitive Paper Session A:

TRAVEL AND TOURISM

Papers From Competitive Paper Session B:

LEISURE AND RECREATION

HOW FAST CAN A SERVICE FIRM GROW?

Edward J. Mayo
Western Michigan University

Lance P. Jarvis
University of Central Florida

Paul A. Lane
Western Michigan University

Abstract

The capacity for firms to grow in the rapidly expanding service sector is examined using the concept of sustainable growth (g*). g* indicates how rapidly a firm's sales can increase while it finances required new assets through additions to retained earnings and new debt alone. g* and its components are examined across 42 service industries and the manufacturing sector for 1986. Average sustainable growth levels in the service sector exceed those found in manufacturing. g* is higher for people-based services than for equipment-based services. Although g* may approximate growth capacity for equipment-based services, other non-financial factors constrain growth capacity in people-based service businesses.

The growing body of literature dealing with the marketing of services during the past decade has clearly shown that service marketing is different. Marketing automobiles or toothpaste is different in many important ways from marketing drug addiction therapy, money market accounts, or family vacations to Walt Disney World.

Important commonalities remain, of course, and these include sales growth and earnings as important organizational objectives. Whether it markets a tangible good or an intangible service, year-to-year sales and earnings growth remain high on the list of marketing and financial objectives for many firms. Unrestrained growth, however, is often inconsistent with sound financial management. At the extreme, the firm experiencing growth beyond its ability to prudently finance such gains has the potential to literally "go broke." This important issue has been studied by others (Higgins and Kerin 1983; Higgins 1977; McCammon and Bates 1977; Robinson 1979), but the focus has not been on firms that market intangible services.

That the service sector of the economy is growing at a much faster pace than the industrial sector is well documented. And it is anticipated that growth in the demand for services will continue to outpace growth in the demand for most tangible goods. The central question posed in this paper is this: how rapidly can service businesses grow and simultaneously maintain financial stability? The answer to this question is addressed by focusing on the concept and measurement of sustainable growth in a service firm context.

1

SUSTAINABLE GROWTH

Sales growth creates a continuous demand for funds to finance that growth. To increase sales, a service firm may, for example, have to increase its cash position, its accounts receivables, and its investment in fixed assets. Potential sources of financing include both internal and external sources -- although most companies prefer, for a variety of reasons, not to resort to issuing new equity to finance their growth (Harrington and Wilson 1983, p. 132). Indeed, this option does not realistically exist for the many service firms organized as individual proprietorships and partnerships.

The typical service firm then must finance its growth through internally generated funds and debt. Conceptually, the sustainable growth rate is the maximum annual sales growth that a firm can support using these two sources of financing. Sustainable growth, it should be noted, has gained increasing prominence as a managerial financial and operating tool in recent years, according to Higgins and Kerin (1983). Furthermore, it has helped to underscore the fact that rapid sales increases are not always a blessing.

Sustainable growth is a tool, then, for assessing how rapidly a firm's sales can increase while it finances required new assets through additions to retained earnings (net income) and new debt alone. Growth is, of course, financed through cash flow rather than net income, per se. However, to keep the sustainable growth model in a simple form, net income will be considered equivalent to cash flow by restricting the analysis to a steady-state situation in which depreciation provides cash flow that must be reinvested in new assets to maintain the existing level of sales (Higgins, 1977, p. 8). (See Higgins (p. 15) for a more complex model that relaxes this restriction.)

Mathematically, the rate of sustainable growth (g*) is expressed as follows (Higgins and Kerin 1983; Higgins 1977):

$$g* = P \times R \times A \times T$$

where g* = sustainable sales growth expressed as a percentage

  P = profit margin after taxes

  R = retention ratio, or fraction of earnings retained in the business

  A = 1 + debt/equity = assets/equity, or financial leverage

  T = sales/assets, or asset turnover

To illustrate, the sustainable growth rate is shown for the average Standard & Poor industrial firm in 1986. In that year, profit margin = 3.8%, retention ratio = 48%, debt-to-equity ratio = 121%, and sales-to-asset ratio = 120%. Solving for sustainable growth,

2

$$g^* = .038 \times .48 \times 2.21 \times 1.2 = .05$$

For the typical manufacturing firm in 1986, therefore, in the absence of new equity financing, the only growth rate in sales that is consistent with stable values of P, R, A, and T was 5 percent.

If the typical manufacturing firm experienced an actual growth rate below 5 percent, it would have had more than enough capital to meet its investment needs. Leftover capital could have been used to increase liquid assets, reduce debt, or increase dividends.

If, on the other hand, the typical manufacturing firm experienced an actual growth rate in excess of 5 percent, it may have incurred a serious set of problems. To finance growth beyond 5 percent, the firm would have had to do one or more of the following:

(1) increase P (improve its profit margin)
(2) increase T (improve asset productivity by increasing its sales/asset ratio)
(3) increase R (reduce its dividend rate)
(4) increase A (increase its debt)

The first two options, of course, represent operating solutions to the sustainable growth problem by increasing the firm's efficiency and effectiveness through achieving a higher return on assets. If these options were not achievable, then the firm would have had to employ one or both of the remaining two options -- and this may have been difficult, unwise, or otherwise infeasible. Finally, should none of the options prove tractable and the firm be averse to new equity as a means to achieve desired growth, it would have to realize a growth rate less than that of the market as a whole, thereby experiencing a decline in market share.

In short, if sales expand too rapidly, something often has to give -- usually to the detriment of financial soundness (Higgins 1977, p. 7). For a firm that desires to maintain a target dividend payout ratio and capital structure without issuing new equity, sustainable growth addresses the question: how much growth can the firm afford?

At first glance, it might appear that the sustainable growth question is germane to financial managers but not so to marketing decision makers. As a practical matter, of course, nothing could be further from the truth. The situation analysis preceding the development of marketing objectives and strategies must, inevitably, consider the firm's financial resources and capabilities.

The firm's sustainable growth rate, then, is a significant factor in the processes of setting marketing objectives and developing marketing strategies. Anderson (1979) underscored the necessary interface between marketing management and finance in this way:

3

Too often marketing tends to focus on sales growth or market share and it fails to recognize the impact of marketing decisions on such variables as inventory levels, working capital needs, financing costs, debt-to-equity ratios, and stock prices. To assume that such factors are purely the responsibility of finance is to be guilty of a kind of marketing myopia no less damaging than that originally envisioned by Levitt (1960).

The remainder of this paper: (a) compares sustainable growth levels across a variety of service industries (and with the manufacturing sector); (b) examines some reasons for differences in the sustainable growth rates among service industries; and, (c) suggests other non-financial factors that serve to limit short-term growth potential for firms in some areas of the service economy.

SUSTAINABLE GROWTH IN THE SERVICE SECTOR

Table 1 lists 42 service sector industries for which financial and operating data are published regularly by the Federal Trade Commission. These 42 industries are arranged in order from those with the highest g*'s to those with the lowest. A number of interesting observations emerge from an examination of the data in this exhibit and also Table 2.

Services vs. Manufacturing

Table 2 shows that the "average" service sector business could have sustained growth through leveraged assets and retained earnings of 28 percent in 1986. This compares with the 5 percent level of sustainable growth computed earlier for the manufacturing sector of the U.S. economy. Intuitively, the large difference between the two g*'s may come as no surprise. After all, the service sector of the U.S. economy, fueled by rapidly increasing demand, has been growing at a much faster pace than the manufacturing sector for a number of years. Nevertheless, this does not explain why the sustainable growth potential is so much higher in the service sector. In order to understand why the service sector has been in a position to respond to this growth in demand, one has to examine the individual components of the sustainable growth model for the average service sector firm.

First, it is noted that the average service firm in 1986 appears to have employed its assets more productively (T = sales/assets) than the average S & P industrial firm. In addition, the average service firm appears to have leveraged its assets to a greater extent than the average S & P firm (A = 1 + debt/equity = assets/equity).

Caution is necessary, however, in interpreting these findings. Because some service firms make heavy use of assets that are "hidden," financial leverage (A) and asset turnover (T) may be inflated in other than accounting terms. That is, for many service providers, the primary "assets" of the enterprise are the skills of the person providing the service. These are not, of course,

TABLE 1

Sustainable Growth Rate and its Components Across SIC Service Sectors for 1986

SIC	Industry	Industry Average				
		P	R	A	T	g*
8111	Legal Services	16.2	.98	2.23	3.6	1.27
8021	Dentists	10.3	.94	3.00	3.0	.87
7361	Employment Agencies	7.3	.77	2.54	5.0	.71
8011	Physicians	7.8	.96	2.46	3.5	.64
7231	Hair Stylists	8.1	.73	2.70	3.5	.56
8931	Accounting/Bookkeeping	14.4	.72	2.00	2.2	.46
7221	Photographic Studios	8.5	.73	3.22	2.3	.46
7342	Exterminating Services	8.0	.77	2.31	3.1	.44
7311	Advertising Agencies	5.4	.65	3.91	3.2	.44
7538	Auto Repair - General	6.2	.77	2.99	3.0	.43
7393	Protection Agencies	5.2	.76	2.83	3.5	.39
7362	Temporary Help Services	4.1	.77	2.38	5.1	.38
7392	Consulting & P.R. Services	7.3	.76	2.68	2.5	.37
8071	Medical Laboratories	6.7	.84	2.94	2.2	.36
7372	Computer Software Services	7.4	.77	2.73	2.2	.34
8911	Engineering/Architectural	6.5	.82	2.60	2.3	.32
7542	Car Washes	6.0	.77	3.07	2.2	.31
7395	Photofinishing Labs	5.5	.76	3.23	2.1	.28
7814	Motion Picture/Tape Prod.	7.6	.73	2.78	1.8	.28
7331	Direct Mail Advertising	5.8	.65	2.95	2.3	.26
4119	Local Transport. Services	5.9	.71	2.79	2.1	.25
7334	Data Processing Services	6.6	.77	2.56	1.9	.25
6531	Real Estate Agents/Brokers	8.0	.99	3.13	1.0	.25
4712	Freight Forwarding	4.7	.64	3.05	2.7	.25
7211	Laundries/Dry Cleaners	6.0	.73	2.62	2.1	.24
7261	Funeral Services	9.8	.73	2.63	1.2	.23
7312	Outdoor Advertising	7.5	.65	3.97	1.2	.23
4722	Travel Agencies	3.7	.55	3.56	3.2	.23
4151	School Busing	6.6	.77	2.49	1.5	.19
7999	Skating Rinks	8.5	.68	3.26	1.0	.19
7299	Health & Fitness Clubs	8.6	.73	2.66	1.1	.18
4511	Air Transportation	3.2	.88	3.80	1.6	.17
6411	Insurance Agents/Brokers	8.0	.43	4.85	1.0	.17
4221	Farm Product Warehousing	4.8	.78	2.74	1.6	.16
4213	Long-distance Trucking	3.3	.57	2.98	2.5	.14
4811	Telephone Communication	14.2	.29	3.02	1.1	.14
7011	Hotels & Motels	5.0	.65	4.41	0.8	.11
8051	Nursing Homes	3.1	.61	4.48	1.2	.10
7996	Amusement Parks	3.1	.72	3.11	1.3	.09
7832	Motion Picture Theaters	2.3	.83	3.21	1.4	.09
4832	Radio Broadcasting	4.1	.70	2.88	1.0	.08
4222	Refrigerated Warehousing	6.3	.57	2.78	0.8	.08
4953	Refuse Systems	7.0	.23	2.78	1.6	.07
4899	Cable T.V.	3.5	.67	4.39	0.6	.06
7997	Membership Sports Clubs	3.8	.68	2.01	0.7	.04
4833	Television Stations	1.4	.71	3.56	0.8	.03
4131	Intercity Ground Transport.	0.9	.77	2.46	1.4	.02

5

TABLE 2

Sustainable Growth Rates in the Service
and Manufacturing Sectors for 1986

	P		R		A		T		g*
Average Service Firm	6.5	x	.71	x	3.02	x	2.0	=	.28
Average S & P Firm	3.8	x	.48	x	2.21	x	1.2	=	.05

reflected in the financial asset base of the business, thereby overstating (A) and (T). At the same time, however, for many manufacturing firms the book value of assets is undervalued relative to their market or replacement value, resulting in similar effects for A and T in this sector, too.

What is clear from Table 2 is that the average service firm earned higher after-tax profits (P) and also retained a higher percentage of its earnings (R) than the average industrial firm. There may be any number of reasons for this. One would expect, for example, P to be higher for a firm in a sector of the economy where demand was expanding rapidly. Profit margins might also be expected to be higher in many service industries because they are, by and large, insulated from foreign competition.

Presumably, many service firms -- due to limited ownership -- also have greater control over the percentage of earnings retained in the business (R) than the typical S & P industrial firm. In addition, the more rapid growth in the service sector should require a higher earnings retention rate to fuel such activity.

All in all, it is evident that most service industries are in a position to grow faster than the typical manufacturing firm. For the foreseeable future, most appear to be capable of sustaining growth at levels of demand that might be reasonably anticipated. This is not the case, obviously, for the typical industrial firm -- even one facing significant growth opportunities.

Differences Among High and Low Sustainable Growth Service Firms

Scanning Table 1 from top to bottom, it becomes evident that there is a pattern to the order in which the various service industries are arrayed. In fact, the ranking by g* value corresponds with the conceptual model developed by Thomas (1978) for classifying services into a continuum according to whether they are "people-based" or "equipment-based." High g* value industries which appear at the top of the list tend to be those of a personal service nature where people are the instrumental service providers. Low g* value industries, on the other hand, which appear at the bottom of Table 1, tend to be those where a significant amount of tangible assets is necessary to deliver the service.

It appears, then, that g*'s are inversely related to the asset intensity required to render the service. This point is further underscored by looking at the positive relationship between T (asset turnover) and g*: high asset turnover ratios are characteristic of service industries with high sustainable growth. As will be explained later, however, the g* value does not encompass all of the factors needed to assess growth potential in a service industry sector.

An obvious point, but one that needs to be made here anyway, is that firms in service industries near the bottom of Exhibit 1 tend to display a great deal of similarity to S & P manufacturing firms in terms of values for specific components of the sustainable growth model. When it comes to managing growth in these low g* service businesses, they will need to be managed much like an S & P industrial firm might. High g* service firms, on the other hand, present very different growth management challenges.

Obstacles to Growth in the Service Sector: g* and Beyond

Much of what has been discussed thus far may be better understood if the challenges to growth in two very different service businesses are examined: a legal service practice (representing a high g* business that is a people-based service) and a hotel company (representing a low g* business that can offer its service only through heavy investment in fixed assets). The components of sustainable growth for these two businesses are presented in Table 3.

Actual growth in any industry will be limited, of course, by growth in market demand. Other important factors that will limit a particular firm's actual growth include the effectiveness of its marketing strategy, as well as the entry of new competitors and actions of other firms which may limit the firm's market share potential. For the present purposes, however, these and other constraints to growth are set aside and, instead, the firm's capacity to grow is examined.

TABLE 3

Sustainable Growth Rates in the Legal
Services and Hotel Industries for 1986

	P		R		A		T		g*
Legal Service Practice	16.2	x	.98	x	2.23	x	3.6	=	1.27
Hotel Company	5.0	x	.65	x	4.41	x	0.8	=	.11

In 1986, g* for the hotel industry was .11. The profit margin for the typical firm in this mature industry was a modest 5 percent, and its sales/asset ratio was 0.8 (a figure that has remained the same for this industry since at least 1976). Thus, increasing its growth potential by improving its operating performance -- through improved margins or asset turnover -- may not offer very much hope to the typical hotel firm competing in a monopolistically competitive market.

Improvements in g* for the "average" hotel company must come instead from either decreases in the dividend rate or else increases in debt. Retaining all earnings (i.e., setting R = 1.00), while holding financial leverage constant would increase the aggregate industry g* to a maximum of .18. One of the most successful companies in the hotel industry, the Marriott Corporation, has fueled its rapid expansion over the past decade in this manner, but presumably many other firms do not have the flexibility to retain all of their earnings.

Alternatively, the hotel firm could leave its dividend rate alone and rely on increased leverage. This, of course, has been the historical pattern in this industry. If we hold P, R, and T constant at the values in Exhibit 3 and raise A to its historic high of the last ten years (6.06), g* increases to .16. Before taking this action, however, the hotel firm would have to carefully assess just how far it can stretch its reserve borrowing capacity.

The typical legal service practice firm faces a very different set of sustainable growth problems. The average legal service organization had enormous capacity to grow in 1986. With g* = 1.27, it had the financial capability to more than double its business by relying entirely on retained earnings and debt. It is probably not surprising that actual growth in the legal service industry came no where near its sustainable growth potential. Nevertheless, actual growth in 1986 was a healthy 14 percent (U.S. Industrial Outlook, 1988).

Aside from the financial considerations encompassed in g*, the capacity for growth in many personal service firms will be hampered by limits on their ability to enjoy significant economies of scale or to mechanize much of their "production."

Perhaps the most severe constraint that will limit the growth of a legal service practice as well as other "high touch" personal service businesses, is the scarcity of time. That is, there is a limit to just how much work a professional staff can accomplish -- and, beyond this limit, the firm can only grow by adding to its staff. Its actual growth, then, will be further influenced by the availability of qualified professionals and the firm's ability to attract them. (Unlike the hotel company, however, the legal service firm can expand its "capacity" without having to invest a great deal of up-front capital, which is a key reason for this service sector's high g*.)

In addition, the personal service provider is typically an individual owner, partnership, or small private corporation with no outside shareholders. The incentives to grow, therefore, are not influenced by the necessity to maximize the wealth of shareholders who are not direct participants in the enterprise itself. The service organization owner's personal goal of achieving a "satisfactory" income rather than the maximum wealth possible, too, may limit the firm's growth potential to well below g* levels.

CONCLUSION

Continued growth in the service sector requires that firms participating in such industries maintain financial stability while financing the assets necessary to achieve their growth potential. Sustainable growth (g*) is a tool for assessing how rapidly a firm's sales can grow while it finances its required new assets through additions to retained earnings and new debt alone.

In comparing sustainable growth rates across 42 different service industries and the manufacturing sector, several conclusions appear warranted:

1. The g* in the service sector presently exceeds that found in the manufacturing sector.

2. Within the service sector, higher sustainable growth rates are associated with people-based services requiring low asset intensity than with equipment-based, asset-intensive service industries.

3. The g*'s found across most service industries reveal that the "average" firm is capable of sustaining growth at levels of demand that might be reasonably anticipated.

Sustainable growth has previously been used to analyze retailing and manufacturing enterprises. The present paper represents, to the authors' knowledge, the first effort to apply the concept to a broad array of service businesses. While g* provides management with a "first cut" at assessing growth capacity in a service business, it does not address several key non-financial issues that may limit short-term growth potential in a people-based service organization. Several such factors include: (a) the scarcity of time available to a skilled personal service provider and the difficulty of adding additional "capacity" through attracting compatible, capable personnel; (b) limitations on mechanizing the "production" of services in such a setting; (c) limits on the ability to achieve significant economies of scale; and (d) "satisficing" behavior by owners of such businesses who are not responsible to outside stockholders for their performance.

Further research in this area would appear to be both warranted and productive. The present paper has drawn tentative conclusions based on one year of data. Longitudinal comparisons of individual service sector growth rates with their g* values and components for corresponding periods would help to understand what financial and marketing strategies service organizations do use to address the growth opportunities facing them.

REFERENCES

Analysts' Handbook, Composite Corporate Per Share Data - By Industries. 1987. New York: Standard & Poor's Corporation.

Anderson, Paul. 1979. "The Marketing Management/Finance Interface." Proceedings of the American Marketing Association Educator's Conference. Chicago: American Marketing Association, 325-329.

Annual Statement Studies. 1987. Philadelphia: Robert Morris Associates.

Harrington, Diana R., and Brent D. Wilson. 1983. Corporate Financial Analysis. Plano, Texas: Business Publications, Inc.

Higgins, Robert. 1977. "How Much Growth Can a Firm Afford?" Financial Management (Autumn), 7-16.

_____, and Roger Kerin. 1983. "Managing the Growth-Financial Policy Nexus in Retailing." Journal of Retailing (Fall), 19-48.

Industry Norms and Key Business Ratios. 1987. New York: Dun & Bradstreet.

Levitt, T. 1960. "Marketing Myopia." Harvard Business Review, (July-August), 24 ff.

McCammon, B., Jr., and A. Bates. 1977. "Reseller Strategies and the Financial Performance of the Firm." in H. Thorelli (ed.), Strategy + Structure = Performance. Bloomington: Indiana University Press, 146-64.

Quarterly Financial Report for Manufacturing, Mining, and Trade Corporations. 1987. Washington, D.C.: Federal Trade Commission.

Robinson, S.J.Q. 1979. "What Growth Rate Can You Achieve?" Long Range Planning (August), 7-12.

Thomas, Dan R. E. 1978. "Strategy is Different in Service Businesses." Harvard Business Review (July-August), 158-65.

Troy, Leo. 1987. Almanac of Business and Industrial Financial Ratios. Englewood Cliffs, New Jersey: Prentice-Hall, Inc.

U.S. Industrial Outlook. 1988. Washington, D.C.: U.S. Department of Commerce.

10

A LIFE CYCLE SEGMENTATION APPROACH TO MARKETING FINANCIAL PRODUCTS AND SERVICES

Rajshekhar G. Javalgi
Cleveland State University

Joseph J. Belonax, Jr.
Western Michigan University

V. Kanti Prasad
University of Wisconsin-Milwaukee

S. R. Rao
Cleveland State University

ABSTRACT

State-of-the-art market segmentation is becoming an important strategic tool in the continuing evolution of the financial services industry. This paper, focusing on a life cycle segmentation approach, indicates that the importance attributed to financial choice criteria and financial services varies as consumers pass through an orderly progression of life cycle stages. Thus, the results suggest that marketers in the financial services industry should adopt a life-cycle marketing based system to more fully satisfy the needs/wants of their customers.

INTRODUCTION

Deregulation, technological advances, new economics of scale, increased competition, shifts in the population's age distribution and the changing structure of the family have altered the structure of the financial services industry. Today, the depository institutions (banks, savings and loans, and credit unions) are being challenged by unregulated non-depository institutions (Sears, American Express, Merrill Lynch, Prudential Bache, etc.). In addition, these changes have altered how institutions function in the financial services marketplace. Increasingly, the services being provided by some financial institutions are being duplicated by others. The financial services industry is becoming so undifferentiated in terms of product/services, pricing, distribution and promotion it has led some authors to believe that in the "minds of consumers" financial institutions are all banks (Donnelly, Berry and Thompson 1987). How does a financial institution successfully differentiate itself in this environment?

11

To begin with, financial decision makers must recognize that they can no longer be all things to all people. But they can be very special to a very special group. Strategically then, financial institutions must engage in, (1) a carefully designed, well researched market segmentation analysis, and (2) thoughtfully conceived marketing strategies for each of the profitable market segments.

Kotler and Bloom (1984) note that "there is no single way to segment a market. An organization has to try different segmentation variables, singly and in combination, hoping to view the market structure." Over the years, demographics have gained broad acceptance for segmentation and have lent themselves easily to consumer classification in order to warrant different marketing strategies. However, it is acknowledged that "isolated demographic variables, such as age, income, educational level, and marital status, individually do not predict which financial services consumers will use" (Yaegel 1987). Rather, it is suggested that "the greatest indicator of financial service usage is made up of a combination of demographics variables generally referred to as "family life cycles" (Yaegel 1987). Changes in family life cycle stages give rise to differences in financial service needs. These differences, in turn, provide marketers with important guidelines for developing market strategies for each of the segments or stages of the family life cycle (FLC).

Conceptualizations of the FLC differs primarily in the number of stages. However, there is a general consensus among researchers on the central idea: that each family passes through a number of distinct stages from its point of formation to its ultimate demise. (Derrick & Lehfeld 1980; Murphy & Staples 1979; Feldman & Feldman 1975; Glick 1977; Jain 1975). The most comprehensive work applying the FLC concept to consumer behavior was presented by Wells and Gubar (1966). Their study reported on consumption behavior across the FLC stages. They identified nine stages, (1) the bachelor stage: young, single people not living at home, (2) newly-married couples: young, no children, (3) full nest I: youngest child under six, (4) full nest II: youngest child six or over, (5) full nest III: older married couples with dependent children, (6) empty nest I: older married couples, no children living with them, head in labor force, (7) empty nest II: no children living at home, head retired, (8) solitary survivor, in labor force, (9) solitary survivor retired.

As individuals enter the financial services market, in particular the banking market, they enter with certain specific wants and needs to be satisfied. The bank marketer must identify how consumer financial needs change through the various stages of the life cycle in order to develop effective marketing strategies. Accordingly, the two broadly stated research goals of this study are: (1) to determine whether the relative importance of the choice criteria, underlying the decision to select a primary financial institution, varies according to stages in the FLC, and (2) to determine whether the relative importance of financial services varies according to stages in the FLC.

12

METHODOLOGY

The initial task was to identify the factors which influenced a consumers' selection of a primary financial institution; i.e., bank. This task was achieved by means of preliminary interviews and a review of the relevant literature (Anderson, Cox, and Fulcher 1976; Dupuy and Kehoe 1976). The concern was to include those attributes perceived by customers to be salient in evaluating a primary financial institution. Eighteen attributes were included in this study (see Table 1) Questionnaires pertaining to the key substantive criteria were constructed, and a nationally respected marketing research firm was employed to administer the mail questionnaire. A total of 3,100 surveys were mailed to a randomly selected sample of the population, drawn from a telephone directory of the Standard Metropolitan Statistical Area, where competition among banks and other financial services providers is intense.

Each respondent was asked to rate the relative importance of eighteen product/ service characteristics in determining their choice of banks. An eight-point scale, ranging from (1) not at all important to (8) extremely important, was used. Each respondent was also asked to rate the relative importance of thirteen services that financial services institutions presently offer or might offer in the immediate future. A five point scale, ranging from (1) not at all important to (5) extremely important, was used. A $1 incentive was offered to encourage respondents to complete and return the questionnaire. The total number of responses was 915 (30%). A total of 44 were not complete, leaving 871 respondents for analysis, of which 110 were in life-cycle Stage 1 (bachelor stage: young, single people not living at home), 186 were in Stage 2 (newly married couples: young, no children), 90 were in Stage 3 (full nest I: youngest child under 6), 103 were in Stage 4 (full nest II: youngest child six or over), 101 were in Stage 5 (full nest III: older married couples with dependent children), 104 were in Stage 6 (empty nest I: older married couples, no children living with them, head in labor force), 158 were in Stage 7 (empty nest II: older married, no children living at home, head retired), 10 were in Stage 8 (solitary survivors and in the labor force), and 9 were in Stage 9 (solitary survivors and retired). These last two stages of solitary survivors were eliminated as there were only 19 in the data base. Thus, in the study the first seven stages of the life cycle were used for the empirical analysis.

ANALYSES AND RESULTS

Relative Importance of Choice Criteria For Each Life-Cycle Segment

To identify the relative importance of the choice criteria across life cycle segments, the mean importance scores for the eighteen criteria were computed and are presented in Table 1. The higher the score, the more important the criteria criterion is to the customers.

TABLE 1
Average Attribute Importance For the Life cycle Segment Types
Segment Type

Attribute	S₁ Mean	S₁ Rank	S₂ Mean	S₂ Rank	S₃ Mean	S₃ Rank	S₄ Mean	S₄ Rank	S₅ Mean	S₅ Rank	S₆ Mean	S₆ Rank	S₇ Mean	S₇ Rank
Located near home	7.22	1	6.76	2	7.32	1	7.33	1	7.43	1	7.44	1	7.46	2
Overall quality of Service	6.98	2	6.21	9	6.39	7	6.54	7	6.70	6	6.58	7	5.96	10
Good reputation	6.64	3	7.28	1	6.92	2	6.93	2	6.45	8	6.70	6	6.22	9
Ease of qualifying for free checking	6.60	4	6.20	10	6.28	9	5.96	13	6.00	11	5.99	11	6.70	5
Fast service	6.58	5	6.25	8	6.18	10	6.09	12	6.20	10	5.55	12	5.12	13
Ability to obtain all financial services in one location	6.51	6	6.14	11	6.01	11	6.46	10	5.67	13	6.40	9	6.50	8
High interest rates on savings	6.21	7	6.61	5	6.30	8	6.51	5	6.75	5	7.10	5	6.77	4
Availability of auto/personal loans	6.00	8	6.37	7	5.56	6	6.75	4	5.94	12	6.26	10	4.10	14
Self service banking machine-TYME	5.95	9	4.88	17	5.40	16	5.80	15	5.35	18	5.20	15	4.01	15
Extended hour-Sat. and evenings	5.90	10	5.52	15	5.92	12	5.89	14	5.60	14	5.25	14	3.90	16
Safety of funds	5.64	11	6.10	12	5.78	13	6.48	9	6.80	4	7.20	2	7.70	1
Giving good financial advice	5.20	12	6.70	3	6.62	5	6.68	5	7.08	2	7.15	4	6.66	6
Low intrest rates on loans	5.14	13	6.66	4	6.70	4	6.80	3	6.40	9	5.15	16	3.85	17
Personal service	5.10	14	6.01	13	5.66	14	5.65	16	6.66	7	7.16	3	7.12	3
Experienced people	4.79	15	5.64	14	5.45	15	6.30	11	6.84	3	6.48	8	6.57	7
Availablity of mortgage loan	4.59	16	6.40	6	6.82	3	6.60	6	5.49	15	3.90	18	3.00	18
Ability to bank-by-mail	4.53	17	5.44	16	4.49	18	4.40	18	5.40	17	4.90	17	5.55	12
Concerned about the community	3.20	18	4.44	18	4.85	17	5.15	17	5.94	16	5.50	13	5.86	11
Segment Type Mean	5.71		6.09		6.10		6.24		6.26		6.11		5.73	

S₁ = Bachelor stage: Young, single people not living at home
S₂ = Newly married couples: Young, no children
S₃ = Full-nest I: Youngest child under six
S₄ = Full-nest II: Youngest child six or over
S₅ = Full-nest III: Older married couples with dependent children
S₆ = Empty-nest I: Older married couples, no children with them, head in labor force
S₇ = Empty-nest II: Older married couples, no children living at home, head retired

Based on Table 1, one can infer that individuals who are in the bachelor stage--young, single people not living at home--emphasized the importance of such criteria as: located near home, overall quality of service, reputation, ease of qualifying for free checking accounts by maintaining a minimum balance, fast service, and able to obtain all financial services at one location. For newly married couples--young and no children, attributes considered important are: good reputation, location, giving good financial advice, low interest rates on loans, and paying highest interest rates on savings. Individuals who are in full-nest I--youngest child under six--rated attributes such as location, reputation, availability of mortgage loans, low interest rates on loans, and giving good financial advice as important choice criteria. Individuals who are in the full-nest II stage consider low interest rates on loans and availability of loans (auto or personal) as relatively more important than the individuals in the preceding stage.

Older married couples with dependent children--the full-nest III stage of life cycle--appear to regard attributes such as location, giving good financial advice experienced people, safety of funds, paying highest rates on savings and overall quality of service as more important. For older individuals, location, safety of funds, and personal service appear to be relatively more important banking needs; whereas, interest rates on loans and availability of loans are of the least importance to them as compared to their younger counterparts.

Among the older individuals, those who are in the empty-nest II stage of the life cycle consider such attributes as safety of funds, paying highest rates on savings, and ease of qualifying for a free checking account by maintaining a minimum balance as relatively more important than their older counterparts who are still in the labor force.

TABLE 2

SIGNIFICANCE OF DIFFERENCES IN MEAN IMPORTANCES
ACROSS SEGMENT TYPES

ATTRIBUTE	Significance Raw**	Adjusted Average Importance Segment Type						
		S_1	S_2	S_3	S_4	S_5	S_6	S_7
Located near home	.05	1.51	0.67	1.22	1.09	7.17	1.33	1.73
Overall quality of service	.05	1.27	0.29	0.30	0.44	0.44	0.47	0.23
Good Reputation	.001	0.93	1.19	0.82	0.69	0.19	0.59	0.49
Ease of qualifying for free checking account by maintaining a minimum balance	.05	0.89	0.11	0.18	−0.28	−0.26	−0.12	0.97
Fast Service	.001	0.87	0.16	0.08	−0.15	−0.06	−0.56	−0.61
Being able to obtain all financial services at one location	.05	0.80	0.05	−0.09	0.22	−0.59	0.29	0.77
Paying highest rates on savings	.05	0.50	0.52	0.20	0.27	0.49	0.99	1.04
Availability of auto/ personal loans	.001	0.29	0.28	0.46	0.51	−0.32	0.15	−1.63
Self service banking machine- TYME	.09	0.24	1.21	−0.70	−0.44	−0.91	−0.91	−1.72
Extended hours-Saturdays and evenings	.05	0.19	−0.57	−0.18	−0.35	−0.66	−0.86	−1.83
Safety of funds	.001	−0.07	0.01	−0.32	0.30	0.54	1.09	1.97
Giving good financial advice	.05	−0.51	0.61	0.52	0.24	0.82	1.04	0.93
Low interest rates on loans	.001	−0.57	0.57	0.60	0.56	0.14	−0.96	−1.88
Personal service	.01	−0.61	−0.08	−0.44	−0.59	0.40	1.05	1.39
Experienced people	.003	−0.92	−0.45	−0.65	0.06	0.58	0.37	0.84
Availability of mortgage loan	.001	−1.12	0.31	0.72	0.36	−0.77	−2.14	−2.73
Ability to bank-by-mail	.15	−1.18	−0.65	−1.61	−1.84	−0.86	−1.21	−0.18
Concerned about the community	.09	−2.51	−1.65	−1.25	−1.09	−0.32	−0.61	0.13

*For each segment type, the mean segment importance across eighteen attributes was subtracted from the importance for each of the eighteen attributes.

**Significance of differences among segment types based on raw average importance score.

15

The seven sets of ranks presented in Table 1 suggest that the importance of choice criteria varies across stages of the cycle. To see if the differences in importance among life cycle segments were statistically significant, eighteen one-way analyses of variance were performed. The relative importance of the attributes can be judged by calculating the difference between the mean attribute importance from the overall mean importance rating for the respective stages in the life cycle. This adjusted importance rating can then be interpreted more easily (a positive importance suggests greater than average importance for the segment type and vice versa) and be compared across segment types.

Table 2 indicates that fifteen of the eighteen variables are statistically significant at the .001 and four are significant at the .05 level. Hence, it is reasonable to assert that the relative importance of choice criteria underlying the financial institution choice decision is significantly related to the stage of the life cycle under consideration.

TABLE 3

Average Financial Service Importance
for the Life Cycle Segment Types

FINANCIAL SERVICE	Mean (S1)	Rank	Mean (S2)	Rank	Mean (S3)	Rank	Mean (S4)	Rank	Mean (S5)	Rank	Mean (S6)	Rank	Mean (S7)	Rank
Regular passbook savings	3.96	1	3.99	1	4.05	1	3.91	1	3.48	4	3.60	3	4.21	1
Preferred loan rates	3.90	2	3.63	3	3.89	2	3.85	2	3.00	8	2.92	9	1.91	11
Personal line of credit	3.56	3	3.05	7	3.40	5	3.46	5	2.63	11	3.00	8	2.10	7
Automated teller machines	3.50	4	2.90	9	2.80	11	2.53	11	2.27	13	1.98	13	1.55	13
Savings certificates	3.45	5	3.57	4	3.01	7	2.97	6	3.45	2	3.82	1	3.94	2
Money market funds/ liquid assets accounts	3.00	6	3.91	2	3.65	3	3.75	3	3.35	6	3.27	4	3.16	4
Financial information newsletter	2.97	7	2.96	8	3.08	6	2.91	7	2.98	9	3.06	7	2.57	5
Advice on tax shelters	2.82	8	3.31	6	2.98	8	2.79	9	3.63	1	3.66	2	1.98	8
Real estate investment advice	2.79	9	3.42	5	3.49	4	2.71	10	2.45	12	2.29	12	1.68	12
Seminars on financial planning	2.68	10	2.75	12	2.84	10	3.54	4	2.76	10	2.54	11	2.22	6
Preparation of income tax forms	2.60	11	2.63	13	2.71	12	2.38	13	3.10	7	3.10	6	3.58	3
Financial advice for retirement	2.50	12	2.79	11	2.61	13	2.45	12	3.54	3	3.20	5	1.80	10
Estate planning	2.45	13	2.84	10	2.92	9	2.84	8	3.40	5	2.85	10	1.94	9
Segment Type Mean	3.09		3.21		3.19		3.08		3.09		3.02		2.51	

Relative Importance of the Services Offered by Financial Service Institutions

The next study objective was to examine the relative importance of a set of services offered by financial service institutions across the life-cycle stages. Table 3 presents the mean importance sources on a variety of financial services. The higher the score, the more important the service attribute is to the consumer.

The seven sets of ranks presented in Table 3 suggest that the importance of services offered by financial institutions varies across the stages of the life cycle. While those who are in the early stages of their life cycle (bachelor stage, young and single people not living at home) view regular passbook savings, preferred loan rates, personal line of credit, automated teller machines, and 21 savings certificates, as relatively more important, newly married young couples, with no children, consider regular passbook savings, money market funds/liquid asest accounts, savings ceritificates, and real estate investment advice as relatively more important.

Among members who are in different stages of the full nest cycle, differences in the importance of financial services are conspicuous. For instance, older married couples with dependent children consider advice on tax shelters, money market funds, and financial advice for retirement as relatively more important than those who are in the preceding stages of the life cycle. Full nest I members view regular passbook savings, preferred loan rates, money market funds, and real estate investment advice as relatively more important, and full nest II members deem important such services as: seminars on financial planning, savings certificates, and financial information newsletters.

Older members who are in the "emptying of the nest" stage of their life cycle differ in terms of their perceived importance of the services offered by the financial institution. Older individuals in the "emptying of the nest" stage and in the labor force view savings certificates, advice on tax shelters, regular passbook savings, preparation of income tax forms, and financial advice for retirement as relatively more important than the older retirees who perceive regular passbook savings, savings certificates, preparation of income tax forms, money market funds/liquid assets accounts, and a financial information newsletter as relatively more important. For empty nest I members, a relatively high importance attributed to specific services such as advice on tax shelters and financial advice for retirement results from the fact that these members are still in the labor force and their financial position is much better than their older retired counterparts who face drastic cuts in income, and thereby tend to view savings instruments (e.g., regular passbook savings) as relatively more important.

To determine if the differences in importance among life cycle stages are statistically significant, thirteen one-way analyses of variance were performed (see Table 4).

17

TABLE 4

Significance of Differences in Mean Importance Across Segment Types

Financial Service	Significance Raw**	Adjusted Average Importance* Segment Type						
		S1	S2	S3	S4	S5	S6	S7
Regular passbook savings	.05	0.87	0.78	0.86	0.83	0.39	0.52	1.70
Preferred loan rates	.001	0.81	0.42	0.70	0.77	-0.09	-0.10	-0.60
Personal line of credit	.001	0.47	-0.16	0.21	0.38	-0.46	-0.02	-0.41
Automated teller machines	.001	0.41	-0.31	-0.39	-0.55	-0.82	-1.04	-0.96
Savings certificates	.05	0.36	0.36	-0.18	-0.11	0.47	0.80	1.43
Money market funds/liquid assets accounts	.05	0.09	0.70	0.46	0.67	0.26	0.25	0.65
Financial information newsletter	.001	-0.12	-0.25	-0.11	-0.17	-0.11	0.04	0.06
Advice on tax shelters	.001	-0.27	0.10	-0.21	-0.29	0.54	0.64	-0.53
Real estate investment advice	.001	-0.30	0.21	0.30	-0.37	-0.64	-0.73	-0.83
Seminars on financial planning	.001	-0.41	-0.46	-0.35	0.46	-0.33	-0.48	-0.29
Preparation of income tax forms	.05	-0.49	-0.58	-0.48	-0.70	0.01	0.08	1.07
Financial advice for retirement	.001	-0.59	-0.42	-0.58	-0.63	0.45	0.18	-0.71
Estate planning	.001	-0.64	-0.37	-0.27	-0.24	0.31	-0.17	-0.57

* For each segment type, the mean segment importance across thirteen financial services was subtracted from the importance for each of the thirteen financial services.

** Significance of differences among segment types based on raw average importance score.

The relative importance of the services be calculated by computing the difference between the mean service attribute importance from the overall mean importance rating for the respective life cycle stages. As indicated earlier, this adjusted importance rating can then be interpreted and compared across life cycle stages. The results (Table 4) indicate that nine services are statistically significant at the .001 level and four services are significant at the .05 level. Hence, the relative importance of financial services is significantly related to life cycle stages.

MANAGERIAL IMPLICATIONS AND CONCLUSIONS

The evidence presented here suggests several important implications for marketers and key decision makers in the banking industry. First and foremost, the findings of the study clearly reveal that differences exist among life cycle segments with respect to the relative importance of financial institution choice criteria, and financial services. These findings suggest several important implications in relation to product/service strategy, pricing (fee) strategy, and location strategy.

Product (Service) Strategy

The most basic marketing decision bank marketers must make is what product/-service offerings to provide to their target groups. As deregulation has loosened restrictions on banks' product/service offerings, banks today can increase the width and depth of their product mix by offering a variety of new products such as loan products, CDs, senior citizen accounts, and a host of other accounts.

The findings of the study clearly suggest to marketers that product needs vary across family life cycle stages. While members in the full nest I stage emphasize the importance of a mortgage loan and availability of loans, these specific products were also viewed important by newly married couples; thus, there is a demand for mortgage loans which are generally available in different forms including "fixed rate mortgage," "variable rate mortgage," etc. Recent work (e.g., Mills and Gardner 1986, Colton et al. 1980) for example, notes that younger people are more willing to adopt variable rate mortgages or adjustable rate mortgages. This provides an opportunity for bankers to discuss their product line width and make their customers familiar with the benefits of these products' variants.

While offering these products they have the opportunity to cross-sell NOW accounts, savings certificates, IRA, and other liquid/nonliquid assets. The results of the study shows that consumers in all stages have some common choice criteria (convenience, bank's reputation); this allows the marketers to carefully examine these banking needs that vary according to life cycle stage. Retired people seem to view personal service and safety of funds as extremely important; while these are not as important to those who are in the early stages of their life cycle. Families with children have needs for such services as availability of loans, money needs for their children to go to college, IRA's, and money market funds; however, some of these products are less important for older couples with no children.

In the area of offering financial advisory services, the findings clearly suggest differing needs. Financial advice for retirement and preparation of income tax forms were relatively more important for older individuals than those who are in the bachelor stage or in the full nest stages of the life cycle. Those consumers in the full nest I or full nest II stage show strong needs for financial advisory services, notably real estate investment advice, while those who are in the full nest III stage emphasize financial advice for retirement and estate planning. From a strategic perspective, bank marketers should consider financial advisory services as the cornerstone of building a relationship with their customers and in establishing a reputation in their service offerings. Banking professionals may be able to attract potential customers by informing them that they have competitive investments and savings instruments. Bankers must also acknowledge that as the customer passes through various stages of the life cycle, different products/services will become appropriate for the customer. Each stage of the life cycle presents marketing challenges in offering products/services and meeting both present and future banking product/service needs of the customer.

Pricing (Fee) Strategy

Price setting has become a much more challenging task to bank marketers in the financial services industry as many financial institutions often compete for the same profitable target market. Different strategies towards price (fee) setting will be dictated depending on the particular market/segment in which the products/services are sold, and consumer willingness to use these products/-services. Pricing strategies involve combinations of specific fees, the interest earned on savings instruments and the interest rates on loans. For example, in the area of mortgage loans which appear to be relatively more important for consumers in the full nest I and II stages, the demand for variety lies in increasing or maintaining the market share for specific mortgage loans, price reductions, if perceived as real reductions, can increase or improve market share by attracting those customers in the full nest I/full nest II group. This particular strategy is perhaps beneficial to bank marketers if they want to introduce new forms of mortgage loans and/or auto or personal loans.

Bank marketers must realize that when it comes to "the emptying of the nest" and retirement, consumers face a decrease in income which usually remains fixed. To attract the retired market, free services such as free checking with a minimum balance requirement, slightly higher interest rates on savings instruments, and/or free checkbooks as a means of building good will and promotion may be some possible suggestions. These special offerings for older members, coupled with low interest rates on loans for those who are in the full nest stages of the life cycle, may generate additional profits and help to attract other potential customers, thereby increasing market share.

From a strategic perspective, other service variables, such as: financial advice for retirement, preparation of income tax forms, estate planning, etc., offer important pricing implications to marketers. Recognizing the timely and interactive nature of services such as financial advisory services (tax advice, investment advice), and the effect of the interaction and perceived importance or value of the service suggests useful strategies for the pricing of different services. The key is that market-oriented strategies would assist in achieving objectives for specific products/services offerings, without ignoring costs which must be carefully examined in the cost/benefit analysis portion of the process.

Location (Place) Strategy

Location/convenience is widely thought to play a central role in attracting retail customers. Regardless of what breadth products/services are offered and at what cost, if the products/services are not easily accessible to the target groups, bankers face a difficulty in selling their products/services. Kotler and Bloom (1984) note that "when service organizations target a portion of its marketing effort toward a given geographic area, whether it is a region, state, country, city, or neighborhood, it should be based on a careful analysis of the market potential of the area."

Convenience is a multidimensional construct which reflects different meanings to different groups of customers. While the findings of the study suggest to bank marketers and other key decision makers that "located near home" is a common need for consumers in all life-cycle stages, the consumers' degee of importance varies for the convenience dimensions "being able to obtain all financial services at one location," "hours of operation," and "self service banking machine--TYME." Recognizing this, professionals in the banking industry must be able to deliver their products/services in a manner that can be easily accessible to their target members. A good location/place can provide bank marketers with strategic advantages that the competition may find difficult to overcome. Furthermore, the very act of accessibility (the degree to which segments can be effectively reached and served) can produce a positive image of the bank in the community, and may help many to consolidate their business at that one bank. Therefore, the actual delivery of products/services which bank marketers choose to provide must be a key part of marketing strategy since the convenience dimension was the most important characteristic perceived by all customers in all stages of the family life cycles.

In conclusion, segmenting the market according to life cycle stages offers a better understanding of the consumers' use of choice criteria and financial services. According to this approach, life cycle stages determine the financial needs/wants of consumers. Marketing of financial services should be based on the financial needs of individuals in different stages of the life cycle. The financial service institutions that focus on identifying the financial needs of families in the various stages of the life cycle and satisfying these needs will have a competitive advantage in the continuing evolution of the financial services marketplace.

References

Anderson, Thomas W., Eli P. Cox III, and David G. Fulcher. (1976), "Bank Selection Decisions and Market Segmentation," *Journal of Marketing*, 40 (January), 40-45.

Colton, Kent W., Donald R. Lessard, David Modest, and Arthur P. Solomon. (1977), "National Survey of Borrowers' Housing Characteristics, Attitudes and Preferences," in *Alternate Mortgage Instruments Research Study*, 1 (November), Washington, D.C.: Federal Home Loan Bank Board.

Colton, Kent W., Donald R. Dessard, David Modest, and Arthur P. Solomon. (1980), "Borrower Attitudes Toward Alternative Mortgatge Instruments," Federal Home Loan Bank Board Invited Research Working Paper No. 31 (January), Washington, D.C.: Federal Home Loan Bank Board.

Derrick, Frederick W., and Alane K. Lehfeld (1980), "the Family Life Cycle: An Alternative Approach," *Journal of Consumer Research*, 7 (September), 214-217.

Dupuy, George M., and William J. Kehoe. (1976), "Comments on Bank Selection Decision and Market Segmentation," *Journal of Marketing*, (October), 89-91.

Feldman, Harold, and Feldman, Margaret. (1975), "The Family Life Cycle: Some Suggestion for Recycling," *Journal of Marriage and Family*, 37, 277-284.

Glick, Paul C. (1977), "Updating the life Cycle of the Family," *Journal of the Marriage and Family*, 39, 5-13.

Jain, Subash C. (1975), "Life Cycle Revisited: Applications in Consumer Research," *Advances in Consumer Research*, Vol. 2, ed. Mary Jane Schlinger, Association for Consumer Research, 39-49.

Kotler, Philip, and Paul N. Bloom. (1984), *Marketing Professional Services*, Prentice-Hall, Inc., Englewood Cliffs, New Jersey.

Mills, Dixie L., and Mona J. Gardner. (1986), "Consumer Response to Adjustable Rate Mortgages: Implications of the Evidence from Illinois and Wisconsin," *The Journal of Consumer Affairs*, 20 (Summer), 77-105.

Murphy, Patrick E., and Staples, William E. (1979), "A Modernized Family Life Cycle," *Journal of Consumer Research*, 6 (June), 12-22.

Wells, William D., and George Gubar (1966), "Life Cycle Concept in Marketing Research," *Journal of Marketing Research*, 8 (November), 355-363.

Yaegel, Thomas. (1987), "Using Life Cycle Segmentation to Build an Effective Sales System," *Journal of Retail Banking*, 9 (Fall), 53-62.

DEVELOPMENT OF A MODEL COURSE OF STUDY FOR TRAVEL-TOURISM FOR A TWO-YEAR DEGREE OR CERTIFICATE

JanHendrik A. Vroom, Ph.D.
California State University, San Bernardino

Abstract

An investigatory study was made of the curricula of seven institutions offering travel-tourism courses, one in Africa, one in Canada, three in Europe and two in the United States. This was supplemented by personal interviews with faculty, directors, students and on-site inspections. It was found that there were similarities in the American institutions, however, all others were quite different. This resulted in the development of a model course of study in Travel-Tourism Administration.

The Problem

> "Travel has become one of the great forces for peace and understanding in our times. As people move throughout the world and learn to know each other, to understand each other's customs and to appreciate the qualities of the individuals of each nation, we are building a level of international understanding which can sharply improve the atmosphere for world peace. . . . The leisure-tourism industry plays a key role in stimulating this flow of world's peoples. . . a most important activity." (Recreation Month, 1971).

Since World War II, the number of Americans traveling abroad has increased greatly. Ninety-nine percent of travel has been by air. Although no area of travel-tourism has declined in popularity, Europe became the uncontested Mecca for an affluent people in search of ancestral identity (Kando, 1971).

In the last thirty years, travel, especially for pleasure, has now become an activity for masses rather than for a privileged few. To service clients, qualified employees had to be found, yet few educational institutions offered courses leading to either a certificate or an associate degree in travel-tourism. An investigatory survey of travel-tourism curricula was made in preparation for the design and development of a model curriculum to be used by junior colleges or with some minor changes and additions, by four-year institutions.

Institutional Research

In order to arrive at a suitable course of study, it was determined to research educational institutions in various geographic locations. Thus a two-year institution in Kenya, two three-year institutions in Germany and the Netherlands, two graduate schools - one in Canada and one in Switzerland, and two community colleges in the United States were selected for an in-depth study of their curricula.

This was accomplished by means of personal visits and interviews with faculty and students of six institutions. Due to time and travel limitations, curriculum and educational topics were discussed with the principal of the Canadian institution. At the same time, the literature of several countries, including those of France, Germany, the Netherlands, Switzerland and the United States was thoroughly reviewed to create a foundation of data on which a model program could be designed.

While an active participant in several European conventions and seminars, special interviews were held with tourism personnel as well as with students and faculty of the Free University of Berlin (Federal Republic of Germany) and the International Tourism Exchange (ITB) in West Berlin. Information obtained from the interviews and literature provided sufficient knowledge so a model program in travel and tourism could be designed.

On-Site Visits (Africa, Canada, Europe and the United States)

In making the selection of these institutions, several guidelines were used, such as a) all seven institutions offered travel and tourism administration programs with student enrollment in each of the institutions resembling one another and b) directors, deans, faculty and students agreed to participate in the survey.

The following institutions measured up to the above standards.

1.   Africa: Kenya Utalii College, Nairobi, Kenya.
2.   Canada: McGill University, Montreal, Quebec, Canada.
3.   Europe: The Institute for Tourism and Transport Economics at the Graduate School of Economics, Law, Business and Public Administration, St. Gallen, Switzerland;

    The Netherlands Scientific Institute for Tourism and Recreation, Breda, the Netherlands;

    The Rhineland-Pfals Fach-hochschule Ludwigshafen/Worms, State University, Worms, Germany.
4.   U.S.A.:   Canada College, Redwood City, California and Foothill College, Los Altos, California.

Research Methodology

Techniques used in the research was to record and observe the components which made up the travel-tourism programs. During the on-site interviews and observations, the researcher made use of his experience gained during the past thirty-three years in the tourism industry.

Materials collected and observations made included: a) class lectures and outlines, b) replies and statements of faculty, and c) institutional catalogs and class handouts. The data received from the personal interviews were placed in three groups: 1) faculty, et al, 2) students and 3) course outlines.

The methodology used was that of personal examination. The course offerings of all seven institutions were scrutinized with regard to contents, such as core course work in travel-tourism administration and general education courses. At its completion, five experts in the travel-tourism industry and education were asked to review the model. This program was then altered to incorporate their recommendations.

Philosophical Guidelines and Aims

The Travel-Tourism Administration program in the African, American, Canadian and European institutions have different philosophical guidelines as well as aims. The purpose of the Netherlands institution is to educate students for management positions within the travel-tourism-recreation industries.

The Swiss institution prepares students for management positions in business and public administration. An array of in-depth lectures and exercises are provided dealing with problems closely associated with the tourism industry. Studies are divided into four semesters with lectures and exercises on political economics, law, industrial administration and languages. According to the program outline, specific exercises and lectures are covered in the following subjects: tourism economics, research, communication and advertising. One foreign language is also required.

The German Professional University first started to offer full-time courses in business administration and tourism during the winter term of 1978. The tourism courses were conceived in close cooperation with leading experts from the tourism industry.

The Kenya Polytechnic was founded in 1969, offering training for careers in the hotel and tourism industry. The college is a comprehensive hotel and training center offering courses in hotel management, travel operations and driver guides education. Of special interest is the Utalii Hotel, which is attached to and part of the college. It is an application hotel providing opportunities for practical training.

The Canadian institution offers graduate studies leading to a diploma in tourism management. It is designed both for those who are already in the travel-tourism industry and those who are thinking about a travel-tourism career.

Canada College instructional offerings cover all of the broad and essential areas of human knowledge, including the arts, science and occupational courses (travel-tourism).

Foothill Community College offers several community programs, some of which are taught in more than thirty off-campus locations.

Continuing Education

The Travel-Tourism Administration program should also include opportunities for interested students and individuals to participate in continuing education courses. The individual who is already employed in the travel-tourism industry would be able to acquire up-to-date skills and pertinent information essential to the industry. This could be easily accomplished by offering special seminars and workshops. A variety of seminars and courses could be offered such as:
- a)   Airline Deregulation
- b)   The Travel Agent and the Law
- c)   Visit U.S.A. Workshops
- d)   Special Interest Tour Design
- e)   Incentive Travel
- f)   Wheelchair Person Travel and Tours
- g)   Tour Escorting

These courses or seminars could be offered as special topics when the need arose. A case in question would be item "c" above. More and more visitors from overseas are entering the United States as prices are very attractive. While the ranks of these visitors have nearly doubled in the past several years, the late eighties will go down in the travel industry books as the first of many in which the number of overseas visitors touring the U.S. exceeded the number of Americans going abroad.

Teaching Staff

The Director, Chairperson or Coordinator of the Travel-Tourism program should be an individual with several years of practicum within the travel-tourism industry. At the same time, this individual should possess a degree from an accredited four-year university or institution.

The responsibility of this person is to not only be a consultant to the students and advisory board, but should also strengthen the travel-tourism program and direct the public relations activities to the public at large and the travel industry.

In order to serve the students and residents of the area, faculty teaching the advanced travel-tourism courses should hold a graduate degree and be well traveled. Another must is the sharing of industry knowledge acquired from years of practical experience. Management courses should be taught by instructors who have management experience.

Each program should use part-time instructors drawn from the travel-tourism industry. Many industry personnel are easily available, such as an airline ticket agent to teach domestic and international ticketing.

The Travel-Tourism industry needs qualified employees now. According to the U.S. Department of Commerce, tourism is the fastest growing industry in the world. In the United States, the tourism industry is currently number three behind food and auto sales. It is already number two in terms of employment behind health services (CHRIE Communique 1988). During the past ten years travel and tourism employment has grown fifty-seven percent, more than twice the growth rate for all jobs in the U.S. economy (Travel Weekly, 1988).

Conclusion:

The primary purpose of this paper was to research the travel-tourism administration educational programs offered in these different institutions. It was found that even though there was similarity in course offerings in both American institutions, the Canadian, European and Kenyan curricula were quite different. Faculty varied substantially with heavier emphasis on full-time instructors with terminal degrees in Europe, while the American, Canadian and Kenyan institutions have a small full-time staff.

After fulfilling the degree requirements, it was found by the researcher that the American institutions conferred the Associate of Arts degree as compared to a three-year Travel-Tourism Diploma in Germany and the Netherlands, a graduate degree in Canada and Switzerland and a Diploma of Tourism and Driver Guide in Kenya.

Placing students varied greatly. The American and Kenya experience showed placements into entry level positions in the travel and tourism industry. However, the Canadian, Dutch, German and Swiss graduates entered management level positions.

Educators desiring to implement a travel-tourism administration program in their course offerings should consider the following:
- a) General education courses as required by the State and core courses should be part of the total program (see Appendix I). All other courses should be left open to the student in selecting the balance needed for graduation.
- b) This selection should be based on the student's area of specialization.
- c) Community colleges or other similar institutions should provide extension courses or continuing education programs to persons who are already associated with the travel and tourism industry.

d) Community colleges or similar institutions should provide a certificate of proficiency or Associate Degree (Technical) of Arts (see Appendix II).

e) Community colleges or similar institutions should teach skills especially in the area of computer ticketing, automation, personnel management, sales and marketing, which would prepare the student for lower management positions.

In order to obtain valuable experience, the Travel-Tourism Administration curriculum should provide for an internship program for which not only a salary but also credit hours are earned. The on-the-job training program will provide the student with insights into the working and operation of a travel agency or other entity within the travel-tourism industry. This internship should take place at the end of the first semester or at its latest at the end of the second semester (preferably during the summer recess) with a total work experience time span of four hundred (400) hours with set rules to guide the evaluation process of the student. The advantage of this internship program is that the student can determine early in the program if employment in the travel-tourism industry would be the right vocation.

APPENDIX I

Curriculum for the Associate of Arts Degree in Travel-Tourism Administration

In order to earn the Associate of Arts degree, students are to complete the core travel courses and must complete the General Education and Business requirements. The student must select approved electives as well as twenty-four units of residency for a total of sixty units.

G. E. and Business Courses	Units
Social Science	6
English Composition	3
Physical Education	4
Health Education	2
Accounting	3
Math	3
Communications	3
Typing or must demonstrate a typing speed of 45 wpm	

First Semester	Units
English Composition	3
Introduction to the Recreation and Leisure Industry	1
Introduction to the Travel Industry	3
Accounting	3
Physical Education	1
World Travel Geography and Tourist Regions	<u>4</u>
	15

Second Semester	Units
Domestic Air Transportation, Computer Ticketing	3
Physical Education·	1
Health Education	2
Cruises and Sea Travel	2
Introduction to the Hospitality Industry	1

U.S. Travel Geography and Tourist Regions	2
Electives	4
	15

Third Semester

	Units
Social Science	3
Physical Education	1
International Air Transportation, Computer Ticketing	3
Math	3
Communications	3
Bus and Rail Travel	2
	15

Fourth Semester

	Units
Social Science	3
Physical Education	1
Travel Agency Management	3
Typing	3
Package Tour Development	3
Special Projects	2
	15

Electives

	Units
Travel Insurance, Liability and Law	1
Travel Sales Techniques	3
Cultural Tourism	3
Anthropology	3
Introduction to Management	3
Communications	3
Business Machines	3
Speech	2
Foreign Languages	10
Introduction to Art	3
Data Processing, Computer Science	3
Management Techniques	3
Conferences and Seminars	2
Group Travel/Tour Management	3
Convention Management and Services	2

Course Descriptions

Introduction to the Travel Industry

An overview of the history and growth of the travel industry, retail and wholesale travel tours, functions and responsibilities, components of the travel-tourism industry.

Domestic Air Transportation and Ticketing

Introduction to the domestic Official Airline Guide, mileage, routes and ticket writing.

International Air Transportation and Ticketing

Introduction to the international Official Airline Guide, ticket writing and usage of other tickets and forms, rules, regulation and special fares.

Cruises and Sea Travel

History of steamship travel, cruise destination and durations, use of steamship guide.

U.S. Travel Geography and Tourist Regions

North American tourist attractions. Use of consolidated Air Tour Manual and tour planning books to design itineraries.

Package Tour Development and Marketing

Develop and design independent tours, folder preparation, travel documents, vouchers, sightseeing, local guides and tours, and charter tours.

Introduction to the Hospitality Industry

Overview of accommodations, hotels, motels and condos, reservations, prepayment receipts.

Introduction to the Recreation and Leisure Industry

The study of leisure time and recreation facilities. Federal, state, regional and private commercial parks.

Bus and Rail Travel

Use of rail guides, Thomas Cook rail guide, Eurail travel and domestic bus guides, routes and scheduling.

Travel Agency Management

Financing, accreditation, advertising, personnel management, office location, general operations, public relations and travel promotions.

Special Projects

To be assigned by the instructor. Primarily research oriented, directed studies and readings.

Elective Travel Courses:

Travel Insurance Liability

Discusses travel laws, consumerism, liability clauses, insurance forms, agent obligations, errors and omission.

Travel Sales Techniques

Student participation in sales techniques, presentation of services, public speaking.

Cultural Tourism

Discusses the history, culture, geography and customs of various nations, nationalities, ethnic background and folklore. Festivals and local recreational activities.

APPENDIX II

In order to earn a certificate in Travel and Tourism Administration, the courses listed below must be completed successfully:

THE CORE	UNITS
Introduction to the Travel Industry	3*
Domestic Air Transportation and Computer Ticketing	3**
International Tourism	3
Cruises and Sea Travel	2
U.S. Travel Geography and Tourist Regions	2
World Geography and Tourist Regions	4
Package Tour Development and Marketing	3*
Introduction to the Hospitality Industry	1*
Introduction to the Recreation and Leisure Industry	1*
Bus and Rail Travel	1
Travel Agency Management	3
Special Subjects	2

*   Minimum C grade required
**   Minimum B grade required

End notes

1.   Kennedy, John Fitzgerald (1971), "Message." Recreation Month, International Recreation Association Bulletin.

2.   Kando, Thomas M. (1975), Leisure and Popular Culture in Transition. St. Louis, Mosby.

3.   "Tourism Week is May 15-21," (May 1, 1988), CHRIE Communique, Council on Hotel, Restaurant, Institutional and Tourism Education. VOL 2 No. 8.

4.   "Tourism Week's Events Will Stress Industry's Impact on Nation," (May 12, 1988), Travel Weekly, p. 45.

FACTORS PERCEIVED AS IMPORTANT BY PACKAGE TOURISTS: A MULTIVARIATE ANALYSIS

Venkatakrishna V. Bellur, Ph.D.
Brian McNamara, Ph.D.
California State University, Bakersfield

Duane R. Prokop, M.B.A.
Gannon University

Abstract

Recognizing the potentials of tourism as an industry capable of providing jobs and generating revenues governments around the world are developing and implementing tourism development strategies. Projected growth in the industry offers tremendous opportunities to the travel agencies in terms of organizing and conducting package tours. This study was, therefore, designed to determine the demographic and socioeconomic profile of those taking package tours; reasons for joining package tours; factors perceived as important in selecting a travel agency; and the degree of satisfaction derived from the selected travel agency. A survey of 204 individuals conducted at the Kai Tak International Airport in Hon Kong during November-December 1985 revealed that the majority were female, single, and belonged to the middle class. Of the 12 attributes, only six were perceived as important in selecting a travel agency. Only five services were important, and of this two were found satisfactory. Travel agencies offering package tours should take a look at the target market and satisfy the customers to grow with the growing tourist industry.

INTRODUCTION

Tourism is the world's largest industry today accounting for about 12% of the gross national product (GNP) [1]. The amount spent on tourism worldwide exceeds the GNP of every country in the world excepting that of the United States. According to the World Tourism Organization, the total spending worldwide for domestic and international travel to places 25 miles/more from home, was estimated at $1.8 trillion [2]. In the past, most state and federal governments viewed tourism as only a means for earning foreign exchange. Recently there is grass-root recognition of tourism as an

31

important revenue generating sector providing jobs lost in manufacturing and agriculture. Consequently, the federal and state governments are taking keen interest in developing the tourism industry.

The U.S. attracts tourists from all over the world. It offers historical sites, scenic grandeur, the most modern achievement of the industrial age -- in short, something for everyone. As a result, Americans are relatively happy to take vacations within the country rather than abroad. A Gallop International Poll taken in 1976 showed the percentage of persons in various countries who wanted to travel abroad. Results of the poll are as follows: 1. France--84%; 2. Scandinavia--84%; 3. Australia--83%; 4. Canada--79%; 5. European Economic Community--74%; 6. The United Kingdom--74%; 7. Italy--73%; 8. Benelux--70%; 9. West Germany--67%; 10. The United States--63%; 11. Japan--42%. Americans, except for the the Japanese, rank lowest in wanting to take vacations outside the U.S. [3].

The tourism industry will be able to maintain a sustained growth only as long as the individuals and households have access to increasing disposal and discretionary incomes. Available information reveals that during the five year period between 1980-84, the median income of the U.S. households increased from $17,710 to $22,415, an increase by 27%.[4] At the same time, vacation periods and paid holidays increased significantly. Three - and four - week paid vacations have become more common [5]

The impact of higher income and more leisure time to enjoy can be seen both in terms of increased expenditure on traveling and the number visiting foreign countries. Over a period of five years, between 1980-84, the travel industry receipts in the U.S. rose from $170.72 to $242.28 billion registering an increase of as much as 42%. During the same time period, the employment in the tourism industry increased from 6.92 to 7.96 million or by 15% [6]. Total number of individuals traveling from the U.S. to foreign countries increased from 8.16 to 12.07 million or by 48% between 1980-84. Amount spent abroad by Americans for the five year period increased from $10.40 to $16.01 billion or by 54%. The per capita expenditure abroad, however, increased by a smaller amount. It increased form $1,274 to $1,327 or by only 4% over the five year period. Number of foreigners visiting the U.S. for the five year period between 1980-84, however, declined slightly. It declined from 8.20 to 7.54 million or by 8%. This may be attributed to the unfavorable exchange rate for the foreigners visiting the U.S. The expenditure, however, increased from $10.59 to $11.39 billion or by eight percent. This can be attributed to the fact that the per capita expenditure of the foreign tourists increased from

$1,291 to $1,511 or by 7% [7].

To promote tourism, both public and private agencies are
spending huge sums of money on advertising. According to the
available information, expenditure on TV commercials --
network, spot, and retail/local for the five year period
between 1980-84 increased from $147 to $478 million or by
225%. For the same time period, expenditure on magazine
advertising rose from $123 to $212 million or by 72% [8].
Available information indicate that there is a concerted
effort by all the 50 states to spend more money on promoting
tourism. Together, the states plan to spend over $234
million during 1986-87 fiscal year, up by as much as 11%
compared to 1985-86. For example, New York state spent $9.39
million for promoting tourism in 1985-86 budget and plans to
spend as much as $14.84 million during 1986-87, an increase
of 58% [9].

Despite a plummeting dollar and lingering memories of reign
of terror during the years 1985 and 1986, American travelers
seem to be resuming their annual European trek. The G7
(Canada, France, Italy, Japan, U.K., U.S., and West Germany)
comprising seven major industrialized nations agreed this
year in Paris to stabilize the falling U.S. dollar. In the
meanwhile, terrorist incidents which prompted a 23% drop in
the U.S. visitors to Europe during 1986 have quieted.
Competition across the Atlantic is keeping air fares low. The
net result of all this is that the travel agents, tour
operators, and airlines are reporting increases of 5 - 50% in
overseas bookings compared to 1986. According to an American
Express executive, winter tourist business is ahead 35%
compared to 1986 and an increase of 50% to Europe is
expected. Bookings at Olson Travelworld, a tour operator in
Culver City, California, are up 50% over the same period last
year. At Pan Am, January 1987 booking to Europe was up
almost 13% over the last year. Discount fares and promotions
have helped boost interest in foreign travel and trans-
atlantic competition is expected to keep peak season fares
from skyrocketing this summer. Even Mediterranean Cruise
lines are luring American tourists with lower prices, betting
that terrorism fears have faded away like last year's suntan
[10].

The U.S. dollar which is taking a beating against the
Japanese yen and has lost some ground against some major
foreign currencies is still holding up against the Canadian
dollar. One U.S. dollar is fetching about $1.30 Canadian.
This has resulted in a tourist boom in Canada, especially in
the province of Ontario. During 1986, a record 24.7 million
Americans crossed the border over the bridges or through the
Detroit - Windsor Tunnel representing a 5% increase over
1985. In the first two months of 1987, the number was up by

approximately 9% compared to the same months during 1986. Among the Ontario enticements are tax rebate programs allowing visitors to reclaim 5% sales tax on accommodations and 7% retail sales tax on products taken out of the province within 30 days. Visitors with original receipts may apply for refunds for up to three years from the date of payment of the tax [11].

Recognizing the importance of tourism as a vital revenue generating activity, several Asian countries are also competing for tourist dollars. For example, the Philippines is attracting tourists following the ousting of president Marcos. In the Philippines, tourism is a natural industry with beaches, sunshine, and friendly people. It is also a major foreign exchange earner, generating over one-half billion dollars for the country even during the hard times of 1985 [12]. Malaysia is also looking to tourism to take up the economic slack caused by the fall in commodity prices. During the 35th annual Conference of the Pacific Area Travel Association (PATA), an organization of 36 member countries, in Kuala Lumpur, the Prime Minsiter made it clear that Malaysia is expected to get its fair share of $100 billion tourist industry. As the cost of travel dropped, the number of tourists visiting Southeast Asian countries rose and 300 million international travelers visited the region during 1984 [13]. Hong Kong, the most popular tourist attraction in the region has been experiencing a steady growth in the tourist traffic. Total number of visitors to Hong Kong increased from 2.3 to 3.5 million between 1980-84, an increase of 37% over a five year period. Per capita spending, however, increased from US$527 to US$552 during the same time period registering an increase by a mere 5%. This shows that visitors to Hong Kong are spending fewer dollars [14]. During 1985, Hong Kong earned an estimated US$1.88 billion from tourism. The tourist revenue went up by 5% and the number of tourists visiting the colony by 9% [15].

PROBLEM STATEMENT AND OBJECTIVES

Information available on the popularity of package tours show a big leap forward in 1983 accounting for an increase by 20% compared to 1982. Most of the growth, however, came from an increase in foreign-bound tours. International travel became attractive during the early 1980s because of strong U.S. dollar. Despite the popularity of tourism, package tours accounted for only 22% of all 1982 trips lasting five nights or longer, leaving the market still ripe with opportunities [16].

Reasons for sluggish growth in tourism industry may be traced

34

to increasing costs of traveling due to rising prices for hotel, meals, and other travel related items. Once an individual lands on foreign soil he/she may be in for a surprise. For the first time in four years, American Express hiked the cost of package tours in Europe by an average of 20%. In addition, in most of Europe, boarding and lodging costs have gone up by as much as 10 - 30%. Europe is not cheap anymore to the U.S. tourists [17].

The competition in the U.S. airline industry has cut down the cost of both domestic and foreign travel. In 1986 air fares dropped by 4.9%, while lodging costs rose 4.6%, meal costs 2.1%, and car rental charges went up by 3.7%. Business travel costs as a whole have gone up 47% since 1980 [18]. To combat rising costs of travel, firms are hiring travel experts. These travel experts can save up to 35% by arranging employee trips rather than letting employees arrange their own. For example, American Express Travel Management System seeks corporate accounts by promising to reduce travel costs by as much as 40%. It does it by seeking out lowest airline, hotel, and rental car rates for its corporate customers. Others helping in curbing travel costs to corporate customers are -- Master Card, and Price Waterhouse. A breakdown of the corporate travel expenses for 1986 was as follows: 1. air fare -- 46.7%; 2. lodging -- 24.2%; 3. meals -- 13.7%; 4. car rental -- 9.6%; and 5. other -- 5.8% [19].

The basic problem faced by an individual catering to the tourist industry is that tourism is one of the most intangible services -- experience is the product to the consumer. All the different aspects of vacation -- travel, meals, entertainment, and service are put together in tourist's mind as one product and one experience [20]. Satisfaction with that one experience will be a result of each tourist's expectation and interaction with the tour features [21]. When the experiences does not meet expectations, the result may be dissatisfaction.

Travel agencies have an extremely difficult task of satisfying customers because of the intangible nature of the product offered. It is equally difficult for customers to evaluate services than products because of its intangibility, lack of standardization, and inseparable nature. Despite the problems associated with satisfying the customers, travel agents account for nearly 70% of the domestic and 90% of the international airline ticket sale, almost all cruise and tour package sales, and 25 - 50% of the hotel reservations. In 1985, over 26,500 travel agencies in the U.S. generated approximately $44 billion in travel related product sale [22].

In Hong Kong, which is perceived as a "tourist mecca," the

number of Hong Konger's traveling abroad increased from less than one-half million to over one million over a period of ten years between 1975-84. During 1985, the colony had over 1,200 travel agencies of all sizes catering to the growing market. It was surprising to note that despite the growing demand for tourism oriented services, no adequate data were available to the travel agencies to develop and implement successful package tour marketing strategies to satisfy the potential customers. This study was, therefore, designed to determine the: 1. demographic and socioeconomic profile of package tour customers; 2. reasons for joining the package tour; 3. factors/attributes perceived as important in selecting a travel agency; and 4. the degree of satisfaction derived from the selected travel agency's services.

RESEARCH PROCEDURE

Data pertaining to the objectives of the study were obtained using a three-page questionnaire in Cantonese, the language used in Hong Kong. Questions included were related to -- whether one takes a vacation; vacationing frequency; whether one had joined a package tour before; reasons for taking package tours; information source about the travel agency; destination; factors/attributes one viewed as important in selecting a travel agency; degree of satisfaction derived from the selected agency; and demographic and socioeconomic characteristics of the respondent and the spouse. A total of 204 individuals taking package tours were randomly selected and interviewed at the Kai Tak International Airport, Hong Kong, during November-December 1985. Information provided by the respondents were coded, tabulated, and analyzed using the SPSSx package available at the University.

Demographic and socioeconomic profile of package tourists was determined by crosstabulating the responses to the question on whether one had joined a packaged tour in the past by the demographic and socioeconomic variables, and estimating Chi-square statistic. To determine factors/attributes perceived as important in selecting a travel agency and the degree of satisfaction derived, discriminant model was used.

Discriminant analysis is the appropriate statistical technique one should use when the dependent variable is categorical, and the independent variables are metric. In many cases, the dependent variable will consist of two groups of classifications. For example, "success" vs "failure"; "good risk" vs "bad risk"; and so on. In other instances, three or more groups are involved.An example of three groups may be a classification in which "above average," "average," and "below average" could be the categories. Discriminant analysis can handle either two groups or multiple groups. When two groups are involved the technique is referred to as two-group discriminant analysis. When the dependent variable classified into three or more categories, the technique is referred to as multiple discriminant analysis.

The technique of discriminant analysis involves deriving linear combination of two or more independent variables that descriminate best between the a priori defined groups. It was first shown by Fisher that if the weights/coefficients for the various independent variables in the discriminant function are chosen so as to maximize the ratio:

$$\frac{\text{between-group variance}}{\text{within-group variance}}$$

then the probability of correctly classifying the dependent variable on the basis of the discriminant score would be maximized. The linear combinations of a discriminant function are derived from an equation of the following form:

$$Y = B1X1 + B2X2 + \ldots\ldots\ldots +BnXn$$

Where:

Y = the discriminant score;
$B1\ldots Bn$ = the discriminant weights/coefficients; and
$X1\ldots Xn$ = the independent variables

When discriminant analysis is used for situations involving only two groups, the mean score for each group is calculated separately and the average of the two means is taken. Any individual/object with a score above the average is assigned to one group, and those with the below average scores to the second group.

In this study, individuals who were going on the package tours were classified into two groups: 1. those who had joined the package tour before; and 2. those who had not, and used as the dependent/criterion variable. In addition to the dependent or criterion variable, 12 independent/predictor variables were used in the discriminant model to determine how important they were in selecting a travel agency for taking package tours and ascertaining the degree of satisfaction derived by the selected travel agency. The independent variables were:

$X1$ = location of the travel agency;
$X2$ = price of the package tour;
$X3$ = knowledgeable staff;

```
        X4 = courteous service;
        X5 = scheduling package tour;
        X6 = programs/activities;
        X7 = food;
        X8 = accommodation;
        X9 = travel guide/escort;
        X10 = document handling;
        X11 = airport transportation; and
        X12 = goodwill of the travel agency.
```

The data were processed twice, first to determine the factors/attributes perceived as important in selecting a travel agency, and subsequently to determine the degree of satisfaction derived from using the given agency.

FINDINGS

Demographic And Socioeconomic Profile of Package Tourists

Responses to the question on whether the individual had joined the package tour before were provided by 200 tourists. Of this number, 156 or 78% had joined a tour before and the remaining 44 or 22% had not. The demographic and socioeconomic characteristics of the respondents were as follows:

1. <u>Sex:</u> a. Male -- 95 or 48%; b. Female -- 104 or 52%;

2. <u>Marital status:</u> a. Single -- 117 or 59%; and
   b. Married -- 41%;

3. <u>Respondent's age:</u> a. 20 yrs./less -- 28 or 15%;
   b. 21 to 25 Yrs. -- 61 or 32%; c. 26 to 35 Yrs. --
   54 or 29%; d. 36 to 45 Yrs. -- 16 or 9%; and
   e. 46 Yrs./older -- 28 or 15%.

4. <u>Spouse's age:</u> a. 25 Yrs./less -- 6 or 9%; b. 26 to 35
   Yrs. -- 26 or 37%; and c. 36 Yrs./older -- 38 or
   54%.

5. <u>Respondent's education:</u> a. Some H.S./H.S Grad. -- 121
   or 64%; b. Some college/College Grad. -- 60 or 31%;
   and c. Professional degree -- 9 or 5%.

6. <u>Spouse's education:</u> a. Some H.S./H.S. Grad. -- 49 or
   73%; b. Some College/College Grad. -- 17 or 25%;
   and c. Professional degree -- 1 or 2%.

7. <u>Respondent's occupation:</u> a. White collar -- 84 or
   46%; b. Blue collar -- 63 or 35%; c. Housewife

--8 or 4%; and Student/retired --27 or 15%.

8. Spouse's occupation: a. White collar -- 21 or 33%;
   b. Blue collar -- 22 or 34%; c. Housewife -- 19 or
   30%; and d. Student/retired -- 2 or 3%.

9. Respondent's monthly income: a. HK$2,000/less -- 84
   or 42%; b. HK$2,100 to 4,000 -- 53 or 26%;
   c. HK$4,500 to 10,000 -- 54 or 27%; and
   d. HK$10100/over -- 9 or 5%.

10. Spouse's monthly income: a. HK$4,500/less -- 175 or
    88%; and b. HK$5,000/over -- 25 or 12%.

11. Monthly household income: a. HK$4,500/less -- 104 or
    52%; b. HK$4,600 to 10,000 -- 62 or 31%; and
    c. HK$10,100/over -- 34 or 17%.

TABLE 1
Relationship Between Demographic And Socioeconomic Variables
And Whether One Had Taken Package Tour Before

Variable	n	Chi-square	d.f.	Significance	C
1. Sex:	199	0.03	1	0.86	0.02
2. Marital status:	197	13.04	1	0.00	0.26
3. Respondent's age:	187	53.97	4	0.00	0.47
4. Spouse's age:	70	1.32	2	0.52	0.14
5. Respondent's education:	190	3.72	2	0.16	0.14
6. Spouse's education:	67	2.16	2	0.34	0.18
7. Respondent's occupation:	182	11.40	3	0.01	0.24
8. Spouse's occupation:	64	2.09	3	0.55	0.18
9. Respondent's income:	200	15.54	3	0.00	0.27
10. Spouse's income:	200	2.40	1	0.12	0.13
11. Household income:	200	12.91	2	0.00	0.25

n = number of observations; C = contingency coefficient.
   d.f. = degrees of freedom.
Answers to the question whether the respondent had joined the

39

package tour before were cross tabulated in relation to demographic and socioeconomic variables and Chi-square values were estimated. Information presented in table 1 shows the relationship between the variables.

It can be seen in table 1 that the relationship between the variables -- marital status; respondent's age; respondent's occupation and income; household income and whether one had previously taken package tour is statistically highly significant. It is, therefore, reasonable to conclude that a typical package tourist is female; single; holds white/blue collar job with an income ranging between HK$2,000/less to 10,000 a month; and a household income ranging between HK$4,500/less to 10,000.

Reasons For Joining Package Tour

Reasons for joining the package tour were to be answered by checking each of the listed five reasons, and a category "others," on a 1 - 5 scale in which 1 represented the most important and 5, the least important. Responses were analyzed by estimating the arithmetic mean, median, and the standard error. To determine whether the ratings/rankings were consistent, Kendall tau was estimated. Results of the analysis are shown in table 2 and matrix 1, respectively.

TABLE 2
Reasons For Joining Package Tour: Mean, Median,
And Standard Error of Rating/Ranking

Reason	Mean	Median	Standard Error
1. Price	2.56	2.60	0.10
2. Destination	1.96	1.59	0.09
3. Guided tour	3.20	3.21	0.11
4. Group travel	2.52	2.32	0.11
5. Accommodation	2.26	2.04	0.10
6. Others	1.31	1.17	0.15

Category "others" included responses such as -- I like it; convenient; and so on.

The mean ratings/rankings presented in table 2 shows that "destination" and "others" were relatively more important compare to the other four reasons. This may be due to the fact that given the destination, a reason which may be unique to each individual, rest of the reasons may be common to all package tours.

MATRIX 1
Estimated Kendall Correlation Coefficients And The Level of Statistical Significance: Reasons For Taking Package Tour

	V1	V2	V3	V4	V5	V6
V1	-	0.52	0.51	0.49	0.50	0.13 (NS)
V2		-	0.57	0.58	0.54	0.11 (NS)
V3			-	0.62	0.59	0.01 (NS)
V4				-	0.53	0.04 (NS)
V5					-	0.06 (NS)
V6						-

NS = not significant; Rest of the correlations were significant at 0.00 level; n = 148; and Variables V1 to V6 represent reasons for taking package tour, listed in table 1.

Data presented in matrix 1 indicate lack of consistency in rating/ranking of the reasons grouped under the category "others." The remaining five with substantially large Kendall Correlation Coefficients and high statistical significance reveal consistency in rating/ranking the reasons for taking package tour.

Factors Perceived As Important In Selecting Travel Agency

Discriminant analysis was used as a statistical tool to determine the factors/attributes perceived as important by the tourists in selecting a travel agency. The dependent/criterion variable, whether the respondent had taken a package tour before was classified into two categories -- 1. those that had taken the package tour before; and 2. those that had not taken. Results of the analysis using 147 observations and 12 independent/predictor variables are shown in table 3.

Information provided about the standardized discriminant coefficients in table 3 indicate that only six of the 12 variables -- X8, X9, X11, X5, X10 and X1, in that order, are significant [23]. Factors/attributes -- airport transportation, schedule, and location have a negative sign. This may be due to the fact that the tourists consider accommodation as important, but they are not necessarily looking for luxurious place to stay and want something that is comfortable enough to stay during the package tour. To

TABLE 3

Standard Discriminant Coefficients And Factor/Attribute
Ranking: Factors/Attributes Perceived As Important In
Selecting A Travel Agency For Taking Package Tour

Factor/Attribute	Discriminant Coefficient	Rank
X8, Accommodation:	-0.78	1
X9, Guide/Escort:	0.57	2
X11, Airport Transportation:	-0.52	3
X5, Schedule:	-0.43	4
X10, Document handling:	0.42	5
X1, Location:	-0.36	6
X4, Courteous service:	0.26	7
X6, Programs/activities:	0.22	8
X2, Price:	-0.11	9
X3, Knowledgeable staff:	-0.10	10
X12, Goodwill of the agency:	0.06	11
X7, Food:	0.01	12

provide luxurious accommodation the travel agency may have to
spend large sums of money and pass this on to the package
tourists in the form of higher package tour prices. Similar
interpretation may be given to the other three variables. In
short, the negative signs may be interpreted as indicating
comforts and economy as the concerns of a travel agency
rather than luxurious and expensive package tours. It is
important, that the travel agencies look at each one of the
factors/attributes that are significant carefully while
developing and implementing package tour marketing strategy.

Degree of Satisfaction Derived From The Selected Travel Agency

Individuals taking package tours were asked to rate/rank the
12 factors/attributes listed in table 4 with regard to
satisfaction derived from the travel agency on a 1 - 7 rating
scale. A rating of 1 represented most satisfied, and 7, least
satisfied. Discriminant technique was used to analyze a total
of 123 observation. Whether the respondent had taken a
package tour before was used as the dependent/criterion
variable and the 12 factors/attributes indicating the degree
of satisfaction were used as independent/criterion variables
in the analysis. Results of the analysis and ranking of the
factors/attributes important in providing satisfaction with
the selected travel agency are presented in table 4.

TABLE 4
Standard Discriminant Coefficients And Factor/Attribute Ranking: Degree of Satisfaction Derived From The Selected Travel Agency

Factor/Attribute	Discriminant Coefficient	Rank
X4, Courteous service:	0.92	1
X5, Schedule:	-0.73	2
X3, Knowledgeable staff:	-0.67	3
X2, Price:	0.45	4
X11, Airport transpo-rtation:	-0.30	5
X12, Goodwill of travel agency:	0.16	6
X7, Food:	-0.14	7
X9, Guide/Escort:	-0.13	8
X10, Document handling:	0.06	9
X8, Accommodation	-0.04	10
X1, Location:	0.02	11
X6, Program/Activities:	0.01	12

Data shown in table 4 reveal that only five of the 12 factors -- X4, X5, X3, X2, and X11, in that order, are significant. Of the five, three service attributes -- schedule, knowledgeable staff, and airport transportation with negative signs indicate dissatisfaction. Package tourists are satisfied with the other two features -- courteous service and price. It is important that the travel agencies try to provide better scheduling, employ staff with adequate travel related knowledge or provide training, and upgrade or provide better airport transportation. Improvement in these areas may result in satisfied customers and hopefully create greater demand for the agency. Moreover, satisfied customers may serve as a source of word-of-mouth promotion to the travel agency.

SUMMARY AND CONCLUSION

Tourism is gaining momentum as one of the fastest growing industries in the world today. The prime reason for the popularity of tourism seems to be its ability to create jobs and as well as generate revenues to fill a country's coffer. Recognizing the importance of tourism in the national economy, countries like Canada, India, and New Zealand have opened up cabinet rank positions with the sole purpose of allocating and directing the available resources for tourism development. In the U.S., both the state and federal governments are showing keen interest in tourism to generate badly needed jobs and revenues. The worldwide recognition of tourism as an industry and the government involvement to promote tourism may open up tremendous opportunities to the travel and tourism agencies.

At a time when the growth in the tourism industry is taking a great leap forward, it is appropriate that those involved in providing tourist oriented services develop and implement marketing strategies to satisfy the potential customers. This study was, therefore, designed to determine the:
1. demographic and socioeconomic profile of the package tour customers; 2. reasons for joining package tour; 3. factors perceived as important in selecting a travel agency; and 4. determine the degree of satisfaction derived from the selected travel agency's services. Data obtained from 204 package tourists at the Kai Tak International Airport in Hong Kong during November-December 1985 showed that the typical package tourist was -- female, single, held white/blue collar job with a monthly income ranging between HK$2,000/less to 10,000, and monthly household income ranging between HK$4,500 to 10,000. The two most important reasons for joining package tours were -- "destination" and "others." Factors/attributes perceived as important in selecting a travel agency were -- accommodation, guide/escort, airport transportation, schedule, travel related document handling, and location of the travel agency. The tourists were satisfied with the service provided and the package tour price, but were dissatisfied with the schedule, staff, and airport transportation. Considering the demographic and socioeconomic profile, reasons for joining package tour, factors/attributes perceived as important in a package tour, and taking a serious look at the factors responsible for tourist dissatisfaction in developing and implementing marketing strategies may help the travel agency attract potential customers and satisfy the current clientele.

REFERENCES

[1] "The Big Picture - 1986," The Travel Industry World Year Book (New York: Child and Waters, 1986),7.

[2] Ibid.,8.

[3] Venkatakrishna V. Bellur and Ramachandran Bharath, "Higher Gas Prices: Will It Affect Tourist Industry," Proceedings: 1980 SE AIDS, February 20-22,1980.140.

[4] U.S. Bureau of the Census, The Statistical Abstract of the United States:1986 (106th ed.),Washington, DC, 1985, 445.

[5] The Conference Board, "Leisure," Road Maps of Industry, No. 1815, September 1977, 2.

[6] U.S. Bureau of the Census, op. cit., 603.

[7] Ibid., 236-37.

[8] Ibid., 552-53.

[9] "States turn on charm, cash to lure tourists," USA TODAY, March 4, 1987, 5A.

[10] Julia Lawler and Peg Loftus, "Europe ho! Travel bug bites USA," USA TODAY, March 9, 1987, 1A-2A.

[11] Deborah Williams, "Flying more 'taxing' than ever," Niagara Gazette, May 3, 1987, 5E.

[12] Anthony Spaeth, "phillipines Is Attracting Tourists Again," Asian Wall Street Journal, May 6, 1986, 1.

[13] Kevin Sinclair, "Looking to prosper from the tourist dollar," South China Morning Post, (Hong Kong), April 15, 1986,1.

[14]"Tourism," Introducing Hong Kong, (Hong Kong: The Hong Kong General Chamber of Commerce, July 1985), 20.

[15] "Immigration and Tourism," Hong Kong 1986, (Hong Kong: Government Printing Office, 1986), 211.

[16] "Package Tours Market," Hotel Management, No. 5, Vol. 199, May 1984, 1.

[17] Julia Lawler and Peg Loftus, op. cit.

[18] "Air fares down, hotel costs rise," USA TODAY, January 19, 1987, 7B.

[19] Susan Voyles, "Tracking travel costs: New agencies specialize in curbing expenses," USA TODAY, February 23, 1987, Section E.

[20] Jofari J. "Anatomy of the Travel Industry," The Cornel H.R.A. Quarterly, May 1983, 71-77.

[21] Bitner, M.J. and B.H. Boones, "New Management Looks for the Successful Tourism Manager," Annals of Tourism Research," 1980, No. 7, Vol. 3, 337-51.

[22] "Travel Agents Are Thriving in 'Glut' of Deregulation,"

Marketing News, No. 19, June 21, 1985, 23.

[23] Joseph F. Hair, Jr. et al., *Multivariate Analysis With Readings* (Tulsa, OK: Petroleum Publishing Company, 1979), 111.

TOURISM AND THE PERCEIVED RISK OF TERRORISM

Judy Cohen
Rider College

ABSTRACT

Negative publicity can cause an increase in consumers' perceptions of risk. Such was the case during 1985 and 1986, when increased terrorist activities caused many tourists to avoid travel to Europe. This paper presents a model of perceived risk as it relates to terrorism in tourist destinations. It then suggests strategies, based on the model, to overcome consumers' perceptions of risk of terrorism. The author concludes that, while fear of terrorism has subsided, tourist marketers must plan ahead to avoid decline in demand resulting from similar incidents.

INTRODUCTION

Marketers have long realized that they must identify and operate within environmental constraints which are not under their control. At times marketers must respond to occurrences in the environment which create negative publicity. Negative publicity has been defined by Reidenback and Sherrel (1986) ". . . as the uncontrollable dissemination of potentially damaging information by providing detracting news about a product, service, business unit or person via print, broadcast media, or word of mouth." (p. 4) This paper examines a specific type of negative publicity which created great problems for tourism marketers - fear of terrorism in European tourist destinations.

Tourism to Europe greatly declined in 1985 and 1986 as a result of terrorist activities. It is estimated that the United Kingdom had a 20 per cent decline in tourism (Upton 1986). Greece lost an estimated $100 million in tourism revenue in 1985 (Waldrop 1986). Early in 1986, a poll of 205 travel agents showed that almost half had had cancellations or changed destinations due to terrorism (Lehrman 1986). For the same time period, a U. S. Travel Data Center study showed that 35 per cent of Americans planning to travel had switched travel plans due to terrorism (Cross 1986). The fear of terrorism has subsided, and tourists are returning to Europe. But tourism marketers must plan ahead should they be faced with a recurrence of this or similar crises.

Fear of terrorism in tourist destinations is an example of consumers' perceived risk. Moutinho (1984) mentions risk as an input into the vacation tourist decision process, but does not elaborate. The concept of perceived risk in consumer behavior was first introduced by Bauer (1960). Several types of perceived risk have been identified, including time, social, psychological, financial, and physical risk. Most studies on perceived risk do not focus on physical risk. For example, Garner (1986) studied perceived risk with respect to realtors, hair stylists, and dry cleaners. For these three services, physical risk was rated as least important. Zikmund and Scott (1977) examined product characteristics which create perceived risk. One characteristic was "dangerous." However, the researchers did not investigate the causes of perceived danger. Further research is needed to better understand perceived physical risk as it relates to risk of terrorism in choice of tourist destination. This paper proposes a model of perceived risk with respect to terrorism and tourism, and suggests strategies for marketers to deal with perceived risk.

Bettman (1973) suggests a model which helps explain how consumers in the high perceived risk category dealt with fear of terrorism. In Bettman's model, there are two components of risk: inherent risk and handled risk. Inherent risk deals with the product class - "the innate degree of conflict the product class is able to arouse" (Bettman 1973, p. 184). Handled risk is on the brand level, i.e., how much risk the consumer perceives when choosing a specific brand. In the case of tourism and fear of terrorism, inherent risk depends on how much the consumer perceives the risk of a terrorist occurrence during a vacation. For handled risk, on the other hand, perceived risk is low when a wide variety of options is possible. This appeared to be true in the terrorism/tourism situation. "Overall traveller concern seemed to be confined to areas associated with terrorism, rather than travel per se." (D'Amore and Anuza 1986, p. 21) Thus the consumer could minimize risk by following a "conjunctive or threshold model, where options (e.g. vacation destinations) are eliminated from further consideration when they are perceived to have certain unacceptable features." (Moutinho, p. 9) During the terrorist crisis, persons in the high perceived risk category dealt with risk simply by choosing destinations with low perceived risk of terrorism, e.g., the United States and Canada (Phillips 1986). The conjunctive model for dealing with perceived risk helps explain consumer behavior, but does not help tourism marketers create strategies for dealing with the outcome - loss of business. In order to develop such strategies, it is necessary to clarify further the nature of this specific perceived risk.

TOURISM/TERRORISM PERCEIVED RISK MODEL

Figure 1 shows a model of perceived risk as it relates to tourism and terrorism. In this section, the model will be described. The following section will then suggest strategies, based upon the model, for tourism marketers.

Perceived vs. Actual Risk

When perceived risk is high for a product or service, marketers should first examine the product/service to determine whether perceptions are accurate. Perceptions of risk of terrorism were definitely high in 1985 and 1986, but what were the real risks? From January 1985 to June 1986, 18 Americans were killed by terrorists; in 1985 alone, 43,500 died in car accidents (Cross 1986). Furthermore, the risk of being killed by a terrorist in the summer of 1985 was less than the risk of being hit by lightening in the U. S. during the same period. Tourism marketers were faced with a difficult problem - perceived risk was much higher, at least in some market segments, than actual risk.

Segmenting the Market by Levels of Risk Perception

Perceptions of risk of terrorism are in part correlated with demographic and psychographic factors, as well as type of travel. On a broad demographic level, the tourism market can be segmented by nationality. During the terrorism crisis, potential travellers from the U. S. had the highest level of perceived risk. In comparison, Canadians, while concerned specifically about Greece, in general did not cancel travel plans, nor did travellers from Italy, the United Kingdom, and Brazil (Philips 1986). Cross-cultural differences in perceived risk are discussed by Hoover, Green and Saegert (1978). They found that Mexicans generally had lower levels of perceived risk (for non-tourism related products) than consumers from the U. S. They attributed this differences to higher levels of fatalism among Mexicans. Mexicans feel ". . . they have much less control over their destiny than people in the United States" (p. 107). Those with higher levels of fatalism would feel they can not avoid their destiny and so should not attempt to do so, e.g., by avoiding certain tourist destinations. Since Americans are generally not fatalistic, their perceptions of risk of terrorism were high.

Those tourist destinations which rely heavily on the U. S. market, such as the United Kingdom, experienced great losses in sales. Italy, on the other hand, may have had a higher actual risk of terrorism. But only four per cent of Italy's tourists in 1985 were from the U. S.; therefore, Italy had less business to lose (Zahradnik and Hall 1986).

Within the U. S., the travel market can be segmented by purpose, i.e., the business/incentive vs. leisure market, as well as demographically and psychographically. Within the business travel market, the conference and incentive travel business was hardest hit, because travel planners did not want to be perceived as sending people to potentially dangerous places and because potential travellers refused to go to those places (Cross 1986, D'Amore and Anuza 1986). Within the leisure market, " . . . affluent and less faint-hearted East Coasters or the more budget-minded back packers" (Upton 1986, p. 21) were less likely to cancel plans due to fear of terrorism than other demographic or psychographic segments. Since these groups did not decrease their travel to Europe, they will not be the focus of this paper. Rather, the rest of the U. S. consumer market will be further examined.

The high perceived risk market can be segmented into viable and non-viable target markets. A viable target market is considered one whose perceptions of risk may be changed by marketing activities. For example, the conference and incentive market would not be a viable target market. Even if travel planners were convinced that risk of terrorism were low, potential travellers' perceptions of risk could still be high.

Insight can be gained into the U. S. tourist/pleasure high perceived risk segment by further subdividing this group. Hoover, Green and Saegert (1978) summarized Cox's (1967) suggestion that the amount of perceived risk depends on "(1) the amount of the loss if consequences are unfavorable and (2) the individual's subjective feeling or degree of certainty that the consequences will be unfavorable" (Hoover, Green and Saegert, p. 103). The segment whose perceptions of risk are high may either not utilize an expected value model, or exaggerate the probability of loss. Each subsegment will be examined further.

A segment which does not follow the expected value risk model was identified in a study by Slovic and Lichtenstein (1968). Slovic and Lichtenstein examined perceived risk in a gambling situation. The expected value for the game was: (probability of winning x amount won) + (probability of loss x amount lost). The researchers found that for a portion of the subjects, the decision whether to play the game depended not on expected value of the outcome, but rather only on the amount that could be lost. Similarly, we would expect to find that for a subsegment of the high perceived terrorist risk market, the amount of loss in the extreme case, i.e., one's life, is the primary consideration upon which perceptions of risk are based. The probability of loss is ignored. Theoretically, in order to lower perceived risk, the tourism marketer would have to convince this subsegment that the amount of loss was not of great value. Since this strategy is not likely to be successful, this subsegment will not be considered a viable segment.

The rest of the high risk segment more closely follows the model that perceived risk equals the amount of lost multiplied by the probability of loss. For this segment, however, the probability of loss has been distorted. In the next section, factors which create a distorted perceived probability of loss will be proposed.

Factors Affecting Perceptions of High Probability of Loss

Very little research has been done on what factors cause high perceived probability of loss, especially with respect to physical risk. One study of relevance to tourism marketers is by Slovic, Fischoff, and Lichtenstein (1984) (hereafter referred to as SFL). This section of the model will rely primarily on their study. Propositions will be made regarding the factors which create high perceived probability of loss and therefore high perceived risk of terrorism in tourist destinations.

SFL examined perceptions of risk with respect to a wide variety of products/services/events, including skateboards, commercial aviation, nuclear reactor accidents, microwave ovens, and smoking. All products studied had a potential physical risk. Most included, ultimately, the risk of death. SFL discuss perceived risk in general, and the propositions made by this author will also refer to perceived risk. However, the reader should keep in mind that, given the common amount of loss, the component which creates the perception of high risk is, in fact, perceptions of the probability of loss.

SFL found that consumers have perceptions of high risk when: (1) the locus of control is outside themselves (i.e., is "uncontrollable"); (2) an occurrence of the feared condition results in many persons dead, wounded, or held captive at one time in one place (i.e., "catastrophic" vs. "individual"); (3) the consumer is not very familiar with the "high risk" product/service (i.e., "new risk"); (4) the consumer himself is at risk, rather than another segment of the population ("affects me"); and (5) the occurrences are

51

perceived as reflecting a general ongoing problem rather than as isolated incidents (i.e., has "signal potential"). An additional cause of perceived risk is when (6) the occurrences are a "media event". Each source of perceived risk will be described in greater detail.

Locus of Control (SFL's "controllable")

Proposition 1: Consumers feel that when they are not "in control" of a situation, risk is higher.

The ability to repel a terrorist attack depends on the effectiveness of the security systems which the government and individual tourist organizations utilize. On the other hand, SFL found, consumers feel relatively in control when they drive a motorcycle, even though the high fatality rate for motorcyclists (2 per 100 annually) indicate they are not all in control. The need to be in control and the perception that one actually is in control is a characteristic of non-fatalistic consumers from the U. S., as indicated by the results of the Hoover, Green and Saegert (1978) study.

Many Victims at One Time/Place (SFL's "catastrophic")

Proposition 2: Perceived risk is high for products/services/events such that when the feared condition occurs, many people are hurt or killed at one time and/or in one place.

Although the absolute numbers of victims of terrorism is small, the concentration of victims at one time and place causes perceptions that risk is much higher than it actually is.

Familiarity with the Product (SFL's "old risk")

Proposition 3: The more infrequent the contact the consumer has with the product/service, the higher perceived risk.

This proposition is supported by Zikmund and Scott's (1977) study on perceived risk. Generally, products scoring high on "newness" and low on "frequency of purchase" (two different measures of familiarity) have higher perceived risk. Similarly, for risk of hazard loss, Roselius (1971) found that the major risk reduction strategy used by consumers was brand loyalty. By buying brands s/he is familiar with, the consumer lowers perceived risk.

The overseas tourist destination decision is a relatively new one to many Americans. Further, most Americans do not travel to Europe frequently. Therefore they can not

reassure themselves on the basis of their own experience
that risk of terrorism is low.

The Consumer Himself is at Risk (SFL's "affects me")

Proposition 4: The public-at-large, or specifically the
American population, must be at risk before the American
public panics.

Proposition 2 - many dead or wounded at the same time - must
be modified by identifying who the population-at-risk is.
When the public-at-large is at risk, so is the risk
perceiver, his family and friends. Thus the fear of
terrorism is bolstered by the perception that terrorists
indiscriminantly choose victims. Perceived risk increases
when terrorist activity is directed against U. S. tourists,
as was the case in 1985 and 1986 (Lehrman 1986).

Risk Perceived as Part of a Larger Problem (SFL's "signal potential")

Proposition 5: Perceived risk is high when the public
believes the feared condition is not simply a cluster of
isolated incidents but is part of a larger ongoing problem.

SFL (1984) describe events with signal potential as those
which "serve as a warning signal for society, providing new
information about the probability that similar or even more
destructive mishaps might occur within this type of
activity." (p. 191) Several factors help create such an
impression. The feared condition is perceived as a signal
when, as discussed above, the consumer starts to feel the
general population, or specifically one's own group, is at
risk. Other factors create a perception of signal
potential. When there is a sudden high incidence of the
feared condition, as there was in terrorist activity in 1985
and 1986 the consumer may consider the problem to be
pervasive (Lehrmann 1986).   D'Amore anbd Anuza (1986) state
"The evidence suggests that we can expect frequent and
bolder (terrorist) action in the future" (p. 20). A final
factor which makes incidents seem like a general problem is
having the subject treated as such by special interest
groups and/or the media.

The Mass Media's Role in Perceptions of Risk.

Proposition 6: To the extent that the mass media treats
terrorism as front-page news, as affecting the American
public-at-large and as having signal potential, perceived
risk will be high.

The mass media serve as gatekeepers for American thought.
Research on mass media's influence on public opinion has
mainly dealt with political issues. Studies by Cohen
(1963), McCombs and Shaw (1972) and Iyengar (1982) found
that in political campaigns, mass media has an
agenda-setting function, i.e., the press ". . . may not be
successful much of the time in telling people what to think,
but it is stunningly successful in telling its readers what
to think about" (Cohen, p. 13). When the press decides to
highly publicize a potentially threatening issue such as
terrorism in Europe, the audience is likely to experience an
increase in perceived risk. How the news is reported is
also likely to have an impact. Finn (1981) found through a
survey of both public relations directors and journalists
that the majority of both groups felt that reporters "play
on public emotions" (p. 10), are inaccurate due to
carelessness, and that how the news is "packaged" is more
important than the facts. How is the news packaged? Nimmo
and Combs (1985) found, using content analysis, three very
different orientations in crisis reporting on the news of
the three national television networks. They found CBS gave
the most factual account and discussed how the situation
would be managed. NBC and ABC gave more emotional accounts
which implied such incidents were not controllable. It
would not be surprising to find that, in response to reports
of terrorist activities, ABC and NBC news audiences had a
higher level of perceived risk than CBS's audience.

STRATEGIES FOR DEALING WITH HIGH PERCEIVED RISK OF TERRORISM

The primary purpose of this paper is to develop a model of
perceived risk as it relates to tourism and terrorism. The
model needs to be empirically tested. However, the author
also proposes strategies based on the model, and where
possible gives examples of tourism marketers who have used
those strategies.

Strategy 1: Reduce the Actual Level of Risk

Tourism marketers have taken measures to reduce the
probability of terrorist attacks. Pan Am, which was
especially hard hit by terrorism, has increased security, as
have other airlines. Both airlines and airports are
following security procedures which El Al and Iseali
airports have used for years. These include matching
luggage to passengers; early check-in so each passenger can
be questioned and scrutinized; more than one check of
baggage and travel papers; and control over who has access
to aircraft. Hotels are also increasing security. For
example, in France, police are called if a suitcase is left
unattended (D'Amore and Anuza 1986, Labich 1986).

Lowering risk by increasing security is necessary, but there are limitations to this strategy. First, national tourism associations and individual tourist organizations do not have control over security measures taken by all airlines, hotels, and tourist attractions. Therefore a megamarketing (Kotler 1986) strategy must be formulated to convince government and other relevant groups to make a concerted national effort to increase security. The second problem for tourism marketers is that when such security measures are successfully implemented, the marketers may be hesitant to inform their target markets of these improvements. One reason for keeping improved security measures secret is to avoid informing potential terrorists about tighter security, thereby helping them plan how to best circumvent these obstacles. Perhaps a greater problem is the fact that in the past, the tourism industry stressed positive news. It was felt that discussing problems only led the consumer to think more about those problems and thus become more concerned. Reidenbach and Sherrell (1986) suggest that such a strategy is appropriate for small incidents. But major problems such as terrorism cannot be ignored. Pan Am is following the open approach, but in a low-key manner. Pan Am executives are informing large corporate clients and travel agents of security improvements (Labich 1986).

Strategy 2: Segment the Market

Different market segments have different perceptions of risk. Marketers should follow a segmentation strategy of differentiation - i.e., use different marketing strategies for different market segments. When a marketer has only one market segment as his target market, he may find that this market segment happens to be the one whose perceptions of risk have increased the most when negative publicity occurs. The implications for marketing strategy are clear: (1) In general, diversify target markets to spread risk. If the demand from one market segment declines (for any reason - currency devaluation, economic recession, fear of terrorism, etc.), demand from other segments will hopefully remain healthy. (2) In the short term, when demand drops, concentrate marketing efforts towards segments whose demand is still strong. British tourism marketers concentrated their marketing efforts on the "less faint-hearted East Coasters"; London theatres remained filled (Upton 1986). (3) In the long run, do not completely eliminate markets which are vulnerable to high perceived risk, since they will eventually rebound (Ibid.)

Strategy 3: Change Perceptions of Risk

In the high perceived probability of terrorism group, the marketer should try to change perceptions of risk. The

55

perceived probability of a terrorist incident occurring is exaggerated compared to the actual probability of occurrence. Suggested strategies will be based on the propositions discussed above regarding causes of distorted perceptions of risk.

Locus of Control: Marketers can try to decrease the perceived risk caused by the locus of control being outside the consumer. They can reassure the consumer that control is in responsible hands. Tourism marketers can inform the public about tighter security measures, especially if a subtle approach is used, as in the Pan Am example discussed above.

Many Victims at One Time/Place: The marketer can help consumers put risk into perspective by statistically comparing the real risk, e.g., of travel in Europe, with the real risk of car accidents, downhill skiing, smoking, etc. This would best be done through publicity. (Media relations are discussed below.) Advertising would not be as effective due to lower source credibility.

Familiarity with the Product: Tourism marketers can try to make their locations more familiar, either through direct or indirect experience, to the potential traveller. In order to lower perceived risk, United Kingdom marketers developed strategies to increase consumers' exposure to the feared object. Through lotteries, British Airways offered the chance to win free flights, a townhouse, and a Rolls Royce. Hotels offered discount prices during peak seasons. By giving consumers deals they "could not refuse," the U. K. refamiliarized consumers with the pleasures of travel in their country (Upton 1986). Greece, very hard hit by fears of terrorism, has arranged special media events to draw back business, e.g., a sailing festival was held (Waldrop 1986). The British Tourist Authority has used vicarious learning to make the U. K. more familiar to Americans. ". . . films of happy American Anglophiles resident in Britain have been sent to the U. S. press" (Upton 1986, p. 24). The BTA has also sent Americans and Britons to appear on U. S. talk shows (Ibid.) The marketer should also have a long-run goal of familiarizing future markets by trying to expose children more frequently to the tourist destination. They will be less fearful of overseas travel if they have had pleasant travel experiences when young. Tourism marketers can use price promotions for families to encourage parents to bring children when travelling.

Consumer himself is at risk: Potential tourists may feel that terrorist victims are chosen at random, and thus risk increases for the public at large. This was certainly the case in the Rome and Vienna airport massacres. Or American tourists may fear they will be targeted because they are American, thus increasing their risk. One strategy for dealing with the perception that all U. S. travellers are at equally high risk is to publicize the fact that certain travellers are at greater risk than others, in the unlikely event of any terrorist action. For example, travellers who wear expensive clothing and/or jewelry, who carry "gold" credit cards, and who carry business cards indicating they have important positions or work at major companies are most likely to be victims of terrorism. People who heed these suggestions should feel that terrorism is less likely to affect them personally.

Perceived Risk as Part of a Larger Problem: The marketer has a particularly difficult job dealing with incidents with signal potential. When the problem relates to the "whole population at risk" , suggestions given above apply. But when an increase in incidents causes consumers to perceive them as a signal portending an ongoing crisis, the strategy is not so simple. Only efforts by the marketer to prevent recurrence, and the passage of time (with the incidents at "normal" or less than normal levels) will prove to the consumer that the series of incidents were in fact just isolated incidents. When a general problem is perceived due to mass media attention, the marketer must sharpen his public relations skills (discussed below).

Perceived Risk and the Mass Media: What can marketers do about inaccurate, sensational reporting about the threat of terrorism? Finn (1981) gives several suggestions for good media relations. They include having good, ongoing relations with media, communicating clearly, and not trying to obstruct negative publicity. Ultimately, the marketers must formulate a strategy to lower the probability of a reccurrence of a terrorist indicent. This will not only gain respect of reporters, but is in any case an essential strategy, and was the first strategy suggested above.

CONCLUSIONS

Negative publicity is always of concern to tourism marketers. This is especially true of the case of terrorism, when a few incidents caused consumers' perceived risk to skyrocket well beyond the level of actual risk. Marketers can and must formulate strategies to deal with such crises. These strategies should not first be considered only after the onset of the crisis; marketers must plan. Several of the strategies discussed above require long term planning. These include: familiarizing young people with the product/service; developing good relations with mass media; and diversifying market segments.

By planning ahead and being prepared, marketers will not eliminate negative publicity. But they will be able to minimize the detrimental effects of unexpected events in the environment such as terrorism, which cause increased perceptions of risk tourists.

FIGURE 1

Model of Perceived Risk of Terrorism
with Respect to Tourist Destinations

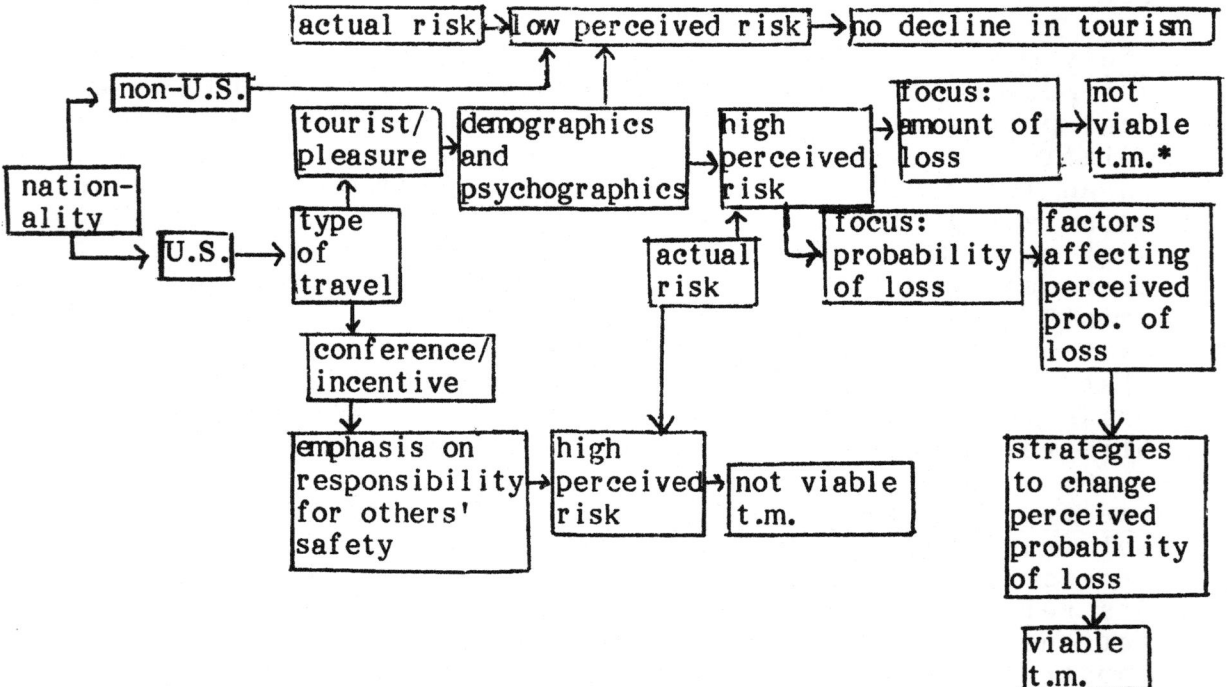

* "t.m." means target market

Note: The author would like to thank John Richardson for his helpful suggestions regarding the model and the final manuscript.

REFERENCES

Bauer, Raymond A. (1967) "Consumer Behavior as Risk Taking," in Donald F. Cox, ed., Risk Taking and Information Handling in Consumer Behavior (Boston: Graduate School of Business Administration, Harvard University).

Bettman, James A. (1973) "Perceived Risk and its Components: A Model and Empirical Test," Journal of Marketing Research 10 (May), 184-90.

Cohen, Bernard C. (1963) The Press and Foreign Policy (Princeton, Princeton University Press).

Cox, Donald F., (1967) Risk Taking and Information Handling in Consumer Behavior (Boston: Graduate School of Business Administration, Harvard University).

Cross, Willaim (1986) "Are Americans Really Staying Away from Europe?," Europe n. 258 (Jul/Aug), 16-17.

D'Amore, Loius J. and Teresa E. Anuza (1986) "International Terrorism: Implications and Challenge for Global Tourism," Business Quarterly 51 (November), 20-29.

Finn, David (1981) The Business-media Relationship (New York: AMACOM).
Garner, Sarah Jane (1986), "Perceived Risk and Information Sources in Services Purchasing," The Mid-Atlantic Journal of Business 24 (Summer), 49-58.

Hoover, Robert J., Robert T. Green and Joel Saegert (1978) "A Cross-National Study of Perceived Risk," Journal of Marketing 42 (July), 102-108.

Iyengar, Shanto, Mark D. Peters and Donald R. Kinder (1982) "Experimental Demonstrations of the 'Not-so-minimal' Consequences of Television News Programs," The American Political Science Review 76 (December), 848-858.

Kotler, Philip (1986) "Megamarketing," Harvard Business Review 64 (March/April), 117-124.

Labich, Kenneth (1986) "Coping with the Fear of Terror," Fortune 113 (May 26), 57-59.

Lehrman, Celia K. (1986) "When Fact and Fantasy Collide: Crisis Management in the Travel Industry" Public Relations Journal 42 (April), 25-28.

McCombs, Maxwell E. and Donald Shaw (1972) "The Agenda-setting Function of Mass Media," Public Opinion Quarterly 36 (Summer), 176-187.

Moutinho, Luiz (1984) "Vacation Tourist Decision Process," The Quarterly Review of Marketiing, 9 (Spring), 8-17.

Nimmo, Dan and James E. Combs (1985) Nightly Horrors (The Knoxville: University of Tennessee Press).

Phillips, Lisa (1986) "Terror Spurs Local Tourism," Advertising Age 57 (January 20), 32.

Reidenbach, R. Eric and Dan L. Sherrell (1986) "Negative Press: Is Your Company Prepared," Business 36 (Jan.-March), 3-10.

Roselius, Ted (1971), "Consumer Rankings of Risk Reduction Methods," Journal of Marketing 35 (January), 56-61.

Slovic, Paul, Baruch Fischhoff and Sarah Lichtenstein (1984) "Behavioral Decision Theory Perspectives on Risk and Safety," Acta Psychologica 56 (August), 183-203.

_____, and Sarah Lichtenstein (1968), "Relative Importance of Probabilities and Payoffs in Risk Taking," Journal of Experimental Psychology Monograph," 78 (November), 1-18.

Upton, G. (1986) "Wooing the Yanks Back" Marketing 25 (June 26), 20-24.

Waldrop, Heidi (1986) "Greece Battles Unsafe Image," Successful Meetings 35 (May), 31-32.

Zahradnik, Rich and Carol Hall (1986) "States of Travel" Marketing & Media Decisions 21 (June), 73-82.

Zikmund, William G. and Jerome E. Scott (1977), "An Investigation of the Role of Product Characteristics in Risk Perception," Review of Business and Economic Research 13 (Fall), 19-34.

INSIGHTS ON PERCEIVED IMPORTANCE OF INFORMATION SOURCES FOR VACATION DECISIONS AMONG THE ELDERLY IN THE UNITED STATES

Alan J. Greco
The University of North Carolina at Charlotte

ABSTRACT

The perceived importance of ten sources of information, including internal and external sources, on vacation trip destination decisions of 94 elderly and 88 middle aged group members was investigated. Data for this study were collected by self-administered questionnaires distributed at the regular meetings of the organizations. Family, experience, and travel agents were the three information sources most often rated as important by both samples, although the elderly perceived all three sources to be less important than the middle aged. Implications of the results are presented.

INTRODUCTION

During the past two decades, a number of primary and secondary research studies have attempted to describe the size and economic importance of the elderly consumer market (e.g., Meadow et al. 1980; Lazer 1985; Greco 1987). This interest in the elderly consumer has been reflected in the travel and tourism literature as well (Guinn 1980; Shoemaker 1984).

The elderly, as travelers, have received increased attention for several reasons. Many senior citizens have the time to travel and they are willing to spend an appreciable amount of their income for this activity (Petre 1986). Older persons also control a large share of this country's discretionary income largely because of freedom from the financial obligations of younger adults (French and Fox 1985). Older people also tend to spend more than average on vacation travel, entertainment, and restaurant meals (Wall Street Journal 1983). Additionally, a national travel survey indicated that more than half of all persons 65 or older had taken a vacation in the year prior to the study (Allen and Bratman 1981, p. 50). Moreover, the elderly market can help fill the peaks and valleys for airlines and hotels because of the flexibility of their travel schedules.

Despite increased attention directed to the elderly market and the implications of their purchasing power, relatively little is known about this market's susceptibility to marketing variables (Phillips and Sternthal 1977). The travel and tourism literature has utilized market segmentation research in over a dozen studies to gain a clearer picture of the composition of various travel markets (e.g. Goodrich 1978; Crask 1981; Etzel and Woodside 1983; Bryant and Morrison 1980; Bartos 1982), but little published research has focused upon sources of information used by the elderly to decide on a vacation trip destination. A better understanding of the perceived importance of information sources by older persons would facilitate the development of communications mixes to serve this important market segment.

BACKGROUND

Most studies of consumer information search activity have found that the amount of information sought by consumers is limited (Hawkins, Best, and Coney 1986, p. 587). However, consumers are more likely to seek external information when confronted with high financial risk, greater differences in product alternatives, higher product/service involvement, less experience, and other situational factors. It is likely that many vacation trip destination decisions—other than family visits—would encourage some formal or informal external information search since both considerable time and money may be invested in the decision.

External information search may involve formal sources such as marketer sponsored mass media, direct mail, and travel agents. Informal external information sources may include interpersonal sources such as family, friends, and neighbors. Internal search, of course, may occur in the form of recollection of past experience with prior vacation trips and may be a valuable information source.

External Information

In a marketing context, Klippel and Sweeney (1974) found information from family and friends to be important to elderly consumers of headache remedies and television sets. Michman, Hocking, and Harris (1979) reported interpersonal communication from friends, spouse, and professional recommendations to be important to senior citizens when purchasing cold remedies. Similarly, friends, spouse, and salespersons were found to be important sources of information for the elderly regarding apparel purchases, however, the elderly were less active information seekers than younger consumers (Lumpkin and Greenberg 1982). These research findings suggest that the elderly do consult informal and formal interpersonal information sources for physical products. It is logical that the propensity for information seeking would extend to high involvement consumption activities such as vacation-travel. Nuclear and extended family influence, in particular, is likely to be a useful information source since many elderly frequently interact with these family members (Phillips and Sternthal 1977).

In addition to interpersonal sources of information, consumers of all ages are exposed to formal, marketer-sponsored communications by the mass media. Research on media usage patterns has provided some useful findings about the

62

elderly. In an extensive review of the communications literature, Kubey (1980) found that nearly all studies have shown that elderly adults watch more television than do middle aged or younger adults. A ten-year longitudinal study comparing the same age cohorts over time has shown that people generally do watch more television as they age (Bower 1973, p. 44). Mornings (before 9:00 a.m.) and evenings (6:00 - 9:00 p.m.) tend to be the periods of heaviest viewing among the elderly (Bernhardt and Kinnear 1976).

Older persons are heavy listeners to radio news at all times of the day (Bartos 1980). With programming formats of big bands and classical arrangements of music, news and talk shows, radio can successfully appeal to elderly listeners.

The print media are also an important information source for the elderly (Kubey 1980). Over half of the elderly read a daily newspaper and nearly 70 percent read Sunday editions (Schewe 1985). The elderly are also well exposed to magazines such as Travel/Holiday, U. S. News and World Report, and Southern Living as well as age-specific magazines such as Prime-Time, 50 Plus, and Modern Maturity (French and Fox 1985). Many of these magazines contain stories and/or advertisements about possible vacation trip destinations.

In addition to the mass media, formal marketing sources include personal selling efforts. In the retail tourism and travel markets the personal selling task often rests with travel agents. While some travel agencies specialize in serving older clients, many do not. Research on personal selling in retail stores suggests that some elderly shoppers wanted store personnel to treat them with more courtesy, dignity, and patience (Lambert 1979). It has also been found that senior citizens would consider patronizing stores that went after the business of retirement age people (Gelb 1978). These findings—to the extent that they can be generalized to the travel industry—may have useful implications for travel agents.

Internal Information

Thus far, informal and formal external information sources have been discussed. It is important to remember that internal information search can also be an important information source, especially among older persons. Experience—both product-specific and generalized—can serve as an internal source of information. Schiffman (1971), in a study of 100 households in an apartment complex catering to the ambulatory elderly in good general health, found that older consumers relied more on experience and less on external sources of information to learn about a new type of salt substitute. Katona and Mueller (1955) found that older families deliberated less when it came to making specific purchase decisions, and Slama and Tashchian (1985) reported that persons 65 and older exhibited less involvement in general, non-product-specific decisions. This behavior could be interpreted as carelessness, or it may suggest that the accumulated experience of older persons makes the seeking of external information less important (Schiffman 1971; Phillips and Sternthal 1977).

63

RESEARCH OBJECTIVE

The objective of this research is to investigate the sources of information perceived to be important when selecting a vacation trip destination other than family visits. The literature reviewed suggests that the elderly are exposed to various types of external information and also possess generalized and specific consumption experience. In order to provide a benchmark for comparison, the study examined a middle aged sample as well as older persons. Since little research has focused on this topic, it is difficult to formulate research hypotheses at this time. Instead, the following research questions concerning selection of a vacation trip destination will be explored.

1. What information sources are most often ranked as important by the elderly?

2. Do the elderly attach greater value to internal or external information sources?

3. Are travel agents perceived to be important information sources?

4. Do the above findings differ from the nonelderly?

METHODOLOGY

Sample

Respondents for this exploratory study were drawn from two age groups—40-59 years and 60 years and older—in a MSA in upstate New York. The elderly subjects were ambulatory members of a senior citizens organization, while the middle aged subjects were members of a Parent-Teachers Association. The middle aged group consisted of 59 females and 29 males. Sixty-nine of the elderly subjects were female while 25 were male. The age distribution in the middle aged sample included 70 respondents in the 40-49 years category and 18 respondents in the 50-59 years group, while the senior citizen sample was comprised of 94 respondents in the 60 years and older category. Thus, there is no evidence of the majority of the middle aged respondents clustering below age 59.

These samples were used since members of organizations tend to be relatively homogeneous and socially active (Tongren 1981). Members of the two groups closely matched the marital status of the U. S. population, but were above average in education. The elderly group consisted of persons of moderate income level, i.e., no household income less than $5,000 and none above $20,000. The middle aged respondents tended to match the general population with respect to income. It is noteworthy that senior centers are accessible to about one-half of the elderly persons in the U. S. and about 18 percent of the elderly attend functions at their center at least once a year (Burton and Hennon 1980). Even though senior centers can provide a social function,

Hanssen et al. (1978) found no difference between center users and nonusers in income, education, marital status, or in frequency of social contact with children or other persons. Similarly, Atchley (1980, p. 314) maintains that members of senior centers do not seem to be very different from other older people.

Questionnaire

Self-administered questionnaires were distributed at the regular meetings of the two organizations. Individual help was available to respondents if needed. To encourage participation among the elderly sample, a donation was made to the center's activity fund. A drawing for prizes was held at the Parent-Teachers Association. All members present at the two meetings participated in the study resulting in 94 responses from the elderly and 88 responses for the middle aged.

As part of a larger study, the questionnaire contained items concerning information sources on a range of products and services including vacation travel. Respondents were asked to indicate the importance of several information sources (see Table 1) when deciding on a vacation trip destination. A five-point Likert-type scale, (1) "not at all important" to (5) very important," was used to measure the degree of importance attached to each information source. An information source was coded as "important" if the respondent indicated the level of importance to be "moderately" to "very important". Frequencies and percentages were used to report the results of the study, while chi-square analysis was employed to test for differences between the elderly and middle aged samples with respect to importance assigned to the information sources.

RESULTS

The data presented in Table 1 indicate that the elderly attach the greatest importance to family members when deciding on a vacation trip destination. Experience and travel agents were ranked second and third respectively. These findings suggest that of the ten information sources ranked, internal (experience) and external (family and travel agents) are most often considered important for the elderly.

When these findings are compared to those of the middle aged, the rankings, in terms of importance, are the same. However, for each of the three information sources, a significantly smaller proportion of the elderly rated them as important.

The elderly also held a relatively high regard for newspapers and friends. The importance assigned to newspapers matched that of the middle aged, while a significantly larger number of elderly respondents ranked friends as important when compared to their younger counterparts.

TABLE 1

FREQUENCIES AND PERCENTAGES OF MIDDLE AGED AND ELDERLY RESPONDENTS WHO RATED INFORMATION SOURCES AS IMPORTANT

Information Source	Middle Aged (N=88)		Elderly (N=94)	
	N	Percent	N	Percent
Experience*	73	83.0	58	61.7
Family*	83	94.3	68	72.3
Travel Agents*	58	65.9	40	42.6
Friends*	7	8.0	32	34.0
Television*	39	44.3	12	12.8
Radio	29	33.0	25	26.6
Newspapers	29	33.0	35	37.2
Magazines	24	27.3	16	17.0
Direct Mail	18	20.5	26	27.7
Neighbors	10	11.4	12	12.8

*p≤.05

The remaining external information sources for the elderly, in decreasing order of importance, are direct mail, radio, magazines, neighbors, and television. With the exception of the elderly's low ranking for television, there were no significant differences on the remaining sources of information when compared with the middle aged.

DISCUSSION AND IMPLICATIONS

In this study, the importance assigned to internal and external sources of information when deciding upon a vacation trip destination revealed some interesting differences among sources as well as between the elderly and middle aged samples. For both samples, family influence, experience, and travel agent recommendations were perceived to be quite important, however, more middle-aged than elderly ranked these sources as important. These results are consistent with Lumpkin and Greenberg's (1982) findings that shoppers over 65 attached less importance to all information sources than did their younger counterparts. These results also seem to support Slama and Tashchian's (1985) conclusion that the elderly may, in general, be less involved in consumption decisions than members of younger age groups. Nevertheless, substantial proportions of the elderly viewed these three information sources as important. It is therefore worthwhile to more fully consider these findings and their implications.

Family, Experience, and Travel Agents

The importance of family influence on the elderly when making purchase decisions has been suggested by Phillips and Sternthal (1977), Klippel and

Sweeney (1974), Michman, Hocking, and Harris (1979), and Lumpkin and Greenberg (1982). The elderly do not appear to make consumption decisions in isolation. Though not directly investigated in the present study, it is quite possible that input from spouse and/or adult children may be sought by senior citizens when deliberating on a vacation trip destination. It would therefore appear advisable to direct promotional appeals to both elderly men and women as well as to younger adults, i.e., the extended family, who may pass the information on to elderly relatives by word-of-mouth communication.

One might expect that experience with a prior vacation trip would be a useful source of information. This finding would suggest that travel charters, hotels, and restaurants should strive to offer quality service and to provide follow-up promotional efforts to the elderly. This is especially important given the findings presented earlier on the sometimes indifferent service offered to elderly retail shoppers (Lambert 1979; Gelb 1978).

Nearly 43 percent of the elderly respondents rated travel agents as an important information source. This is an encouraging finding and is congruent with the findings of other studies of physical products which found that the elderly value the opinions of specialists in their respective fields (Michman, Hocking, and Harris 1979; Lumpkin and Greenberg 1982). Travel agents should be reminded of the continuing importance of the elderly travel market and should be provided with promotional materials designed with the older traveler in mind. The respondents who did not view travel agents as important information sources may be reached directly through newspapers or direct mail.

Other Information Sources

The remaining information sources, while less often ranked as important, offer some useful insights about the elderly market. Of the mass media, newspapers were most often ranked as important. This finding, combined with the results of a study which found travel advertising in newspapers to be more effective than magazine advertising in terms of return-per-dollar-spent (Woodside and Ronkainen 1982), suggest that newspaper advertising may be an effective way to communicate with elderly and nonelderly markets alike. Consistent with the Woodside and Ronkainen study, magazines were viewed as important in the present study by only 17 percent of the elderly sample and 27 percent of the middle aged group.

Direct mail was rated as important by about 28 percent of the elderly sample, placing it above radio, magazines, and television. This finding may be explained by the widespread availability of mailing lists and membership in organizations and clubs such as the American Association of Retired Persons and Sears's Mature Outlook. Direct mail offers the advantage of selecting various segments among the elderly (Baier 1983, pp. 170-175). Nearly 27 percent of the elderly perceived radio to be important, thus placing it ahead of television as an information source. It may be that radio programming, as discussed earlier, has more closely targeted older audiences with age-specific programming thus serving as a more selective medium.

Interestingly, friends and neighbors as information sources were ranked quite differently by the elderly respondents. Friends and neighbors were viewed as important information sources by 34 percent and 12.8 percent of the elderly, respectively. This finding suggests that, at least among friends, discussion about vacation trips occurs. This is an especially plausible explanation given the nature of the sample utilized in this investigation. This finding would further emphasize the importance of providing friendly and competent service to older travelers on the part of service providers.

LIMITATIONS

The findings of this exploratory study are limited by the usual problems of a field study design. While previous works have suggested that members of senior centers may not be very different from non-members, future studies should incorporate a probability-based sample of senior citizens. It should be noted as well that since respondents were asked to indicate the perceived importance of various information sources on making a vacation trip destination decision, the study's findings were based on projective responses.

It is hoped that the findings presented here will stimulate further investigation into this important topic. The high numbers of respondents reporting experience and family as important information sources, may be an indication that respondents tend to be near-home travelers who are likely to repeat their travel experience (Etzel and Woodside 1983). Future research on the elderly should more closely examine distance traveled and benefits sought as segmenting variables. Additionally, future studies should examine the impact of demographic factors such as education, income, health status, employment status (part-time, full-time, retired), and lifestyle variables such as patterns of adjustment to retirement, venturesomeness, opinion-leadership, and similar variables. These variables are likely to be especially useful for identifying segments of older travelers who are prone to visiting new places.

REFERENCES

Allan, Carol and Herman Bratman. 1981. Chartbook on Aging in America. Washington, DC: White House Conference on the Aging.

Atchley, Richard C. 1980. The Social Forces in Later Life. Third edition. Belmont, CA: Wadsworth.

Baier, Martin. 1983. Elements of Direct Marketing. New York: McGraw-Hill.

Bartos, Rena. 1980. "Over 49: The Invisible Consumer Market." Harvard Business Review 58 (January-February): 140-148.

Bartos, Rena. 1982. "Women and Travel." _Journal of Travel Research_, 21 (Spring): 3-9.

Bernhardt, Kenneth L. and Thomas C. Kinnear. 1976. "Profiling the Senior Citizen Market" in _Advances in Consumer Research_ Vol. III. B. B. Anderson ed. Urban, IL: Association for Consumer Research: 449-452.

Bower, Robert T. 1973. _Television and the Public._ New York: Holt, Rinehart, and Winston.

Bryant, Barbara E. and Andrew J. Morrison. 1980. "Travel Market Segmentation and the Implementation of Market Strategies." _Journal of Travel Research_ (Winter): 2-8.

Burton, John R. and Charles B. Hennon. 1980. "Consumer Concerns of Senior Center Participants." _Journal of Consumer Affairs_ 14 (Winter): 366-382.

Crask, Melvin R. 1981. "Segmenting the Vacationer Market: Identifying the Vacation Preferences, Demographics, and Magazine Readership of Each Group." _Journal of Travel Research_ 20 (Fall): 29-34.

Etzel, Michael J. and Arch G. Woodside. 1983. "Segmenting Vacation Markets: The Case of the Distant and Near-Home Travelers." _Journal of Travel Research_ (Spring): 10-14.

French, Warren A. and Richard Fox. 1985. "Segmenting the Senior Citizen Market." _The Journal of Consumer Marketing_ 2 (Winter): 61-74.

Gelb, Betsy D. 1978. "Exploring the Gray Market Segment." _MSU Business Topics_ 26 (Spring): 41-46.

Goodrich, Jonathan N. 1978. "The Relationship Between Preferences for and Perceptions of Vacation Destinations: Application of a Choice Model." _Journal of Travel Research_ 16 (Fall): 8-13.

Greco, Alan J. 1987. "Linking Dimensions of the Elderly Market to Market Planning." _The Journal of Consumer Marketing_ 4 (Spring): 47-55.

Guinn, Robert. 1980. "Elderly Recreational Vehicle Tourists: Life Satisfaction Correlates of Leisure Satisfaction." _Journal of Leisure Research_ 12 (No. 3): 198-204.

Hanssen, Ann M. Nicholas J. Meime, Linda M. Buckspan, Barbara E. Henderson, Thea L. Helbig, and Steven H. Zarit. 1978. "Correlates of Senior Center Participation." _The Gerontologist_ 18 (April): 193-199.

Hawkins, Del I., Roger J. Best, and Kenneth A. Coney. 1986. _Consumer Behavior: Implications for Marketing Strategy._ Third edition. Plano, TX: Business Publications, Inc.

Katona, George and Eva Mueller. 1955. in Consumer Behavior. L. H. Clark ed. New York: New York. University Press.

Klippel, R. Eugene and Timothy W. Sweeney. 1974. "The Use of Information Sources by the Aged Consumer." The Gerontologist 14 (April   ): 163-166.

Kubey, Robert W. 1980. "Television and Aging: Past, Present, and Future." The Gerontologist 20 (February): 16-35.

Lambert, Zarrel V. 1979. "An Investigation of Older Consumers' Unmet Needs and Wants at the Retail Level." Journal of Retailing, 55 (Winter): 35-57.

Lazer, William. 1985. "Inside the Mature Market." American Demographics 7 (March): 23-25, 48, 49.

Lumpkin, James R. and Barnett A. Greenberg. 1982. "Apparel Shopping Patterns of the Elderly Consumer." Journal of Retailing 58 (Winter): 68-89.

Meadow, H. L., Cosmas, S. C. and Plotkin, A. 1980. "The Elderly Consumer: Past, Present, and Future" in Advances in Consumer Research Vol. VIII. K. Monroe ed. Proceedings of the Association for Consumer Research: 742-747.

Michman, Ronald D., Ralph T. Hocking, and Lynn Harris. 1979. "New Product Adoption Patterns of Senior Citizens for Cold Remedies." in Proceedings of the Southern Marketing Association. R. S. Franz, R. M. Hopkins, and A. G. Toma eds., Lafayette, LA: Southern Marketing Association: 309-311.

Petre, Peter. 1986. "Marketers Mine for Gold in the Old." Fortune (March 31): 70-78.

Phillips, Lynn W. and Brian Sternthal. 1977. "Age Differences in Information Processing: A Perspective on the Aged Consumer." Journal of Marketing Research 14 (November): 444-457.

Schewe, Charles D. 1985. "Gray America Goes to Market." Business 35 (April-June): 3-9.

Schiffman, Leon G. 1971. "Sources of Information for the Elderly." Journal of Advertising Research 11 (October): 33-37.

Shoemaker, Stowe. 1984. "Marketing to Older Travelers." Cornell Hotel and Restaurant Administration Quarterly 25 (August): 84-91.

Slama, Mark E. and Armen Tashchian. 1985. "Selected Socioeconomic and Demographic Characteristics Associated With Purchasing Involvement." Journal of Marketing 49 (Winter): 72-82.

Tongren, Hale N. 1981. "Retailing to Older Consumers." Proceedings. Southern Marketing Association.

Wall Street Journal. 1983. "Older Americans." (February 17): 1.

Woodside, Arch G. and Ilkka A. Ronkainen. 1982. "Travel Advertising: Newspapers versus Magazines." Journal of Advertising Research 22 (June-July): 39-43.

QUALITY SERVICE IN HEALTH CLUBS:
DO EMPLOYEES KNOW WHAT CUSTOMERS WANT?

Jeffery M. Ferguson
Kathleen M. Malone
University of Colorado at Colorado Springs

Abstract

Understanding customer preferences and expectations is critical to the delivery of quality service. This paper reviews a study which compares customers' evaluations of service dimensions with employees' perceptions of those evaluations. The results suggest that in a global sense employees are aware of their overall performance. However, on specific service dimensions employees differ significantly from customers on the perceptions of the quality of service delivered. The paper discusses the marketing implications of the results of the study.

INTRODUCTION

A major trend in the 80's has been the interest in health and fitness which translates into big business. In 1984 Americans spent $31 billion on diet and fitness programs (Thresher 1986). This trend appears to be continuing with a projected sales increase for diet and fitness centers of 12% in 1988 over 1987 (USA Today 1988). To fully capitalize on this national trend, businesses need to develop a better understanding of consumers' needs and preferences. Unfortunately, the notion of service quality is not easily articulated by consumers or comprehended by service providers. As a result, service quality has been the target of numerous research efforts (cf. Zeithaml, Berry and Parasuraman 1988).

An example of the attempts to focus attention on this important issue is the Service Quality Model developed by Parasuraman, Zeithaml and Berry (1985). Formulated from a series of focus groups with consumers and in-depth interviews with executives, this model suggests that a set of "gaps" exist between management's perception of service quality and the tasks necessary to deliver service to the customer (Figure 1). Closing these gaps is an essential element to providing quality service from the consumer's point of view.

This paper demonstrates a research approach for determining the differences between provider perceptions and customer expectations -- Gap 1. An example is given of comparisons of the assessments of service quality by customers and service providers from an existing fitness center.

FIGURE 1
Conceptual Model of Service Quality

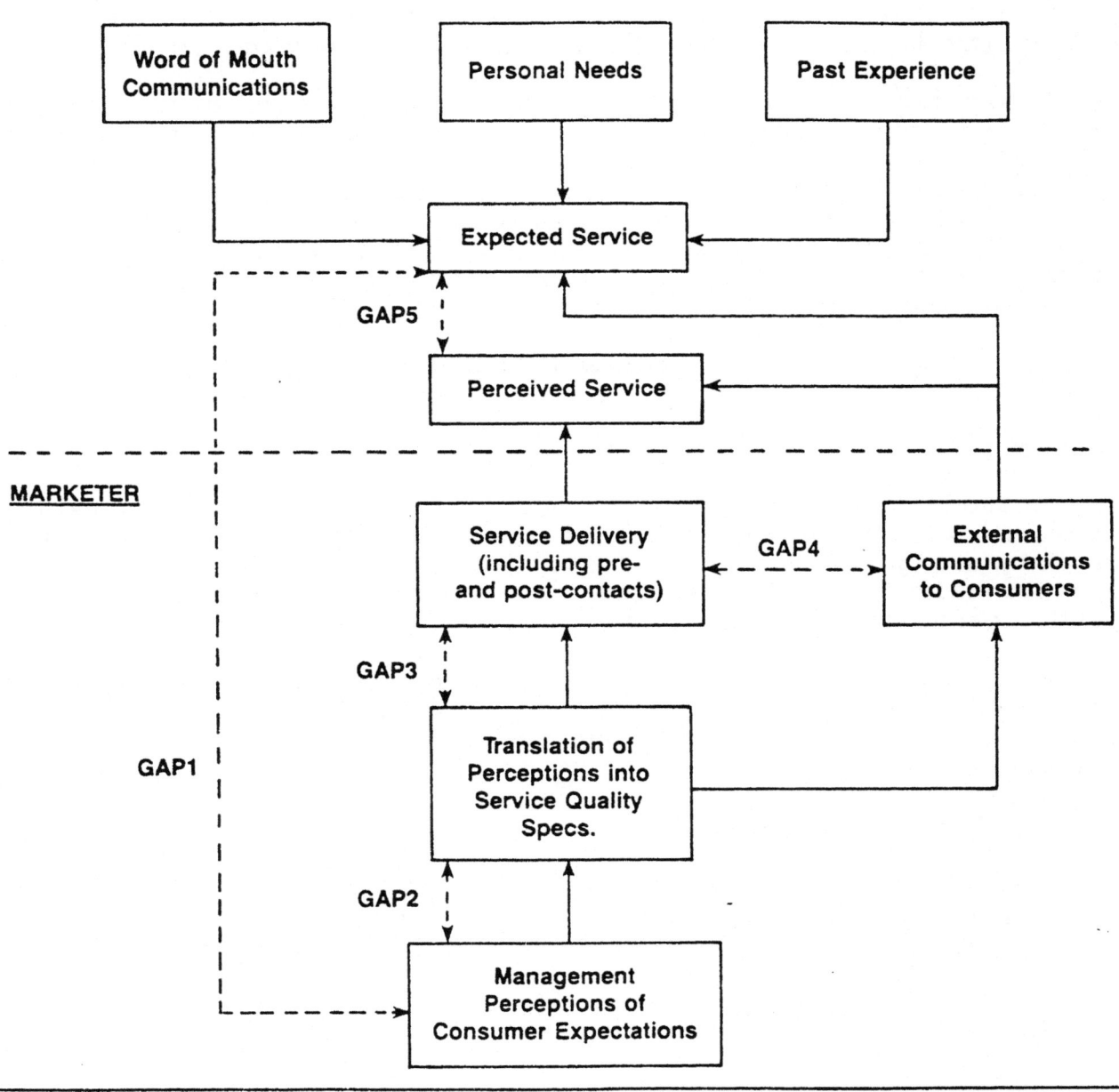

RESEARCH QUESTIONS

The Service Quality Model indicates that one potential barrier to the providing of high quality service is the discrepancy between the service expectations of customers and management's perception of those expectations. Previous research (Schneider and Bowen 1985) indicates that customer contact personnel can accurately predict customer expectations of the service as well as customer evaluations of those services. If indeed the service delivery personnel are highly cognizant of customer expectations, the capability to provide appropriate levels of service is enhanced.

The basic research questions for this study are to determine: (1) If differences exist between customer expectations and employees perceptions of service expectations? and, (2) If those differences exist, on which service dimensions are the differences most significant? In more general terms, the study is designed to determine the extent of Gap 1 for a particular fitness center and identify the specific service areas which need to be addressed in order to close the gap.

RESEARCH DESIGN

Subjects

The customer sample was determined by eliciting the cooperation of members as they signed in at the facility during a one week period during the spring of 1987. Using this approach 143 user questionnaires were completed. A demographic profile of the participants is provided in Table 1.

Seventy employee questionnaires were completed during a regularly scheduled staff meeting. Due to the vastly different staff schedules this was a good way to reach the majority of staff members.

Service Quality Dimensions

Ten service quality dimensions were assessed by both customers and employees. These dimensions were adapted from a list of service quality determinants developed by Parasuraman et al. (1985) and included:

    --Responsiveness to customer needs
    --Reliable service
    --Quality of facilities
    --Accessibility of services
    --Customized, individualized attention
    --Information about available services
    --Price of services

TABLE 1
DEMOGRAPHIC PROFILE OF CUSTOMERS

SEX

Male	48%
Female	52%

AGE

Under 18	4%
18-24	5%
25-34	39%
35-49	45%
50-64	4%
65 or older	2%

INCOME

$0 - 10,000	4%
10,001 - 15,000	5%
15,001 - 20,001	8%
20,001 - 15,000	8%
25,001 - 30,000	11%
30,001 - 40,000	21%
over $40,000	43%

--An appropriately skilled staff
--Courteous service
--Prompt service

The importance of these service dimensions was assessed on a 5-point scale where 1=not very important and 5=very important. Both customers and employees rated these dimensions in terms of their perceived importance to customers. In addition to the importance ratings, these same service quality dimensions of the fitness center were evaluated through the use of ten 5-point semantic differential scales. Appropriate descriptive adjectives were used as anchors for these scales. For example, the reliability of service question was anchored by "not reliable" and "very reliable". The responses were coded so that 1 corresponds to an unfavorable rating and 5 corresponds to a favorable rating.

In addition to the assessments of individual service dimensions, global measures were taken of the perceived satisfaction with the center. Specifically, subjects were asked how well the center satisfies fitness needs, and overall satisfaction with the services provided by the center.

Analysis

The multiple dependent variables suggests the use of MANOVA for investigating relationships when the dependent variables are correlated due to measuring the same factor or collecting multiple measures from the same subjects (Hair et al. 1979). This is due to the tendency of Type I error through the repeated applications of ANOVA. In the case of this study it seems unwise to assume that ten service dimensions are independent from one another. The Pearson product-moment correlations for the ten service dimension importance ratings show that 95% of the correlations are significantly different (p<.01) from zero. For the evaluation scores, 86% of the correlations are significantly different from zero.

The importance scores were analyzed via MANOVA to test for significant differences between employees and customers. There was a significant effect with Wilks' F=4.13, p<.001. Univariate analysis of variance tests revealed significant differences for responsiveness to customer needs, individualized attention, information about available services, and prompt service. As shown in Table 2, in all cases with significant differences the employees perceived the service quality dimension to be more important to customers than the customers own ratings.

Multivariate analysis of variance also showed a significant effect (Wilks' F=2.10, p.<.02) for the service evaluation scores. Univariate analysis of variance revealed significant differences for individualized attention, and appropriately skilled staff. As was the case with the importance scores, employee evaluations of the service dimensions with significant differences were

76

TABLE 2
CUSTOMERS AND EMPLOYEES RATINGS OF
IMPORTANCE OF SERVICE DIMENSIONS

Service Dimension	Customers' Ratings (N = 143)		Employees' Ratings (N = 70)		
	M	SD	M	SD	F
Responsiveness to Customer Needs	4.357	.826	4.629	.594	6.052*
Reliable Service	4.608	.617	4.729	.448	2.108
Quality of Facilities	4.729	.546	4.643	.638	1.003
Accessibility of Services	4.587	.609	4.457	.736	1.869
Individualized Attention	3.217	1.133	3.971	.761	25.411*
Information about Available Services	3.951	1.122	4.314	.826	5.795**
Price of Services	4.196	.988	4.343	.796	1.176
Appropriately Skilled Staff	4.434	.844	4.600	.668	2.082
Courteous Service	4.587	.705	4.714	.542	1.755
Prompt Service	4.392	.639	4.614	.572	6.096**

*p < .001
**p < .02

higher than the customer evaluations (Table 3). Unlike the comparisons of the ratings of the individual service dimension, there were no significant differences in the ratings of overall service quality.

DISCUSSION

Consistent with prior research (Schneider and Bowen 1985), the overall measures of service quality show no significant differences between customers and employees. This finding lends support to the contention that service delivery personnel are in a good position to know and understand the customers' expectations and evaluations of service quality.

On the level of specific service dimensions, however, the evidence is not as supportive of this position. Four out of ten (40%) of the importance ratings and two out of ten (20%) of the service evaluation scores are significantly different between groups. This finding suggests that while, in the global sense, employees know how well they are doing at satisfying customer needs, their understanding of the specific elements of service may be lacking. It is interesting to note that for all the ratings with significant differences, the employee scores are higher than the customer scores (Figure 2 and Figure 3). For the evaluation scores it is easy to speculate that since employees perceive differently the time and effort they expend toward customers, their evaluations of themselves would be higher.

For the importance scores it is more difficult to explain the higher values of the employees. One reason might be that because working at the fitness center is their job employees have a higher level of involvement and as a result tend to place more importance on all aspects of what they do. Another reason might be that management emphasizes particular service dimensions to the employees which makes them more important to employees than to the customers. In this study, the four dimensions with significant differences were all related to personal interactions with the customers; these types of contacts are likely to be priority issues with fitness center managers.

Whatever the reason, discrepancies between the perceptions of service delivery personnel and customers is a source of concern for management. In general the discrepancies are due to one of two factors: (1) employees are not performing up to customers' expectations, or (2) customers don't realize the quality of the service they are receiving. In either case management faces a challenge of either improving the service, or doing a better job communicating with customers about the quality of the services delivered.

The analysis performed in this study does not reveal the reasons for the discrepancies between employees and customers ratings. However, it does point to areas which need further study. Using

TABLE 3
CUSTOMERS AND EMPLOYEES EVALUATIONS
OF SERVICE DIMENSIONS

Service Dimension	Customers' Evaluations (N = 143)		Employees' Evaluations (N = 70)		
	M	SD	M	SD	F
Responsiveness to Customer Needs	3.746	.986	3.900	.745	1.309
Reliable Service	4.052	.928	4.171	.659	.912
Quality of Facilities	4.045	.900	4.143	.748	.610
Accessibility of Services	3.948	.870	4.029	.680	.457
Individualized Attention	3.157	1.047	3.643	.869	11.098*
Information about Available Services	3.858	1.005	3.943	.866	.357
Price of Services	2.806	.770	2.943	.700	1.54
Appropriately Skilled Staff	3.679	.962	4.057	.796	7.949*
Courteous Service	4.209	.935	4.143	.767	.258
Prompt Service	3.940	.891	3.843	.927	.535

*p < .01

FIGURE 2

COMPARISON OF IMPORTANCE RATINGS

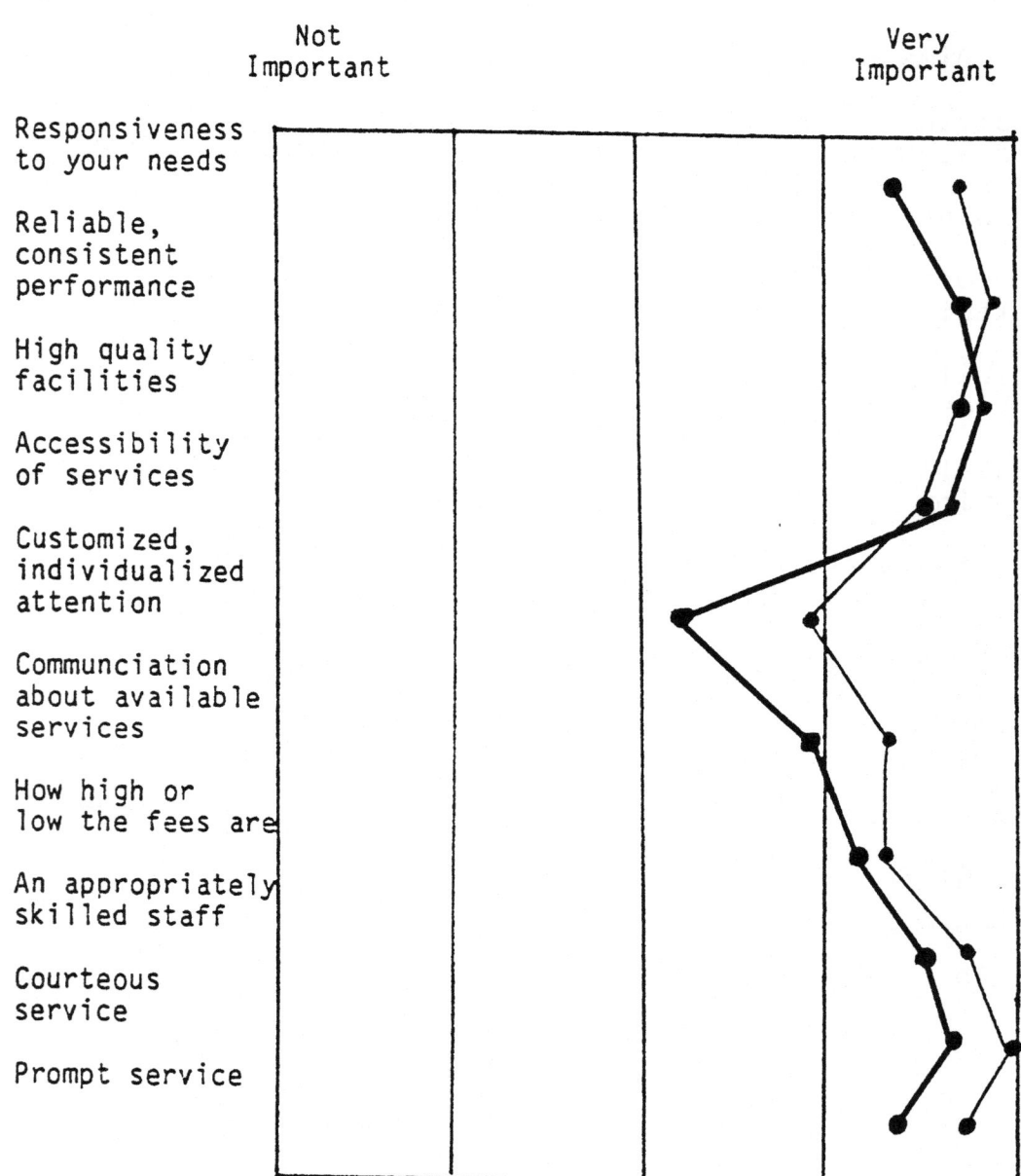

Narrow line -- staff
Bold line -- customer

FIGURE 3

COMPARISON OF EVALUATION SCORES

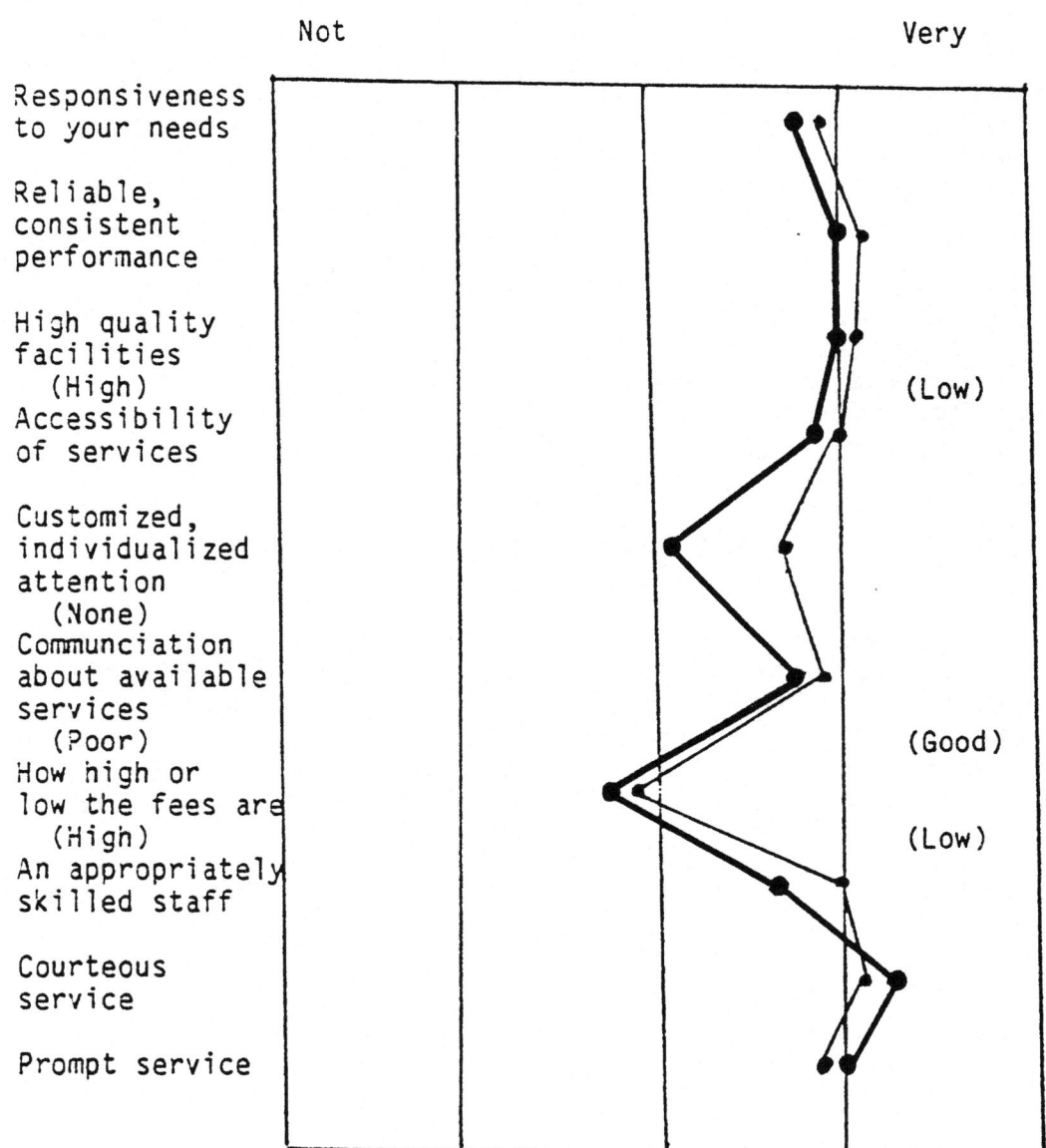

Narrow line -- staff
Bold line -- customer

a technique such as the critical incident approach (Bitner, Nyquist and Booms 1985) it is possible to uncover how customers define for themselves the various service dimensions, and what cues they use as indicators of quality service.

Eliminating these discrepancies should be a high priority because a firm's ability to satisfy customer needs hinges on the thorough understanding of their expectations. The entire service plan is based on the assumption that customer needs are accurately identified and understood. Misreading expectations can lead to inappropriate programs, emphasizing less important service dimensions, and an overall misallocation of resources. Clearly, the successful fitness centers will be the ones which know the needs of the customers and deliver commensurate programs.

In conclusion, it appears that for the fitness center studied in this project there is a good assessment of the overall quality of service delivered. On the other hand, the understanding of specific service quality dimensions is lacking. In the future, to remain competitive, service firms will need to expend more effort analyzing their customers before implementing service programs.

SUGGESTIONS FOR FUTURE RESEARCH

It would be interesting to compare the level of the discrepancy in the perceptions of service across different services industries, and across firms in a given industry. It is likely that certain industries are more attuned to their customers than others. Additionally, further study needs to be done to measure the depth of understanding by companies of specific service dimensions.

REFERENCES

Bitner, Mary J., Jody D. Nyquist, and Bernard H. Booms (1985), "The Critical Incident as a Technique for Analyzing the Service Encounter," in Services Marketing in a Changing Environment, Thomas M. Bloch, Gregory D. Upoh, and Valarie A. Zeithaml, eds., Chicago: American Marketing Association, 48-51.

Hair, Joseph F. Jr., Rolph E. Anderson, Ronald L. Tatham, and Bernice J. Grablowsky (1979), Multivariate Data Analysis, Tulsa: The Petroleum Publishing Company.

Parasuraman, A., Valarie A. Zeithaml, and Leonard L. Berry (1985), "A Conceptual Model of Service Quality and Its Implications for Future Research," Journal of Marketing, 49 (Fall), 41-50.

Schneider, Benjamin and David E. Bowen (1985), "Employee and Customer Perceptions of Service in Banks: Replication and Extension," Journal of Applied Psychology, 70 (August), 423-433.

Thresher, Allison (1986), "Girth of a Nation," Nation's Business, (December), 50-51.

USA Today, February 11, 1988, 8B.

Zeithaml, Valarie A., Leonard L. Berry, and A. Parasuraman (1988), "Communication and Control Processes in the Delivery of Service Quality," Journal of Marketing, 52 (April), 35-48.

TOURING THE FOURTH DIMENSION:
LEISURE TIME FOR SERVICES MARKETERS

Paul M. Lane, Ph.D. and Jay D. Lindquist, Ph.D.

Western Michigan University

ABSTRACT

The recreation and leisure markets are important service marketing opportunities. The literature on leisure from several disciplines including anthropology, economics, finance, leisure, management, marketing, and sociology has been reviewed as it applies to leisure time allocation decisions. The literature has been examined on the basis of a person's time orientation, and put into the Lane and Lindquist (1988) time classification system. The classification system includes income producing time, and four other subcategories of particular interest to those in the leisure and/or recreation markets: committed, (obligated and non-obligated) and uncommitted (planned and unplanned).

INTRODUCTION

The study of time is increasingly becoming important in the marketing of leisure services. Time is a very limited resource that all potential customers have to allocate carefully to optimize their satisfaction. Advances in understanding the leisure and recreational consumer can be made from a better grasp of how leisure time allocation decisions are made. Lane and Lindquist (1988) developed a classification system for the study of time based on an extensive review of the time literature. See Exhibit 1. This classification system provides a method for segmenting leisure service marketing opportunities by time category that may not have been previously considered.

This paper uses a cross disciplinary literature review to explore the concept of leisure services marketing in three primary ways: 1) definitional problems in the leisure and recreation areas, 2) time orientation views of leisure, and 3) leisure articles arrayed on the Lane and Lindquist (1988) model.

WHAT IS LEISURE?

In order to write about leisure time it would seem essential to have an operational definition of leisure. There is no universally accepted definition of leisure, (Unger and Kernan 1983). It is, in fact, this lack of a definition of leisure and the synonymous use of the word with free time, play, recreation (Miller and Robinson 1963), and vacation, that makes this exploration important to marketers.

For some authors the definition of leisure seems to revolve around freedom of choice (Chick 1986, Gerstl 1983, Hornik 1982, and Vickerman 1980). Gerstl (1983) discusses leisure as a time free from work or other obligations and finds youth to be synonymous with leisure. Similarly Vickerman (1980) views leisure as time left after commitments.

According to Unger and Kernan (1982), leisure may be divided into two categories, namely, objective definitions focusing on observable behavior and subjective definitions focusing on leisure as a state of mind or a psychological experience. These authors provide examples of objective definitions including, non-work time, and participation in particular types of activities. Both of these fit well into the Lane and Lindquist classification system. Non-work can be assigned to other than income producing time, and specific activities can be assigned to either committed or uncommitted activities as appropriate.

Unger and Kernan (1982) found six subjective conditions for leisure discussed in the literature: intrinsic satisfaction, perceived freedom, involvement, arousal, mastery and spontaneity. These six when subjectively defined, with the exception of arousal and mastery, fit well into the Lane and Lindquist time classification system (Exhibit 1). Intrinsic satisfaction would not include income producing time for a number of individuals. However, it could be included within the committed or uncommitted areas. Perceived freedom would appear to limit leisure even further by eliminating both income producing time and committed obligated time, leaving only committed non-obligated and uncommitted time. Involvement does not fit as well but suggests total absorption or commitment. Finally spontaneity, Unger and Kernan (1982) suggest, is not obligatory, routine, planned, or anticipated. Spontaneity would appear to fit only in the uncommitted unplanned area of the classification system.

The empirical results of Unger and Kernan's (1982) work point toward there being only three subjective determinants of leisure: intrinsic satisfaction, perceived freedom, and involvement. The remaining three appear to be more activity specific.

One could argue that the lack of a precise and common definition for leisure makes it imperative that the time allocation process be understood. It is through a better understanding of this allocation process that it may be possible to better comprehend the market for leisure services, including both tourism and recreation.
This will be done through a review of the literature in terms of time orientation and its fit into the Lane and Lindquist (1988) time classification model.

LEISURE AND TIME ORIENTATION

Several different types of time orientation have been hypothesized. Settle (1980), for example, suggested that there are three broad classifications of time orientation, Economic, Socio-Cultural, and Psychological (also see Lane and Lindquist 1988). When reviewing the literature on leisure and time this basic division was useful. Each of these orientations, as it applies to the literature on leisure and time, will be presented in turn. An organized array may be found in Exhibit 2.

Economic Orientation

The economic view treats clock time as a commodity. In the case of leisure the primary interest of researchers has been the exchange or trade off with other activities. In some cases this has been looked at from the entire lifecycle of individuals (Ryder et al. 1976 and Driffill 1980). The lifecycle approach is important to capture the exchanges made among leisure, education, and work as a person moves from stage to stage that might not surface in the shorter time frame. In other cases the exchange is assumed to occur in a shorter time period (Linder 1970, Cesario 1976, Best 1978 and Marscak 1978).

Part of the exchange issue with leisure time is its macro economic impact. For example, how closely tied are discretionary income and discretionary time use (Financial World 1974)? If, as suggested by Best (1978), workers would trade income for increased free time, how would the reduced discretionary income resulting impact their leisure choices. Presumably they will have fewer dollars to spend on leisure. The related question that surfaces is, where will discretionary dollars be channeled? If they are channeled into labor intensive, low productivity sectors of the economy then the shift to more leisure may have far reaching consequences for the national economy as a whole (Vickerman (1980). The leisure industry includes businesses such as motels, marinas, ski complexes, and campgrounds which tend to be labor intensive and, therefore, experience lower productivity than manufacturing. Marscak (1978) has already raised the issue of the impact of massive exchanges of time for more leisure, and away from exchanging time for goods. This is of particular importance when considering the increasing affluence (Vickerman 1980) within the U.S. What will the impact of these changes be on the social welfare equilibrium?

Other macroeconomic issues may be raised. Stunkel (1979), for example, offers the thought that if time is a resource, the distribution of free time may be less equitable than the distribution of income over a life time. People may have difficulty getting "free time" for leisure activities. There is also the increasing shift by women in the U.S. from unpaid household production to income producing work. This may also be impacting the scope of leisure (Vickerman 1980). While average hours worked per week have decreased, the additional labor force activities at the household level (Kokoski 1987) and the reduced availability of leisure time to women who are in the work force (Kim and Lee 1988) has the total effect of reducing leisure time available.

Technological advances may help in this area as time saving devices permit people to accomplish more in the same amount of clock time. In some cases the same income producing job task may be accomplished in less time thus permitting an increase in discretionary time and, potentially, in leisure time.

The economic issues are, as suggested by Unger and Kernan (1982), objective ones. Simply stated, what are employees doing in terms of time choices and exchanges. The collective impact of these choices will effect the future growth of the U.S. economy. For example, the consumption of recreational or leisure activities has no market value established (Cesario 1976) but the value of time allotted to the consumption of the activity is conditioned by a trade-off in the form of not dedicating time to other activities.

Understanding time as a resource constraint in the study of leisure and identifying one-to-one trade offs, such as one with money, is not conceptually difficult. The subject of time becomes more complex when it is realized that not all the world sees time from the same perspective. In fact, in the same culture, in the same social class, and even in the same household, people may view time differently.

Socio-cultural Orientation

Socio-cultural time focuses on a person's approach to time as learned in their socialization process. This impacts on an individual's subjective relationship with time --or how a person manages to live within the time milieu (Meerloo 1970). The socio-cultural writers have attempted to reveal systematic differences in the treatment of time among various cultures, sub-cultures and/or social strata (Settle 1980). As the world becomes more interdependent, the importance of culture and language in understanding time perception and time allocation are significant.

Our society is going through a number of major changes that impact on leisure choices. These include the change from housewives to workwives, expansion of jobs for females, more refined family planning procedures, increased life expectancy, rising expectations of standard of living and the resulting cost, growth of labor saving devices, satisfaction of women with their jobs, and the acceptance of the concept of the workwife Mccall (1977). The dramatic changes in the role of women in the U.S. society has had and will continue to have an impact on leisure decisions (Lane 1988) regardless of the definition selected. Women, specifically, and families, in general, have less time over which they exercise control. This reduces the amount of time available to devote to leisure activities for women, and makes the scheduling of leisure activities increasingly difficult. It is interesting to note how one's environment impacts one's leisure choices. Kim and Lee (1988) found that working wives, more frequently than housewives, pursue leisure activities away from the home, while less frequently participating in home centered activities.

Even when the time for leisure is available and the funds are at hand as well, people in the U.S. are seen to have difficulty dealing with the concept of leisure. The "problem" is triggered by a preoccupation with the work ethic. This condition results in individuals not knowing how to handle the idea of the "idleness" of leisure (Linder 1970, Mayo & Jarvis 1981 and Hennefrund 1987). Hence, people are going to have to learn how to "guiltlessly" make use of acceptable leisure time activities.

Opportunities and time for leisure will continue to increase in our society into the foreseeable future. This will partially be a function of technology in the work place which will reduce work load. It will also almost certainly be a result of both reduced travel times as technology permits work to be done at home or in other settings away from the office, and as technology, through such things as cellular phones and portable computers, allows us to make better use of out commuting time. Further it will be a result of the increases in medical technology, knowledge and practice that will allow people to live longer and be in better health than ever before (Business Week Sept 3, 1979). Therefore, services aimed at leisure activities will find a growing market.

There appears to be increasing interest in looking at the patterns of leisure. For example, is there any good reason why large blocks of leisure time must wait for use until the end of.life at retirement (Stunkel 1979). Now being explored are ways that people may accumulate and use blocks of leisure time during their working years. This might be achieved through innovative work scheduling practices, thereby creating opportunities to amass bigger blocks of free time (Best 1978). This movement could create substantial new opportunities for those marketing services for the leisure industry. That is, the mix of physically demanding and non-physically demanding leisure time activities could be shifting if the age factor were less dominant.

Much of the available leisure time for all ages is currently used in passive entertainment, specifically, watching t.v. (Walsh 1983). In fact according to Hill (1985) television represents 60% of passive leisure and 50% of all leisure activities. This has lead to a situation where in the United States passive leisure is dominated by the spoken word (television or radio) as opposed to the written word (the reading of literature of all types).

Education seems to be a determinant of in the kind of activities selected. Russell (1981) suggests that education correlates well with an interest in the arts. He goes on to suggest that the time for leisure is shrinking from a 1975 median of 24 hours per week to a 1980 median of 18 hours per week. Walsh (1983) found larger amounts of time for leisure: Seniors have 37-41 hours per week, "empty nesters" 31 hours per week, single parents, dual career and traditional families 23-25 hours per week, and childless couples, teenagers, and singles 37-41 hours per week. It appears that our life time pattern of leisure is logically curvilinear. One starts with greater amounts of leisure as singles and this is reduced through the family years and then increased as one progresses through what might be called the active retirement years to the more passive final years for those who disengage voluntarily, due to health, or because of a lack of an active cohort group.

Psychological Orientation

To the extent that people in the same cultural or sub-cultural group are able to incorporate significantly different, durable predispositions and perspectives towards time, these differences are evidence in a person's psychological time orientation (Lane and Lindquist 1988). After recognizing the economic view, and socio-cultural changes that may be impacting leisure time, it is important to guard against thinking of time as an objective and/or logical event. Leisure service customers may have different economic or socio-cultural time orientations but, within any given group, individuals will also have different psychological orientations toward leisure and/or leisure time use.

Some people use their leisure activities to justify their existence to others (Hughes 1972). Community service involvement could be an example for a person who did not see his/her job as having worth. Leisure may also be used to satisfy needs that are not met at work (Kiechel 1983), for example, one might seek a chance to exercise leadership as captain of a softball team. Many do not find psychic rewards from their job and need the intrinsic satisfaction (Unger and Kernan 1983) that comes from proving themselves in their leisure. Others will use their leisure time to experience something new (Kotler 1984) such as a physical challenge like climbing Mount Everest, a change in time such as staying in an English castle, a different lifestyle such as a city dweller going to the farm, and so forth. These are all active forms of leisure. For many this is the only type of leisure that they grasp.

Workaholics have difficulty being idle (Hennefrund 1987). They feel guilty about what Lane and Lindquist (1988) call uncommitted unplanned time. For others the essence of leisure is that it implies freedom of choice (Chick 1986 and Hornik 1982).

Others may define leisure not in terms of experience or activity but in terms of intrinsic satisfaction and involvement as suggested by Unger and Kernan (1983).

Overall, there are many economic, socio-cultural, and psychological reasons that will impact on an individual customer's allocation of time to leisure. In our changing society the pressure is on to be successful at everything including using our leisure time. With time becoming increasingly the most precious resource that individuals have to allocate, leisure service marketers need to focus on the kinds of time allocation systems that their target markets are likely to be using—and appeal to it.

CLASSIFICATION OF TIME USAGE

Numerous authors have attempted to address the issue of how time is used. In Exhibit 1, authors are listed chronologically along with the time usage proposed by Lane and Lindquist (1988). The exhibit is organized around their proposed time usage classifications. Exhibit 3 is a chronological listing of articles involving leisure time organized within the same model.

The latter exhibit provides an opportunity to look at leisure time as defined and described by numerous authors. It is not hard to see why there were problems in developing a definition when leisure shows up in some cases in every category but Income Producing Time (McCall 1977, Guenther and White 1979, Driffill 1980) and in other cases appears to be primarily confined to uncommitted unplanned activities (Vickerman 1980, McKendrick 1983, Walsh 1983). The lack of clarity is a function of the difficulty in carrying out empirical research beyond basic time budgeting. Individual time allocation systems and practices are complicated by a multitude of choices and the opportunity to often engage in multiple simultaneous activities.

Exhibit 3 brings into focus important elements in the study of leisure. First, early studies dealt with leisure as everything beyond Income Producing Time and Household Production Time. This was apparently driven by the seeking of an objective definition of leisure such as "non-work." Leisure activities span all of the committed and uncommitted categories.

In the 1980 to 1983 period most of the published work seems to have concentrated on the concept of leisure as free or uncommitted time. This makes for a more coherent definition of leisure. Authors even experimented with better terms such as "passive leisure and vacation." This was an important step forward in the study of time and leisure, since individuals began to differentiate between active and passive leisure.

After 1983, increasing amounts of published work on leisure were devoted to active leisure (Hill 1985, Kim and Lee 1988). The recognition that people are making more choices to engage in active leisure is important to the services marketing industry. Understanding how consumers use their leisure time and in what ways that may be changing will be critical to future successes in leisure marketing.

The examples of specific activities that people call leisure have been particularly helpful in understanding how leisure fits into the classification system that is being used. The use of activities to define leisure or the specific leisure area that a researcher is interested in may help understand the time allocation decision better than other methods at this nascent stage in the study of time.

Based on the literature reviewed, a classification system built on the amount of choice involved seems to work well for the study of leisure time and how it is allocated. The ability to sort the research literature into a common classification system may help with future work related to the conceptualization of leisure and time allocation decisions.

Understanding the element of time, as a critical resource allocation for leisure and recreational customers may help find new ways to meet the needs and wants of consumers. The issue may not be time-money trade-offs as was suggested by early economists. It may be reframed as trade-offs between types of time available for leisure activities, committed and uncommitted or between disposable time (committed and uncommitted) and disposable income. The selling of more recreational and tourism services would require customers making transfers within their leisure time blocks from uncommitted to committed time. Customers are already continually making decisions on the adjustments between disposable time and money. If money were everything, everyone would be working to increase their hoard even at the cost disposable time. In fact, there appears to be a reverse trend where one works less in order to have more disposable time. For example, many academicians have made a trade-off of income for increased uncommitted time.

RESEARCH IMPLICATIONS

In the marketing of services it will be increasingly important to understand consumer's time allocation priorities. This will be particularly true in the leisure areas of travel and recreation. There are a lot of activities that compete for leisure dollars and, more importantly, leisure time. The way that these time choices are made should receive further study.

There are many aspects to the study of leisure time allocation behavior. One of the most important is encouraging researchers to more clearly define the facets of time relevant to leisure. This paper offers a structure for thinking about time allocation in leisure, that parallels and extends the classical economic model in Exhibit 3. This review of the literature on time and leisure has been a portion of a much larger hypothetical framing process in which the authors are engaged. Research needs to be continued in other areas of the time literature. The proposed classification system, as it applies to leisure, needs empirical verification in order to: (1) extend leisure time allocation research to a more practical and usable level; (2) develop a research platform for the future of consumer behavior and other disciplines; and (3) to begin the work of assigning values to different time classifications, understanding the unique situation of leisure in customers time allocation decisions.

Future research should lead to a better understanding of the choices that customers make regarding leisure with their committed and uncommitted time. It is clear from the literature that leisure customers are unlikely to value their disposable time in a way identical to that used to value their work or income producing time. Also, disposable time is used for different purposes than work time.

Increasing role demands on women are creating greater pressure for prioritizing disposable time (Lane 1988). Additionally, research is necessary to determine how consumers allocate their disposable time. This may lead to a method of valuing disposable time. Such valuation of time would provide insight and decision guidance for service marketers. They could then begin to clarify at what price level different market segments may be willing to make adjustments in their disposable time allocations. Simply put, we must grasp the trade-off values of different types of leisure and recreational activity times with the dollar, socio-cultural and psychological values of these times.

MARKETING MANAGEMENT IMPLICATIONS

Providers of leisure services will have to become more attuned to the diversity of views that people have of time. The tendency to think only in economic terms, ignoring both the socio-cultural and psychological views, will stunt the leisure time growth potential within the U.S. and other countries. In this sense growth does not mean strikingly more time available for leisure, but richer time -- or more well-presented leisure time.

The key will be for marketing managers to assess how those people within their target market view time. If there is a dominant view concerning time in leisure it should be considered in positioning and promoting the leisure time service or product.

For example, if dealing, with a potential customer segment which perceives leisure as "idleness" then educational promotion showing how leisure contributes to physical and psychological "battery charging" this could open the doors to these people. Feeling obligated to leisure rather than repelled by "idleness" is the thought.

Marketing managers should also consider teaching people--or exploring with them--the idea that leisure should be "committed" to a greater extent, rather than "uncommitted." "You owe it to yourself to set aside those hours, days or weeks," to travel, ski, bus to a concert, etc. Such an appeal based on an understanding of time and commitment status techniques could open the doors wider for the tour and fixed recreation site leisure operators.

The manager must also be aware of the life cycle position. People with leisure time are at both ends (bachelor, young married without children and retired) of the spectrum. So possibly we should be talking about "Yad" leisures (young adults) and "Geri" leisures (senior citizens). These are potential markets to focus on.

For example, the marketing manager for leisure services could be focusing on the Geri leisures. These seniors will live longer in better health. They will need new opportunities for spending their leisure time. There should be a shift in emphasis for seniors to less physically demanding activities than those their younger counterparts enjoy. Opportunities for touring by bus, or other travel where the Geri leisure is picked up at the home, processed for the trip, aided in boarding, met and escorted at the destination which often has closed complete leisure systems or where conducted tours/activities are abundant.

Time profiles and perceptions of target markets for arts devotees ("Arts" leisure), education leisures ("edu"leisure), cultural leisures ("cultu"leisures) and the like should be investigated also.

Company managers should be thinking about work-leisure programs for their employees. Since many employees, from line workers to executives, garner more or equal intrinsic reward from leisure versus work time. Hence work plus leisure packages could be promoted by the leisure service industry to increase employee satisfaction.

There are innumerable opportunities for the leisure industry that will continue to surface as the perception of time and its value and use is more fully understood.

Time, it appears, will continue to be one of the most constraining resource commodities for customers of services in the future. It will be of key importance for marketers to study and understand this crucial resource limitation. Understanding the types of trade-offs that leisure customers are willing to make, within their disposable, committed and uncommitted, time (or perhaps across their entire time perspective) will be an essential element in the creation of a competitive advantage for those sensitive to this important consumer base.

BIBLIOGRAPHY

Becker, Gary S. (1965), "A Theory of the Allocation of Time," The Economic Journal, 75 (September), 493-51.

Bellenger, Danny N. and Pradeep K. Korgaonkar (1980), "Profiling the Recreational Shopper," Journal of Retailing, 56 (Fall), 77-92.

Blinder, Alan S., and Yoram Weiss (1976), "Human Capital Labor Supply: A Synthesis," Journal of Political Economy, 84, 449-472.

Business Week (1979), "More Leisure in an Increasingly Electronic Society," 206, 208-212.

Cesario, Frank J. (1976), "Value of time in Recreation Benefit Studies," Land Economics, 52 (February), 32-41.

Chick, Garry E. (1986), "Leisure, Labor, and the Complexity of Culture: An Anthropological Perspective," Journal of Leisure Research, 18 (3), 154-168.

Darmon, Rene Y. (1981), "Optimal Compensation Plans for Salesmen Who Trade-Off Leisure Time Against Income," Journal of the Operational Research Society, 32 (5), 381- 390.

Driffill, E. J. (1980), "Life-Cycles With Terminal Retirement," International Economic Review, 21 (February), 46-62.

Financial World (1974), "The Serious Business of Leisure Time," 142 (11), 18 & 30.

Gramm, Warren S. (1987), "Labor, Work, and Leisure: Human Well-Being and the Optimal Allocation of Time," Journal of Economic Issues, 21 (March), 167-188.

Griffin, Marie (1985), "The Importance of Play at Meetings," Successful Meetings, 34 (January), 19-21.

Guenther, Harry and Joseph White (1979), "EFT System Privacy Safeguards: A Preliminary Inquiry Into the Privacy-Leisure Time Trade-Off," Journal of Bank Research, Autumn, 136-144.

Hennefrund, William (1987), "Breaking Away," Association Management, 39 (August), 65-68.

Hill, Martha S. (1985), Time, Goods, and Well-Being. Edited by F. Thomas Juster and Frank P. Stafford. Survey Research Center, Institute for Social Research, The University of Michigan.

Holman, Rebecca H. and R. Dale Wilson (1980), "The Availability of Discretionary Time: Influences on Interactive Patterns of Consumer Shopping Behavior," Advances In Consumer Research, 7, ed by Olson, Jerry C., (Ann Arbor: Association for Consumer Research), 431-436.

Hornik, Jacob (1982), "Situational Effects On The Consumption Of Time," Journal of Marketing, 46 (Fall), 44-55.

Hughes, Meredith (1972), "Recreational Vehicles, Promoted For Leisure Time, Travel U.S.," Advertising and Sales Promotion, 20 (May), 26-33.

Kiechel, Walter III (1983), "What Your Vacation Says About You," Fortune, 108 (6), 205-208.

Kim, Chankon and Hanjoon Lee (1988), "Working Status and Leisure Activities of Married Women," In Press, Proceedings of the Academy of Marketing Science Conference, Spring 1988.

Kokoski, Mary F. (1987), "Indices of Household Welfare and the Value of Leisure Time," The Review of Economics and Statistics, 83-89.

Kotler, Philip (1984), "'Dream' Vacations: The Booming Market for Designed Experiences," Futurist, 18 (October), 7-13.

Lane, Paul M. and Jay D. Lindquist (1988), "Definitions for the Fourth Dimensions: A Proposed Time Classification System," In Press, Proceedings of the Academy of Marketing Science Conference, Spring.

Leuthold, Jane H. (1981), "Taxation and the Value of Nonmarket Time," Social Science Research, 10, 267-281.

Liebermann, Yehoshua, and Jaques Silber (1983), "Household Economics and Market Segmentation," European Journal of Marketing, 17, 13-25.

Linder, Staffan C. (1970), <u>The Married Leisure Class</u>, New York: Columbia University Press.

Lioukas, S. K. (1982), "Choice of Travel Mode and Value of Time in Greece," <u>Journal of Transport Economics and Policy</u>, May, 161-180.

Marscak, T. A. (1978), "On the Study of Taste Changing Policies," <u>American Economic Review</u>, 68 (May), 386-391.

Martin, W. H. and S. Mason (1976), "Leisure 1980 and Beyond," <u>Long Range Planning (UK)</u>, 9 (April), 58-65.

Mayo, Edward J. and Lance P. Jarvis (1981), <u>The Psychology of Leisure Travel</u>, Boston: CBI Publishing.

McCall, Suzanne H. (1977), "Meet the 'Workwife'," <u>Journal of Marketing</u>, 41 (July), 55-65.

Meerloo, Joost and Abraham Mauritis (1970), <u>Along the Fourth Dimension: Man's Sense of Time & History</u>, New York: Day.

Menefee, John A. (1982), "The Demand for Consumption Time: A Longitudinal Perspective," <u>Journal of Consumer Research</u>, 8 (March), 391-397.

Oppenheimer, Margaret (1979), "Time as a Scarce Resource in Economic Planning," <u>Journal of Economics and Business</u>, 31, 218-221.

Robinson, John P. (1967), "Time Expenditure on Sports Across Ten Countries," <u>International Review of Sport Sociology</u>, 2, 67-84.

Russell, Cheryl (1981), "Profile: America's Arts," <u>American Demographics</u>, 3 (November), 40-41.

Ryder, Harl E., Frank P. Stafford and Paula E. Stephan (1976), "Labor Leisure and Training Over the Life Circle," <u>International Economic Review</u>, 17 (October), 651-674.

Schary, Philip B. (1971), "Consumption and the Problem of Time," <u>Journal of Marketing</u>, 35 (April), 50-55.

Settle, Robert B. (1980), "A Discussion of 'Time' Research," <u>Advances in Consumer Research</u>, 7, ed by Olson, Jerry C., (Ann Arbor: Association for Consumer Research), 448-450.

Shaw, Susan M. (1986), "Leisure, Recreation or Free Time? Measuring Time Usage," <u>Journal of Leisure Research</u>, 18, 177-189.

Stunkel, Edith L. (1979), "Let's Abolish Retirement," <u>Futurist</u>, 13 (October), 325-328.

Tavernier, Gerald (1978), "Car Workers Shift to Flexible Leisure Time," <u>International Management</u>, 33 (October), 39-40.

Unger, Lynette S. and Jerome B. Kernan (1983), "On the Meaning of Leisure: An Investigation of Some Determinants of the Subjective Experience," <u>Journal of Consumer Research</u>, 9 (March), 381-392.

Vickerman, R. W. (1980), "The New Leisure Society: An Economic Analysis," <u>Futures</u>, 12 (June), 191-200.

Voss, Justin (1967), "The Definition of Leisure," <u>Journal of Economic Issues</u>, 1, 91-106.

Walsh, Doris (1983), "Dual-Career Sex and Other Mundane Topics," <u>American Demographics</u>, 5 (September), 38-39.

AUTHORS PROPOSED MODEL (Sample Allocations)	INCOME PRODUCING TIME		COMMITTED		UNCOMMITTED	
	(Labor)	(Work)	Obligated (Childcare)	Non Obligated (Housework) (Shopping)	Planned (Book to Read)	Unplanned (Spontaneous) (Activities)

Findings From the Literature Arrayed on Author's Proposed Classification System

	INCOME PRODUCING TIME		COMMITTED		UNCOMMITTED	
ECONOMIC MODEL	Production Income Producing Time		Consumption Disposable Time		Discretionary Time	
BECKER (1965) Hypothetical	Labor		Leisure			
ROBINSON (1967) Empirical	Work Related		Team Sports	Adult Education-Organizations Housework Childcare	Free Time Active Leisure Passive Leisure <Sports as a subset> Social Entertainment Individual	
VOSS (1967) Hypothetical	Work (Paid directly or indirectly)		Non Discretionary Time[1]		Leisure (Discretionary Time)	
LIBERMAN AND SIVER (1970) Empirical	Market work		Housework Education Timechild "Eatosleep" "Orgapart" "Goodsbuy" "Sociallife"		Active Leisure Passive Leisure (Individual)	
SCHARY (1971) Hypothetical	Compensated		Non Compensated			
BLINDER (1976)[2] WEISS Hypothetical	Work		Education		Leisure	
OPPENHEIMER (1979) Hypothetical	Paid Production		Transaction Interaction	Unpaid Production Consumption	Leisure	
SETTLE (1979) ALRECK BELCH Hypothetical					Leisure Entertainment Competitive Sports	
HOLMAN (1980) WILSON Empirical	Work Time		Fixed Time	Discretionary	Freetime	
MENAFEE (1982) Empirical	Work Time		Consumption Non Work Time			
SHAW (1986) Empirical			Leisure ———— Freetime[3]			
GRAMM (1987) Hypothetical	Labor (Manual)	Work[4] (Skilled Intellect)			Leisure[5] (Residual)	

1. Nondiscretionary time includes a sense of legal moral, social or physiological compulsion or obligation when deciding how to allocate time.
2. These were considered over the lifecycle of the individuals.
3. All recreation is free time, but not all free time is leisure, free time not as experimental as leisure. Part of leisure can occur during inobligatory activities such as: coffee and work break, childcare, personal care, home and garden care, mealtime.
4. Embodies elements of direct satisfaction and direct utility.
5. Non labor, nonwork. Sacrificed effort, the cost of giving up the future. Active as opposed to passive.
Note: 1.   Discrepancies in the placement of identical terms is due to the different author's definitions. Words like "leisure," "freetime," "discretionary," have different meanings in various studies.
         2.   An author's definition requires dual placement under the proposed model.

EXHIBIT 2
TIME ORIENTATION: A LITERATURE REVIEW

AUTHORS	ECONOMIC	SOCIO CULTURAL	PSYCHOLOGICAL
Hughs 1972 H			Leisure for Significance
Financial World 1974 H	Discretionary Time Used for Leisure Time Products		
Ryder, et al. 1976 H	Leisure in Economic Model of Life-Cycle Training, Enriches Modeling		
Martin and Mason 1976 E	Trade-Off Between Leisure and Free Time		
McCall 1977 E		Workwives Cultural Acceptance; Job Satisfaction; Family Planning; Standard of Living; Labor Saving Devices	
Cesario 1976 H	Recreation Consumption Has No Market Value; Time Trade-offs		
Travernier 1978 H			Workers Want to Choose Leisure Time
Best 1978 E	Exchange of Income for Free Time Format	Workers Want to Choose Leisure Time	Individual Life-Cycle Planning
Marscak 1978 H	Shift in Leisure Impacts Social Welfare		
Guenther and White 1979 H	Non Work Time Consumed in Transaction and Leisure Varies With Wage Rate		
Business Week 1979 H	Technology Increasing Productivity	Leisure Time Increasing with Improved Technology and Health	
Stunkel 1979 H	Inequitable Distribution of Income	Free Time and Life-Cycle	
Bellenger and Korgaonkar 1980 E		Recreational Shopper Uses Leisure Time for Shopping	
Driffill 1980 H	Utility Maximization of Leisure Time Over Life Cycle		
Vickerman 1980 H	Workwife's Transfer From Home Production to Labor Macro: Work/Leisure Substitution; Leisure Spending Low Productivity Sectors		

97

EXHIBIT 2 (continued)
TIME ORIENTATION: A LITERATURE REVIEW

AUTHORS	ECONOMIC	SOCIO CULTURAL	PSYCHOLOGICAL
Darmon 1981 H	Salesmen Not Income Maximizers		
Leuthold 1981 E	Leisure as Consumer Good and Tax Implications		
Mayo and Jarvis 1981 H		Uneasiness About Leisure	Guilt About Time Off; Work Ethic
Russell 1981 H		Shrinking Leisure Time	
Hornik 1982 E			Situational Effect on Consumption; Leisure Is Free and Uncommitted
Lioukas 1982 E	Travel Time is a Component of Leisure		
Gerstl 1983 H	Leisure Time Increasing Importance and Structured by Work		Leisure: Diversity; Future Flows, and Social Relations
Kiechel 1983 H		Leisure Models: Spillover Model - Work & play Alike; Compensation Model: Leisure Satisfaction Needs Not Met at Work	
Unger and Kernan 1983 E	Objection Definitions; Non-Work Time; Participation in Certain Types of Activities		Subjective Definitions; Intrinsic Satisfaction; Percieved Freedom Involvement
Walsh 1983 H		Amounts of Leisure Time Vary with Life-Cycle Stage	
Kotler 1984 H		Leisure Experience with Significance	
Griffin 1985 H			Leisure Provides Physical & Emotional Outlet
Hill 1985 E		Importance of Television in Leisure; Passive Leisure is Dominated by the Spoken Word	
Chick 1986 H		Cultural Complexity, Evolution, and Leisure Time; 1. Surplus Theory 2. Time Scaricity Hypothesis 3. U-Shaped Curvilinear 4. Unrelated	Freedom of Choice
Hennefrund 1987 H		Increasing Potential Conflicts with Leisure and the Work Ethic	Workacholics feel for Uncommitted Planned
Kokoski 1987 E	Decreasing Household Leisure Consumption		
Kim and Lee 1988 E	Despite Work Constraint Workwife Makes Time For Leisure	Workwives Pursue Non-Home Leisure; Housewives Home Centered	

Proposed Classification System

AUTHORS PROPOSED MODEL (Sample Allocations)	INCOME PRODUCING TIME		COMMITTED		UNCOMMITTED	
			Obligated	Non Obligated	Planned	Unplanned
	(Labor)	(Work)	(Childcare)	(Housework) (Shopping) (Personal Needs)	(Book to Read)	(Spontaneous) (Activities)

Findings From the Literature Arrayed on Author's Proposed Classification System

	INCOME PRODUCING TIME	COMMITTED	UNCOMMITTED
ECONOMIC MODEL	Production Income Producing Time	Consumption Disposable Time	Discretionary Time
Linder 1970 H	Working Time	Personal Work ---------------------Consumption Time--------------------- -----------------Cultivation of Mind and Spirit-------------------	Idleness
McCall 1977 E		---------------------------------------Leisure---------------- [Housewife] civic work school volunteer transport children bridge / [Workwife] boating camping crafts	
Gunther and White 1979 H	----------Work--------------------	---------------------------------Transaction and Leisure---------------------------------- sleep / recreation / socializing	
Bellenger and Korgaonkar 1980 E		---------------------------Recreational Shopping-------------------------	
Driffill 1980 H	-----work------------training-----	--Leisure---------------------------	
Vickerman 1980 H		(May include some committed time if not work or personal care) visiting relatives	------------Leisure------------------ listening to music gardening television
Mayo and Jarvis 1981 H		Maintenance Time ----------------------------Consumption Time---------------------------------- ------------------------------Social Time----------------------------------- ----------------------------Cultural Time--------------------------- ---------------------------------Leisure Time-------------------------------	Idle Time
Hornik 1982 E			-----------Leisure-----------------
Gerstl 1983 H			-----------Leisure-----------------

Exhibit 3 (continued)

AUTHORS PROPOSED MODEL (Sample Allocations)	INCOME PRODUCING TIME		COMMITTED		UNCOMMITTED	
	(Labor)	(Work)	Obligated	Non Obligated	Planned	Unplanned
			(Childcare)	(Housework) (Shopping) (Personal Needs)	(Book to Read)	(Spontaneous) (Activities)

Findings From the Literature Arrayed on Author's Proposed Classification System

ECONOMIC MODEL	INCOME PRODUCING TIME	COMMITTED	UNCOMMITTED
	Production Income Producing Time	Consumption Disposable Time	Discretionary Time
Kiechel 1983 H		Dreams to reality	------------Vacation------------ Time for Adjustment Avoid Obligations Set the child in you free Active interests follow
McKendrick 1983 E			--------Passive Leisure------------- Television Television Reading Reading Music Music
Unger and Kernan 1983 E		---------------------------Intrinsic Satisfaction---------------------------	 ------------Perceived Freedom---------
Walsh 1983 E			---------Free Time or Leisure-------- Television
Kotler 1984 H			------------Dream Vacations---------
Hill 1985 E			-------------Passive Leisure-------- radio, records or tapes; reading: books, magazines or newspapers con- versations: telephone & face-to-face (T.V. average 14.3 hours per week)
	team sports performance arts	----------------------------------Active Leisure----------	individual sports --------individual arts/literature--------- -------hobbies and domestic crafts--------

Kim and Lee 1988 E		Cultural activities
		Participation Games
		Spectator Games
		Social
			------------------Domestic------------------
			  Household- Woodworking
			  Renovation Gardening
			              Dressmaking
			              Knitting
			              Reading for Pleasure

	Downhill skiing Horseback riding Camping trips	----------------------------------Outdoor------------------------- Cross-country- Ice Skating Skiing Swimming Boating Jogging/Running Archery Horseback Riding Cycling	

AN EMPIRICAL INVESTIGATION OF THE UTILITY OF SELECTED ENVIRONMENTAL VARIABLES IN EXPLAINING CONSUMER LOYALTY TO SELECTED RECREATION SERVICES

Sheila J. Backman
University of Illinois

ABSTRACT

The current stage of loyalty research reported in recreation studies is similar to early brand loyalty research in that it is plagued by an abundance of behavioral definitions which inhibited comparison and generalizability of the research findings. This paper discusses consumers' loyalty to a selected recreation service as a two dimensional construct comprised of a psychological and a behavioral dimension. It was hypothesized that selected environmental factors, side bets, price sensitivity, perceived constraints, and perceived skill level would discriminate between consumers exhibiting differing degrees of loyalty. Results of the discriminant analysis support the hypothesis.

The issue of understanding how and why consumers use recreation services has been of interest to leisure behavior scholars and administrators for at least the past two decades. Studies have been successful in distinguishing participants from non-participants (Snepenger & Crompton, 1984) and in identifying constraints to participation in recreation services. However, very little is known about why some consumers repeatedly use selected recreation services while other consumers discontinue their participation. Buchanan (1985) hypothesized that consistent participation in selected recreation services is related to the notion of commitment or attachment. The notion of attachment was referred to Crompton and Lamb (1986) who postulated that consumers' level of attachment may influence which services consumers use.

The propensity to concentrate use on one or a few services has been termed loyalty in the consumer behavior literature, and has been one of the most widely researched topics. It is now generally acknowledged by consumer behavior theorists that loyalty involves more than repeat use of goods and services. Most current loyalty definitions in consumer behavior acknowledge that loyalty is a two-dimensional construct encompassing both psychological and behavioral components.

<u>Conceptualization of Recreation Service Loyalty</u> The current stage of loyalty research reported in recreation studies is similar to early brand

loyalty research in that it is plagued by an abundance of behavioral definitions which inhibited comparison and generalizability of the research findings. For example, amount of past participation, frequency of participation, number of years, have typically been used to assess loyalty to recreation services.

Loyalty to recreation services, viewed as a two-dimensional construct, refers to consumers consistent use of a selected recreation service that is influenced by an affective attachment to that service. It suggests that although a service may have many repeat users, it is erroneous to assume that all of these consumers are highly loyal to the service. A conceptual definition of loyalty towards a recreation service, like brand loyalty must consider both psychological and behavioral components. (Figure 1). The psychological component of loyalty assess the affective component of loyalty while the behavioral component assess the intensity of participation. Service loyal behavior is defined as repeat participation (behavioral consistency) of a service. Psychological service loyalty refers to the underlying processes which predispose individuals to behave in a selective manner. A two-dimensional concept of loyalty which incorporates behavioral and psychological dimensions affords investigators the opportunity to assess consumers' strength of loyalty by distinguishing between spurious behavior and highly loyal behavior.

High loyalty describes those participants who have a high degree on affective and behavioral commitment to a service. The behavior of highly loyal participants is resistant to change because consumers perceive the activity or resource to be a central life interest which is personally important. Highly loyal consumers have been found to be opinion leaders with respect to a selected service.

Spurious loyalty characterizes those participants with high behavioral loyalty but low psychological loyalty. To these consumers the activity is not perceived as central to their life-style. This type of consistent behavior in the absence of positive attachment to the activity describes simple repeat participation use which may be due to extrinsic factors. The tendency to discontinue participation, perceive conflict, or substitute activities is likely to be higher for spuriously loyal participants than for those who are highly loyal.

Latent loyalty refers to those participants who, despite having high positive attachment toward the service, exhibit low behavioral loyalty to a service. Their frequency of participation, or use is low. To these consumers, the service is perceived as important, but they cannot participate as frequently as they desire.

Low loyalty describes consumers exhibiting low psychological attachment and low behavioral loyalty to the service.

There is a paucity of published research, however, which has focused on loyalty to recreation services. Loyalty to a selected recreation service may influence consumers perception of constraints, accumulation of side bets, level of price sensitivity and perception of skill level and hence continued use of a service. Past research (Romsa & Hoffman, 1980; West, 1977, 1985; Searle & Jackson, 1985; Witt & Goodale, 1981), has demonstrated that constraints do influence use of recreation services, but have not investigated the relationship between loyalty and constraints. Becker (1960) suggested that consumers accumulate investments (side bets) such as club memberships, magazine subscriptions, learning cost, and equipment, when engaging in committed behavior. Similarly, Bryan (1977, 1979) and Graefe (1980) have shown that consumers at different levels of specialization own differing types of equipment. However, Buchanan (1985) speculated that reliance on observables may lead to erroneous assumptions because they do not assess a consumer's affective attachment to a service. Loyalty rather than intensity may influence the accumulation of side bets due to consumers' affective attachment to a service. In the context of consumer goods, Muncy (1983) and Pessemeier (1959) have shown that highly loyal consumers were less influenced by level of price sensitivity than were consumers exhibiting low loyalty. However, very little is known about consumers of recreation services price sensitivity. Finally, Iso-Ahola & Mannell (1985) postulated that the final variable, consumer's perception of his or her skill level would influence consumers consistent participation.

Method: The purpose of this study was to formulate a loyalty paradigm for recreation services and to identify differences between selected environmental characteristics, perceived constraints, side bets, price sensitivity and perceived skill level, of consumers exhibiting differing levels of loyalty to golf. The following hypothesis: Consumers' side bets, price sensitivity, perceived constraints, and perceived skill level will discriminate between high, spurious, latent, and low loyalty consumers, was formulated.

The study was conducted at three 18 hole municipal golf courses in Austin, Texas. Golf was selected as the recreation service on the basis of the following criteria:

1. Golf had shown changes in aggregate participation levels during the past five years.

2. Golf is a relatively discretionary service with wide opportunities for consumers to use or not to use it.

3. Golf had shown varying levels of participation.

A modified shopping center sampling approach was used to select the sample of 420 golfers. The target sample size for the service was computed in relation to the intensity of use at the three public golf courses. A self-administered questionnaire was distributed at each of the three golf courses during June 1987 to collect data. The questionnaire was divided into three sections consisting of questions which assessed: (a) continuer's loyalty; (b) marketing characteristics and (c) demographic characteristics. Golfers were asked to mail the completed survey. A response rate of 71.5 percent for golfers was achieved following the initial distribution and follow-up. Responses elicited from a random sample of non-respondents were compared to respondents to determine if non-respondents differed from respondents. Results revealed no significant differences between respondents and non-respondents, for age and intensity of participation.

Consumer's service loyalty was operationalized as a categorical variable. (See Figure 1). Golfers were assigned to one of four loyalty groups based upon their behavioral and psychological scores as follows: high loyalty; strong psychological commitment, strong behavior; latent loyalty; weak psychological commitment, weak behavioral commitment; spurious loyalty; weak psychological commitment, strong behavior and low loyalty, weak psychological and behavioral commitment. Behavioral loyalty was assessed by a consumer's intensity of recreation participation. Golfers were assigned divided ex-post facto into two groups (low and high) using the median as the dividing point. Golfers whose participation was high were defined as strongly behaviorally loyal. In contrast, respondents classified into the low participation category were defined as weakly behaviorally loyal. Psychological loyalty was measured using a semantic differential scale composed of 15 items selected from the evaluative domain. Cronbach's alpha was used to assess the reliability of the scale and found to be .92. Golfers were divided into two groups using the median (high, low) according to their overall score across the 15 item scale.

Consumers' side bets were assessed by summing over an 8 item Likert-type scale (alpha = .86). Price sensitivity was operationalized as the price level necessary to induce discontinuance and was measured following a procedure suggested by Pessemier (1959). Perceived skill level was assessed by asking respondents to compare their skill level to that of other golfers. Finally, the 21 item Likert-type scale used to assess constraints were derived from a taxonomy of constraints developed by Crompton and Lamb (1986) (alpha = .94). Factor analysis was performed on the constraints scale for the purpose of data reduction. The resulting dimensions were subjected to an oblique rotation and used as criterion variables in hypotheses testing.

Results: Multiple group discriminant analysis was performed using side bets, price sensitivity, perceived constraints, and perceived skill level as predictor variables. The criterion variables were based on the respondent's type of service loyalty (high, spurious, latent, and low). The results suggest that only one function, Function 1, was statistically significant (.01) (See Table 1). Function 1 explains 86 percent of the variance in the data set. The most important predictors for this function were

---

Insert Table I about here

---

side bets, a perceived high level of skill, a perceived skill level (about the same), miscellaneous constraints, promotion failings, pricing and distribution constraints and social constraints. The group means on the canonical variable indicate that the greatest difference appears to be between high and low loyalty groups. Comparing the low loyalty group means on the canonical variable with the total structure coefficients revealed an inverse relationship between low loyalty golfers and the three most important predictor variables. However, comparing group means on the canonical function for high loyalty golfers with the total structure coefficient revealed a direct relationship between the high loyalty group and the three most important predictor variables.

The discriminant function correctly classified 50 percent of respondents into the loyalty paradigm. The discriminant function performed best for the low loyalty and latent loyalty groups, and was least effective for the spuriously loyal group.

Discussion: Consumers' repeated use of selected recreation services was postulated to be related to their type of loyalty to the service. Consumers' service loyalty was conceptualized as a two dimensional concept; integrating psychological and behavioral components. It was anticipated that environmental variables would discriminate between high, spurious, latent, and low loyalty consumers of golf. Two variables, side bets and perceived skill levels discriminated between high, spurious, latent and low loyalty continuers for golf. However, three additional variables, perceived constraints, perceived skill level and price sensitivity were important discriminators of golfers' type of loyalty.

Consumers' service loyalty has substantial importance for the marketing of recreation services. Inclusion of the psychological dimension facilitated identification of marketing characteristics among continuers exhibiting high intensity of participation. The data suggest that reliance on intensity of participation as a surrogate of consumer loyalty appears to be erroneous.

A second area of application is related to the market share achieved by a service. Howard (1985) suggests that agency managers develop a unique set of marketing strategies targeted at current users in an attempt to retain consumers and build market share. However, Raji (1985) points out that the quality of the market share depends on more than the number of consumers comprising the share, the share's quality depends on the relative percentage of loyal consumers. Similarly, Exter (1986) noted that brand loyalty was positively associated with market share; brands which lost market share also declined in the same ratio as brand loyal consumers in the share. It is easy for managers to assume that continuers are loyal to a service, but the data show that in the context of service loyalty if behavioral measures alone were used 70 percent of the golfer sample percent would have been classified as high, whereas when the two-dimensional measure was used, only 42 percent of golfers exhibited high loyalty. Thus, defining loyalty from a behavioral perspective overstates the strength of the share. This finding suggests that managers may have a false sense of the strength of their share of the services market if the composition of the share is examined only from a behavioral perspective.

REFERENCES

Becker, H. (1960). Notes on the concept of commitment. American Journal of Sociology, 66, 32-40.

Bryan, H. (1977). Leisure value systems and recreational specialization: The case of trout fisherman. Journal of Leisure Research, 9, 174-187.

Bryan, H. (1979). Conflict in the great outdoors: Toward understanding and managing for diverse sportsmen preferences. University of Alabama, Birmingham: Bureau of Public Administration Press.

Buchanan, T. (1985). Commitment and leisure behavior: A theoretical perspective. Leisure Sciences, 7, 401-420.

Crompton, J., & Lamb, C. (1986). Marketing government and social services. New York, NY: John Wiley and Sons.

Exter, T. (1986). Looking for brand loyalty. American Demographics, 4, 32-56.

Graefe, A. (1980). The relationship between level of participation and selected aspects of specialization in recreational fishing. Doctoral dissertation, Texas A&M University, College Station, Texas.

Howard, D. (1985). An analysis of the market potential for public leisure services. Journal of Park and Recreation Administration, 3, 33-40.

Iso-Ahola, S., & Mannell, R. (1985). Social and psychological constraints on leisure. In M. Wade (Ed.), Constraints on leisure, (pp. 111-154). Springfield, IL: C. C. Thomas.

Muncy, J. (1983). An investigation of the two-dimensional conceptualization of brand loyalty. Doctoral dissertation, Texas Tech University, Lubbock, Texas.

Pessemier, E. (1959). A new way to determine buying decisions. Journal of Marketing, 24, 41-46.

Raji, S. (1985). Striking a balance between brand popularity and brand loyalty. Journal of Marketing, 49, 53-59.

Romsa, G., & Hoffman, W. (1980). An application for non-participation data in recreation research: Testing the opportunity theory. Journal of Leisure Research, 12, 321-328.

Searle, M., & Jackson, E. (1985). Non-participation and barriers to participation: Consideration for management of recreation delivery systems. Journal of Park and Recreation Administration, 8, 23-25.

Snepenger, D., & Crompton, J. (1984). Leisure activity participation models and the level of discourse theory. _Journal of Leisure Research, 16_, 22-23.

West, P. (1977). A status group dynamics approach to predicting participation rates in regional recreation demand studies. _Land Economics, 2_, 251-259.

West, P. (1985). Status differences and interpersonal influence in the adoption of outdoor recreation activities. _Journal of Leisure Research, 2_, 251-259.

Witt, P., & Goodale, T. (1981). The relationships between barriers to leisure enjoyment and family stages. _Leisure Sciences, 1_, 29-49.

BEHAVIOR	PSYCHOLOGICAL COMMITMENT: ABSENT	PSYCHOLOGICAL COMMITMENT: PRESENT
ABSENT	LOW	LATENT
PRESENT	SPURIOUS	HIGH

Figure 1. **Conceptual Model of Loyalty**

TABLE 1

Results of Discriminant Analysis, Using Marketing Variables as Predictors of Loyalty to Golf

Function	Wilks' Lambda	Approximate F	NDF	DDF	Significance
1.	.77	1.84	30	605.3	.01
2.	.96	.43	18	-414	.96
3.	.98	.29	8	208	.87

Function	Canonical Correlation	Adjusted Canonical Correlation	Squared Canonical Correlation	Eigenvalue	Proportion	Cumulative
1.	.44	.39	.19	.24	.86	.86
2.	.16	---	.02	.02	.09	.95
3.	.10	---	.01	.01	.05	1.00

Predictor Variables	Structure Coefficients	Group Means				Univariate	
		High Loyalty	Spurious Loyalty	Latent Loyalty	Low Loyalty	Signif- F	cance
Individual Constraints	-.23	-.09	.12	.01	-.06	.63	.58
Social Constraints	-.79	-.09	.07	.04	.09	.55	.64
Pricing and Distribution Constraints	-.55	-.03	.01	.06	.02	.07	.97
Misc. Constraints	.95	.11	-.00	.24	-.34	2.32	.07
Promotion Failings	.67	.01	.03	.30	-.19	1.15	.32
Price Sensitivity (under $3.00)	.56	.27	.29	.47	.18	1.83	.14
Price Sensitivity (from $3.00 to $5.00	-.01	.35	.36	.19	.32	.81	.48
Perceived Skill Level (about the same)	-.83	.55	.57	.52	.59	.11	.95
Perceived Skill Level (higher)	.99	.38	.29	.38	.18	1.80	.14
Side Bets	.99	30.62	28.05	29.71	25.29	12.48	.001

TABLE 1 (Continued)

Group Means on Canonical Variable

Canonical 1

High Loyalty	.41
Spurious Loyalty	-.11
Latent Loyalty	.31
Low Loyalty	-.96

Confusion Matrix

From	High Loyalty	Spurious Loyalty	Latent Loyalty	Low Loyalty	Total
High Loyalty	50[a]	18	17	5	90
	55.5[b]	20.0	18.8	5.5	
Spurious Loyalty	17	31	11	12	71
	23.9	43.6	15.4	16.9	
Latent Loyalty	3	1	13	4	21
	14.2	4.7	61.9	19.5	
Low Loyalty	2	5	3	27	37
	5.4	13.5	8.1	72.9	121[c]
					219
					55.0[d]

a- frequency, b-percent, c-total number of cases classified correctly, d-total percent of cases classified correctly

110

AN INVESTIGATION OF THE RELATIVE IMPORTANCE OF RECREATION PARK AND CULTURAL AMENITIES IN BUSINESS RELOCATION AND ECONOMIC DEVELOPMENT

Jill Decker
Jackson County Parks and Recreation

Abstract

The purpose of this study was to investigate the importance of recreation, park and cultural amenities relative to four other quality of life attributes in the location selection processes of four types of companies. The study solicited input from three sets of factors: company officials, economic development professionals and relocation consultants. Relative importance of the attributes was determined by a constant sum scale and multiple comparison tests. Results suggest that recreation and cultural amenities are less important than other factors such as cost of living and education. Several explanations are suggested as well as ideas for future research.

INTRODUCTION

The economic growth and well being of most communities, whether they are cities, counties, states, or even larger regions, has been substantially dependent on the location of businesses in those communities engaged in the manufacturing of goods and services (Moriarty, 1980). As the United States shifts from an industrial manufacturing economy to an informational society companies are becoming more mobile and more selective in their location decisions (Litz, 1979; Sneath, 1978). This has caused a highly competitive situation to develop between economic development groups vying to attract business and industry to their communities. Many economic development organizations have begun to take a more systematic approach to economic development rather than the traditional shotgun approach. Sophisticated marketing plans are becoming increasingly common. The ability of a community to attract relocating companies requires an understanding of a company's basic requirements and desired attributes in an area and its ability to supply those requisites (Thornton, 1984).

People have become the major resource of many companies and their needs are also becoming a consideration in the business location selection process. Many companies require highly skilled, professional employees and therefore are more likely to require a locale offering a lifestyle that will aid in the attraction and retention of this mobile workforce (Breckenfeld, 1987). Quality of life factors have been cited in the

111

literature as being of particular importance in the location decisions of four types of companies: corporate headquarters, high-technology, research and development, and services (Carson, 1986; Gerard, 1986; Lund, 1986). Many scientists, engineers, technicians, intellectuals, and entrepreneurs share a new "inner-directed" system of values. These "gold collar" workers place a high value on education, cultural richness, amenities, clean water, and other factors contributing to the quality of life (Austin Chamber of Commerce, 1985).

Recreation, park and cultural amenities are central components of an area's quality of life (Fridgen, 1986). They are among the elements reportedly considered important by relocating companies for employee attraction and retention. The extent to which they influence business location decisions, however, is unknown. In contrast to studies into the location of industrial manufacturing industries, most of the evidence concerning the location of services, high-technology companies, research and development firms, and corporate headquarters is anecdotal.

How important are parks, recreational and cultural amenities in attracting these types of businesses to an area? Are these factors considered at all in the business location decision process? Do those communities rich in recreational and cultural opportunities have a competitive edge over those communities that are not? These questions are of great importance considering the increasing emphasis being placed on economic development and the possibility that local government expenditures for public recreation could be justified on that basis. Despite their importance, these and other questions remain largely unanswered. The purpose of this study, therefore, was to identify the importance of quality of life and more specifically, recreation, park and cultural amenities, relative to other factors, in the location decisions of corporate headquarters, high-technology companies, research and development firms, and services. The study was of an exploratory nature and was limited to the state of Texas in its scope. It did not attempt to make causal inferences or to provide exact answers to any questions. Rather, it was intended to provide insights and to stimulate further thought and formulation of more exact research questions concerning the role of recreation, park and cultural amenities in business location decisions.

THE LOCATION EVALUATION AND SELECTION PROCESS

The process of business location and economic development follow the basic principles of traditional product marketing in which the locating company takes on the role of the consumer, the community represents the product,

112

and the economic developer is associated with the marketer. In product marketing the decision to purchase a particular brand of product is based on a consumer's perception of differences in the brands. To evaluate alternative brands, consumers establish specific criteria against which they seek to measure product attributes and each criterion may be weighted in importance. These criteria are of 2 kinds: (1) those which are necessary and (2) those which are not necessary, but desired. Necessary criteria can not be traded off and are referred to as non-compensatory. Secondary or desired criteria may be traded off for other criteria if necessary. Such criteria are referred to as compensatory.

A consumer possesses an awareness set of available product brands. Each brand in this awareness set is judged on its ability to meet the necessary criteria. The product attributes which enable the product to meet these criteria are termed qualifiers. Those brands which satisfy the qualifying criteria form a set of possible alternatives referred to as the consumer's evoked set (Howard and Sheth, 1969). These are the alternative brands the consumer will consider for purchase. Further evaluation is conducted. If more than one brand equally satisfies the most important criteria, secondary or desired attributes may be used to make the final decision.

In many cases the qualifying attributes are not those that distinguish competing brands from one another. Lovelock (1984) gives the following example:

> Most travelers rank "safety" as their number-one consideration in air travel. But since major U.S. airlines are generally perceived as equally safe, safety is not usually an attribute that influences consumer choice between several major domestic carriers.

Determinant attributes (those that do determine choice) may be low on a list of priorities, but they are often the attributes where significant differences between competing alternatives are apparent to consumers (Lovelock, 1984). The consumer will then arrive at an expected level of satisfaction for each brand based on the degree to which it meets the original need criteria. The brand perceived to provide the greatest satisfaction will be the preferred brand (Assael, 1984).

These concepts may be applied to the location decisions of (re)locating companies. The model of brand evaluation has been adapted to business location decisions (Figure 1). The company defines a set of needs or criteria and prioritizes them. Schemenner (1982) indicates that the most common way to simplify the multitude of influences documented as location factors is to designate certain factors as "musts"--conditions which must exist in an area if the company is to consider moving there (qualifying attributes). Uthe factors may then be categorized as "wants"--desirable attributes which are sought in a new location but which could be foregone

if other influences, including the "musts", would be too severely
compromised. Executives in a company, like individual consumers, are
likely to possess an awareness set of locations which meet their needs
based on their passive accumulation of information concerning the areas or
communities. In most cases not all communities in the awareness set will
be feasible alternatives for location of the company. A preliminary,
non-compensatory evaluation involving an active search for additional
information about these communities is conducted to eliminate those areas
which do not possess the attributes necessary to fulfill the "must"
criteria. The remaining communities which do possess the "necessary"
attributes become the company's evoked set; communities which may be
considered as prosepective sites. These sites are then evaluated for
secondary criteria or "wants". These secondary factors may be foregone or
traded out for other factors if necessary. For example, a higher cost of
living may be endured in order to locate in proximity to a large research
iniversity, or a company may forego a desirble physical environment in one
area if another offers a more convenient transportation system. This
evaluation of "wants" is therefore considered to be compensatory.

Although many factors may be considered in business location decisions,
only a few are likely to be crucial to a firm's success among the types of
companies defined as the population of interest in this study. Industrial
location factors have been categorized in a variety of ways. Miller
(1977) refers to primary factors (cost of transportation, labor, market
access, raw mateials, energy, capital) and secondary factors (government
policies, physical environment, taxes, research, management, regional
perception, and personal considerations).

Uther companies, such as the four types in this study, are different.
They tend to be rather footloose in that they have fewer qualifying
criteria and these criteria are easily satisfied in many locations. They
have a much larger field of feasible locations from which to choose. In
this situation, desired factors take on more importance and may be
weighted more heavily in the decision process. Since there are fewer
"musts" to be satisfied in the location, desirable criteria become more
readily considered and are also less likely to be traded off in order to
satisfy other needs.

Quality of life attributes have generally been categorized as secondary--
"desired" but not "necessary". However, many companies today,
particularly the types included in this study, tend to have fewer
constraints on their location. Is it possible then, that for at least
some of these companies, quality of life factors may be perceived as
necessary rather than simply desired attributes in a community? Could
recreational opportunities ever be determinant attributes in decisions
between alternative locations?

The study solicited input and perspectives from three sets of factors: (1) representatives of businesses which had recently relocated to the state of Texas, (2) independent relocation consultants, and (3) representatives of economic development organizations in Texas communities. All three groups are involved in business relocation but in different ways. A judgement sample was selected from each population. A comprehensive list of economic development organizations in metropolitan and non-metropolitan areas of Texas was obtained from the 1986 and 1987 Geoeconomic editions of the Site Selection Handbook. The sample was limited to the 126 organizations identified in metropolitan areas and in non-metropolitan cities with populations of 20,000 or more. Many rural communities have chambers of commerce but their functions rarely include active economic development so they were not included in the study.

Thirty-five firms believed to be involved in relocation consulting were identified through contacts with economic development professionals, company advertisements in trade magazines, and articles in the literature which mentioned specific firms. Few of these firms were located in Texas, but the nature of their involvement in the relocation process did not require that they be from within the State.

Economic development organizations in the thirty metropolitan Texas cities were requested to provide a list of the companies which had relocated to their respective areas in the five years prior to the study. Company lists were received from eleven organizations including those representing the six largest cities in the state. Each list was reviewed and seventy-four headquarters, high-technology companies, research and development firms and service businesses were identified for inclusion in the study bringing the total sample size to 235. Every organization was contacted by telephone to obtain contact names and current mailing addresses.

The collection of primary data for this research was accomplished through a mail survey. The design and implementation of the survey followed the Total Design Method (TDM) developed by Dillman (1978). Twenty-two individuals were eventually dropped from the study due to ineligibility for various reasons decreasing the overall sample size to 213. The response rates from each population are listed in Table 1.

A separate survey questionnaire was developed for the three populations, each designed to solicit similar information but also including questions specific to each population. Each survey instrument focused on the decision making process in business relocations and the relative importance of quality of life, recreation/parks/open space, and cultural opportunities in that relocation process. Economic development professional and relocation consultants responded to questions according to their own perceptions developed through working with companies in the four categories. The company officials in the four categories responded to questions as they related to their own recent relocations.

The importance of an area's quality of life relative to seven other general location criteria (labor, transportation, levels of taxation, proximity to suppliers, proximity to research universities/colleges, energy and utility costs, state and local government incentives) was obtained by the use of a constant sum scale. The relative importance of recreation/parks/open space and cultural opportunities among a total of six quality of life factors (primary/secondary education, cost of living, health/medical services, and personal safety/crime rate) were determined by the same technique. Respondents were asked to indicate the importance of the presented criteria in the location selection process by allocating among them a total of 100 points. Again, company officials responded for their own firms while relocation consultants and economic development professionals indicated their perceptions of importance in each of the four company categories. The attributes presented in these scales included those reported to be of greatest importance in the existing literature. This is recognized as a limitation of this study. It would not be feasible to include every location attribute that influences the decision.

Analysis of variance was conducted on multiple repeated measures to determine if the mean point allocations given to each of the general location attributes and to the quality of life attributes were significantly different from each other. If the analysis of variance was significant, Tukey's multiple comparison procedure was applied to determine where the difference or differences were.

RESULTS

The mean points allocated to each of the eight general location factors by company officials are listed in Table 2. The responses were not separated by company categories due to the small number of research and development firms participating in the study (4) and because the category of corporate headquarters was not exclusive of the other categories.

The analysis of variance test was significant with a p-value of .0001 indicating that at least one mean score differed from the others. Tukey's multiple comparison test was calculated at alpha=.05 and produced a critical range (difference between two mean scores necessary to declare them significantly different) of 11.3 suggesting no significant difference between labor and transportation nor between transportation and quality of life. Labor, however, was significantly more important than quality of life. No significant differences were found between quality of life, levels of taxation or proximity to suppliers or research universities. Energy and utility costs and government incentives were not significantly different from each other but were significantly less important than quality of life. These results, summarized in Table 2 (solid vertical line represents no significant difference), indicate that the location factors can not be ranked in importance by their mean scores. Quality of life does, however, seem to be of considerable importance.

The mean points allocated to each of the eight location factors by the relocation consultants are shown in Table 3 with the summarized results of the Tukey's multiple comparison test. The analysis of variance was significant in each company category with p-values less than .001. Tukey's test at alpha=.05 produced the following critical range values: headquarters 11.2, high-technology 12.7, services 15.8, and research and development 15.0.

The mean scores for most factors fell into two or three categories with few significantly different mean scores. This made it difficult to assess which location factors are actually perceived to be more important than others. Quality of life was considered significantly more important than several other factors in the headquarters and research and development categories but was not considered significantly different from the factors with the lowest mean scores in the services and high-technology categories.

The mean points allocated to the eight location factors by economic development professionals (Table 4) were similar to those of the relocation consultants. Quality of life received the highest mean score in the survey from the economic development respondents in the headquarters category. It also received the second highest mean score in the high-technology and research and development categories after proximity to research universities. Quality of life once again appeared to considered less important in the location decisions of service related businesses than other factors.

The analysis of variance test was again significant in each company category with p-values less than .001. Tukey's critical range values were: headquarters 4.8, high-technology 4.6, research and development 4.7, and services 4.9. These results are summarized in Table 4. Quality of life was perceived by economic development professionals to be significantly more important than most other attributes in the location decisions of all four types of companies.

The mean points allocated to the six quality of life attributes by company officials are presented in Table 5. The analysis of variance was significant with a p-value of .0001. At alpha=.05, Tukey's multiple comparison test produced a critical range of 8.027 indicating that cost of living was considered significantly more important than all other attributes. Recreation/parks/open space and cultural opportunities received the lowest mean scores but were not found to be significantly different from either personal safety or health services.

Cultural opportunities fared better in the perceptions of the relocation consultants. The analysis of variance was significant in each company category with p-values each less than .001 and Tukey's test calculated the following critical ranges: headquarters 10.2, high-technology 9.9, research and development 12.8, and services 9.9. The mean point allocations and summary of Tukey's test are shown in Table 6. The relocation consultants generally perceived cost of living and primary/secondary education to be significantly more important than the remaining four attributes which do not differ significantly in importance. For headquarters, however, results indicate that cultural opportunities are significantly more important than recreation/park/open space amenities.

More significant differences were discovered in the responses of the economic development professionals. This may be due partly to the greater number of respondents from this group. The analysis of variance test was significant with p-values all less than .0001. Tukeys critical range (in parentheses) and summary findings are shown in Table 7. These results indicate that in the perceptions of the economic developers education and cost of living are the most important quality of life attributes in the location decisions of company officials in each of the four company types. With the exception of services, cultural amenities were also perceived as being significantly more important than health services, personal safety, and recreation/parks/open space.

CONCLUSIONS AND INTERPRETATIONS

The findings of this research imply that quality of life is a significantly important consideration in the location decisions of companies in the four business categories but that recreation, park and cultural amenities, although they may be considered, are generally less important than the cost of living and primary/secondary education and, in some cases, other quality of life factors as well. These findings are not generalizable beyond the state of Texas. This limitation of the study may, in fact, provide explanations for these findings which seem to contradict the existing literature.

After observing the relative importance of the quality of life components in business location decisions it became apparent that the importance of quality of life among other general factors may have been primarily a reflection of the importance of the cost of living. The reason cost of living was found to be so important may also have been the reason recreation, park and cultural amenities appeared to be so much less important and both may be explained by the nature of the study. Since the cost of living is known to be relatively low in Texas compared with many other regions of the country, it could be expected that the state would be attractive to company officials who consider a low cost of living as a high priority. In keeping with this view, Texas cities (except Austin, perhaps) are not generally reknown for their quality parks or for the recreational and cultural opportunities available. It seems plausible to suggest that those firms which do consider recreation, park and culture amenities to be very important, for whatever reason, would decide to locate in other areas of the country that are well-known for having those amenities. Perhaps Texas cities are not considered as potential locations by those company officials who place great importance on recreation, park and cultural amenities.

A study of the importance of six quality of life factors in business location was conducted by Biscomb (1979). He also found recreation and cultural amenities to be considered important in the location decisions of fewer companies than other quality of life factors which he tested. When he separated the companies by region of the country, however, he found that recreation rated most important in the Eastern and Northeastern regions of the country. O'Connor (1986) also found recreational opportunities ranked first as quality of life components in the New England region. If these areas were perceived to possess exceptional recreational and cultural opportunities then it is likely that those firms which consider recreation, park and cultural amenities important would locate there rather than in an area which does not possess the desired attributes.

Another explanation for the lack of importance of recreational amenities relative to the other quality of life attributes is derived from Allen and Beattie (1984). They found that community satisfaction dimensions could be placed in a hierarchy similar to that of Maslow (1943). They argued that some dimensions were considered essential to subsistence while others were satisfiers and that until subsistence needs were met satisfiers would not be considered. Leisure was considered a satisfier. Recreation, park and cultural amenities may be less important than other attributes which may be considered more necessary for life satisfaction. Following this line of thought -- many people, particularly professionals and executives, may be willing to travel further to participate in recreational or cultural activities or visit a park, than to take children to a good school or receive medical services. Also the cost of living and crime rate cannot be disregarded. It seems logical that recreation and cultural amenities would be less important than these other factors no matter how important they are. Forcing respondents to indicate the "relative" importance of the quality of life factors may have forced recreation, park

119

and cultural amenities to appear less important than they actually are.

These explanations, though they seem logical, are conectural. The purpose of this exploratory study, as stated earlier, was not to provide direct answers but to develop more specific problems and pose more exact questions.

SUGGESTION FOR FUTURE RESEARCH

Why were recreation, park and cultural amenities found to be of relatively less importance to companies located in Texas than to companies which relocated in other regions of the country (according to Biscomb's study, 1979)? Is there support for the explanations given in the preceding paragraphs? At what stage in the location decision are quality of life attributes considered? Do they influence the subjective selection of an awareness set of potential locations, or are they considered after locations have been narrowed to only a few serious contenders (evoked set)? Recreational and cultural amenities may not attract a company to a certain location but they could be the determining factor in the final choice between two locations. What factors influence what company officials define as important and can these factors be used by economic development professionals in recruiting relocating businesses? Each of these questions provide the basis for a separate and intensive study.

A study of relocated companies which considered a particular area, in this case Texas, but located elsewhere could provide valuable information concerning determinant attributes. A national study similar to that of Biscomb (1979) is suggested. Rather than asking company officials why they located where they did, maybe they should be asked why they did not consider certain locations. How many times would quality of life and recreational opportunities be mentioned?

Finally, studies concerned with determining the importance of quality of life attributes in business relocation should be conducted at different demographic levels. Reasons for locating in one city rather than another may vary greatly from the reasons for locating in that state or region of the country. Are quality of life factors more important at the community level or at the regional level?

Although this study does not provide justification for local government investment in urban parks and recreation it does ask questions that should be considered before troubled communities decide to cut back on this type of funding.

120

REFERENCES

Allen, L.R., & Beattie, R.J. (1984). The role of leisure as an indicator of overall satisfaction with community life. _Journal of Leisure Research, 16,_ 99-109.

Austin Chamber of Commerce. (1985). _Creating an opportunity environment._ SRI Project 7799 Research Report. Austin, TX: Austin Chamber of Commerce.

Breckenfeld, G. (1987, February 2). The economy of the 1990s: Where to live --and prosper. _Fortune,_ 52-55.

Carson, R.H. (1986). _Locating the factories of the future._ Norcross, GA: Industrial Development Research Council.

Dillman, D.A. (1978). _Mail and telephone surveys._ New York, NY: John Wiley & Sons, Inc.

Fridgen, J.D. (1986). _Recreation and tourism: Creative interrelationships._ Paper presented at the National Recreation and Parks Association Leisure Research Symposium, Anaheim, California.

Gerrard, K. (1985, May). Why they fled the big apple (and do they regret it?) _Across the Board,_ 56-63.

Lund, L. (1986). _Locating corporate r&d facilities._ Report No. 892. Washington, D.C.: The Conference Board, Inc.

Maslow, A.H. (1943). A theory of human motivation. _Psychological Review, 50,_ 370-396.

Moriarty, B.M. (1980). _Industrial location and community development._ Chapel Hill, NC: University of North Carolina Press.

Sneath, W.S. (1978). Business and the states: The elements of a productive partnership. _Vital Speeches of the Day, 45,_ 17-19.

Thornton, L.W. (1984, Summer). Targeting industries for economic development. _Economic Development Review,_ 23-28.

Zitz, M.E. (1979, Winter). Corporate headquarters relocation: The war among the states. _Directors and Boards,_ 21-31.

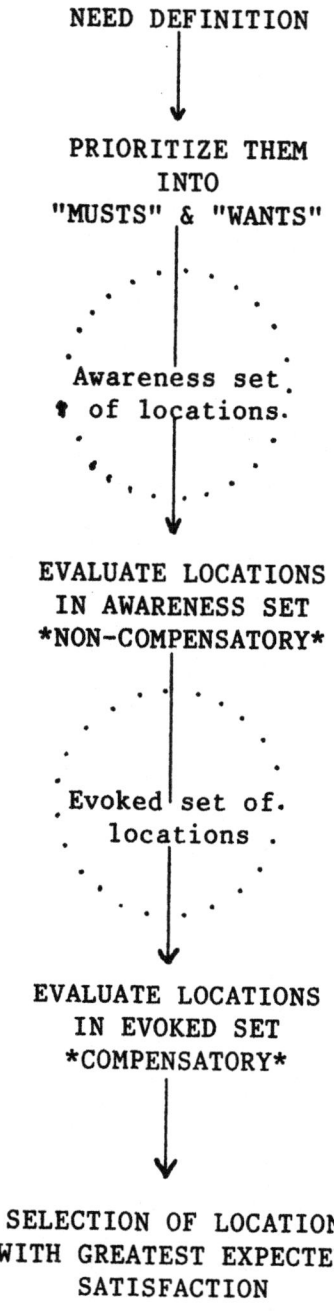

NEED DEFINITION

PRIORITIZE THEM
INTO
"MUSTS" & "WANTS"

Awareness set
of locations.

EVALUATE LOCATIONS
IN AWARENESS SET
NON-COMPENSATORY

Evoked set of.
locations .

EVALUATE LOCATIONS
IN EVOKED SET
COMPENSATORY

SELECTION OF LOCATION
WITH GREATEST EXPECTED
SATISFACTION

Figure 1. Model of Business Location Evaluation

TABLE 1
Summary of the Survey Response for the Three Populations

	Economic Development Professional	Relocation Consultant	Relocated Business	Total
Original Sample Size	126	35	74	235
Dropped	5	6	11	22
Returned	91	13	41	145
Response Rate	75.2%	44.8%	65.1%	68.1%

TABLE 2
Mean Point Allocations for Location Factors by Company Officials
and Summary of Tukey's Multiple Comparison Test

Labor (LAB)	26.8
Transportation (TRAN)	21.3
Quality of Life (QOL)	16.8
Levels of Taxation (TAX)	8.9
Proximity to Suppliers (SUPP)	8.8
Proximity to Research Universities (UNIV)	8.0
Energy and Utility Costs (ENER)	5.3
State and Local Government Incentives (INCEN)	4.2

TABLE 3
Mean Points Allocated to Location Factors by Relocation
Consultants and Summary of Tukey's Multiple comparison Test

Headquarters		High-Technology		Services		Research & Development	
QOL	23.3	UNIV	25.0	LAB	28.0	UNIV	28.5
TRAN	16.1	QOL	17.7	INCEN	15.0	QOL	21.5
TAX	15.8	LAB	17.5	TRAN	14.5	INCEN	13.0
INCEN	13.8	INCEN	8.6	TAX	10.5	LAB	12.1
LAB	10.4	TRAN	8.4	SUPP	10.5	TAX	6.8
UNIV	10.0	SUPP	8.3	QOL	10.1	SUPP	6.2
ENER	5.0	TAX	7.6	ENER	5.4	TRANS	6.1
SUPP	4.7	ENER	6.8	UNIV	5.1	ENER	5.9

TABLE 4
Mean Points Allocated to Location Factors by Economic Development
Professionals and Summary of Tukey's Multiple comparison Test

Headquarters		High-Technology		Services		Research & Development	
QOL	30.5	UNIV	26.8	LAB	22.3	UNIV	35.2
TRAN	16.6	QOL	18.1	SUPP	16.7	QOL	20.2
INCEN	11.3	LAB	16.9	TRAN	15.4	LAB	11.0
TAX	10.7	TRAN	9.2	QOL	13.4	INCEN	9.2
LAB	9.9	INCEN	7.9	TAX	11.6	TRAN	8.2
UNIV	9.2	SUPP	7.6	ENER	9.4	ENER	6.1
ENER	6.2	TAX	7.5	INCEN	7.8	TAX	5.2
SUPP	5.6	ENER	6.4	UNIV	4.0	SUPP	4.7

TABLE 5
Mean Points Allocated to Quality of Life Attributes by Company Officials and Summary of Tukey's Multiple Comparison Test

Cost of Living (COL)	28.1
Primary/Secondary Education (ED)	19.9
Personal Safety/Crime Rate (SAFETY)	14.9
Health/Medical Services (HEALTH)	13.7
Recreation/Parks Open Space (REC/PARK)	11.8
Cultural Opportunities (CULT)	11.6

TABLE 6
Mean Points Allocated to Quality of Life Attributes by Relocation Consultants and Summary of Tukey's Multiple Comparison Test

Headquarters CR= (10.2)		High-Technology (9.9)		Services (9.9)		Research & Development (12.8)	
ED	26.8	ED	28.0	COL	31.5	ED	29.4
COL	23.6	COL	26.0	ED	22.0	COL	20.0
CULT	17.7	REC/PK	12.0	HEALTH	12.0	CULT	18.3
HEALTH	13.6	CULT	11.5	SAFETY	11.5	HEALTH	12.2
SAFETY	11.6	HEALTH	11.5	REC/PK	10.0	REC/PK	10.3
REC/PK	6.5	SAFETY	11.0	CULT	10.0	SAFETY	9.3

TABLE 7
Mean Points Allocated to Q of L Attributes by Economic Development Professionals and Summary of Tukey's Multiple Comparison Test

Headquarters CR= (3.6)		High-Technology (3.8)		Services (3.4)		Research & Development (4.0)	
ED	23.1	ED	28.1	COL	25.8	ED	30.1
CULT	20.1	COL	18.3	ED	22.1	CULT	18.0
COL	17.9	CULT	17.4	HEALTH	14.8	COL	16.8
HEALTH	14.6	HEALT	12.9	SAFETY	14.6	HEALTH	13.1
SAFETY	13.1	SAFETY	11.8	REC/PK	11.7	SAFETY	11.6
REC/PK	11.4	REC/PK	11.4	CULT	10.7	REC/PK	10.9

SURVIVAL STRATEGIES FOR STATE-OWNED AIRLINES:
The Case of Arabian Gulf Carriers

Professor M. Sami Kassem and Professor Bhal J. Bhatt
College of Business Administration
University of Toledo
Toledo, Ohio 43606

ABSTRACT

Arab carriers besieged by growing international competition are operating in a turbulent environment. Now with the plummeting oil revenues and the levelling off in infrastructural development, their load factor is declining. Besides, the prevailing winds of deregulation that swept the entire airline industry coupled with escalating regional tension have compounded the felony and depressed air traffic even further. Consequently Arab carriers are feeling the pinch and fighting a battle for survival as their direct pipeline the to state treasury is ruptured. After identifying the common structural features of Arab carriers and the key environmental forces threatening their survival, the authors have explored several strategies aimed at lowering operating costs and improving load factors without hurting their service image. They then offer some specific alternative proposals geared to help Arab carriers in implementing new strategies and adapting themselves successfully to the demands of their turbulent environment. The authors conclude by arguing that the performance of state-owned enterprises should be made by reference to their stated objectives rather than to the commonly accepted economic criteria.

To what extent should state governments continue to run unprofitable airlines in a fiercely competitive international industry? The answer should, no doubt, depend upon the objectives with which the airlines were started in the first place. If these objectives were _not_ purely economic, then it hardly makes any sense to use their economic performance to make important decisions regarding both their future and direction of growth. Alternatively, if the objectives were political, social, or national in scope, then we need to re-examine the performance and future directions of national airlines within such relevant and appropriate terms. What might these terms of reference be? What are the _attainable_ goals? What strategic alternatives are available? These and other related questions are examined in this paper with particular focus on the Arab Airline carriers.

Employing a case research approach, we have attempted an analysis of economic performance of the Arab airline industry and explored existing "turn around" strategies. However, our primary concern here is to understand the severe constraints on implementation of available business strategies, even though they might prove effective. Further, we have identified several and strategies for attaining long-term desirable goals and plans that might prove both attractive and appropriate for the airlines in question.

I. THE CHALLENGE

The Arab airline industry is heading the list of Arabian Gulf service industries facing hard times. The great boom of the 1970's -- fueled by the oil bonanza -- is ending and with it, the familiar long waiting lists for hotel rooms and airline seats. Sales are sagging, profits are rapidly declining, jobs are vanishing and careers are being disrupted. Ambitions are reappraised. Some service operations are overhauled. Others are shut. Competition intensifies among service operators as companies try to improve sales at rival's expense.

Today's recession has affected the region's air carriers the most. The expatriate labor force -- the core market segment for the Arabian Gulf Carriers -- is being sent home in droves. The full-fare business traveller who used to flock the region in search of juicy construction contracts is rapidly disappearing. Today, the average traveller to the region is a technician on his way to service and maintain equipment installed by his predecessors.

In addition to these recessionary pressures, Arab air carriers are plagued by excess capacity, uncompetitive cost structure, many new types of competitors both from within and outside the region and by escalating regional wars. In view of the fact that all Arab airlines are state-flag carriers, it is unclear whether they will be able to survive these environmental challenges without adversely affecting the quality of their service image. This paper maps out several strategies to help Arab air carriers cope with these environmental challenges. First, however, it will briefly identify the common structural features of Arab carriers along with the problems they collectively face.

In 1970, Arab carriers had a combined fleet of 137 aircraft, carried a total of 5 million passengers a year and employed about 25,000 persons. Fifteen years later, they had a combined fleet of 322 aircraft, carried 33 million passengers, employed about 81,000 person and achieved an average seat factor of about 58% and a load factor of about 53% (see Exhibit 1).

A. Shared Characteristics

Arab carriers, in general and Gulf carriers in particular, share the following attributes in common:[1]

1) With the exception of Saudia, they are all small in size. Individually, they can't benefit from economies of scale in training, purchasing, maintenance and computerization. But collectively, they can.

2) With the exception of the Middle East Airline, they are all state-owned and state-run corporations. This has, all too often, led them to assume too much and function in a less than competitive manner.

127

3) With the exception of Saudia, they are operating without the benefits of a sizable domestic network. This built-in geographic handicap compel them to devote the bulk of their energies and resources in the service of their international network -- a fact which brings them in direct competition with the giant experienced European carriers and with the lean and mean Far Eastern carriers as well (e.g. Singapore Airline and Cathay Pacific). This pattern of outward orientation partly explains the failure of some Arab carriers to meet the regional and domestic needs of Arab passengers.

4) Arab carriers operate at a competitive cost disadvantage. Virtually everything needed to run an airline -- the plane, the spare parts, the computer, the crew, the meal offered the passenger -- is imported and at a premium price. For instance, 35% of the pilots, 50% of the cabin crews, and 35% of the engineers and technicians employed by Arab carriers are foreigners. This fact explains why the average payroll bill, particularly for Gulf Carriers, tends to be twice as high as the industry average. After all, foreign labor have to be offered high salary plus an attractive housing, hospitalization, schooling, and repatriation allowance or else they would rather stay home.

B. Environmental Turbulence

In the past five years, the following environmental forces have threatened the survival of the Arab air carriers.

1) Glut in Oil Market

The glut in the oil market has depressed oil prices and sharply reduced the revenues of the Arab states. To balance their national budget, these oil-producing states have slashed their capital expenditure programs and curtailed their spending budget. The impact of these cutbacks on the operation of the state flag carrier was direct and swift. Lower revenues translate into lower spendings which eventually translates into fewer jobs and fewer passengers. Lower spending also means lower subsidies for the national carrier and fewer opportunities for foreign business travelers. In a word, plummeting oil revenues led to the erosion of the two major market segments of the Arab carriers: expatriate labor and foreign business travelers. The former was sent home, the latter was kept from leaving home.

2) Liquidity Crisis

Sharply reduced oil revenues mean sharply reduced government subsidies for the flag carrier. It also means that the national carrier is more likely to encounter slowdown in payments for its services from its governments and corporate clients. These cash flow problems are compounded as the airlines have to modernize their fleet and as the recession deepens.

3) Excess Capacity

The strategic location of the Arab world makes the Arab travel market one of the busiest in the world directly behind the North Atlantic and the Far East. This market is worth about 7 billion dollars, the bulk of which is taken by non-Arab carriers. Virtually most European and Far Eastern carriers make a daily stop or two in the region. Besides, the introduction of wide-bodied aircraft right in the midst of the oil boom whetted the appetite of Arab airline executives to buy more "big birds" in the name of customer appeal. Most of these jumbo jets were delivered just in time the band stopped playing and the party was over -- giving rise to the phenomenon of too many seats chasing fewer passengers.

4) Increased Competition

The Arab airline industry is experiencing competition it has never seen before. About 40 air carriers -- Arab and foreign alike -- are battling fiercely to expand their customer's base and to improve rapidly deteriorating load factors, carried by weakened demand, excess capacity and fare wars.

Thanks to their low-cost structure and aggressive marketing skills, foreign carriers serving Arab airports are able to promote fare wars and innovate better services. Most thrive on fifth and sixth freedom traffic to fill their planes and lower their fares. The elite European and Far Eastern carriers (such as Air France, Lufthansa, Swissair, and Singapore Airlines) target the business traveller and offer him a first-class service at an economy class fare. The budget class carriers of the Far East and Europe capitalize on their low-cost position to offer the labor traffic emanating from or destined to their base cities cheap fares, decent services and direct flights to major Gulf cities. Due to their uncompetitive cost-structure and unmotivated front-line personnel, Arab carriers are condemned to play a catch-up game with their foreign competitors. Individually, they can neither champion a low-fare nor a better service strategy for a long period of time.

Competition is getting tougher and stiffer not only among the 40 or more carriers serving the Arabian Gulf but also among the region's airports. Dubai is becoming a very popular destination for all giant carriers who use it as a stopover of convenience on their East-West around the world trips. These carriers can afford to "dump" their empty seats in Arab markets at a huge discount thereby making the going rough for the endogenous high-cost carriers of the region.

5) Deregulation

The initial response of Arab carriers to the unfriendly competition taking place in their local markets was uneven. Carriers of the oil-rich states have fought it teeth and nail. They blacklisted travel agents suspected of dumping foreign carriers tickets. When these campaigns did not put a stop to "illegal discounting," these carriers reluctantly and selectively joined the intruders in the discounting game. This protectionist urge stems from the fact that most of the route networks of the oil-rich Arab carriers are made up of routes with seasonal peaks and limited room for growth. They cater primarily to expatriate employees who travel on these routes at their employers expense. Travel on these routes is restricted by visas.

By contrast, airlines of tourist-oriented Arab countries (such as Egypt and Jordan) resigned themselves to the new game of deregulation and tried to adapt. They joined the discounting wave to stimulate traffic on their dense routes. They relaxed restrictions on visas. Quietly, they capitalized on their geographic location and tourist appeal to compete for fifth and sixth freedom traffics. Fortunately, Arab carriers do not have to choose between the extremes of rigid protectionism and unbridled competition. The former suits nations with their international routes, while the latter nations with developed airlines, dense routes and open skies. Since Arab countries do not strictly fit either profile, they would be better off adapting themselves to the new game, at least in the short run. In the long run, it behooves them to pool their resources, experiment with joint ventures to reduce unit costs, operate long routes, diversify their gateways and tap new markets.

6) Escalation of Intraregional Rivalries and Tension

The Arab world is plagued by at least four problems: the Arab-Israeli conflict, the Iran-Iraq War, the Civil War in Lebanon and inter-Arab rivalries and sensitivities. These problems have taken their toll and left their mark on the Arab airline industry. They have affected the movement of people and goods, changed the face of nations and the established norms of airlines operations (e.g. excessive delays due to extensive security checks, exorbitant insurance premiums caused by high risk of hijacking, unusually high fuel bill).

To illustrate the debilitating effect of intra-regional rivalries and hostilities, let us consider the case of Gulf Air. As of late, this regional carrier has been threatened by a disagreement among its shareholding states concerning free trade and open-sky policy. This disagreement has led Dubai to break ranks and launch its own carrier - Emirates Airline. This newcomer has already forced Gulf

Air to switch its services away from more popular Dubai to nearby and less accessible Sharjah. And consider the Iranian attack on the Holy Shrine of Mecca in the Summer of 1987. This incident prompted the Saudi government to sever political relations with the Iranian government and the subsequent cessation of air travel between the two neighboring states. The continuation of political strife in the region have prompted many international carriers to discontinue their service to Beirut, Baghdad and Tehran. Ali Ghandour Alia chairman and an articulate spokesman for the Arab airline industry, summed up the impact of political turmoil in the Middle East, on airline operations as follows:

"Until we have peace, there can be no real strategic business planning. We find ourselves buying aircrafts not on the basis of pure economy or comfort but after detailed consideration of such factors as range and ability to operate under adverse conditions. So, you see, without peace we must live each day as it comes: the victims of perpetual crisis management."[2]

II. STRATEGIC ALTERNATIVES AND CONSTRAINTS

A. Competitive Strategies:

Given the environmental challenge just described and the prospect of continued economic slowdown and political instability, what Arab carriers can do to compete with their foreign counterparts?[3] Can they ever become lean and mean and still offer high-quality service? Can they become aggressive marketers? The answer depends on what each Arab government wants out of its national carrier and what it plans to do with it. If airlines are intended to make profit only, the answer is negative. If, by contrast, they are intended to serve as a means for developing skilled manpower and infrastructure, then the answer is in the positive.

A content analysis of the strategies used by Alia, Kuwait Airways, and Gulf Air suggests the following pattern of commonalities.

1. Downsizing

The key issue in downsizing is finding out how small an airline can be and still operate effectively.[4] One useful tool for answering this practical questions is a proforma income and expense model that takes account of the main influences on a carrier's costs and revenues. These should include projected load factors, staffing, variable adn fixed costs. Using such a model analysts can pose a series of "what if" questions to helpestimate the financial, competitive, and quality of service effects of various downsizing scenarios (such as dropping unprofitable routes, selling underutilized aircraft, divesting out of marginal anciliary activities). Although downsizing is an unpopular strategy with airline executives, it is not a bad medicine given the huge, idel capacity in fleet and facilities among Arab air carriers.

2. <u>Low Cost Provider</u>

Being a low-cost provider is a strategy that every airline must attempt.[5] This is particularly the case with Arab carriers, the bulk of which is victimized by an uncompetitive cost structure, and low level of resource productivity.

Several tactics are used to control costs. One of these is to rely heavily on travel agents for booking and selling tickets. Another tactic is to hire fewer employees while increasing their individual productivity -- through better training and incentives. Alia's labor costs are only 18% of expenses compared to 37% for the Arab carriers as a group. Still another cost-control tactic is the use of better scheduling techniques to increase aircraft productivity. Alia's plans are utilized daily 10.1 hours per plane compared to 7.1 hours for the Arab carriers as a group. Another cost-cutting tactic is to perform all fleet maintenance work in-house for oneself and for others, too. Alternatively, it may be wiser to replace aircraft every three years to minimize maintenance costs and maximize customer appeal.

One issue that is sure to arise in controlling costs is the impact on quality of service. Field observation suggests that today's travellers are sensitive to the costs of high quality levels and are willing to accept some reductions in service, especially if they are paying for their own tickets.

3. <u>Market Niche</u>:

Arab air carriers may innovate better services to fit special needs of their markets. For example, expatriates constitute a key segment of the Arab travel market and they may respond favorably to any of the following:

1) Offering expatriates Round the World (RTW) tickets with a small differential between the allowed home leave fare and the (RTW) fare.

2) Allowing expatriates to visit a point or two en route to their home country during their annual home leave. The traditional policy of Arab carriers of issuing non-refundable and non-reroutable tickets hurts the image of Arab carriers in the long run.

132

Similarly, the leisure travel segment could be stimulated by:

1) Promoting short package tours to favorite destination cities such as London, Paris, Malga, Vienna, Geneva, and Cairo;

2) Promoting packaged holy land tours to the Moslem communities in Europe and the Americas;

3) Offering expatriates an annual pass for unlimited trips between the home base of the Arab carrier and the home city of the expatriate -- at an attractive price.

Although the Arab travel market is stagnant and relatively small in size, its spending power is relatively high -- making it a lucrative market whose penetration is much simpler than entering a single country market. This may provide mutually beneficial joint venture possibilities with other major non-Arab airlines.

B. Constraints

In considering the foregoing strategic alternatives, one must recognize various constraints in implementing them that are deeply rooted in the Arab society.

(1) Heads of Arab states -- rich and poor alike -- are adamant about the need of their coutnries for a respectable national airline. To them, the prime job of the national carrier is to serve as a tool for the social, economic and political development of the shareholding state. Thus, there is a lesser concern for a competitive strategy for the national airline among Arab heads of states.

(2) Bureaucrats don't want to loose their power and authority over such a strategic and high visibility enterprise. Turf protection and pure self interest make them reluctant to relinquish their grip on their national airline.

(3) Managers of Arab carriers are ambivalent about privatization. Most are well-socialized to work with their senior top-governmental officials and they have grown accustomed to operate with a sizeable budgetary slack. Therefore, they are likely to lobby against privatization, in whole or in part. Few of these managers welcome privatization as an opportunity to depoliticize management and to free their hands to run the airline as a business, not as a government agency. In other words, political mangement is the norm, professional management is the exception.

(4) Neither Arab consumers (of airline services) nor Arab airline employees favor a change in the status quo. The former oppose change that threatens suspending services to remote and

133

unprofitable markets while the latter oppose change that threatens their job security and generous incentive system. Only the local minority of Arab airline employees may be interested in stock ownership. The majority are expatriates who -- due to restrictive legislation -- are denied property rights expecially in the oil-rich Arab Gulf states. So, stock-ownership as a means of providing production incentives and of achieving wage concessions from labor is not likely to work in the Arab airline industry the way it did elsewhere.

C. New Directions

Turn around strategies might be successfully implemented despite the foregoing severe constraints. However, the end results are likely to prove detrimental to the greater national goal of modernization through industrialization. Costs associated with turn around strategies with regard to loss of jobs, pride, economic dislocation and prestige are likely to have far reaching and lasting consequences for the Arab States. Instead, if airlines industry were to be used as an agent for change aimed at developing an industrial infrastructure with all its requisites, then the search for new strategic directions becomes imperative.

The cost of running an unprofitable airline could be construed as: i) an investment toward the development of skilled manpower and managerial cadre, ii) a membership fee for participating in a global industry through building the requisite infrastructure (e.g. airports, catering, maintenance, training and ground handling facilities), iii) important foundation and learning vehicle for exposing the present generation of Gulf nationals to space-age technologies.

Policy makers and managers will need to articulate their respective needs and prioritize goals that will include broad societal and national objectives. Such an undertaking will also require national consensus with regard to adoption of criteria against which the performance of a given airline will be measured. Reward structures will require the inclusion of such new criteria. For example, if the stated goal was the creation of a skilled manpower and managerial cadre, then airline executives will have to be rewarded on the basis of attaining such a goal. And, if the stated goal was to serve as a bridge for promoting tourism, cultural understandings and trade, as in the case of ALIA, then the performance of airline executives has to be judged on the basis of achieving this goal.

Failure to clearly articulate what specific objectives a particular state-owned industry is expected to attain will surely lead to further confusion and chaos, and eventual demise of a promising investment.

III. CONCLUSIONS

In choosing appropriate and effective survival and growth strategies for state owned industries, it is imperative to clearly establish objectives, goals, performance measures, and meaningful organizational structure for such undertakings. If the objectives are economic, then adoption of economic performance criteria and appropriate business strategies appear to meet the needs. If not, one must clearly define what the societal or national objectives the state wants the enterprise to attain. Performance measurements have to be based on operational definitions of these goals and results obtained. Choice of appropriate strategies will then depend upon how to make an enterprise attain these goals through appropriate and relevant policies, organizational structure, style of management and systems. Failure to do this might result in the early demise of an otherwise promising undertaking. In our case of Arab Airlines, we strongly feel that their economic performance alone should not determine the future direction of that industry. Instead, we recommend that a serious effort be made to re-examine and re-evaluate the purpose and objectives such carriers are expected to fulfill in the long run.

ENDNOTES

1. For a detailed comparative analysis of the Arab Airline Industry see Kassem, S. and Habib, G. Strategic Management of Services in the Arabian Gulf States, New York: Walter de Gruyter, 1988 (in press), Ch. 4.

2. Ghandor, A. "Politics in the Middle East: Its Effects on Air Transportation and Communication." Address before the Council for World Affairs. Los Angeles, Sept. 10, 1979.

3. _____ "The Role of Air Carriers in Developing Air Transport in the Arab World." A paper presented at the Civil Aviation Forum sponsored by the Arab League Civil Aviation Council. Rabat, July 7-11, 1983. (Amman: Alia P.R. Dept.).

4. James Lynch. Airlines organizations in the 1980's. An Industry Report on strategies and structures for coping with change, London, MacMillan, 1984.

5. D. Hambrick, and S. Schecter. "Turnaround Strategies for Mature Industrial-Product Business Units." Academy of Management Journal, 26:2:(1983).

IS THERE AN INTERNATIONAL LIFE CYCLE FOR FOREIGN BANK ADVERTISING?

William Renforth
Florida International University

Abstract

Advertisements by foreign banks in the U.S. were examined using standard content analysis procedures to determine services advertised, promotional themes utilized, and the degree of internationalization of the strategy depicted. Results indicate that the overwhelming majority of ads emphasize general institutional characteristics and only occasionally focus on specific services. Further, themes stress size-assets, internationality, experience, and competitiveness. Significant differences in services advertised, themes stressed, and degree of internationalization were noted between the first half and the last half of the period studied. This supports the notion of an international advertising life cycle, whereby foreign banks change their ad strategies as they gain more experience in the U.S.

The volume of foreign bank activity in the United States has increased sharply in recent years. In 1973 the U.S. offices of foreign banks accounted for 3.8 percent of total banking assets in the United States and 1.7 percent of total deposits. By 1982 their assets had increased to $299.4 billion or 14.4 percent of total U.S. banking assets, and deposits stood at $154 billion or 10.3 percent of total deposits (Park and Zwick, 1985).

The rapid expansion of foreign bank activities in the U.S. during the 1970's has, in many respects, paralleled the expansion of U.S. banks abroad in the 1960's, in that comparable factors of economics and government regulation account for the expansion. Foreign banks frequently set up operations in the U.S. during the period to follow their domestic customers who had undertaken direct foreign investment activities in the U.S. The prolonged U.S. balance of payments deficits in the period provided the initial dollar balances required. Another attraction is the size and sophistication of U.S. financial markets, which provide a convenient source of dollar financing and an outlet for investment of surplus funds. The dominant role of the dollar in international finance made a dollar based operation especially attractive for foreign banks with significant international business operations. Opportunities for profitable retail operations, often focused on a specific ethnic market, were also inducements in some cases.

The very favorable regulatory environment of the 1970's also attracted foreign banks to the U.S. Until the passage of the International Banking Act of 1978, U.S. branches and agencies of foreign banks were regulated only at the state level (Reed, 1984). This meant that, compared to U.S. domestic banks, foreign banks were not subject to Federal Reserve requirements, deposit interest rate ceilings, or restrictions on interstate banking, all of which resulted in cost advantages. Prior to the passage of the IBA, foreign banks were especially active in purchasing U.S. banks and establishing branches to beat the consequences of these new regulations.

One survey (Ricks and Arpan, 1976), indicated that the increase in foreign banks in the U.S. is a rather recent phenomenon, with over 30% of the activities being established since 1970. This research also revealed that the inflow has resulted in increased competition for U.S. domestic banks, especially in the area of international services, since many foreign banks enter the U.S. to compete as "full service" banks. The priority ranking of activities planned by the foreign banks in the U.S. were, in order:

      to serve foreign subsidiaries,
      to serve U.S. corporations,
      to handle foreign exchange operations,
      to provide retail service.

The increased volume of foreign bank activities in the U.S. has aroused interest in how these foreign banks have conducted their business in this country. The purpose of this paper is to examine one specific aspect of foreign bank business, namely the pattern of advertising strategy by these banks in the U.S. market. Since advertising often mirrors business strategy, it is reasonable to expect that foreign bank advertising in the U.S. will reflect the services, competitive approaches, and business philosophies used by those banks for their entry into the U.S. market. However, no known studies have examined empirically the themes and portrayals used by foreign banks in the U.S. Specifically, this paper provides a description of the themes and appeals used in foreign bank advertisements in the United States. The evolution in the emphasis on specific themes over time is also examined to determine if advertising strategies have changed following increased experience in the U.S. economy.

METHOD

In order to study the changing pattern of advertising strategies of foreign banks in the United States, every page of Business Week magazine from 1976 through 1985 (520 issues) on which the advertisements of foreign banks appeared was analyzed. Two reasons influenced the selection of the time period 1976 to 1985: (1) the number of foreign banks operating in the U.S. increased significantly during this period, thereby insuring a sufficient number of relevant banks with diverse experience in the U.S. market; (2) the period was sufficiently long to detect changes and trends.

The communications media are so diverse that it is impractical to consider every possible type of advertisement for the purposes of this research. Magazine print media was selected, based on its convenience for content analysis, availability of advertisements over a long period of time, and widespread use by advertisers. Business Week was utilized based on its wide regard as a leading national circulation business magazine, and its appropriateness as a bank advertising vehicle in terms of circulation, audience, and editorial content. Although utilization of only one magazine is a limitation imposed by practical considerations, it is assumed that the advertisements placed in this magazine also appeared in other communications media. Thus, the results obtained from this sample are applicable to other media and can be generalized.

Following the general operational definitions developed by Suzuki (1980), each foreign bank advertisement was content analyzed in terms of three different, general types of information:
1. the services advertised,
2. the themes, promotional appeals, and information presented, and
3. general thematic classification.

The content analysis procedures utilized defined the services advertised in terms of seven categories: foreign exchange services, international services, project lending, domestic banking services, others, general supportive, and general information. The general supportive category was assigned in those cases where the advertisement mentioned a variety of specific services, but did not emphasize clearly any one offering. The general information category was used to indicate advertisements which did not mention services, but merely presented bank background, financial information, or other such general, non-service related, information.

The purpose of the theme or promotional appeal category is to identify the overall talking point or basic idea highlighted by the advertisement. The ideas of convenience, expertise, experience, size-assets, creativity, internationality, services, competitive status, special offers, and other, are included in this section.

The general thematic classification is intended to measure the degree of internationalization of advertising themes. The Suzuki procedures, replicated in this present study, were used to identify four developmental stages of advertising, as follows:

Stage 1   Nationality Supportive. Advertisements in this category emphasize the national origin of the bank involved and its performance in its domestic market, suggesting by implication that its record at home demonstrates its superiority to competitors in the U.S. market. Non-product attributes, such as the bank's high level of performance in its home country, long business history, or well established branch network at home, are emphasized. The nationality supportive theme can be regarded as premature from the standpoint of internationalization of ad themes, since its reliance on national origin does not stand on its own merits in describing bank attributes and competitiveness.

Stage 2   Product Attributes. This ad theme emphasizes the attributes of the banking service featured. Product characteristics, information, and attributes such as rates, timeliness, or the like are stressed. Here the national origin of the bank or the competitive superiority of services are not emphasized; only the essential features of the offering are described. For this reason the theme is regarded as neutral in terms of internationalization, since only attributes are described.

Stage 3 and 4 Competitiveness and Global Market Orientation. Ads in these categories emphasize the superior characteristics of the banks, compared to the competition, or view customers and competitors in the international perspective, respectively. "Our bank is the world's leader" and "No competitor in the world" are examples of messages contained in the advertisements classified at this stage. As defined by Suzuki, these two categories of ad themes are grouped together and defined as matured advertisements from the standpoint of internationalization of ad themes.

Stage 5 Bank information. This category includes advertisements which could not be classified in any of the four stages mentioned above or where the idea is to merely announce or highlight the presence of the bank in the U.S. market. This category is considered neutral from the standpoint of internationalization.

Two judges separately content analyzed each of the advertisements in the sample according to their answer to the questions "What services are advertised?" "What themes or promotional appeals are utilized?" and "What general thematic classification applies to the advertisement considered?" In addition, each judge also noted the date of the ad, the size of the ad, the country of origin of the advertising bank, and the section of the magazine in which the advertisement appeared. The average interjudge reliability for all categories in this study was 91.3 percent. The suggested minimum interjudge reliability for content analysis studies is 85 percent (Kassarjian, 1977). This suggests there is a relatively high degree of interrater consistency in this study. Thus, inconsistencies due to possible evaluator bias or the degree of subjectivity involved in classifying the ads appears well within the standard acceptable limits for studies of this type.

A total of 809 foreign bank advertisements appeared in Business Week from 1976 through 1985. The general section of the magazine contained 619 ads and special advertising sections the remaining 190. Special sections promote a particular country for investment purposes, the idea being to encourage U.S. firms to invest in the country advertised. Many of these bank ads were generally supportive of a national image, or placed by banks not actually operating in the U.S. Given the non-commercial, general focus of these ads, only ads appearing in the general section were included in this study. Of the 619 ads so considered, many were multiple placements or repetitions. To avoid distorting the analysis by varying frequencies of advertisement placement, only distinct ads were considered. That is, each specific individual ad was included in the study only once, regardless of the number of times it may have appeared in various issues. This resulted in a total of 220 ads, which provides the data base for this paper.

FINDINGS

Table I indicates the number of ads, classified according to services advertised, by year since 1976. The bank ads identified in the table represent 15 countries of origin. Five countries, Canada, Germany,

139

Switzerland, Japan, and the U.K., in order of frequency, account for 82% of the placements. This generally corresponds with the proportion of foreign banks operating in the U.S. The common market countries account for 42% of foreign bank assets in the U.S. (41% of ads) and Japan 24% of foreign bank assets (18% of ads).

As Table I indicates, foreign banks tend to be very general in the selection of services to advertise. Over half of the themes were generally supportive, emphasizing no one specific service or offering. General information about the bank was provided in about 8 percent of the ads. Of the specific services advertised, only international services and project lending provided the focus for more than 5% of the ads. The picture presented, then, is one of generalized, non-specific promotion. Ads do not tend to emphasize specific services, but instead focus on the bank as an institution or the entire range of bank activities. Only about one third of the ads highlighted a specific service; among those two services, project lending and international services dominated, accounting for the vast majority of specific services promoted.

TABLE I
SERVICES ADVERTISED

Number of ads, by year

	Total	1976	1977	1978	1979	1980	1981	1982	1983	1984	1985
Foreign Exchange	9	1	1	-	1	1	1	-	2	1	1
Int'l. Services	20	2	-	2	3	1	-	-	3	6	3
Domestic Services	1	-	-	-	1	-	-	-	-	-	-
General Support	119	16	14	18	16	15	13	11	7	5	4
Project Loans	18	3	3	2	3	-	-	1	2	4	-
Gen. Info	18	3	2	1	-	1	2	-	2	5	2
Other	35	3	3	2	6	2	2	4	6	4	3
Total	220	28	23	25	30	20	18	16	22	25	13

Source: 220 non duplicated foreign bank advertisements appearing in Business Week, 1976-1985.

This general tendency is not uniform over time, however. In the first half of the decade covered by this analysis, specific services were featured in 31% of the ads, compared to 46% in the second half. This difference, significant at the .95 level, suggests that the use of specific service themes seems to increase as more banks develop more experience in the U.S. market and become more sophisticated or competitive in targeting customers.

TABLE II
ADVERTISED THEMES

Frequency, by year

	Total	1976	1977	1978	1979	1980	1981	1982	1983	1984	1985
Convenience	3	1	-	1	1	-	-	-	-	-	-
Expertise	30	5	5	2	3	3	-	2	4	5	1
Experience	64	9	9	10	8	5	3	4	4	8	4
Size-Assets	128	19	15	16	13	1	10	8	11	15	9
Creativity	21	2	1	3	5	-	2	2	3	3	-
Interna- tionality	123	12	9	15	15	10	12	12	15	13	10
Services	26	1	-	1	2	5	3	1	5	5	3
Competitive	77	5	3	5	12	8	4	8	11	15	6
Special Offers	1	-	-	-	-	-	-	-	-	1	-
Others	27	4	5	3	4	2	1	1	2	3	2

Source: 220 non-duplicated foreign bank advertisements appearing in Business Week, 1976-1985.

Table II presents the frequency distribution of the promotional themes utilized. Foreign banks seem to consistently emphasize two advertising themes: size and internationality. These two themes account for 50 percent of those utilized. Only two other themes, experience and competitive status, account for more than 10 percent each. Analysis of theme frequencies by first half and second half of the period covered reveals only three significant differences in frequency (at the .95 level). Experience and size were more frequently used as themes in the early part of the decade covered. Services offered was more frequently utilized in the second half of the period. This suggests a movement away from general themes based on experience, which is consistent with that noted in the discussion of services advertised.

TABLE III
ADS CLASSIFIED ACCORDING TO DEGREE OF INTERNATIONALIZATION

Number of ads, by year

Stage	Total	1976	1977	1978	1979	1980	1981	1982	1983	1984	1985
1. Nationality Supportive (Premature)	56	13	12	11	4	1	3	4	5	2	1
2. Product Attribute (Neutral)	12	1	-	1	2	3	2	-	1	1	1
3. Competitiveness (Matured)	49	6	3	3	6	3	1	2	7	14	4
4. Global Orientation (Matured)	75	6	6	8	13	10	8	9	8	3	4
5. Bank Information (Neutral)	28	2	2	2	5	3	4	1	1	5	3
TOTAL	220	28	23	25	30	20	18	16	22	25	13

Source: 220 non-duplicated foreign bank advertisements appearing in Business Week, 1976-1985.

Table III classifies the ads analyzed according to the degree of internationalization, using the categories developed by Suzuki. Foreign banks have utilized the global orientation theme most frequently (34%), followed by nationality supportive (26%) and competitiveness (23%).

Product attributes and bank information are used relatively infrequently.

142

IMPLICATIONS

As discussed previously, the degree of internationalization of advertisements can be measured quantitatively by classifying the themes as premature, neutral, and matured, as discussed in stages 1-5. Following the procedure and formula suggested by Suzuki, the degree of internationalization of ad themes was calculated for each of three periods: 1976-1985, 1976-1980, and 1981-1985. The calculations result in a coefficient, ranging from 1 to -1, which reflects the relative proportion of matured (positive) or premature (negative) international themes in the sample. A coefficient of one, for example, would indicate a sample with every ad theme in stage 3 or 4, the matured stage. The internationalization coefficients for the bank ads analyzed are:

1976-1985	1976-1980	1981-1985
.21	.11	.38

This suggests an overall picture of a relatively high proportion of internationalized themes in the ads studied, given the positive coefficients. To place these findings in context comparable coefficients in the period 1972-1977 for Japanese car ads were .15, Japanese TV ads .1, Japanese cameras .16 and Japanese calculators .25. In this sense, then, foreign bank advertisements in the U.S. seem relatively internationalized.

Comparison of the coefficient in the early and later half of the time period studied reveals several interesting facts with implications for future research. First, during the period 1976-1980 only a slight development of advertisements toward the matured stage of internationalization was detected. This low profile of internationalization existed even considering that a number of banks had been operating in the U.S. for significant periods prior to 1976. Second, the period 1981-1985 evidenced a rapid movement toward the matured stage of internationalization, with the coefficient equal to .38. This means that foreign bank advertisements have become more aggressive in the international dimension than the previous period. This may reflect growing confidence as foreign banks gain experience in the U.S. market and an increased tendency toward direct, specific competition.

Third, research results seem to indicate in a general way a parallel relationship between increased foreign bank presence in the U.S. and increased utilization of internationalized ad strategies. This observation supports the notion of an advertising spiral in international marketing noted by Kleppner (1979) and confirmed by Suzuki's research. The advertising spiral is a graphic representation of the advertising stages of products which, according to Kleppner, "provides a point of reference for determining which stage or stages a product has reached in a given market and what the thrust of the advertising message should be. In many cases the advertising spiral parallels the life cycle of a product, except that it shows what has to be done at each stage and where the product can go when it reaches a high level of success."

The results of this research confirm Suzuki's observation that the advertising spiral can be extended into an international dimension, and also builds on

143

this work by applying the methodology successfully to service industries. As suggested by Suzuki, the progress of product and service advertisements through the internationalization stages is similar, with the exception of a very weak emphasis on the product attribute stage for services. Although this stage was not skipped entirely by service advertisements, as Suzuki assumed, it was utilized much less frequently.

The research also provides important implications for service marketers. Perhaps the most obvious implication arises from the documentation of an international life cycle for bank service ads. This suggests that the themes and services featured in a foreign bank's advertisement follow a more or less predictable pattern, depending on a bank's longevity in the foreign market. Although not all newcomers will necessarily want to follow previous patterns, the existence of a fairly consistent path followed by prior entrants is suggested. A second implication is the necessity to make continual adjustments to advertising strategy to prevent business declines and target new clients. Appeals that are successful in reaching one set of customers in early stages are not those that are appropriate for attracting additional clients at a later time. Emphasis on home country performance, for example, must give way to broader orientations after foreign market experience develops. A final implication arises from the relative generality of the themes and messages presented. Focus on single, specific services or other selling points is relatively rare. This suggests that abundant opportunities for differentiation and specialization are available.

Naturally, several limitations must be kept in mind in interpreting the results of this study. First, the sample of advertisements includes only one magazine. Moreover, the sample time span, although relatively long, might not be sufficiently long to detect all longitudinal changes in the complex phenomenon studied. Different samples, from different magazines or covering different time periods, might yield different results. Second, the technique of content analysis is relatively subjective and capable of detecting only large differences. For these reasons the results are best thought of as exploratory in nature, indicating the possibility of detecting differences over time in the themes used by foreign bank advertisers. These limits notwithstanding, the findings are interesting for marketers. Clear indications of changes in thematic emphasis and support for the concept of an internationalized "advertising spiral" or advertising international life cycle for banking services is provided.

REFERENCES

Kassarjian, Harold H. (1977), "Content Analysis in Consumer Research," Journal of Consumer Research, 4 (June), 8-18.

Kleppner, Otto (1979), Advertising Procedure, Englewood Cliffs, New Jersey: Prentice-Hall.

Park, Yoon S. and Jack Zwick (1985), _International Banking in Theory and Practice_, Reading, Massachusetts: Addison-Wesley Publishing Company.

Reed, Edward W. (1984), _Commercial Banking_, Englewood Cliffs, New Jersey: Prentice-Hall.

Ricks, DAvid, and Jeffrey S. Arpan (1976), "Foreign Banking in the United States," _Business Horizons_, 19 (1 February), 84-87.

Suzuki, Norihiko (1980), "The Changing Pattern of Advertising Strategy by Japanese Business Firms in the U.S. Market: Content Analysis," _Journal of International Business Studies_, 11 (Winter), 63-72.

STRATEGIES PERCEIVED AS EFFECTIVE BY ENTREPRENEURIAL
SERVICE MARKETERS: ILLUSTRATIONS FROM THE TRAVEL INDUSTRY

Jeffrey C. Dilts and George E. Prough
University of Akron

Abstract

Marketers of services are increasingly facing environments which are
turbulent and uncertain. To survive, greater emphasis may be placed on more
proactive patterns of strategies. One such industry is travel. With recent
dramatic growth and deregulation (airlines in 1978 and travel agencies in
1985), the industry is changing markedly. This paper reports on a survey of
travel agents in the northeastern and midwest U.S. Explored are questions
related to the existence of strategic patterns in the industry and
especially those related patterns showing a correlation with the more
entrepreneurial mentality.

BACKGROUND

Academic and applied researchers in marketing have seen the literature
change dramatically in the last few decades. One of the changes has been
away from the traditional view of marketing of only manufactured products to
the broadened view of marketing to include a wider spectrum of
possibilities, including services. And the growth of services as a part of
the U.S. economy has been considerable.

Another change has been a movement from the consumer orientation of the
1960's to the positioning of the 70's and the strategic planning of the 80's
(Gluck, Kaufman, and Welleck 1980). In the decade of the 80's, marketers
have turned greater attention to strategic planning and long-range issues
affecting the organization.

As the decades have progressed, more and more of the energies of management
has been spent on matters external to the organization--its environments.
And as research in strategic planning developed, marketers began to
incorporate the notions of environmental turbulance and uncertainty
(Zeithaml and Zeithaml 1984) into their literature. This heightened even
more the concerns strategic thinkers had regarding environmental scanning
and assessment. In addition, more attention was paid to the meshing of the
two bodies of literature on strategic marketing and strategic management.

Among the results of the still uneven merger of the the two areas are two
viewpoints: first that the organization can seek to manage its environments
(Galbraith 1977, Miles and Snow 1978) rather than react to them, and second

146

that in so doing patterns of strategic hevavior or "generic" strategies may be developed (Robinson and Pearce 1985).

The environmental management view proposes that among the options available to managers are those with which the organization can seek to develop structures, prodedures, and/or strategies which enable the organization to minimize the extent to which it is dependent on various elements of the environment with which it interacts (e.g.-suppliers, certain customer groups, etc.) or to maximize its opportunities. It is a proactive posture in which the manager seeks to create opportunities, minimize dependencies, and position the organization in the best possible environmental context.

Such an orientation will not be found in all managers. In fact, it can be argued that those who hold this view are more likely to be the most entrepreneurial types, individuals who see opportunities in situations, not problems. And as may be expected, a significant body of literature has grown dealing with entrepreneurial management styles. The point is clear: as today's business environment becomes increasingly more turbulent and unpredictable, successful managers may have to be more innovative, more entrepreneurial in their approaches to the types of competition which are emerging. This paper attempts to investigate the patterns of strategies which are viewed as effective by entrepreneurial managers in a specific setting: that of the travel agent.

THE TRAVEL AGENCY SITUATION

The need for environmental management is especially acute in deregulated industries, where environmental change of dramatic proportions is legislated into existence as the deregulation is enacted and its effects begin to be felt. Among the most recently deregulated businesses is that of travel agents, one of the fastest growing service industries of the last decade (Banks 1985). Major changes in the industry began in 1978 when airlines were deregulated. The effects of this action are still being felt. But to further complicate matters, the Civil Aeronautics Board was legislated out of existence as of January 1,1985, thus resulting in the deregulation of the sale of airline tickets, and changing the nature of competition in the marketing of them (Civil Aeronautics Board 1984). What had been 40 years worth of protection from competition became a fairly wide open market. And travel agents are now faced with possible competition from such diverse groups as banks, hotels, Ticketron, retail chain stores, corporate travel offices, automated tellers of tickets and the like (Bitner and Booms 1981, Business Week 1985).

So the travel agent not only is facing a situation of major change in terms of products and suppliers (as a result of the deregulation of airlines and the tremendous changes in that part of the industry), but also in terms of the competition within the industry (as a result of the deregulation of travel agents themselves in terms of the marketing of airline tickets).

Therefore, travel agents were selected to be the target of this study. Lessons to be learned from travel service providers who are undergoing significant changes from within and without their industry can prove beneficial to other service marketers faced with varying degrees of change themselves.

RESEARCH DESIGN

The implicit hypothesis in this report was the belief that there were distinct, competitive patterns of strategies that retail service agencies in the travel agency industry may employ. And secondly, of these strategies certain patterns are more likely to be associated with an entrepreneurial style of management. Among these are options which may be used proactively to alter the task environment, such as seeking out new markets or combining with other parties (e.g., agencies) to reduce their dependencies on the environment (e.g., suppliers).

Sample

The sample consisted of 1484 travel agency managers located in major metropolitan areas in the northeastern and mid-western regions of the U.S. A specialty mail directory firm was employed to compile the list. A systematic sampling procedure was used to select every nth agency from a total universe located in designated areas. Due to frame error (e.g., firms out of business), the operational sample was reduced to 1473.

A self-administered mail questionnaire was employed to gather the data. The survey instrument was designed to obtain perceptual measures on a number of issues salient to airline deregulation and the changing competitive environment in which travel agencies operated. Contact with potential respondents involved an initial mailing and a follow-up. Of those contacted, there were 201 useable responses. Although low, the response level was not unexpected given the length of the questionnaire and the low response rates encountered in surveys of the retail trade.

Sample classification data was compared to industry estimates reported in the trade press to determine the sample's representativeness. This showed that the sample was commensurate with the population of U.S. travel agency operations. For example, single site agency operations accounted for 62% of those responding. This compares to the industry estimate of 65% (Sturken 1987). When revenues are classified as to business-related or pleasure travel, respondents reported a breakdown of 45% to 55%. This compares to an industry ratio of 43% to 57% (Newman 1987).

Method and Findings: Strategic Options

In developing a taxonomy of competitive strategies common to the industry, various strategic options suggested by the literature (Galbraith 1977, Porter 1980, Zeithaml and Zeithaml 1984) were considered and a set of strategy statements were developed. A seven-point scale, ranging from "1 = very undesirable outcome" to "7 = very desirable outcome," was used to measure the perceived financial consequences of employing the various strategic options. Since variables of strategic choice may be categorized into distinct, competitive patterns of strategic activity, a principal components procedure was employed to identify the grand strategies among the twenty-seven separate strategies previously identified.

Factor analysis is a useful procedure in that it provides summary statistics by which the presence of meaningful patterns may be detected among a set of variables. Nine significant factors (i.e., eigenvalues $\geq$ 1) were obtained, accounting for 63.5 percent of the variation in the data.

To aid in interpretation of the strategic patterns, a varimax rotation was conducted. Factors were interpreted based on items loading at .50 or better on the related factors. These loadings may be considered to be a conservative criterion (Dess and Davis 1984, Kim and Mueller 1978). Several items (5, 6, 20, 26) failed to load heavily on any of the nine factors and were excluded from further analysis. The factors are displayed in Table 1 and are ranked according to the proportion of total variance explained.

Respectively, the nine factors reflected the perceived financial consequences of employing the following actions: (1) enhancing the agency's competitive position by improving services and operational efficiency, (2) establishing closer working relationships with preferred suppliers so as to increase the agency's bargaining position, (3) giving greater attention to long-term planning that focuses on diversifying agency offerings, (4) jointly acting with trade associations regarding matters that impact agency's performance, (5) combining formally or informally with other agencies to achieve mutual benefits, (6) dramatically altering the agency's focus by targeting new, more attractive markets, (7) discouraging demand for unprofitable services and focusing on selected existing market niches, (8) maintaining the status quo by continuing to use past policies that were successful, and (9) coopting representative of various external parties in return for their support.

Based on the above analysis, indices were created for each of the nine dimensions of strategic options. These were obtained by adding the individual's original response score for the items that loaded highly on a given factor and dividing that sum by the number of items. The averaging step was taken to allow comparisons over factors with different numbers of loadings. Summary statistics, including means, for each of the nine indices are reported in Table II.

Methods and Findings: Entrepreneurial Index

Of the identified strategic options, certain patterns were felt to be more associated with an entrepreneurial style of management. To investigate this, an entrepreneurial index was developed. Part of the questionnaire included a set of Likert-scale statements reflecting managerial philosophy.

A multiple-item index was developed from these (using the 7-point scale), making use of statements consistently found in the literature as reflecting an entrepreneurial orientation (e.g., "The environment in which my agency operates represents more of an opportunity than a threat to my business."). The previously created indices were correlated with this multi-item measure of entrepreneurial philosophy.

Five of the nine patterns of strategies were significantly associated with an entrepreneurial style of management. These are reported in Table II. This finding would appear to be consistent with the suggestion of various writers (e.g., Carland 1984) that entrepreneurial managers are more likely to make use of a variety of strategic options because of their innovativeness and their willingness to take risks.

Dramatically altering the agency's focus by targeting new, more attractive markets, diversifying present offerings, and establishing preferred suppliers were all moderately correlated with an entrepreneurial approach. Enhancing the agency's competitive position by improving services and operational efficiency and combining with other agencies to achieve mutual benefits were also significantly related, but at a lower level of association.

DISCUSSION

The factor analytic routine utilized produced nine strategy factors which serve to illustrate the pattern of strategic options viewed as valuable by a representative sample of travel agents. Though these strategies are primarily marketing based, the search for patterns of strategies ("generic strategies" as used by some) at the corporate level has been receiving increased attention of late (Herbert and Deresky 1987). And the existence of distinct patterns was confirmed in this research.

One strategy pattern found, though discussed little in the research, was that of Status Quo, the strategy of least change, the maintenance of patterns, policies, and strategies which had worked in the past. It can be expected that some travel agents would find this desirable in this situation of extreme change and uncertainty -- at least the status quo is predictable. But the environmental management literature ignores this strategy because environmental management implies a more proactive stance.

The Galbraith and Zeithaml and Zeithaml (Z & Z) schemes noted above identify three types of environmental strategies: independent, cooperative, and strategic maneuvering. Independent strategies involve enhancing the firm's position with its customers against its competitors. The organization does so on its own, without assistance from others.

Two of the strategy factors found in this research correspond to the Independent strategy category. The Competitive factor was rated the most attractive by sample respondents. It fits the Independent strategy of competitive response in the Z & Z and Galbraith schemes, and suggests that the organization attempt to more effectively compete by improving services and operational efficiency. The other factor which fit the Independent strategies was that of Selectively Segment (in which the competitor attempts to discourage demand for less profitable service offerings and to focus only on selected market niches).

Several factors found fit the Galbraith and Z & Z category of Cooperative Strategies. With these strategies, the organization attempts to reduce its uncertainties or dependencies on either suppliers or customers by combining with others either implicitly or explicitly. While such strategies give the competitor extra leverage in some areas or minimize dependence in others, they can cause the competitor to lose some degree of autonomy or control in the process. Strategies which fit this type were Preferred Suppliers (in which closer working relationships with selected suppliers could be established to give the competitor greater bargaining power), Trade Associations (acting in some way with trade associations in the gathering and sharing of information useful to the competitor in planning and performance), Combine (the informal or formal combination with other competitors through agreements, exchange of services, commitments, etc.), and Coopt (bringing in representatives of important external parties to participate in policymaking in exchange for support).

The Galbraith and Z & Z strategy category of maximum change and maximum risk is that of strategic maneuvering. These strategies involve changing the focus of the organization in a more dramatic way such as merger, acquisition, repositioning of the firm, etc. The three strategy factors found in this study to belong to this category are Alter Market Targets (in which the firm's focus is dramatically altered by targeting new, more attractive markets), Plan/Diversify (in which added attention is given to long-term planning focusing on diversifying the offerings), and Combine (such as merger and acquisition with others).

According to the frameworks proposed by Galbraith and Z & Z, of the environmental management strategies, strategic maneuvering is viewed as the most risky because of the greater uncertainties and degree of change involved. Independent strategies, on the other hand, involve less risk and do not put the organization in a position where it may lose some of its autonomy relative to other organizations (as would be true with the cooperative strategies). In the present study, then, it can be expected that the strategies involving the most risk (such as strategic maneuvering) would be attractive to those most willing to assume that risk, namely the more entrepreneurial managers.

Correlations of the strategy factors with the entrepreneurial index show that the more entrepreneurial respondents were more likely to perceive as valuable the riskier environmental management strategies. The factors which were not correlated with the entrepreneurial index were those with low risk or little action. These include Status Quo (clearly the lowest risk alternative), Trade Associations (no real competitive action), Co-opting (with limited perceived competitive gain) as well as the strategy of Selectively Segment.

The strongest correlation was found with the strategy Z & Z and Galbraith view as most risky: Alter Market Targets. This type of strategic maneuvering attempts to alter the focus of the organization and to target newer markets. Though slightly less strong, the other two strategic maneuvering strategies, Plan/Diversify and Combine, also were highly correlated with the entrepreneurial index.

In addition, entrepreneurial managers would likely be more aggressive in pursuing competitive activities (as noted by the high correlation with the Competition factor) and in pursuing dependence-reducing activities with suppliers (as noted by the high correlation with Preferred Suppliers).

The levels of some of these correlations may be exaggerated by the conditions found in the travel agency business. Rapid change, fast growth, and the emergence of new and nontraditional competitors may increase the need for riskier strategies or for more aggressive ways of doing business (Arrendell 1988, Bitner and Booms 1982). And it may be that the entrepreneurial mentality thrives on such unsettling conditions where both the risks and the potential rewards are great. Whatever the case, at least in the dynamically changing business of marketing travel services, the entrepreneurial managers studied exhibited decided preferences for the patterns of strategies involving greater risks and greater market change.

REFERENCES

Arrendel, Stephen (1988), "Profile of Tomorrow's Successful Agent: Adaptable," Travel Weekly, February 29, 10.

Banks, Howard (1985), "The Start of a Revolt," Forbes (October 7), 41-42.

Bitner, Mary J. and Bernard H. Booms (1982), "Trends in Travel and Tourism Marketing: The Changing Structure of Distribution Channels," Journal of Travel Research, Spring Vol. 21, 39-44.

Carland, James W. et al. (1984), "Differentiating Entrepreneurs From Small Business Owners: A Conceptualization," Academy of Management Review 9, 2, 354-359.

Dess, Gregory G. and Peter S. Davis (1984), "Porter's (1980) Generic Strategies as Determinants of Strategic Group Membership and Organizational Performance," Academy of Management Journal 27, 3, 467-488.

Galbraith, Jay R. (1977), Organization Design, Reading: Addison-Wesley.

Gluck, Frederick W., Stephen P. Kaufman, and A. Steven Walleck (1980), "Strategic Management for Competitive Advantage," Harvard Business Review 58 (July-August), 154-161.

Herbert, Theodore T. and Helen Deresky (1987), "Generic Strategies: An Empirical Investigation of Typology Validity and Strategy Content," Strategic Management Journal, Vol. 8, 135-147.

Kim, J. and C.W. Mueller (1978), Factor Analysis: Statistical Methods and Practical Issues, Beverly Hills, California: Sage University Press.

Newman, David (1987), "What Do Agents Think?" Travel Weekly Focus 46, 12 (January 31), 18-19.

Porter, Michael E. (1980), Competitive Strategy, New York: The Free Press.

Robinson, Richard B. and John A. Pearce II (1985), "The Structure of Generic Strategies and Their Impact on Business Unit Performance," Robinson and Pearce (eds.) Academy of Management Proceedings, 35-39.

Sturken, Barbara (1987), "Take over Targets," Travel Weekly Focus 46, 12 (January 31), 16-17.

Zeithaml, Carl P. and Valarie A. Zeithaml (1984), "Environmental Management: Revising the Marketing Perspective," Journal of Marketing 48 (Spring), 46-53.

TABLE I
FACTOR ANALYSIS OF STRATEGIES

STRATEGIES	DERIVED FACTORS									h²
	(1)	(2)	(3)	(4)	(5)	(6)	(7)	(8)	(9)	
1. Improve operational efficiency	(.719)	.172	.031	.085	.010	.031	.144	-.104	-.062	.592
2. Stimulate primary demand	(.740)	.044	.125	.003	.107	.122	-.048	.029	.047	.595
3. Informal cooperative arrangements	.100	.065	.019	-.011	(.544)	.077	.035	-.243	.417	.552
4. Alter focus-targeting new markets	.143	.082	-.017	.109	-.037	(.085)	.168	-.113	.026	.731
5. Differentiate agency's offerings	-.034	.319	.440	.009	.052	.456	.193	.180	-.166	.606
6. Minimize agency's costs	.249	-.143	.355	-.061	.035	.289	.057	.260	.090	.377
7. Establish formal agreements others	.078	.148	.325	-.010	(.608)	.114	.029	-.253	.029	.584
8. Offset irregular/slow demand	.125	.095	.337	-.007	.278	(.568)	-.210	.010	.227	.591
9. Diversify agency's offerings	.225	.126	(.692)	.119	.107	.288	-.135	-.041	-.161	.702
10. Emphasize long-range planning	.198	.183	(.704)	.251	.120	-.107	.195	-.092	-.009	.705
11. Promote favorable image	(.514)	.118	.312	.044	.180	.058	-.069	.439	.178	.644
12. Adhere to stricter standards	(.540)	.140	.366	.104	-.170	.061	-.013	.244	.222	.598
13. Discourage unprofitable demand (fees)	.013	-.034	-.002	.038	.007	.181	(.816)	-.008	.107	.713
14. Employ similar actions as competition	.217	-.018	-.098	.199	.306	.086	(.591)	.080	-.306	.698

154

STRATEGIES	DERIVED FACTORS									h²
	(1)	(2)	(3)	(4)	(5)	(6)	(7)	(8)	(9)	
15. Merge with/acquire other agencies	.074	.139	.030	.050	(.769)	.000	.021	.104	-.006	.632
16. Retrench markets	.017	(.579)	.095	-.212	.166	-.074	.364	.123	-.044	.573
17. Increase supplier's dependency on agency	.286	(.674)	.139	.163	.056	.231	.015	.015	.115	.653
18. Coopt external parties	.032	.140	-.116	.290	.122	.083	.091	-.030	(.701)	.642
19. Continue with past successful strategies	-.011	.064	-.059	.042	-.111	-.069	-.024	(.840)	-.101	.744
20. Engage in legal action	-.231	-.185	-.053	.493	.469	-.008	.069	.084	.022	.567
21. Engage in political action	.160	-.344	.152	(.592)	.211	-.110	.118	-.026	.186	.624
22. Act jointly with trade associations	.030	.152	.065	(.726)	-.000	.013	.044	.027	.111	.571
23. Gather external information	.204	.158	.148	(.720)	-.092	.244	.001	.013	-.009	.676
24. Focus on selected markets	-.109	.319	.327	.070	-.158	-.046	(.624)	-.221	.257	.758
25. Establish preferred suppliers	.183	(.757)	.100	.071	.097	.055	-.060	.013	.171	.668
26. Adapt procedures to change	.413	.401	.326	.219	.266	.181	-.028	-.117	-.241	.663
27. Offer innovative services	(.542)	.435	.069	.231	.095	.398	.048	-.036	-.168	.743
Eigenvalues	2.59	2.34	2.10	2.06	1.98	1.77	1.73	1.32	1.23	17.16
Percent of total variation	9.6	8.6	7.7	7.6	7.3	6.6	6.4	4.9	4.5	63.57

TABLE II

SUMMARY STATISTICS

STRATEGIES	MEAN*	S.D.	Entrepreneurial Management Style r**	p≤
1. Enhance Competitive Position	5.93	0.99	.157	.03
2. Preferred Suppliers	5.43	1.01	.262	.0003
3. Diversify	5.42	1.23	.224	.001
4. Trade Associations	4.57	1.11	.060	.41
5. Combine with others	4.53	1.33	.160	.02
6. Alter Market Targets	5.30	1.14	.319	.0001
7. Selectively Segment	4.25	1.23	.040	.58
8. Maintain Status Quo	4.79	1.59	−.008	.90
9. Coopt External Parties	3.74	1.66	.11	.10

*   Values ranged from "1 = Very Undesirable Outcome" to "7 = Very Desirable Outcome".

**   Pearson Correlation

CHANGES AND DEVELOPMENT IN UK TOURISM MARKETING

D C GILBERT
UNIVERSITY OF SURREY, UK

ABSTRACT

The aim of this paper is to identify those factors which have led to the introduction of marketing and the pressures which continue to mould its future. Progress within the structural formation of marketing departments is examined along with the role of research.

The importance of tourism marketing is shown through the contemporary stance taken by the government and also marketing's role within the hotel industry.

In conclusion, the future of tourism marketing is highlighted with a discussion of some of the existing developments already taking place.

The paper assumes the reader understands the premise of marketing and therefore issues of pricing, promotion, product and distribution are subsumed into a management overview. It is believed that the dynamics of societal change and marketing adoption offer a more fertile basis for understanding the emergence and establishment of the nature of marketing in tourism, than other approaches.

International tourism, once the prerogative of the wealthy or the true adventurer, is now a more freely available product for the mass to enjoy. Pioneers of tourism marketing, such as Thomas Cook and subsequently his son, showed the imagination and flair, as well as attention to detail, which was to become the touchstone of many successful tourism entrepreneurs. The enterprising few, with a blend of missionary zeal and an eye for profit rolled back the frontiers of travel. Today no self-respecting organisation would be without a Marketing department. If we look back 20 years, we would find the absence of the Marketing department in the majority of company structures. This is not to say marketing was totally absent, just that it had not been formalised or developed fully.

The Adoption of Marketing

The nature of the tourism industry is one where custom and tradition are particularly strong. This is not surprising, given that many sectors of the service industry exhibit this tendency. It is this author's belief that the adoption of marketing has taken place in the tourism industry within a conflict between traditionalism and need.

The tourism industry has been characterised by customs of procedure which have long required change. Holloway and Plant (1988) illustrate the traditional role taken by the UK industry. They relate that there has been a tendency in tourism to believe that the best way of 'learning the business' is to recruit staff straight from school and 'train them up'. They argue that this system has led to a lack of innovation and skilled market analysis as well as inhibiting the development of modern marketing techniques. Schmoll (1977) in parallel to this, points out that many of the changes brought about in the tourism industry came from those who had been initially trained or had worked outside the industry. This was not easy as there was a mistrust of highly qualified or formally trained marketing people in many companies.

In order to examine why companies adopt marketing, we need to understand both the internal and external forces which bring this about. If we consider first the internal factors, we have to be aware of the dynamic nature of any organisation. Companies are more than just collections of individuals. Companies are social systems in miniature with norms, values and status groups which are controlled by means of rewards and punishments. The business system can be viewed as an organism with the sole purpose of survival and proliferation. When a system is threatened, it takes functional steps to improve the situation. Michael Baker (1987) utilises the case of a simple organism whose cells divide and grow exponentially. If the cells are placed in a test tube containing nutrients, they will reach a ceiling point of growth and then either try to mutate (diversify) or settle into equilibrium (stagnation). (The brackets are this author's attempt at classification).

In a similar way in the case of threat, Marketing departments become essential in the planning of tactical action. On the other hand, in times of shortage – such as war and post war periods, production systems can dominate because there are few demand problems. Within periods of over-supply, mass production and market saturation, marketing assumes a key role in the system. This is even more important with tourism products which are high risk perishable products, where an airline seat, hotel bed, or meal not sold is lost forever. Burkart and Medlik (1981) identified that marketing assumed a new significance in the 1970s. They argued that this was linked to over-production within the airline and hotel industry and also the rapid growth of inclusive tours to Europe. In the 60s and 70s, in the UK, many tourism industry companies set up Marketing departments because of the high risk nature of the product they were selling. Unfortunately, many of these departments did not function properly and companies became disillusioned with the results. Much of the problem lay in the inability to understand what a Marketing department should do, and how marketing should be integrated throughout the company.

British Airways offers a recent case example of success due to the adoption of a marketing orientation for the company. Although British Airways had announced a massive loss in 1981-82 of £544m it created an operating surplus of £272m in the financial year 1983-84.

158

This represented one of the fastest and largest changes in fortunes ever achieved by a major commercial concern. This was mainly due to a marketing revolution led by Sir Colin Marshall. The company reported (Marketing, 10 May, 1985) that until a re-organisation British Airways had not been truly marketing led. Even though it had a Marketing department, it had been operations led. The key change was to ensure operations delivered what the Marketing department requested due to an identification of consumer needs. The overall success was explained as attributable to three main thrusts: satisfying customer requirements; becoming more people oriented and the creation of overall long-term strategies.

Various social and business pressures have formed the current tourism industry structure. The speed of change in disposable income, business competition, the availability of tourism products and attitudes towards debt, all began to change the boundaries and structure of the business tourism environment. The collapse of tour operators such as Clarkson in the UK and airlines such as Braniff and Continental, in the USA, are evidence of the new pressures to create high levels of demand in order to achieve the necessary economies of scale.

In understanding marketing fully, we have to establish the pressures and forces which have, and will, mould tourism's future. Tourism has continued to grow even though there has been an end to unbridled western, economic expansion. Heller (1984) argued that the oil price explosion was a major factor in determining a change in economic and business management throughout the western world.

World markets have been shattered apart and have regrouped again within a market place of new opportunity and a range of new technology. Much of the change we have witnessed is due to the advance of electronics. According to R Heller, (1984) the electronic age has performed three feats at once in the camera market:

o   It has lowered manufacturing costs; Raised reliability and led to innovation.

Tourism has felt the impact of electronics in the form of: centralised reservation systems for hotels, airlines, tour operators, car hire etc which has led to more cost-efficient distribution systems; teletext services to the consumer providing more information through the home TV or travel agent; computer aided design for cars and aircraft which has given rise to more fuel efficient transport; computer applications for marketing research so that information can be gathered and analysed more effectively, the rise of marketing information systems where models and statistical techniques can forecast more accurately and for the consumer home electronics have led to a range of labour saving devices which allow more leisure time. Margaret Bruce's paper (1987) "New technology and the Future of Tourism", reviews the main technological developments in the travel industry and considers developments in terms of opportunities and threats. She also examines the way that a company's strategy may be affected by the role of technology. Along with these changes, the industry has been faced with specific pressures:

1. Krippendorf (1987) has identified that the consumer of tourism requires new types of marketing. He identifies the emerging force of new tourist values. The new tourist is seen as holding beliefs relating to a desire to enjoy life, maximise their leisure time and earn sufficient money to be able to consume. However, he identifies that tourism-oriented marketing will have to become more socially responsible in relation to both the environmental and social aspects of development.

2. The battle for market share has been intensifying and profit returns for some sectors have suffered - internationally, nationally and regionally. This has resulted in the growth of large retail multiples, airlines and tour operators due to takeovers or mergers. Watkins (1986) has argued that there has been a general shift of power during the past 20 years to the multiple retailer.

3. Competition has increased. This can be seen in the distribution channels following the deregulation of the retail price maintenance or in the deregulation of airline routes in America. The struggle within markets has led to the collapse of many tourism concerns, eg Braniff, Continental Airlines, etc.

4. The service industry, faced with rising labour costs and an inability to recruit suitable staff, have provided different forms of service, eg, there is an increase in self-service.

5. Many nationalised industries have been returned to private ownership, including BA. The belief in private not public enterprise can be gauged by the rise of marketing bureaus for tourism in preference to town hall control. Gurney (1984) explains how new initiatives have proved to be successful in the partnership between local authorities and commercial interests.

6. The modern worker expects more from their employment. There has been a move towards improved inward marketing within companies (see Berry's (1981) dictum that marketing must first be sold to the employee). The emphasis is now on the 'communication' of the goals and objectives of companies so that personnel understand what they have to achieve and what they are responsible for.

7. The public are much more interested in life-style and self improvement as a way of gaining status, ie, you are the product you buy which conveys symbolic meaning. Lifestyle, not class, is the new provider of status. For marketing trends, see Burdenski (1986) Economist Intelligence Unit (1981).

160

The Management Function

New technology and emerging consumer needs have led to responsive action with the industry. Within the Marketing department, progress has been shown in the development of both main line marketing management functions as well as planning functions. Marketing planning sections have been set up in Marketing departments with the responsibility for setting up marketing information systems, which enable more effective pricing patterns due to analysis of competitors price offers. These departments are given the responsibility for forecasting or late offer decision making. The progress has occurred due to the ability to harness computer power to information systems. Reservations for airlines, tour operators and hotels are computerised and this lends itself easily to different modelling inputs. The industry has developed a fixation on the price sensitive nature of demand patterns, perhaps to the detriment of creating campaigns which encourage brand loyalty as develop added value. Because the tourism market is volatile, short run profitability and cash flow become focal points for marketing strategy. Such low horizon planning is a serious deterrent to improvement in product planning or long term image building of a brand. The high risk nature of the industry brought about by excess capacity directs planning into short run sales campaigns.

As mergers and take-overs progress in the industry there is greater emphasis on companies providing an adequate return-on-investment rather than brand building investment. The recent acquisition of the Rank Holiday company by Horizon is an example of how a large organisation was more interested in short term returns on investment than investing in growth in market share. The Rank Organisation arguably paid too much money for what was originally Wings and OSL and then never invested enough back into the company to develop the brands.

If we look at the Japanese system of planning we find that they gear their objectives on financial return to longer term corporate marketing strategies. The Japanese example may be an important guideline for the tourism industry.

The role of marketing within the Tourism and Hospitality industry has changed within leading companies. This has led to demands for wider expertise from the key marketing personnel. Historically we have already seen the business need to develop sales skills into marketing skills. This change is dynamic. As marketing is taking on more financial accountability the natural course of development is for the Marketing Director to evolve in relation to business pressures and requirements. This will probably lead to the role of a Commercial Director whereby Marketing Directors will have responsibility for an integrated company wide marketing role.

This type of development will only occur if Chief Executives in companies understand the benefits of such a system and actively promote it. It may mean that because the Tourism and Hospitality industry is primarily a service industry, where the interaction of individuals and the performance of staff throughout the company is of key importance for success, that marketing expertise will be required in the role of other divisional heads. A Commercial Director could co-ordinate the integrated effort and also cut through the bureaucracy which is sometimes a feature of larger companies.

One author has recently identified the need for the development of entrepreneurial skills in management. H Strage (1986) has referred to a 'profound shift' from a managerial to an entrepreneurial economy in the USA. His hypothesis is that entrepreneurs are on a collision course with those who have thrived and prospered in the traditional corporations and who have determined the corporate culture. He cites the fact that in the USA during 1981 to 1986 small firms created 10 million jobs whilst the Fortune top 500 companies generated a net decrease. In the UK during the period 1975 to 1980 there was a similar pattern of activity. Strage concludes that most large organisations are mixed in bureaucratic red tape and often unconscious prejudices about how things should be done. He identifies the failure to produce entrepreneurial skills and the ability to grasp new opportunities.

The majority of textbooks related to tourism marketing, stress the importance of tourism as a service product (Middleton, 1988; Holloway and Plant, 1988; Buttle, 1986; Foster, 1985; Schmoll, 1977). A service product is normally described in terms of the characteristics of heterogeneity, intangibility, perishability and inseparability. However, only some of these authors have attempted to show that there is some debate within the wider literature as to the general acceptance of this notion. Buttle is the clearest in his discussion of the issues. Some authors also fail to develop theories of customer service provision, out different marketing mix strategies which would obtain more to services than goods marketing.

In relation to this point, there have been particular theorists who have taken more of a services management stance and have consequently emphasised the service encounter move. Within tourism we are selling both the combination of a product and service but the emphasis is on service. Davidson, (1978) has noted that the service industry manager is only as important as the delivery of friendly, polite and well-trained customer contacts. Collier has reinforced this (1983-84) by stating that in the service business, you cannot make happy guests with unhappy employees. Albrecht & Zenke, (1985) suggests that when service encounters go unsupervised, the quality of service regresses to mediocrity. Service has been rediscovered by many organisations in tourism as the main factor of customer satisfaction. Government Tourist Boards have made videos in order to encourage customer care and heighten the awareness of personal hygiene and presentation. British Rail and British Airways have invested millions of pounds into training schemes to improve customer service interactions. However, customer service training is not always handled correctly and may not achieve Gronroos' objectives, (1981) for internal marketing which is the development of 'motivated' and 'customer conscious' personnel which will secure increases in productivity. British Rail advertised the fact that it was 'getting

162

there' in terms of service, prior to finding out whether there had been any perceptual improvement in service provision on behalf of the commuter. Whereas progress may have been made in the emphasis placed on training staff to deliver a better service, it is not training which brings about the most effective means of customer service provision. It is the corporate culture of the organisation which passes on the norms and values of customer interaction procedures and, therefore, we may see more emphasis in the future on inward marketing to change or reinforce corporate culture, rather than short term training schemes which lead to higher expectations from the public, who then feel dissatisfied if the reality of the product consumption experience is too low. Davidson's solution, (1978) is to remove employees out of the system if they do not measure up to the service task but this approach has been attacked by organisational theorists who suggest such an approach has not been successful. In order to improve overall service levels we may have to focus on those individuals in an organisation who are capable of influencing the performance level of interpersonal situations. Following this argument certain individuals who could become culture-carriers would be rewarded for exhibiting positive patterns of behaviour and values within the organisation.

Bitner et al, (1985) has developed the use of critical incident analysis to assess the service encounter. In the research, respondents specify incidents in which 'good' or 'poor' service was delivered. The respondent has to be sure in stating the way the incident was critical to the outcome of the activity. By utilising Gronroos, (1985) typology of technical versus functional service quality dimensions, the authors discovered that 77% of the service encounters mentioned as either satisfactory or unsatisfactory pertained to the functional aspects. The negative functional aspects related to rudeness, indifferent treatment, unprofessional behaviour, lack of apologies for system breakdowns etc or the positive aspects which included apologies, helping with the children etc. Technical quality negatives involved lost baggage, poor food, lateness of flights etc.

Tourism organisations, as service providers, may want to study the techniques of those industry leaders who have adopted the strategy of adopting a service culture. Disney, Marriott Hotels and McDonalds would seem to be leading the way at the moment.

Marketing is all about consumer orientation because it stresses the fundamental importance of the consumer and suggests the best way to remain viable and continue to stay in business in the long run is to define correctly what consumers desire and then deliver it more efficiently and effectively than the competitors. An essential to this philosophy is that organisations research what consumers want and then are flexible enough to respond and adapt in order to create consumer satisfaction. Yet this does not always occur.

163

There are museums, zoos and heritage centres which are not geared to consumer satisfaction. The exhibits are thought to be sufficient in themselves and methods of interpretation, display and layout are sometimes thought too costly or irrelevant.

Marketing management techniques for attractions would seem to be fundamental in order for them to be successful. Apart from a concern with resource protection, enhancement of the visitor experience and the promotion of the sites benefits, there is a need for strategic planning. Walt Disney Productions correctly identified they were in the entertainment business. They adopted a marketing strategy which emphasised resource should be released for theme parks, television programmes and motion picture directed at family markets with 6 to 12 year olds (Business Week, 31 July, 1978). However, management having recognised the decline in the younger age market and the emerging emphasis on education with leisure looked for new markets. This led to the development of the Epcot centre in Florida on what had previously been cheap low-lying swamp and agricultural land. Successful marketing management is always concerned with analysing emerging needs and demographic trends. There is always the need to develop a sustainable competitive advantage for tourism attractions and products. Butlins in the UK had ignored the fact that consumer holiday needs had become more sophisticated during the 1980s. They are now embarking on a multi-million refurbishment programme of their sites to improve the experience of their product offer and to enable them to offer a year round programme.

The UK now has attractions such as a theme park at Alton Towers which has adopted a sophisticated approach to marketing and customer care, the Jorvik Centre, in York, which has understood interpretation and display of heritage; even to the level of utilising aromatic oils to recreate the smells of a pig sty, apples or a cesspit. Centre Parc, a holiday centre in Nottingham, which has identified that the needs of the modern holiday maker do not necessarily have to include a beach setting and that there is potential demand for high quality standards and all weather facilities. The new developments in tourism are all based upon providing consumers with products which satisfy their needs. This has placed a heavy reliance on market research activity.

There is a developing belief in research as an important aid to feedback and decision making. The corollary of this is that systematic marketing research is both the font and catalyst of any marketing decision making. However, some authors (Samuels, 1973; Copstick & Riley, 1977) attack the weakness of the availability of relevant information regarding service provision in the tourism and recreation industry. Some authors even point to the irrelevance of research to applied decision making processes (Rossi et al, 1978; Dimaggio and Useem, 1980; Driver and Knopf, 1981). However, we may place some of the blame of this weakness on the manager who fails to specify their objectives clearly or who lacks the logical rigour necessary to define specific research needs. Beaman (1978) has identified that appropriate research has not been carried out due to the weakness of those involved in early tourism research work. We

164

should also remember that research is only the means by which to reduce uncertainty. As Luck (1980) stresses: 'Research is the handmaiden of competent management, but never its substitute'.

Within companies, there is now the adoption of research systems which can provide part of a structured decision making support process. These systems are either Decision Support Systems (DSS) which can provide clerical or database analysis systems (Keen and Scott-Morton, 1978) or Management Information Systems (MIS) which produce routine information in an automated process.

Hotel Marketing

Much of the hotel industry is sales-oriented according to Buttle (1986). He observes that since hotels are immobile and structural alterations costly, they can neither be moved to locations where demand is higher nor are they readily converted to new uses such as offices, flats or retail outlets without considerable expense. He therefore concludes hotel marketers have been required to demonstrate sales skills. In addition, Schmoll (1977), views the whole tourism industry as being characterised by a large number of small and medium sized enterprises which have not invested in specialist marketing staff. This author's experience in research into the strategy formulation of medium and large hotels would seem to indicate it is only some of the larger hotel groups which are truly marketing oriented. However, given the pressures of the marketplace and the arguments expressed earlier, regarding marketing adoption, changes in hotel marketing would seem to be imminent. The following paragraphs outline the main changes which have occurred recently in the hotel industry.

The demand for hotel accommodation in the US has grown approximately in line with the overall growth in the economy but has not kept up with the growth shown in many sectors of the tourism market, R J Goeglein (1986). There are early signs that hotel demand patterns may be changing. There is a great deal of activity in the budget sector of the market where new, good quality standard accommodation is being offered. Strategically, the hotel as a product in the UK has always been viewed as requiring constant upgrading and refurbishment. Hotel management have equated status of their role in comparison to the star rating of the hotel. In terms of product positioning this has led to a constant desire to upgrade the star-rating of hotels. At the same time, new hotel development for many years has been targeted towards the top end of the market. These factors combined to create a gap in the market for good quality two-star accommodation. This gap was identified not by the marketing departments of UK companies but mainly by the French companies who are now developing what has been termed the 'budget hotel' in the UK, accommodation market. This description seems inadequate as the association of the word budget is that of poor quality. This category of hotels is reported to have high demand patterns in the USA where Marriott and Holiday Inns are developing low price, no frills chains.

A major change in hotel marketing has been the development of short-break or mini-break holidays. These holidays, once known as 'bargain breaks', are now a common package offer supplied in the hotel market. However, nowadays, there is a vast variety of forms and promotions linked to these products.

Marketing is all about identifying opportunities which arise from emerging consumer needs. The modern weekend break has developed into many different forms, from activity to education leisure, since its inception by Grand Metropolitan back in the mid 1960s. The Grand Met holidays were marketed successfully under the brand name 'Stardust' holidays and offered a weekend in London with rail travel included in the package. These holidays were promoted at rail stations and priced to be attractive to average wage earners in regional areas. Planning of these holidays was perhaps the initial departure from what were in the 60s Sales departments, into a marketing orientation of satisfying consumer needs at prices which offered good value for money.

The initial packages for 'bargain breaks' were planned on the basis of discounting the under-utilised weekend bed supply of hotels in urban locations. The emphasis now is to package different experiences. This has led to an expansion of the product into midweek periods and created a highly developed market for mini-breaks based around the themes of interest or activities. For many hotels who have realised that the market is not solely price based there have been successful partnerships between regional Tourist Boards, who can help with the addition of local features or heritage products. Marketing initiatives shown by those who realise the attractions of an area and good accommodation, which is priced competitively, have led to the evolvement of an important segment of the domestic tourism market.

The other important change which has occurred within the hotel market is the trend towards co-operative ventures by individual hotels. This development occurred to counteract the economy of scale benefits which accrue to the larger chains of hotels. Hotels have been steadily concentrated into fewer large scale operations of national or international importance. Growth in consortia membership is attributable to the security afforded by membership (Slattery, 1985). Independently owned hotels have either combined into a consortium of hotels or joined groups such as Best Western in return for a percentage of turnover or fee basis. These consortia can then more easily promote a common brand name and obtain reductions for bulk orders or credit card charges. The future will probably be characterised by an increasing concentration of hotel units into the control of fewer groups. These groups whether consortiums or not will, because of the ability to raise large marketing budgets, be able to place a heavy emphasis on building corporate identities through effective use of the marketing mix.

166

Government and Tourism Marketing

Governments have considered tourism a business which is essential to economies because of the direct effects on employment, the balance of payments and society, in terms of educational and cultural benefits. Tourism is characterised by the fragmentation of supply, the complimentarity of tourist services and the predominance of small enterprises. As Schmoll (1977) has pointed out, it is not surprising that official organisations - whether local, regional or national or international - have important functions and responsibilities in tourism marketing. Governments have, therefore, been involved in the provision of help and guidance to the industry in setting up boards which include departments with tourism marketing expertise. The boards have attempted to improve the industry's marketing expertise by providing a range of booklets, pamphlets and guidelines which help explain marketing functions and give ideas for the solution of problems. An example of this is a regular English Tourist Board publication featuring ways of improving low season demand.

More recently as world economies have suffered, there has been even greater emphasis on creating employment through both domestic and international tourism demand, especially in areas where alternative economic development is not a cost effective alternative. A sign of change in the UK's support of tourism projects is the indication by David Trippier (1987) that grants for tourism ventures will be made more available for the larger projects. This is because it is the larger projects which are seen to create the most benefit in terms of job creation.

Significant steps are being taken in the UK to market regional areas in order to disperse tourists from London. The improvement of an area's image brought about by marketing can enhance a community's pride in their area. The improvement and marketing of cities such as Bradford, Liverpool, Cardiff and Bristol have brought about a resurgence of pride in heritage and place. A major objective of the 'I love N.Y.' marketing promotion was to improve individual citizen pride for New York City as well as to create wider awareness for the City throughout the world.

The emphasis placed upon the creation of images is due to particular tourism products being very similar to each other in what they offer. For example, one airline flight is very similar to another flight. This has led to a greater emphasis on creating an improved or better image for individual tourist products. Schmoll (1977) takes the standpoint that it is evident if a tourist's experience is mainly subjective in nature then ideas or expectations associated with a product and how these correspond to the reality, or are transformed, will have a significant bearing on both the choices made by potential tourists and the satisfactions and benefits they gain. Lawson and Baud Bovy, (1977) have written of image as the expression of all objective knowledge, impressions, prejudice, imaginations and emotional thoughts associated with place or product. The importance of images is that they form part of our decision making process and influence the choices we make. This has been more fully understood and therefore the creation of image utilising PR, advertising and sales literature has been an important aspect of tourism marketing. However, some tourism products are created with multi-images because of the number of different segments they will be sold to. Each segment has a different marketing mix targeted to it. In this way, places such as cities can be marketed to many different customers for different uses.

Governments have also attempted to control and improve standards of product quality. Award schemes such as the 'Dragon Award' scheme in Wales for caravan parks and annual awards such as the BTA's 'come to Britain' trophy award are all planned to encourage excellence in product formulation. The ETB has also expanded its classification scheme to all types of establishment from hotels to guest houses by utilising up to 5 'crown' symbols per unit to categorise standards.

The Future

The future for tourism marketing is an exciting one. This is because technology and social change are continually providing new opportunities and challenges. Societies are moving towards shorter working weeks, flexible working patterns, more paid holiday entitlements, freelance working arrangements, earlier retirement opportunities and increases in real disposable income. Whereas the treat for working hard in the 60s was the chocolate bar the compensation now is to partake in leisure activities. The annual holiday is becoming treated as a 'necessary reward' for having worked throughout the year. Even business travel is changing with the inclusion of pleasure excursions being added to the business itinerary. This is even more important in the decision process for agreeing a conference venue location.

The home has continued to be the centre for entertainment and leisure. America is leading the way with the inclusion of exercise rooms in many homes. The convenience of home leisure provision will lead to a continuing demand for domestic leisure equipment. Hawkins (1988) has argued that this may lead to image libraries where large flat panel display screens will be able to generate all the great works of art from any gallery in the world. Commentaries will explain the background to the painting and the painter. These library screens would be able to show any subject which would be commercially viable. The development from this would be to create simulation modules whereby someone could enter a motorised device which not only would project images but would also have the capability of movement (See Booth, 1986; Long, 1987). Such devices could simulate canoe or raft rides, skiing, hot air balloon rides or even piloting a jet aircraft.

The most advanced systems would include complex sensory stimuli such as temperature, humidity, smell changes to create as realistic experience as possible. Whereas this may seem non-commercial at the moment we should consider that all the technology is available for production.

Interactive video whereby a programmed laser disc linked to a computer is capable of answering questions or teaching is already being introduced into the tourism industry. As the cost of this equipment is reduced we will see the use of touch sensitive screen training prior to sailing, scuba diving, water skiing etc. This type of instruction will introduce the leisure user to all types of activity. Hotels will be able to offer in room TV checkout, room service options and onward reservations (McCoy, 1987; Cetron and Roda, 1987). Interactive video is also being used to help people in large stores or cities find their way to where they want to go. Another application is for the sale of products and in this respect the next generation of machines will be able to sell direct to people who have 'smart' cards. The introduction of this for travel agencies or other forms of retail outlet may revolutionise the way distribution channels work.

Travel agents are developing into information centres and this type of technology will become important to them in enabling an improved standard of information to be available for clients.

The future of transportation may soon be revolutionised if the advances in super conductor materials continue. Energy use for magnetic trains, or buses will be minimal and this will lead to price reductions for travel. It may be possible to travel between Los Angeles and Las Vegas faster than by air (Black, 1984; Lemonick, 1987).

As the world economies develop peoples' satisfaction with the marginal utility of increased consumption of material goods will decline. Given people will have more discretionary time, there will be an increase in the consumption of leisure based products, spectator sports, entertainment and travel. We all need to understand how the future may affect tourism because we will then be in a stronger position to harness the changes rather than be led, or controlled, by them.

REFERENCES

Baker, M.J., 1987, One more time - what is marketing, The Marketing Book, Institute of Marketing, Heinemann.

Bartos, R., 1982, Women in travel. Journal of Travel Research 20 (4) pp 3-9.

Beaman, J., 1978, Leisure research and its lack of relevance to planning management and policy formulation: A problem of major proportions, Recreation Research Review, Vol 6 (3) pp 18-25.

Bitner, M., Nyquist, J. and Booms, B., The critical incident as a technique for analyzing the service encounter, in Bloch T et al Services Marketing in a Changing Environment Chicago: A M Marketing Ass 1985, pp 48-51.

Black, R., 1984, magnetic trains take off, Science Digest, August, p26.

Booth, S., 1986, Future vision Popular Mechanics, July, pp 67-69.

Bruce, M., 1987, New technology and the future of tourism, Tourism Management, Vol 8 (2) pp 115-122.

Burdenski, H., 1986, Tourism, America's hottest industry, Tourism Services Marketing Conference, Vol 11 pp 3-12.

Burkart, A.J., Medlik, S., 1981, Tourism past, present and future, Heinemann, London.

Buttle, F., 1986, Hotel and food service marketing, Holt, Rinehart and Winston, London.

Capstick, M. and Riley, S., 1973, Problems of implementing tourism policy to achieve optimum economic impact'. Tourism as a tool for regional development. Edinburgh Leisure Studies Association Conference.

Cetron, M.J. and Rocha, W., 1987, Travel tomorrow. The Futurist, July-August, pp 29-34.

Collier, D.A., 1983-84, Managing a service firm: A different management game, National Productivity Review, Winter, pp 36-45.

Davidson, D.S., 1978, How to succeed in a service industry. Turn the organisation chart upsidedown. Management Review, April, pp 14-16.

Dimaggio, P. and Useem, M., 1980, Small scale policy research in the arts, Policy Analysis, Vol 6 (2) pp 171-191.

Driver, B.L. and Knopf, R.C., 1981, Some thoughts on the quality of outdoor recreation, research and other constraints on its application, social research in national parks and wilderness areas, pp 85-99. Atlanta, USDT National Park Service, South East Region Office. Economist Intelligence Unit, Forecasts to 1990, 1981, Special Report, No 93.

Edgell, D., Managing the research function for effective policy formulation and decision making, Travel, Tourism and Hospitality Research, Ritchie, J.R.B., et al. Eds pp 35-43 J Wiley, New York.

Foster, D., 1985, Travel and tourism management, MacMillan Education Ltd., London.

Frechtling, D.C., 1987, Five issues in tourism marketing in the 1990s, Tourism Management, Vol 8 (2) pp 177-178.

Goeglein, R.J., 1986, The technology and tourism: A growing partnership. TTRA 17th Conference Proceedings.

Gronroos, C., 1981, Internal marketing - An integral part of marketing theory in Marketing of Services. Ed by Donnelly and George, Chicago, Am.M.Ass. pp 236-238.

Gurney, J., 1984, Tourism and Local Authorities: Firming up for the future, Hospitality No 50, pp 2-4.

Hartley, C., 1987, Video dreamland Audio Visual Communications, June p41.

Hawkins, D., 1988, Rural areas and new demands in tourism marketing, Conference Paper, Valencia Tourism Institute.

Heller, R., 1984, The naked market, Sidgwick and Jackson, London.

Holloway, J.C., Plant, R.V., 1988, <u>Marketing for tourism</u>, Pitman, Great Britain.

Lawson, F. and Baud-Bovy, M., 1977, <u>Tourism and recreational development</u>, London, Architectural Press.

Lemonick, M., 1987, Superconductors, <u>Time</u>, May, pp 62-72.

Long, M., 1987, The 1987 Seers catalogue, <u>Omni</u>, Jan. pp 37-40.

Luck, D.J. et al, 1970, <u>Marketing research</u>, 3rd edition, Prentice Hall, New Jersey.

McCoy, M., 1987, Technology update. <u>Lodging Hospitality</u>, May, pp 72-73.

Middleton, V.T.C., 1988. <u>Marketing in travel and tourism</u>, Heinemann, Oxford.

Murphy, P.E., 1985, <u>Tourism : A community approach</u>, Methuen, New York.

Rochester, P., 1986, The unreal thing, <u>Omni</u>, Dec 3rd.

Rossi, O.M., Wright, J.P. and Wright, S.R., 1978, The theory and practice of applied social research, <u>Evaluation Quarterly</u>, **Vol 2** (2), pp 171-191.

Samuels, J.A., 1973, Research to help plan the future of a seaside resort, The Marketing of Tourism and Other Services: Proceedings of the 12th Marketing Theory Seminar, Lancaster, England, University of Lancaster.

Schmoll, G.A., 1977, <u>Tourism promotion</u>, Tourism International Press, London.

Slattery, P., Roper, A. and Boer, A., Hotel consortia: their activities, structure and growth', <u>Service Industries Journal</u>, **Vol 5** (2), pp 193-199.

Strage, H., 1986, Corporate star wars: Can entrepreneurs and marketers co-exist? <u>Business Graduate Journal</u>, April, USA.

Trippier, D., 1987, Tourism in the 1990s - UK Government view, <u>Tourism Management</u>, **Vol 8**, No 2, pp 79-82.

Watkins, T., 1986, <u>The economics of the brand</u>, London, McGraw Hill.

Title: Changes In Distribution Channels Under Airline Deregulation

Terrence J. Kearney, DBA
Marquette University

William Hickey, MBA
Ask Mr. Foster Travel

Abstract

The 1978 deregulation of the domestic passenger airline system has resulted in major changes in all aspects of that industry. The number of carriers has increased, as has the number of passengers. Fares have fallen, along with the quality of service in the industry (Kearney 1988). Along with these changes, the channels of distribution for airline services have been substantially altered by deregulation. This paper will examine the scope and causes of these changes and look at the future of the distribution of air line services.

AIRLINE DEREGULATION

The Airline Deregulation Act of 1978 ended forty years of federal economic regulation of the domestic airline industry. The end of regulation meant that new airlines were allowed to enter the industry. Old carriers were free to enter new markets and to abandon unprofitable old markets. Carriers were free to compete on price as well as service.

The result of this new freedom was to increase competition in the industry and in many markets. While the number of markets served increased by five percent between 1978 and 1984, the number of monopoly markets declined by almost ten percent. During this same period, the number of markets with five or more carriers nearly tripled, increasing from 77 to 228 city pairs (Kearney 1988).

As markets became more competitive, airlines competed more intensely. From the earliest days of deregulation, airlines offered discounts on tickets. Prior to the end of regulation, the only reduced prices available for airline tickets were restricted to senior citizens, military and student standby and some charter operations. After deregulation, discounts were available to any passenger willing to abide by certain restrictions (Meyer, Oster et al 1981).

With the proliferation of fare and restriction combinations, consumer carrier selection has become more and more complicated. In a long-haul contested market, such as Chicago to Los Angeles, there can be as many as 250 fare/restriction combinations. This system has caused a major increase in the number of passengers using the services of travel agents. These agents can be seen as surrogate decision makers acting for consumers faced with complicated decisions (Solomon 1986). Table 1 shows the increase in

172

the number of travel agents and in the volume of their business.

Table 1
Growth of Travel Agencies

Year	Number of Travel Agents	Gross Dollar Volume Travel Agent Airline Ticket Sales (Millions of $)
1970	6700	3000
1972	8000	4500
1974	10260	6200
1976	12240	9400
1978	14804	11800
1981	19203	19500
1983	22633	27530
1985	27193	33660
1986	29933	----
1987	30169	----

Source: Travel Weekly

The increase in travel agent activity shown in Table 1 indicates an increase in the dependence of the consumer on the travel agent in processing the mass of data involved in selecting a flight. At the same time, the airlines have become more dependent on travel agents to direct passengers to them and to handle the administrative details of selecting flights and ticketing passengers. During the period 1974 to 1987 the proportion of airline passengers ticketed by agents rose from about forty percent to just under ninety percent (Bitner and Blooms 1982; Travel Weekly 1987).

Technological Changes

In addition to the changes in the market and regulatory environment, there have been major technological changes in the travel industry during the 1980's. The most important of these changes involves computer reservation systems. With advances in computer technology, travel agents are able to have access to up-to-date reservation, schedule and fare information. Agents anywhere in the country can find out the latest fares, the availability of seats on individual flights and changes in schedules and equipment. Agents can also make and confirm reservations on the system without having to talk to airline employees. The rapid increase in the number of passengers carried, the number of fare/restriction combinations and the changes in the availability of those fares would not be feasible without these computer reservation systems.

The computer reservation systems used by nearly all travel agents are operated by subsidiaries of major airlines. These systems are offshoots of the reservation systems used by each carrier. Table 2 illustrates the market share for the four major reservation systems and the airline that developed each.

Table 2
Computer Reservation Systems

System	Developing Carrier	Approximate 1987 Market Share
Saber	American	.42
Appollo	United	.33
System One	Texas Air	.16
PARS	TWA	.05

Source: Travel Weekly.

The costs of developing these systems were lower for the carriers than they would have been for other developers, because the carriers were able to use much of the equipment and softwear they used in developing their own systems. The systems are major profit centers, as other carriers must pay a fee to the operator of a system in order for agents to be able to make reservations on that carrier's flights. Each travel agent must pay an installation fee and a monthly access fee to the operator. In addition, each time a reservation is made using the system, a fee of about $1.85 is paid to the operator, per segment booked. In addition to fees, the systems were supposed to give the sponsoring carrier an advantage in attracting customers (Thornton 1986). While the systems are not perfectly unbiased, the operators have been forced to remove most of this advantage by a series of lawsuits and regulatory complaints (Travel Weekly 1987).

The Rise of Wholesalers

There are two categories of wholesalers in the air travel channel of distribution: tour operators and consolidators. Tour operators put together and sell packages of travel services. A package might include air travel, hotel accomodations, rental car, sightseeing and admissions to attractions. Tour operators buy blocks of seats from airlines at a substantial discount, and resell them as a component of tour packages. The operator also gets a discount on the other elements of the package. Since the tour is sold as a bundle, the price of each part cannot be determined. The operator can offer a combination of services at a price lower than the consumer would find if the services were purchased separately.

Salvage wholesalers purchase leftover tour seats and sell them to travelers who are willing to take a risk on seats not being available or who are not selective concerning where they spen their vacations. Since tour operators pay for seats whether or not they sell them, they are willing to sell leftover tickets to salvage operators at a low price.

Consolidators guarantee that they will buy a minimum volume of seats from an airline in return for a discount on the ticket price. They then sell these seats directly to the public or through travel agents, and the consolidator is free to charge what the market will bear.

Deregulation has encouraged the development of a gray market form of wholesalers. The coupon broker buys free flight coupons from milage club members and resells them at a major discount from the list price. Since all frequent flyer milage programs state that awards are not transferable, the airlines claim that this activity is illegal. There have been a number of lawsuits concerning this matter. In a suit against The American Coupon Exchange (ACE) of Newport Beach, California, TWA claims that ACE has cost TWA between $3 million and $4.5 million by trading frequent flyer coupons. In another suit, TWA received a judgement enjoining The Coupon Bank from buying, selling or trading TWA coupons. Northwest Orient Airlines has sued World Connection in a similar case (Travel Weekly 1987). These gray market operations can be seen as an alternative to conventional channels, offering an alternative to travel agents while costing the airlines much more than the conventional markets.

The Threat of Mega-Retailers

One of the possible avenues of growth for a nationwide travel agency is the mega-retailer. If one of the retailing giants were able to create a national in-store chain of travel outlets, the size of this organization would cause a major shift in channel power. As part of its strategy of diversifying out, Sears experimented with allowing a travel agency to open branches in some of its stores. This was a natural extension of the total service concept that had previously put stock brokers, realty agents, insurance agents, dentists, optometrists and a host of other service providers into Sears' retail outlets. This experiment fell through, however, due to contractual problems with the vendor. K-Mart has also had an unsuccessful experience with an outside firm setting up branch travel offices in some of its stores. J C Penney is currently experimenting with a company owned travel system. If J C Penney is successful, it is possible that other retailers may try to get into the travel business.

In House Travel Departments

Another possible long-term complication in the channel of distribution is the rise of corporate travel offices. In a 1986 survey of business travelers reported in Travel Weekly, thirteen per-

cent of business travelers reported using a corporate travel office or manager to make airline reservations. About a quarter of
those reservations were placed with a travel agent by the corpo-
ate travel office.

There is no legal impediment to corporate travel offices entering into the business of in house travel agencies. Until 1985,
however, the Airline Reporting Corporation (ARC) would not certify
a travel agency unless it met three criteria. First, no more than
twenty percent of an agency's business could be with one party or
firm. Second, all commissions collected had to be for third party
transactions. This false agency provision was similar to the practice in the advertising industry, in that a firm selling a product
cannot accept commissions if the firm places its own ads. Only a
true agent may accept an agent's commission. The third restriction
that the ARC enforced until 1985 was that while an agency could
operate a branch office on the premesis of a client, the agent must
have made at least one office accesible to the public.

In 1985 the ARC dropped these requirements under fear of an-
ti-trust litigation. Since the ARC is dominated by the air
carriers, there was some fear that restrictive rules could be seen
as a combination in restraint of trade. In the place of ARC rules,
the major airlines individually took over the task of screening
travel agents for accreditation. They have adopted the same three
rules that the ARC used (Pestron 1987).

There has been some fear among travel agents that airlines
would begin to pay commissions to corporate travel offices. The
airline could offer a commission rate to the firm lower than the
rate paid to travel agents, saving the carrier and the firm money.
Some in-house travel offices do a larger volume of business than
many independent travel agents. No major carrier has entered into
any agreements like this. To some extent the airlines each fear
being the first one to try this. The travel agents would be sure
to retaliate. The fact that the airlines have resisted this option is an indication that travel agents wield considerable power
in the channel.

Changes in Channel Power

The relative power of channel participants is proportional to
the sources of power available to them (Hunt and Nevin 1974).
These sources can be seen as either coercive or non-coercive.
Non-coercive sources include referent, expert and reward (Lusch
1976). To some extent, coercive power can be viewed as the converse
of non-coercive power, in that the withholding of a reward or of
expertise can be a form of coersion. Power can be seen as a function of dependence to the extent that one member of the channel
(for example a retailer) depends on another member of the channel
(for example, a wholesaler) to reach the goals the channel member
(the retailer) has set for the product (El-Ansary and Stern 1972).
It is this dependence, often on non-coercive power sources, that

gives a channel member an opportunity to exert leverage in a coercive manner.

In the air travel channel, there is a high degree of mutual dependence. In the era of deregulation, the proportion of airline tickets sold through travel agents has risen from about thirty percent to about eighty. At the same time, airline tickets represent over sixty percent of travel agent business. If hotel and car rental business sold as a complement to airline tickets is included, the proportion rises to about ninety percent. It would seem that these numbers indicate a rough parity in power, in that each industry depends on the other for a vast majority of its business. During the five years following deregulation, the average rate of commission on the sale of domestic airline tickets rose from about seven percent to about ten percent indicating some rise in travel agent channel power during this time.

The rise in computer reservation systems has made the travel agent dependent upon the airline operating the system. In a speech reported in <u>Travel Weekly</u> Judith Jacek, Director of the Institute of Certified Travel Agents, stated that without the computerized reservation system, travel agents would not be able to function in this rapidly changing environment. With the practice in the industry of rewriting the contract each time a change is made, the agent is kept dependent. Since the contracts include heavy damage clauses, the agent has no ability to change systems. Therefore, the agent has no source of coercive power available (<u>Travel Weekly</u> 1987). Airlines also gain power from their ability to control special travel givaways and commission rates. The carrier can set quotas or goals for ticket sales or for market share and reward agents that achieve those goals. The agent also depends on the carrier's help to maintain customer good will. It is important to the agent to be able to offer special treatment to regular customers, such as special seating or meals. Only the airline can offer these extras.

The wave of mergers that swept the system in 1986-87 has had an effect on the travel industry. There are less airlines competing for the travel dollar. In some markets, merged carriers have established monopoly or near-monopoly market control. Travel agents are less able to steer passengers to competing carriersand power has shifted toward the airline.

The airline is dependent upon the travel agent to steer passengers to it. The customer, faced with hundreds of fare/restriction combinations, depends upon the agent to find the airline that offers the best deal. In general, airline passengers are interested in low fares, convenient schedules, on-time arrivals and good service. While passengers may have preferences or aversions among airlines, the nature of airline route systems and schedules means that consumers move from carrier to carrier. Anything that increases pasenger brand loyalty decreases travel agent channel power. The rise of frequent flyer programs has raised the level of carrier loyalty, the travel agent lost the ability to divert these frequent flyers from one airline to another. As a result, the travel agent has lost power in the channel.

Travel agents get much of their power from their role as travel consultants to businesses. The firm depends upon the travel agent to ensure that the firm's employees are using cost-effective travel services. Many firms recognize the tendency of some employees to choose flights based on milage club membership instead of expense. The brand loyalty the individual passenger might have is diminished due to the role of the travel agent in making the reservations. The agent is free,then, in the absence of major price differences, to ticket the passenger on whichever carrier the travel agent chooses. The main influences on the agent are the long-term relationship with the firm and the relationship with one or more airlines.

The rise of the travel agent franchise system has increased the power of travel agents in the channel. If a major billion dollar a year airline has a conflict with a million or two million dollar a year agency, the agency cannot threaten the airline with any action that would really hurt. On the other hand, if a franchise system has hundreds of offices, the carrier has more to lose. The travel agent is in a stronger position to bargain.

Conclusions

The regulatory, technological and market changes that the airline industry has undergone in the last ten years have produced changes in the channel of distribution. New institutions have grown while old institutions have taken on new roles or adopted new ways of performing old functions. These changes have produced changes in the relative power of institutions in the channels. Travel agents have increased their power as the market became more complicated and as they gained technological power. The rise of franchise travel agencies has also added to agent power. Mergers, ownership of reservation systems and the development of frequent flyer programs have increased the power of the airlines. The development of consolidators, salvage operators, tour operators and gray market coupon brokers have further complicated the marketplace.

While the future of the industry is hard to predict, some trends are appearant. The growth of franchise travel agent systems should increase the power of and the services offered by travel agents. The continuing mergers in the airline industry should give the consumer less choice (Thorton 1986). These two trends suggest the eventual pitting of giant against giant, which could develop into a test of channel power.

Suits now in court will determine the influence of computer reservation systems on channels of distribution. If the courts uphold the heavy cancellation damages called for in the system contracts, the big two, Appollo and Saber, will become even more powerful. Another set of suits could spell the end to the gray market in frequent flyer coupons and the brokers who trade in coupons.

As the airlines go through a shakeout, there could be a corresponding shakeout of the travel agent ranks. Both industries have gone through a period of unprecedented growth. Both have strong firms competing with weak ones. For a travel agent to survive it must find a winning strategy. An agency must choose whether to affiliate with a franchise operation or stay independent. It can concentrate on a niche in the market, such as business travel or cruise packages, or try to remain independent. It can enter the consolidator or tour operator business. The travel agent has to plan carefully to survive. The airlines have to be careful of their relationship with the travel agents. In a very competitive market only the best survive.

Bibliograghy

Bitner, M.J. and Booms, B.H. (1982) "Trends in Travel and Tourism Marketing," _Journal of Travel Research_, Spring Pp.39-44.

Brown, J.R. and Day, R.L. (1981) "Measures of Manifest Conflict in Distribution Channels," _Journal of Marketing Research_ XVIII August PP. 263-274.

El-Ansary, A.I. and Stern L.W. (1972) "Power Measurement in the Distribution Channel," _Journal of Marketing Research_ IX February Pp. 47-52.

Gaski, J.F. (1984) "The Theory of Power and Conflict in Channels of Distribution," _Journal of Marketing_ Summer Pp. 9-29.

Hunt, S.D. and Nevin, J.R. (1974) "Power in the Channel of Distribution: Sources and Consequences," _Journal of Marketing Research_ XI May Pp. 186-93.

Kearney, T.J. (1988) "Quality of Service Under Airline Dergulation," Proceedings of the 1988 American Marketing Association Winter Educator's Conference.

Lusch, R.F. (1976) "Sources of Power: Their Impact on Interchannel Conflict," _Journal of Marketing Research_ November Pp. 382-390.

Meyer, Oster et al, (1981) _Airline Deregulation: The Early Experience_. Auburn House Publishing Co. Boston, Mass.

Pestron, M. (1987) "Appointment Rules: The Ins and Outs," _Travel Weekly_ September 21, Pp. 13.

Solomon, M.R.,(1986) "The Missing Link: Surrogate Consumers in the Marketing Chain," _Journal of Marketing_ 50, October Pp. 208-218.

Thornton,R.L. (1986) "Airlines and Agents: Conflict and the Public Welfare," _Journal of Air Law and Commerce_ Pp. 371-96.

Travel Weekly, Continuous Issues 1985-88.

THE IMPACT OF DEREGULATION ON THE RETAIL BANKING INDUSTRY: CAN THE SMALL BANK COMPETE?

Tony L. Henthorne
University of Southern Mississippi

Abstract

Degregulation of the retail banking industry has given rise to questions concerning the relative importance of various marketing mix variables in the acquisition of market share. Additionally, the role of the smaller retail bank in a deregulated and openly competitive environment is questioned. A conclusion of this research is that the smaller banking institutions may have reason for concern in this new environment.

Concurrent with the introduction and implementation of the 1980 deregulation in the retail banking industry, a decrease in average ROA was experienced (average ROA of .91% in 1980 as compared to .60% in 1986 (Business Week 1987)); the entire decade of the 1970's saw ROA hover at around one percent (Koch and Steinhauser 1982). Several factors have been linked to this decline in average profitability, including the invasion into the "traditional" banking markets by nonbank financial intermediaries (e.g., savings and loans, credit unions, retail organizations (Benston 1983; Haegele 1982)), and the slowness of the traditional banking organizations in reacting to a marketplace characterized by natural competition (Brown 1983; Cobb 1981). Retail banks must learn to adapt to this competitive environment.

PURPOSE

This research is concerned with examining some of the variables which have a direct impact on the competitiveness of retail banking institutions. In particular, the study looks at the use of marketing effort and its relationship to deposit share. Additionally, the ability of the smaller retail bank to efficiently compete in the newly competitive environment is examined.

BACKGROUND

Much has been written concerning the impact of deregulation on the retail banking industry and the ability of that industry to effectively and efficiently cope with the dynamically changing environment (e.g., Dubinsky and Clayton 1983; Kaufman, Mote, and Roseblum 1983; Wall 1985). As an example, Kaufman, Mote, Rosenblum (1983) forsaw a financial services industry significantly altered from what then existed, in large part due to the inability of the traditional retail banking industry to react aggressively to changing environmental conditions. This prophecy has, to a degree, been realized.

The effective and efficient use of the various components of marketing effort has long been viewed as one of the principle aspects of the competitive organization. However, the use of marketing in the various service related industries (e.g., retail banking) has been shown to be somewhat less efficient than in the traditional consumer and industrial goods industries (George and Barksdale 1974). Unfortunately, since the advent of banking deregulation, little has been published concerning the relationship between marketing effort and market/deposit share. Of particular concern has been the fate of the small, locally owned retail bank (Kolari and Fraser 1984; Smirlock 1985).

The development of thought concerning the fate of the smaller retail bank has been primarily along two opposing avenues: (1) due to the economies of scale inherent in any large organization, the small, independent retail bank will be at a distinct disadvantage, unable to compete effectively with the larger, well financed banking organizations for deposits; and (2) retail banking does not profit through economies of scale to any great degree, therefore, the implementation of deregulation into the financial services market should not adversely affect the small retail bank (Brown 1983; Kaufman, Mote, and Rosenblum 1983; Kolari and Fraser 1984). In particular, Kaufman, Mote, and Rosenblum (1983) point out that the small retail bank may even prosper in the new, deregulated environment given that there is a genuine demand for the personal services that only a smaller, local bank appears to be able to efficiently provide. Additionally, it has been shown that the smaller retail banks appear to be quicker in the adoption and incorporation of some innovations (Hunter and Timme 1986).

RESEARCH QUESTION

Using the above discussion as a base, this research seeks to address the following question:

Question: Are small banks more efficient in their marketing effort activities than their larger competitors?

METHOD

The optimal combination and utilization of marketing effort has long been viewed as one of the prerequisites for a successful and profitable organization (Bartels 1976; Lambin 1970; Schoeffler, Buzzell, and Heany 1973). The industry, requiring a specific definition of marketing effort for the given industry (Bartels 1976; Little 1975).

An accepted definition of marketing effort does not currently exist within the retail banking environment, therefore, a necessary first stage of this research was the determination of the marketing mix variables applicable to retail banking. Through a jury of executive opinion and a review of the cost accounting practices of retail banks, the following categories were determined to comprise the definition of the marketing mix variables (i.e., marketing effort) applicable to retail banking for the present study. It should be noted that the following is not offered as a general definition of marketing effort for all retail banks, only those in the present study.

Table 1

Marketing Mix Components
for Retail Banks

Advertising   Promotion

Charitable Contributions

Travel and Entertainment   Dues   Public Relations

Salaries and Wages   Branch Locations

Automated Teller Machines (ATM)

The marketing effort variables detailed in Table 1 were reduced to three broader sets of variables in an effort to avoid the potential problem of multicolliniarity. A "naive factor analysis" was undertaken with the result being three distinct composite variables: (a) Promotion -- composed of the expenditures for advertising, charitable contributions, travel and entertainment, dues, and public relations; (b) Service -- composed of expenditures on wages and salaries; and (c) Distribution -- composed of expenditures on branch locations and ATMs. Subsequent analysis of correlation matrices revealed no serious problems associated with multicolliniarity.

The Sample

Longitudinal data were collected from banks comprising a local market. Nine banks of varying size (representing approximately 95% of deposits) were determined to comprise the local market. The local market was one characterized by relative stability. No major competitive disruptions occurred, no banks merged or were taken over, no one institution dominated new product introductions. Data were collected for the period 1981 through 1985 (in quarters) for a total of 20 data points for each bank within the market area. The data consisted of expenditures in each of the marketing effort categories previously defined and total retail deposits (on a quarterly basis). 1981 was chosen as the base point as this was the first full year in which the impact of deregulation could be measured. Earlier data was determined to be unsuited for the current research.

The Model

Since it can not be assumed that the impact of marketing effort is totally realized in the period of the expenditure (Telser 1962), a distributed lag model was utilized in the analysis. The form of the multiple component model utilized in the present study follows.

$$DS_{j(t)} = a + B_1(Promo_{(t-i)}) + B_2(Ser_{(t-i)}) + B_3(Dist_{(t-i)})$$

where:

$DS_{j(t)}$ = deposit share of bank j, time period t

a = intercept

B_x = standardized b weight for variable X

Promo = expenditures on promotion related activities

Ser = expenditures on service related activities

Dist = expenditures on distribution related activities

Varying combinations of promotion, service, and distribution expenditures were modeled so as to permit maximum significant relationship between the components of marketing effort and deposit share (as measured by R^2 values and the greatest individual significance of each component in the model.

RESULTS AND DISCUSSION

A review of Table 2 indicates the amount of time required for each component of marketing effort to exert maximum significant impact on deposit share. Fisher's r to z transformation was utilized in the determination of maximum significance level (Hays 1981). It is interesting to note that no clear pattern emerges as to length of time required for the individual components of marketing effort to maximally relate to deposit share. It appears that Service and Promotion typically impact deposit share more rapidly than Distribution.

Table 2 also exhibits the R^2 values associated with each model. A general trend which may be seen is a decrease in the amount of variance explained by the three marketing effort components as the size of the bank decreases (moving from Bank 1 to Bank 9). Ancillary to this is a weaking in the significance level of the models (as measured by F). These findings suggest that the larger banks within the sample may be more efficient in their expenditures on marketing related variables than their smaller competitors. This lends support to the stream of thought that the smaller retail banks may be at somewhat of a competitive disadvantage in the deregulated environment (Brown 1983).

Generalizing these findings of this study beyond the current exploratory sample must be cautioned; however, the results of this limited study suggest that smaller banks are not more efficient in their marketing effort activities than their larger competitors. It appears the reverse may, in fact, be the case.

Table 2

Model R^2s and Marketing Effort Component Relationship
to Deposit Share

Bank		Model R^2	F	Component	Lag (qtrs)	Significance of B
1	l	.914	.000	service	1	.030
	a			promotion	1	.048
	r			distribution	6	.000
	g					
2	e	.721	.004	service	6	.049
	r			promotion	1	.048
				distribution	4	.007
3		.926	.000	service	0	.016
				promotion	2	.009
				distribution	1	.000
4		.827	.000	service	4	.040
				promotion	4	.078
				distribution	4	.000
5		.270	.155*	service	5	.036
				promotion	2	.188
				distribution	na	na
6		.626	.012	service	2	.002
				promotion	4	.052
				distribution	5	.471
7		.962	.000	service	1	.001
				promotion	4	.003
	s			distribution	5	.000
	m					
8	a	.495	.014	service	1	.005
	l			promotion	5	.196
	l			distribution	na	na
	e					
9	r	.500	.011	service	4	.062
				promotion	3	.004
				distribution	na	na

*model not significant

REFERENCES

Bartels, Robert (1976), THE HISTORY OF MARKET THOUGHT, 2nd edition, Columbus, OH: Grid, Inc.

Benston, George J. (1983), "Federal Regulation of Banking: Analysis and Policy Recommendations," JOURNAL OF BANK RESEARCH, 13 (Winter), 216-244.

"Bank Scoreboard," (1987), BUSINESS WEEK, (April), 114.

Brown, Judy (1983), "How High-Performance Community Banks Cope With the Effects of Deregulation," JOURNAL OF BANK RESEARCH, 5 (Fall), 17-24.

Cobb, Joe (1981), "Deregulation of Banking: How Far, How Fast," JOURNAL OF RETIAL BANKING, 3 (September), 39-45.

Dubinsky, A.N.J. and Ronnie J. Clayton (1983), "The Impact of Newly Available Financial Products: Banks - vs - savings and Loans," JOURNAL OF RETAIL BANKING, 5 (Fall), 44-51.

George, William R. and Hiram E. Barksdale (1974), "Marketing Activities in the Service Industry," JOURNAL OF MARKETING, 38 (October), 65-70.

Haegele, Monroe (1982), "Financial Deregulation and the Commercial Loan Officer," JOURNAL OF COMMERICAL BANK LENDING, (September), 30-44.

Hays, William L. (1981), STATISTICS, 3rd edition. New York: Hold Rinehart and Winston, Inc.

Hunter, William C. and Stephen G. Timme (1986), "On Deregulation, Concentration, and Innovation in Commercial Banking," Working Paper (86-8), Federal Reserve Bank of Atlanta.

Kaufman, George E., Larry Mote, and Harvey Rosenblum (1983), "Implications of Deregulation for Product Lines and Geographical Markets of Financial Institutions," JOURNAL OF BANK RESEARCH, 14 (Spring), 8-21.

Koch, Donald L. and Delores W. Steinhauser (1982), "Challenges for Retial Banking in the 80s," ECONOMIC REVIEW, (May), 13-19.

Kolari, James W. and Donald R. Fraser (1984), "The Effects of Deregulation on Bank Profitability: Can Small Banks Survive?" JOURNAL OF BANK RESEARCH, 6 (Fall), 1-11.

Lambin, Jean-Jacques (1970), "Optimal Allocation of Competitive Marketing Efforts: An Empirical Study," JOURNAL OF BUSINESS, 43 (October), 468-484.

Little, John D. C. (1975), "BRANDAID: A Marketing-Mix Model, Part 1: Structure," OPERATIONS RESEARCH, 23 (July-August), 628-655.

Schoeffler, Sidney, Robert D. Buzzell, and Donald F. Heany (1973), "PIMS: A Breakthrough in Strategic Planning," Working Paper (73-120), Marketing Science Isntitute, Cambridge, Mass.

Smirlock, Michael (1985), "Evidence on the (Non) Relationship Between Concentration and Profitability in Banking," JOURNAL OF MONEY, CREDIT, AND BANKING, 17 (February), 69-83.

Telser, Lester G. (1962), "Advertising and Cigarettes," JOURNAL OF POLITICAL ECONOMY, 70 (October), 471-499.

Wall, Larry (1985), "Why Are Some Banks more Profitable Than Others?" JOURNAL OF BANK RESEARCH, 14 (Winter), 240-256.

DIMENSIONS OF QUALITY FOR
FINANCIAL INVESTMENT SERVICES

Joseph L. Orsini
California State University, Sacramento

Abstract

Several methods of developing dimensions of service quality have been proposed recently in the literature. This study uses secondary sources, recommendations by "experts", to derive a substantial list of quality characteristics for financial investment services. These characteristics are then categorized into strategic dimensions. The usefulness of the approach, and suggestions for further research, are discussed.

The decade of the 1970's witnessed two important economic phenomena: the acknowledgement of the importance of services to the American economy (e.g. Ginzberg and Vojta 1981), and an increasing awareness of the competitive importance of product quality (e.g. Schoeffler, et al. 1974). The current decade has seen the merging of these interests: an increasing concern for service quality (e.g. Quinn and Gagnon 1986). This has led to the search for components of service quality for design and strategy purposes (e.g. Parasuraman, Zeithaml and Berry 1985).

While the literature in this area is fairly recent, important strides have been made in both developing a set of universally applicable quality dimensions, and in devising methods to derive specific quality characteristics for any particular service industry. The purpose of this paper is to utilize a recently suggested method to derive a list of characteristics of financial investment service quality; these characteristics are then categorized into eight broad dimensions useful for strategic planning purposes.

BACKGROUND AND METHODOLOGY

Service quality theory has hypothesized a heirarchical relationship among the concepts of total service quality, dimensions of service quality, and characteristics of service quality (e.g. Garvin 1984, Parasuraman, et al. 1985). Total quality is composed of the quality dimensions which are, in turn, composed of individual quality characteristics. Figure 1 illustrates this hierarchical order using an example of the nursing home industry.

The managerial use of dimensions differs from the use of characteristics. Knowledge of quality characteristics is necessary for service design purposes, while the knowledge of dimensions (aggregated characteristics) is most useful for purposes of strategic planning. For example, a nursing home

FIGURE 1

Service Quality Hierarchy - Nursing Home Example

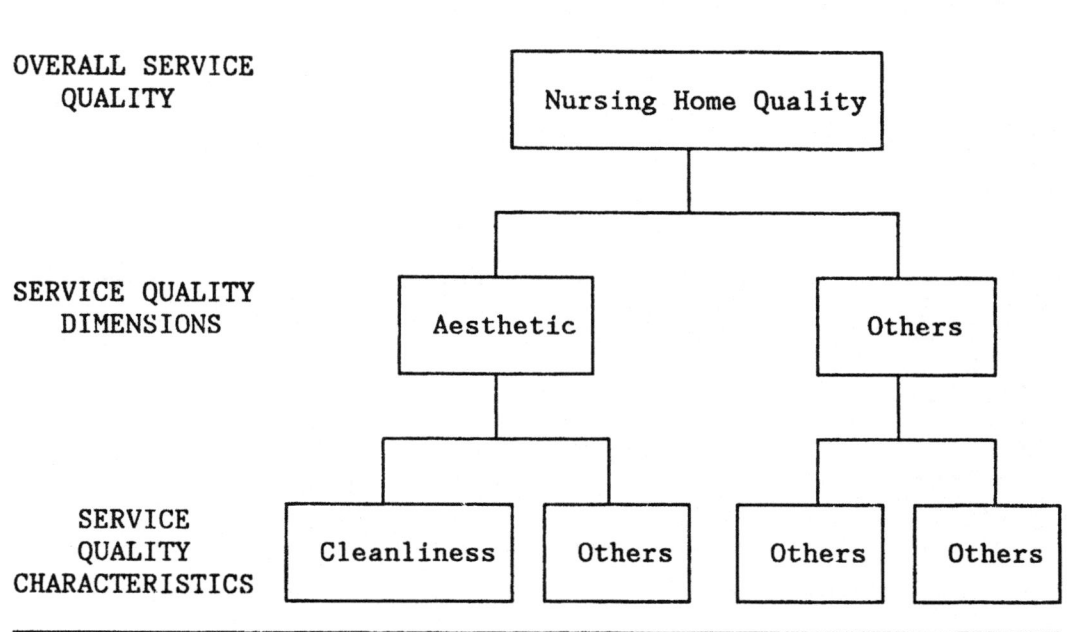

OVERALL SERVICE
QUALITY

SERVICE QUALITY
DIMENSIONS

SERVICE
QUALITY
CHARACTERISTICS

Nursing Home Quality

Aesthetic

Others

Cleanliness

Others

Others

Others

may make the strategic decision to compete on an aesthetic dimension (e.g. Garvin 1984). This decision, in turn, would result in specific character- istic design considerations, e. g. processes to assure that the facility is clean (Orsini 1988).

Methodology

The characteristics of financial service quality found in this study were derived qualitatively: by examination of popular literature which contains advice to consumers regarding their purchase of the services of a given industry. Newspaper articles, for instance on "how to choose a nursing home", invariably list characteristics the consumer is to look for in making the selection decision. In essence, the article writer serves as a qualita- tive researcher, typically reporting the results of a study, and performing further investigation by interviewing people with expertise in the industry. A recent article by Wolff (1987) on nursing home selection, for example, was based on a report produced by the Friends and Relatives of Institutionalized Aged, supplemented by personal interviews of consumer advocates involved in evaluating nursing homes.

Sources of Quality Characteristics

A variety of sources of financial investment service quality may be found using this approach. Figure 2 indicates a list of indices and agencies in which to find these articles. An important benefit of this method is that these sources not only reflect consumer thinking on aspects of the particular service industry, they also serve to guide consumer thinking in their decision making (Beales, et al. 1981). That is, these sources are the popular media, read by consumers interested in making decisions concerning purchase of the product class, thereby influencing their decision processes.

FIGURE 2

Information Sources for
Expert-Based Secondary Research

1. The National Newspaper Index
2. The Magazine Index
3. Consumer Reports
4. Local newspapers and magazines
5. Reports of private consumer agencies
   e.g. the American Association of Retired Persons
6. Public consumer agencies
   e.g. the California Department of Consumer Affairs

The types of financial investment services investigated in this study include: financial planners; the general topic of financial investment; and stockbrokers. A review of the sources of Figure 2 resulted in a total of 14 articles, which yielded 85 characteristics recommended for consumer consideration in determining the quality of the service provided.

Defining Dimensions

Defining the dimension categories in this study was also accomplished subjectively. While Parasuraman, et al. (1985) utilized services research to derive their dimensions, Orsini (1988) concluded that their dimensions were too restrictive, and those suggested by Garvin (1984, 1987) better fit a list of nursing home quality characteristics. Those suggested by Garvin (1984) are: the primary service performance characteristics; supplemental features; reliability; conformance to design; durability; serviceability; aesthetics; and indirect measures of quality.

While these dimensions appeared to form a better basis for categorization, their origin in manufactured goods quality control required some modification to accomodate service differences. The Conformance dimension's applicability is suspect, as the consumer may not be able to differentiate between the service design specification (if one exists) and its performance. Durability was also viewed to be not substantially applicable, as services are usually produced and consumed simultaneously.

190

Some additional dimensions appeared to be warranted, however, to accomodate services theory. This includes dividing the Serviceability dimension into two categories: Technical Personnel quality and Functional Personnel quality (e.g. Gronroos 1984). These relate to what the service provider supplies, and how it is supplied. An example would be a doctor's technical competence vs. his/her "bedside manner". A further category suggested by Orsini (1988) is a Transaction dimension, which relates to the quality of the exchange process itself (possession utility). A salesperson providing sufficient information for the consumer to make a confident decision is an example.

In summary, the approach to deriving financial service quality characteristics used in this study is based on review of the popular literature advising consumers on criteria to use for their purchase decisions in the product class. The dimensions used to categorize these characteristics are based on production quality theory, modified by findings in the services literature. These derived characteristics and dimensions are discussed in the following section.

FINDINGS

The primary, or basic, financial investment service quality characteristics are indicated in Table 1. These are defined as the fundamental reasons for purchase of the service; unless these exist, the consumer may just as well not make the purchase. It will be noted that there are some which apply only to financial planners, others which apply only to investors, and some which apply to both, is evident in all the tables below. Managers interested in design issues should have no difficulty in differentiating those characteristics not applicable to their particular industry.

TABLE 1

Service Performance Dimensions

Definition: primary service characteristics

1. Liquidity of the investment (access to funds)
2. Detailed financial plan is prepared
3. The plan matches the financial goals of the client
4. Financial records are computerized
5. A variety of products are offered (not just one or two)
6. There is periodic review of the plan
7. The planner/investor represents more than one company
8. Assistance in implementation is part of the plan
9. Past successes of the organization are documented
10. The yield to risk ratio is maximized

The characteristics listed in Table 2 are those which are not absolutely necessary for the basic service, but which enhance or supplement it. Included in this dimension, as indicated in Garvin (1984), is service customization, e.g. understanding client needs. That is, an investment may yield a profit (a Performance dimension), but be more desirable if it was the type of investment more appropriately suited to the particular needs of the client's financial situation (e.g. yielding short-run rather than long-run profits).

TABLE 2

Service Supplemental Features

Definition: characteristics that supplement basic service functions

1. An initial free consultation is provided
2. Investment biases are specified
3. Available services meet client needs
4. Products offered meet client needs
5. The organization investment style meets client needs
6. The plan and all advice is personalized
7. Interviews are held with both spouses
8. Clients are enlightened on general financial matters
9. Client financial areas needing help are identified
10. Discussions are in "plain English"
11. The client deals with only one person in the organization
12. The client is regularly advised on important financial matters.
13. The investment needs of the client are understood
14. Personnel are available without appointment
15. There is a large staff

Interestingly, the reliability dimension generated the most characteristics of any dimension. Reliability, in the financial investment services area, was interpreted to mean the likelihood of investment failure due to incompetance or, as was more heavily reflected in the literature, fraud.

TABLE 3

Service Reliability Dimensions

Definition: avoiding the liklihood of service failure due to
fraud or incompetance

1. The organization is financially sound
2. All claims are in writing
3. The organization will list its principles and officers
4. The exact location of the investment is supplied willingly
5. The plan has three to six months cash reserves
6. The organization is willing to disclose the source of
   receiving your name
7. Counselors are not compensated purely on commission
8. The organization is registered with the appropriate regulatory
   agencies (such as the SEC, if advising on securities)
9. No complaints, or a low complaint rate, with the BBB
10. Appropriately licensed and certified
11. Products offered in addition to those earning high commission
12. Stated fees are not discounted as an inducement to invest
13. A financial questionnaire is completed prior to the interview
14. There is ample opportunity to ask questions (no high pressure)
15. Tax shelters are not recommended too quickly
16. The organization is listed in the phone book
17. Investments are traded on a regulated exchange
18. The names of the regulating agencies are disclosed
19. The organization has existed in the community for some time
20. There is no organization or employee history of crime or fraud
21. Indicated returns are reasonable, not substantially above market
22. The organization will supply information through the mail
23. There is willingness to explain the offer to your banker,
    attorney or accountant

While one of the characteristics of services is "the person is the service",
Orsini (1988) suggests a differentiation between those items pertaining to
the actual provider of the service and those items pertaining to management
policy. Characteristics relating to organization/management policy have been
discussed in Tables 1, 2 and 3 above, while characteristics relating to the
person providing the service are included in Tables 4 and 5. Table 4
includes those characteristics which seemed related to the technical performance of the individual provider, such as continuing training and offering
new ideas to the client. As in all these tables, frequently a given characteristic could arguably be categorized in a different dimension.

193

TABLE 4

Service Personnel Technical Dimensions

Definition: technical competance of personnel in performing the service

1. Experienced with rate cycles
2. The client is assisted in decision making
3. Transactions are performed in a timely manner
4. Personnel possess appropriate education and training credentials
5. Personnel possess appropriate previous experience
6. Personnel are continuing their education
7. A variety of solutions are offered
8. Personnel are competent in non-investment areas
9. Personnel are knowledgeable about the market
10. An implementation time frame is suggested
11. Periodic review is suggested
12. The plan is discussed in specifics, not generalities
13. The clients attitude toward risk is discussed
14. The client is given sufficient time to make decisions
15. The client is offered new ideas
16. The advisor has personnally researched the recommended products

---

Table 5 considers the functional characteristics of the service provider, that is, the __way__ in which the service is provided. Insofar as the major

TABLE 5

Service Personnel Functional Dimensions

Definition: interpersonal abilities of personnel in performing the service

1. Full explanations are given
2. Personnel are helpful
3. The advisor listens to the client
4. The advisor provides ample opportunity for questions
5. Client's questions are fully answered
6. The advisor serves as a sounding board for client ideas
7. Personnel are available
8. Personnel are courteous
9. Complexities are fully explained

---

concern of most of the articles was the prevention of fraud, quite possibly this dimension received less attention than it would have in other services.

While the source articles were highly concerned with reliability issues, they evidenced little concern with physical items related to the service, compared to the latter's importance in quality theory (e.g. Parasuraman, et al. 1985). Apparently none of the article authors felt that much useful information could be derived from the physical appearance of people or equipment. Given the unanimity of opinion in service quality theory that tangibles are important factors of consideration, it is unclear as to why the source articles do not include more of these characteristics. It may be that they were overlooked, or it may be that where fraud is an item of high importance, physical aspects of the service, such as appearance, are so easy to provide that they do not provide reliable cues for assessment. Further research will be necessary to make this determination.

TABLE 6

Service Tangibles Dimensions

Definition: physical facilities, equipment, and appearance of personnel

1. The advisor is willing to meet in the organization office

One of the strong points of the quality dimensions proposed by Garvin (1984) is the inclusion of a category for indirect indicators of service quality. Most of the items in this category do not fit well in the other dimensions, but are important in both quality theory and the source articles of this study. Ratings by regulatory agencies, for example, were included in virtually every article examined.

TABLE 7

Service Indirect Dimensions

Definition: indirect measures of organization and attributes

1. The organization has high ratings by regulatory agencies
2. The organization is well established and stable
3. The organization is willing to supply references
4. Sophisticated computer programs are used
5. The organization is recommended by friends and coworkers

The service transaction dimension of Table 8 is suggested by Orsini (1988) as a separate dimension. While it is understandable that this is not included in Garvin's (1984) list of production-based dimensions, it is interesting that it was also not included in the original dimensions of Parasuraman, et al. (1985), insofar as transaction, or exchange, is the basis of marketing theory. While it is possible to include these characteristics in other dimensions, possession utilities (those related to the transaction process) have been considered as "value added" items within the marketing discipline since its origin.

TABLE 8

Service Transaction Dimensions

Definition: characteristics related to the exchange process

1. There is a rapid response to telephone inquiries
2. Thorough information regarding the transaction is supplied
3. Rates meet client needs and are reasonable
4. The deposit or minimum charge requirements are affordable
5. Samples of the plan are provided
6. Fees and other client costs are supplied willingly

CONCLUSIONS

This study has illustrated a method of deriving characteristics of financial service quality based on their inclusion in the popular literature which advises consumers on their purchase of those services. These characteristics were further grouped into broader dimensions of quality in accord with the theoretical quality literature. While the characteristics themselves are useful for service design purposes, the dimensions are managerially useful for strategic planning purposes.

As with any research, certain limitations should be noted. The method of deriving these characteristics and dimensions is subjective, thus they may vary with the individual researcher. It is quite possible, for example, that the reader may feel that some of the characteristics were miscategorized and more properly belong in a different dimension. Another important limitation is the scarcity of the consumer literature from which the characteristics were derived. Since local newspapers were an important source, there would undoubtedly be variation by another research effort for the same industries.

While this method is applicable to a wide variety of service industries, the marketing manager should not rely exclusively on this list or any other list derived by this method. However, it does provide a suitable base from which to proceed to further primary research, both qualitative and quantitative, in that it provides a minimum of items to consider. Depending on the individual segments pursued, and variation in the importance of the characteristics to those segments, service design should be industry-specific rather than more global in nature.

In conclusion, for the individual financial investment manager, the findings of this study provide a valuable basis from which to begin research. For other service managers, the method provides an illustration which is applicable to a wide variety of service industries. The method is relatively simple, and may be largely accomplished by minimally trained personnel. For those interested in the development of services quality theory, the method and findings add to the understanding of an area which has, at this time, only begun to be explored. Undoubtedly, service quality dimensions and their uses will see substantial changes in the future.

REFERENCES

Beales, Howard, Michael B. Mazis, Steven C. Salop and Richard Staelin (1981), "Consumer Search and Public Policy", Journal of Consumer Research, 8 (June), 11-21.

Garvin, David A. (1984), "What Does "Product Quality" Really Mean?", Sloan Management Review, (Fall), 25-43.

Garvin, David A. (1987), "Competing on the Eight Dimensions of Quality", Harvard Business Review, 65 (November-December), 101-109.

Ginzberg, Eli and George J. Vojta (1981), "The Service Sector of the U.S. Economy", Scientific American, 244 (March), 48-55.

Gronroos, Christian (1983), Strategic Management and Marketing in the Service Sector, Cambridge: Marketing Science Institute.

Orsini, Joseph L. (1988), "Defining Components of Service Quality: An Alternative Approach", unpublished working paper, California State University, Sacramento.

Parasuraman, A., Valarie A. Zeithaml, and Leonard L. Berry (1985), "A Conceptual Model of Service Quality and Its Implications for Future Research," Journal of Marketing, 49 (Fall), 41-50.

Parasuraman, A., Valarie A. Zeithaml, and Leonard L. Berry (1986), Servqual: A Multiple-Item Scale for Measuring Customer Perceptions of Service Quality, Cambridge: Marketing Science Institute.

Quinn, James Brian and Christopher E. Gagnon (1986), "Will Services Follow Manufacturing Into Decline?", Harvard Business Review, 64 (November-December), 95-103.

Schoeffler, Sidney, Robert D. Buzzell and Donald F. Heany (1974), "Impact of Strategic Planning on Profit Performance", Harvard Business Review, 52 (March-April) 137-145.

Wolff, Craig (1987), "Finding a Nursing Home: Some Guidelines", The New York Times, August 29, Style p. 1.

MARKETING FINANCIAL SERVICES: PRELIMINARY FINDINGS FROM NORTHERN IRELAND.

Kate Stewart, University of Ulster, Northern Ireland

Abstract

This paper looks at the banks in Northern Ireland and the implications for their marketing of personal financial services, given a rapidly changing environment. This change is occuring on many fronts, those examined are competition, regulation, society and technology. Cowell's four-level analytical framework for the definition of service products is heavily utilised. Qualitative findings are summarised in a systemic representation. The author states that
a.   it is unclear whether current marketing strategies will provide the means to achieve competitive advantage; and,
b.   Northern Irish banks have been slow to adopt the marketing orientation.

INTRODUCTION

The services marketing debate remains an academic tease. What is generally agreed, though with some exceptions (eg. Buttle 1985), is that marketing services is different. Following Geshuny and Miles (1983) who use the term 'services' in four analytically distinct ways, this paper will focus on a particular service industry and its service products. The personal financial services industry illustrates well the issues of services marketing and the behaviour of an industry in a changing environment. Empirical research findings, which are of a qualitative nature, are ordered using Cowell's (1984), four-level analysis. Accordingly this paper falls into the following sections: the service product, the financial services environment, Northern Ireland banks, systemic representation of empirical findings and early conclusions.

THE SERVICE PRODUCT

The service product is one element of the marketing mix. Much debate has centred on whether the marketing mix for services requires expansion from the 4P's (product, price, promotion and place) of McCarthy (1960). Perhaps the source of this debate lies in the original abbreviation of all marketing variables to the 4P's. The four Ps,' by offering a seductive sense of simplicity to teachers, students and practitioners of marketing, has become an article of faith'. Kent (1986) criticises the lack of empirical study into what the key marketing variables are and how they are perceived and used by marketing managers. This study is one attempt to contribute to such investigation.

An organisation's success is dependent upon its product policy. The product, however, is one of a number of interdependent elements in the marketing mix. This presents difficulties to the researcher wishing to 'unpackage' the mix and focus on one element . Cowell (1984) recognises the service product to be a complex phenemenon. In order to trace the linkage between the service product from the consumers' and the providers' viewpoints he suggests analysis at four levels – the consumer benefit concept, the service concept, the service offer and the service delivery system. Although not wholly discrete, each level of analysis is a progression from the other and relates demand and supply.

The consumer benefit concept is concerned with the benefits customers seek. These are difficult to measure and monitor by virtue of their elusive nature. Yet the service marketer is fundamentally obliged to discover what the consumer seeks as distinct from what is produced. The service concept defines what general benefits the service organisation will offer. Cowell suggests that decisions are required on service elements (ingredients of the total service offer); service forms (how these ingredients are put together); and service levels (the level of quality and quantity provided).

The service delivery system is suggested as the final level of analysis necessary to define the service product. Consideration must be given to the people and physical evidence involved in the performance of the service. Managing these elements, according to Cowell, requires to understand them and the interrelationships. Successful management entails integration of these elements with respect to the providers and consumers viewpoint. It is Cowell's four-level analysis which is used to order the findings of research conducted with Northern Ireland's five banks.

ENVIRONMENTAL IMPACT ON NORTHERN IRELAND PERSONAL BANKING INDUSTRY

The key environmental changes are regulation, technology, competition and society. Although each of these will be examined separately, it is important to remember that they are interactive forces.

Regulation

The Financial Services Act (1988) is the latest and most comprehensive in a series of acts aiming to revise financial services legislation (Whittaker and Morse 1987). The main provisions of the Act are strict rules governing any business involved in offering any kind of investment advice, and compulsory registration of all investment businesses. Polarisation implies that all these businesses must elect either to be independent intermediaries with regard to the advice and products they recommend, or tied agents selling only their own products. A plethora of self regulatory oragnisations (SROs) and Representative Professional Bodies (RPBs) has emerged, all of which are supervised by the Securities and Investments Board (SIB).

Of the five banks operating in NI, the Ulster and Northern who together account for over 65% of the market have opted for the independent route, with TSB, Bank of Ireland and Allied Irish Banks having chosen or are assumed to be choosing to be tied agents. As tied agents, they are barred from recommending other companies and restricted to giving general advise on generic differences between, for example, types of policy. One implication for tied agents is that they risk losing customers by not being able to give independent advice or having an incomplete portfolio of products. To overcome these problems, a conduit may be used. The Banks have also been impacted by the Building Societies Act 1986 which allows building societies to provide a much wider range of services than before.

Technology

Banks initially invested in computers in the sixties. These were used principally for computerisation and centralisation of consumer credit and debit account records. This was followed by the establishment of an interbank cheque-clearing system. During the seventies technological changes contributed to a rapid increase in branch productivity. As for the eighties, 'technological changes are increasingly affecting banking operations but at markedly different scales and time frames.'(Wield and Smith 1987).

Technology's indirect impact on the customer may well be an efficient service. Its more direct impact is in terms of distribution or access. More flexible money transmission services such as credit cards, automated teller machines (ATMS) and so on, are advances based on technology, Watkins and Wright (1986).

Technological advance is a double edged sword. Branches may be less congested but if customers are less likely to visit the branch its potential as a selling outlet is not fully realised.

Competition.

It would be erroneous to suggest that competition in personal financial markets is confined to that between banks.. Research in Britain (Carter, Chiplin and Lewis 1986) by the Nottingham Institute of Financial Studies (NIFS) in 1985 suggests that building societies and stockbrokers are perceived by banks to be competitive threats. For their part building societies see banks as their major competitors, while life assurance companies are wary of the banks and building societies. Carter (1986) comments that this blurring of the distinction between banks and savings institutions is a feature of American as well as UK markets.

Other competitors may well emerge from the retail sectors, though the NIFS research found that retailers were not perceived as very important sources of competition for banks. A position of advantage for retailers is implicity endorsed by Cowell who cites 'reputation' as being one means of building a strong competitive position in service businesses.

Wield and Smith (1987) see competition as comprising a set of instruments, namely: higher interest rates to savers; lower margins between borrowing and lending rates; flexibility and ease of credit; more flexible money transmission services and breadth of branch network.

In Northern Ireland, the banks are cash rich at the moment and therefore have little immediate need to attract savers with higher interest rates. With competition between banks and building societies bringing down the interest rate on borrowing, the building societies may well be forced to reduce their interest rate on deposits, which is tradionally higher than that given by banks. The banks are strongly resisting following building societies in providing interest bearing current accounts which are successful with the customer but which are losing substantial money according to industry sources. Competition is therefore changing in institutional and instrumental respects.

Society and Customers

Societal changes have impacted many markets including those for financial services in the past decade. Some of these changes are in the areas of - home and motor car ownership, educational opportunity, types of employment, working women and the age profile. Mc Ivor and Naylor (1980) point out that with personal customers these changes mean that financial services producers can think in terms of a much wider potential market than they had before. The customer is also becoming more sophisticated and aware of their ability to shop around. Indeed Tansey (1985) has commented that 'the customer now holds the power, not the bank'. Increasing disposable income has been accompanied by a disproportionate increase in consumer spending. Bank borrowing has therefore increased as have loans for business. Transaction services are also the subject of a great deal of activity with numbers of current account holders increasing and more extensive usage of automated services such as direct debit, credit card and cash card transactions (Watkins and Wright 1986).

These trends in society and customer markets are reflected in the number of segments which banks may now target. Channon (1986) cites the following segments: very rich private banking, middle market private banking, higher net worths (HNWs), professionals, self employed, white collar older marrieds, retirees and the savings conscious. Although each of these developoments suggests opportunities for creative marketing it is important to respect the role of customer confidence in the industry, (Zavvos 1988). Because of feduciary responsibility, McIvor and Naylor (1980) argue 'the marketing style of a financial services organisation can never be as uninhibited as that of , let us say, a manufacturer of fast-moving packaged goods.' Banks looking to the 1990's and beyond may well disagree. One local senior bank director has stated that marketing of financial services is no different from marketing any good. Another marketing director confessed to borrowing the sales techniques of car-salesmen. The banks are keen to use

202

marketing to help progress their image from an 'institutional' one to that of being financial services providers.

It has been shown that changes have occured in many of the environments in which the banks operate. To use the words of one key informant, the impication is - "marketing's time has come".

NORTHERN IRELAND BANKS

The five banks operating in Northern Ireland are Bank of Ireland; Allied Irish Banks; Northern Bank; Ulster Bank; and Trustee Savings Bank (TSB). The National Girobank, owned by the Post Office is a sixth player, though its market share is so small that it was not included in the investigation. Unlike some other countries, the process of consolidation of Irish banks was well established by the early years of the century.

The head offices of Allied Irish Bank and Bank of Ireland are located in Dublin. Both banks have only recently established marketing departments in Belfast. In the past this has meant that policy was made in Dublin, primarily with the Republic of Ireland in mind and then simply replicated for Northern Ireland. This applied to product development and planning. Key informants in both banks indicated that Belfast departments would have a much more proactive approach and design products for the Northern Irish market.

The Northern Bank is in a similar situation following its disengagement from Midland Bank PLC and its new Australian owners giving complete responsibility to it for marketing. Although this would imply that products developed will be much more tailored to the NI market, it puts a tremendous onus on the capabilities of its now expanded marketing department. By contrast, the Ulster Bank can use the substantial marketing resources of its London-based parent company. The Ulster's marketing department was established in Belfast in 1985 though it is supplemented by the longer established Planning and Development Department which is responsible for concept generation. All key informants agreed that, in the past, head office officials were recruited from branches on the basis of length of service. This system has now changed so that these positions are filled on the basis of relevant skills.

Branch networks are seen to be an important part of marketing strategies, though some key informants judged Northern Ireland, with a population of 1.5 million, to be overbanked. The number of branches operated by each of the banks in Northern Ireland ranges from 45 to 120. Respondents expect this number to decline so as to achieve cost savings.

SYSTEMIC REPRESENTATION OF EMPIRICAL FINDINGS

Following Cowell, the four level analysis of financial services products of NI banks are: consumer benefit concept; service concept; service offer; and service delivery system.

Consumer Benefit Concept

All of the banks use similar sources of information and indeed, one respondent stated that they all share the same view of the market place. Ad hoc research is commissioned to identify benefits sought. One informant expressed concern at the capabilities of market research to overcome the sensitivity and retiscence of consumers regarding their finances. In order to monitor these and trends in the market place the five banks also buy into the local Financial Research Survey - a recently established omnibus. There was little variation in the informants' views of what benefits consumers seek from a bank. All initially stated service as a primary benefit sought, followed by convenience, advice, long-term relationship, efficiency and so on. Varying interpretations of the term 'service' would seem to be employed and this is evidenced in the service concept level. For some it was taken as quality service, while for others the emphasis was put on the friendliness of service. Both of these interpretations involve subjective judgement and are difficult to define fully.

Lewis (1986) sees financial services as directed towards satisfying the need to make payments, the desire to accumulate wealth for later consumption by means of saving or borrowing for house purchase, and the provision of financial security. It is around these needs that the benefits are sought.

Given a thorough understanding of the consumer benefit concept it can then translated into the service concept.

Service Concept

This is a general notion of what the provider, in this instance the banks, offer. The broadest view of this is that banks take deposits, lend money and perform transmission services. This three-fold definition relates to the three-fold needs of consumers outlined by Lewis.

More specific attention is required on several areas. The first of these is how the service will be produced and consumed. Production of bank services entails the cooperation of many departments: legal, computing, personnel, marketing and branch network. What is produced are three core products with various attributes. This will be elaborated under the service offer section.

Attention also needs to be directed to segment identification. Informants all mentioned segmentation as being of increasing importance - the following segments have been targetted by some or all of the banks in N.I.:- babies, primary school children, 11 - 15 year olds, 16 - 18 year olds, school leavers, students, graduates, professionals, solicitors, house buyers and retirees. In many cases the background to the targetting of segments suggested that this was a reactive decision. On discovering that a high proportion of its customers were in the 40+ age bracket, one bank targeted newly born babies (or more accurately their parents), as a source of new customers. Age and occupation are the most widely used segmentation variables and although one bank defines theirs as lifestyle segmentation, in effect age is the surrogate indicator used.

The interface between the customer and provider also requires consideration. In banking terms it is inevitably the branch network which undertakes this role. If this interface is assumed to involve selling a service product then staffing implications arise. Product knowledge is regarded by all the banks as an essential component of the selling mix. Accordingly, many of the banks have developed training programmes for their staff, with an apparent emphasis on product knowledge. Some of the banks ensure that all branch staff fully understand a dozen products identified as the most important. Head office support is available for information on the others. For new products, specific staff may be trained in aspects of the product. It is also important that providers consider the image of the service offer and ensure clarity in communications.

According to Nystrom (1985), service companies are expected to engage in 'holistic imagery'. This approach contrasts with the more explicit price and quality competition of goods marketers. Informants held different views on this. Northern Bank, for example have placed only one corporate advertisement. In contrast to the Ulster, the Allied Irish Bank is seeking to move away from product driven to 'people and quality of service' driven advertising. Looking at some recent advertisements it would appear that some of the banks are opting for product and price-led messages. With the number of products in the banks ranges increasing an emphasis of this type is to be expected.

In general, policy decisions are being made which indicate a move from implicit marketing strategies. Segmentation is being increasingly used, the importance of interface between the banks and customers is leading to enhanced staff training and the number of products which banks offer is increasing.

The Service Offer

Cowell comments that decisions on the detailed shape of the service offer are intertwined and indissoluble from decisions on the service delivery system and are derived from those on the service concept. The elements or ingredients of the financial services marketing mix include the type of service product to be offered - lending, depositing or transmission - plus decisions on issues such as convenience, access, delivery, service and so on. Given the banks current cash-rich situation, products being developed are predominantly of a lending nature: an example of this is the mortgage product now offered by all the banks. Shostack (1977) comments that the physical evidence of those products is easier to manage than their intangible aspects. This is, perhaps, one reason for the great emphasis which the banks place on their sales literature, which is so abundant in any of the branches.

The wide array of elements available to financial service marketers means that decisions are required on the forms in which they are offered to the market place. One innovation in this area is the Northern Bank's one-sell concept. Working on the premise that customers dislike having to come to the bank to ask for a loan, on opening an account, customers are given a credit-line. This is based on credit scoring and differs from the past system where customers were given a loan for a specific purpose for a specific time period. An analysis is required of the levels of quality and the volume, timing and flow of service delivered in a service product. All the banks are increasingly attempting to 'cross-sell' their products to overcome the high proportion of customers who buy or own only one product. It is interesting that all of the banks stress the quality of customer service and intend to increase this quality. This would imply that a similar positioning policy has been adopted by all the banks. If this is the case, then its use as a means of differentiation and competitive advantage is lost.

Timing of service delivery is a topical issue. Only recently have NI banks stopped closing at lunch time and this is at a limited number of locations. This move was a reactive one to the competition of building societies which open for longer hours. Resistance from the Irish Bank Officials Association will have to be overcome if Saturday opening is to happen.

The analysis of the service offer is a complex issue but provides an understanding of many of the tactics which may provide competitive advantage. In many respects, however, it would appear that this distinctiveness is not being achieved by NI banks.

Service Delivery System

Cowell contends that specifying the delivery system and the elements of which it is composed is an essential ingredient in defining the service product. This can be attributed to the inseparability of the service product and its delivery. Recognition of the importance of people in services marketing is reflected in the growth of internal marketing. This is described by Mudie (1987) as the process '...whereby selling the job to employees must precede selling the service to customers.'

NI banks would appear not to have separate internal marketing programmes but rather place emphasis on the value of staff product knowledge and therefore, training. Changing attitudes from production orientated to consumer orientated is a long process in which the NI banks have, only recently, engaged. Some of the informants seemed very cynical of what they termed the 'have-a-nice-day syndrome.' Indeed a subjective judgement of the findings would indicate that the banks are staffed with an 'old guard' and 'new guard'. The latter are more appropriately skilled in marketing and enthusiastic. The 'old guard' still protects the institutional aspect of banking and respects the head office reccruitment system from branch management. One comment indicates a rather quaint view of the customer – 'any customer worth his salt will ring their bank manager to find out about a loan before accepting that of a car salesman'. Perhaps the decline of this type of attitude will lead the NI banks to realise the potential of their staff through internal marketing.

The importance of physical evidence in the service product is well established (Groroos 1980). Physical resources are part of the total customer experience and include branch building, signage, equipment, facilities layout, documents, forms and so on.

Traditionally teller facilities have been the dominant physical feature of branch layout and these are designed with security as the uppermost concern. Queuing facilities also mean that, on entry to the branch, the customer is 'regimented'. Bank of Ireland has successfully piloted an open plan layout with teller windows a much more subtle feature. This creates a different atmosphere and suggests easy access to bank staff. The Northern Bank has recently changed its signage to incorporate a new logo which was designed to reflect its new status as a more autonomous Irish bank. One informant also spoke of the importance of user friendly forms, attractive sales literature and the use of colour. Whatever form physical evidence takes, the banks are mindful of the role of a branch as a sales outlet and the need to create a selling environment.

EARLY CONCLUSIONS

Some brief conclusions are now drawn, though it should be borne in mind that the research is at an early stage. Figure 1 represents a summary of the findings.

> i) Cowell's framework allows an analysis of the service product and can be applied to personal banking products. It is, however, inappropriate for a comprehensive analysis of an industry and the changes affecting it.
>
> ii) The analysis illustrates the difficulty of analysing one marketing variable alone and, indeed, the complexity of decision-making in marketing.
>
> iii) The analysis suggests that changes in the service product in personal banking, are initiated by environmental changes as well as changes in the consumer benefit concept.

207

iv) Marketing is gaining increasing recognition in NI banks.

v) Analysis of the service product may enhance the banks understanding of how they may achieve competitive advantage. At present their marketing suggests little innovation or creativity.

REFERENCES AND FOOTNOTES

Buttle, F. (1986) 'Unserviceable Concepts In Services Marketing' Quarterly Review of Marketing. Volume 11, No. 3 (Spring), 8-14.

Carter, R.L., Chiplin,B. and M.K. Lewis (eds) (1986) Personal Financial Markets. Philip Allen. Oxford.

Channon, D.(1986) Bank Strategic Management and Marketing. Wiley. Salisbury.

Cowell, D. (1984) The Marketing of Services. Heinemann. London

Gershuny, J.L and Miles, L.D. (1983) The New Service Economy. Frances Pinter in Buttle, F. ibid.

Gronroos, C. (1980) 'An Applied Service Marketing Theory' Swedish School of Economics and Business Administration. Working Paper 57.

Kent, R.A.(1986) 'Faith in four Ps: An Alternative' Journal of Marketing Management, Vol. 2 No. 2, 145 - 154.

Lewis, M.K.(1986) 'Provision of Retail Financial Services' International Journal of Bank Marketing 5,2, 33 - 46.

McCarthy, E.J.(1960) Basic Marketing. Irwin. Illinois.

McIvor, C. and Naylor, G.(1980) Marketing Financial Services. Institute of Bankers. London.

Mudie, P.M.(1987) Internal Marketing: Cause for Concern' Quarterly Review of Marketing. Spring/Summer, 21-24

Nystrom, M.(1985) 'Marketing Strategies for Service Companies' in Gronroos, C. and Gummenson, E (eds) Services Marketing: Nordic School Perspectives, University of Stockholm.

Shostack, G.L.(1977) 'Breaking Free From Services Marketing' Journal of Marketing, vol. 41, no. 2. American Marketing Association. April.

Tansey, W.J. (1985) 'What Marketing Offers Banks' The Banker. June.

Watkins, T. and Wright, M.(1986) Marketing Financial Services. Butterworths, London, 25.

Wield, D.V. and Smith, S.L.(1987) 'Banking on the new technology- Choices and Constraints' International Journal of Information Management. 7. 115-129.

Zavvos, G.(1988) 'EC Strategy for the Banking Sector: The Perspective of 1992' European Affairs, Spring, 100-108.

Figure 1. The Personal Banking Service Product : A Systemic View

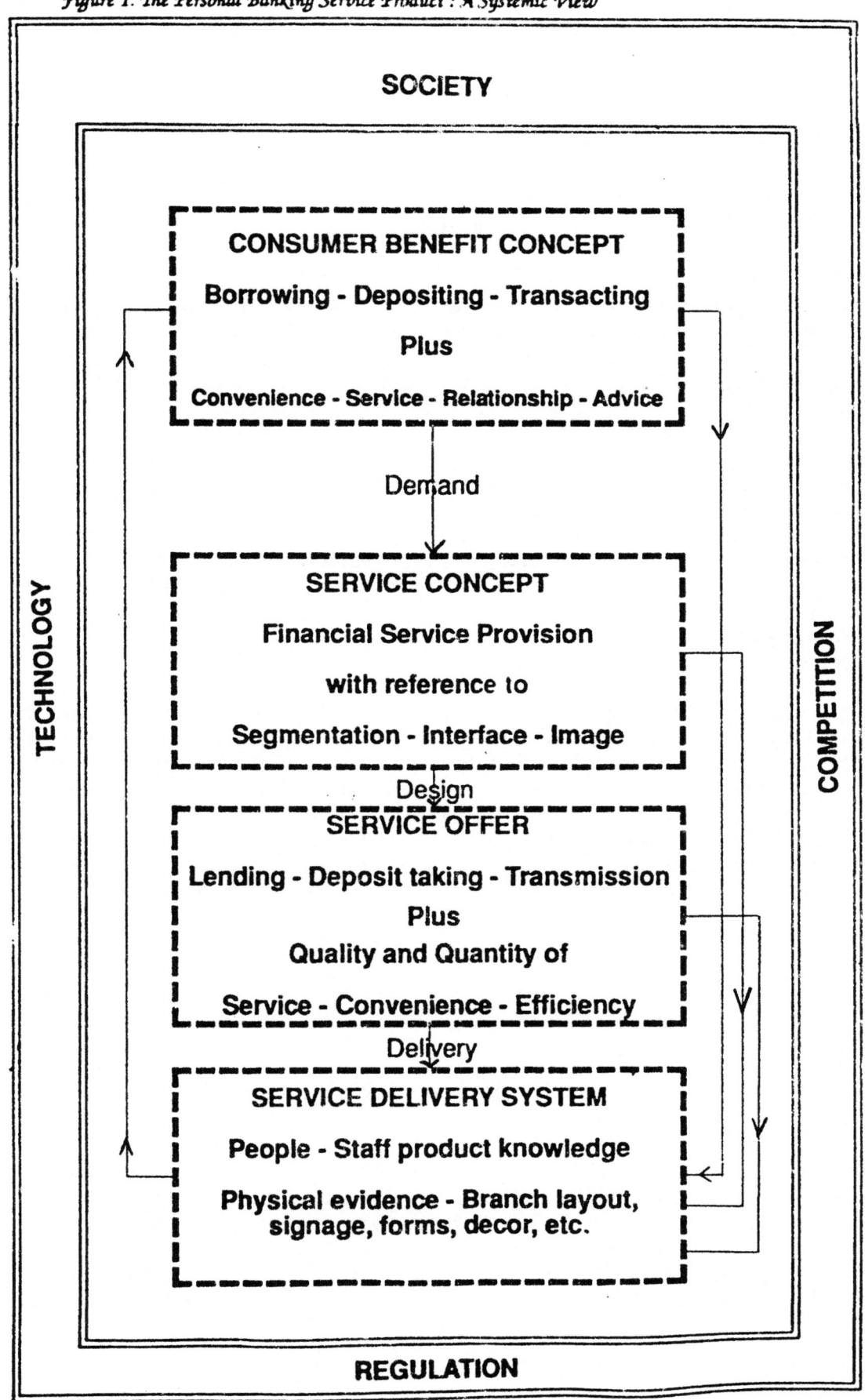

PROMOTIONAL STRATEGIES AND TECHNIQUES IN SERVICES MARKETING

Gideon Falk and Casimir F. Bozek
Purdue University Calumet

Abstract

The service economy is rapidly increasing; reaching approximately 75% of the GNP in the United States. Marketing scholars and practitioners have long struggled to identify the similarities and differences of marketing and promoting services and products. The questions the authors wish to address are:

1. Can one apply traditional promotional techniques to services marketing?
2. What adaptations do companies have to make to be effective in the promotion of services?
3. How should the marketing, and in particular, the promotional mix be changed for effective promotion of services?
4. Is the timing of the promotion process in services different from that of products?
5. How does the content of the advertising message vary when one promotes a service?

The paper relates the special characteristics of services: intangibility, perishability, variability, and inseparability, to the promotional techniques of price discounts, personal selling, trade shows and exhibits, free samples, advertising, branding, public relations and referrals and references.

The authors provide several key insights into the differences in the promotion of services (as compared to products) which could provide guidelines for practitioners. Finally, suggestions for future research are presented.

INTRODUCTION

Nearly one-half of every dollar spent by consumers goes for the purchase of services. Government figures show that in the early 1980's about two thirds of the private, non-governmental labor force was engaged in supplying services. Further government projections into the later 1980's and early 90's indicate that services will attract an even larger portion of consumer spending and employment. Today, the United States economy is becoming a "service economy", where the important economic activities include trade, transportation, communication, finance, health and education services, professional services, personal services, and governmental services.

Most people in service industries have recognized the unique challenges in service marketing and the underlying differences between products and services, which lead to a clear conclusion: service marketing is different (Upah, 1985). The literature on the uniqueness of services marketing continues to expand dramatically (Kotler, 1988; Upah, 1985). Thus, one could see the emergence of a consensus that the differences between goods and services lead to differences in marketing.

This paper will focus on how the special characteristics of services -- intangibility, perishability, variability, and inseparability -- (Kotler, 1988), relate to the promotional techniques of price discounts, personal selling, trade shows and exhibits, free samples, advertising, branding, public relations, and referrals and references.

KEY DISTINGUISHING CHARACTERISTICS OF SERVICES

The four major unique characteristics of services that affect the design of marketing programs are: intangibility, perishability, variability, and inseparability. These characteristics are key to an understanding of the uniqueness of services and will be briefly explained.

Intangibility

Because services are essentially intangible, it isn't possible for consumers' senses to sample or try the services before they purchase them. Service marketing personnel are under pressure because of this limitation. Much of the burden in this case falls on the company's promotional program.

The intangibility characteristic increases the buyers' uncertainty about the degree of need satisfaction achieved by purchasing the service. To reduce uncertainty, the buyers will seek signs or evidence of the service quality. They will draw inferences about the quality of the service from the place, people, equipment, communication material, symbols, and price that they recognize (Kotler, 1988).

Therefore, the service providers' challenge is to "manage the evidence", to "tangibilize the intangible". Whereas product marketers are challenged to add abstract ideas, service marketers are challenged to put physical evidence on their intangible services (Kotler, 1988).

Perishability

The perishability of services means that a capacity (or potential) to provide a service, which is not used in a given day, is a lost opportunity which can't be recovered. Since most services can't be stored, unused services represent business that is lost forever.

Perishability is not a problem if demand is steady, or at least predictable, because it is then possible to plan and staff the personnel needed to provide the service in advance. The market for services (as with products) fluctuates by season, by day of the week, and by the hour of the day. When a peak occurs, service firms have different problems in satisfying all customers since they can't sell from inventory as product companies do. Thus, they must develop promotional strategies for producing a more suitable match between demand and supply of their services.

Variability

The nature, characteristics and quality of people oriented services vary much more than those of products. Manufactured products are more consistent because of the use of machines and equipment which usually have less variations than people. Service industries seem to differ on the extent to which they are "people based" or "equipment based" (e.g., Automatic Teller Machines). An implication of this distinction is that the "results" of people based services have a tendency to be less standardized than the outcomes of equipment based service or goods. Because of heavy people involvement in the "production" of services, there is a higher degree of variability in the provision of services which occurs infrequently when machines are dominant.

Relying on people means being subject to "human variability", in other words, depending on their motivation and efforts, skills and competence, their understanding of policies and procedures, their interpretation of the rules and guidelines, and their daily moods and energy levels. Thus, services dependence on people will lead to significant variations in the process, delivery, performance and outcomes of services. Because of the large number of service industries that are labor intensive this consideration is very important.

Inseparability

Many services are typically produced and consumed simultaneously. This characteristic of services requires people and equipment to be present in a given location in order to provide the needed service. For example, medical services cannot be transported, like products. Many services cannot be mass produced in one location and then transported to be sold to customers in other locations.

The inseparability characteristics of services, and the resulting inability to transport the service(s) to another location creates limitation on organizational growth.

The implications of these four service characteristics on the promotion of services will be discussed below. While many promotional techniques and tools used for products can be effectively used in services, the overall promotional mix is frequently different due to the above characteristics.

212

A CLASSIFICATION OF TRADITIONAL PROMOTIONAL STRATEGIES

There are multiple classifications of promotional services. Some of the traditional promotional services are: price discounts, personal selling, trade shows and exhibits, free samples, advertising, branding, public relations, and referrals and references.

Pricing and Price Discounts

Price operates as a major determinant of buyers' choice. The issue of pricing a product or a service has two key dimensions. First, each company needs to establish a pricing policy for its products and/or services depending on its overall strategy and positioning. Second, each firm has to determine whether it will use price discounts as a promotional strategy and if so, how frequently they will be used, how big the discounts will be, will they be on one, a few, or all items and when will they be used. The first of these falls under pricing and will not be covered here. This paper will take the first as given, and will focus on the second one, i.e., on price discounts. Price discounts take the form of "sales", rebates, coupons, discounts, and two for one sales.

Personal Selling

Personal selling is an oral presentation by a salesperson to a prospective purchaser for the purpose of making a sale. Within this category we include sales presentations, sales conferences, telemarketing, incentive programs, and salesmen samples. Personal selling is essential when one attempts to develop close relationships between a buyer and a seller.

Personal selling is the most effective tool at certain stages of the buying process, particularly in building up buyers' preferences, conviction and action. The reason for this effectiveness is that personal selling, when compared with advertising, has three distinctive qualities: personal confrontation, cultivation of relationships, and immediate response.

Personal selling is very expensive to implement. Personal selling is the firm's most expensive contact tool, costing companies an average of about $300 a sales call in 1987. In 1981, American firms spent over $150 billion on personal selling compared with $61 billion on advertising (Kotler, 1986).

Trade Shows and Exhibits

Trade shows are one of the most frequently used forms of promotion. Trade shows are an excellent place and time to discuss customers' needs with numerous buyers assembled under one roof. This area has been widely used in the promotion of products.

Free Samples

These are free offers of a product or service to a potential consumer in order to make him try it and see its benefits and value without a direct expense to him. Frequently, the free sample comes in a smaller package than the purchased product. The sample may be delivered to one's home, picked up by a customer, mailed or found attached to another product. Sampling is a very effective but occasionally expensive way to introduce a product or a service to new users (depending on variable costs).

Advertising

Advertising is delivering a non-personal communication message to potential consumers or clients. It includes all types of communication except for personal selling and publicity. The purpose of advertising is threefold: 1. to inform potential buyers of the existence of the product or service; 2. to persuade potential buyers to buy the service; 3. to remind and reinforce customers to continue to buy it (Kotler, 1986). As part of the second function, one could include a reference to other promotional tools like the availability of price discounts, free samples, additional services or prizes and gifts.

Advertising is used in a variety of ways, such as TV and radio advertising, print advertising (newspapers and magazines), direct mail, billboards, packaging, brochures and promotional gifts (a "Cubs" hat, a "Coke" T-shirt). In discussing advertising, one can examine the content of the message (copy) as well as its form, its image and atmosphere, its colors and music and other non-content elements.

In most product advertising the product is shown as part of the content of the message. Obviously, in most services this can't be done since the service is intangible and is a process and a set of activities.

Branding

Branding is a strategy of companies to label one or a set of products with a special name. The purpose of branding is to ease a customer's decision making by assuring him of a given quality or other important characteristics (e.g., taste in "chiquita bananas"). Thus, the purpose of branding is to reduce the customer's uncertainty about the consistency, reliability and quality of a product or service. If the customers "accept" the brand name as standing for these characteristics the likelihood of repeat purchase and customers' brand loyalty is increased. Branding tends to be more effective in complex products where most customers cannot pre-judge the quality by the way a product looks (e.g., vcr, tv, bicycle) and less so in commodities which have low differentiation.

Public Relations

Public relations is the activities and process by which an organization builds its external image other than through the sales of its products and services by disseminating information to outsiders about its contributions to society and to employment, export, technology, and knowhow. Public relations typically involves providing positive information on organizational achievements and contributions to society to external organizations in general, and to the mass media in particular. Public relations is really the marketing of the organization as a whole, rather than its products or services (Kotler, 1986). Public relations, if successful, provides unpaid advertising to the firm and creates a positive public image of the firm which is very beneficial to the promotion of its products and services.

THE APPLICATION OF TRADITIONAL PROMOTIONAL TECHNIQUES TO THE MARKETING OF SERVICES

The challenge for service marketing people is to see whether the traditional promotional techniques, previously discussed, are relevant to and effective in service marketing. Simultaneously, should one vary the promotional mix? Should one vary the timing of any of these promotional tools? Which ones are currently under-utilized? These are the questions we will address below.

Price Discounts

Price discounts, sales, or coupons are widely used in the promotion of consumer products. Price discounts are, as a rule, used less frequently in the promotion of services. The main reason for this is a combination of two factors — the "variability" dimension of services (i.e., the quality of the service could be high, medium or low depending on the firm or the specific employee in the firm) and strong perceived price-quality relationship (Curry, 1985; Goering, 1985; Wheatley, 1981). Thus, frequently, if a company temporarily reduces the prices of its service(s) (without a reason) the potential customers are likely to perceive that the services will be of lower quality. Thus, the price is one of the differentiating factors, and changing it may confuse the potential customers.

However, there are firms and situations when price reductions could be used by service companies. These situations have the following characteristics:

1. An established, well known company, whose quality of service is well known.
2. This company's industry is subject to seasonal fluctuations in demand (sales).
3. The company has significant unused resources (people, equipment, etc.).

Examples of companies who fit into these type of situations are United Airlines and Magikist. The airline can afford to promote sales in off season or off peak periods since the quality of its services is well known by most customers and most people understand the seasonal nature of the industry (i.e., they understand the reasons for the discount). Similarly, Magikist promotes its rug cleaning services using price discounts at slow periods.

Price discounts should be clearly distinguished from a low price strategy as used by Southwest or Piedmont Airlines which clearly provide fewer services for the lower price.

A second situation where coupons or price discounts could be used as a promotional device is by a new business which is looking to build up a customer base (in repeat buyer's industries). In this case, in order to reduce the negative impact of the perceived price-quality relationship the company needs to inform the potential customers that the lower prices are only "introductory prices" and do not reflect a low price strategy (interpreted by customers as low quality service).

We have made two observations about the use of price discounts:

(1) Price discounts are not heavily used in the promotion of services due to service "variability" and perceived price-quality relationships.
(2) Due to "perishability", reputable companies do use price discounts to promote their sales during slow periods.

Personal Selling

Personal selling is a major promotional tool whose total cost to U.S. organizations has been larger than any other promotional tool (Kotler, 1986).

Personal selling is used frequently and heavily in the promotion of professional services (e.g., financial planning, insurance, consulting) and the promotion of many business services. The importance of personal selling in the marketing of services is increased due to the "intangibility" of services. Since the buyer cannot see the service (as compared to a product) the role of personal selling is frequently more important and significant. Since the benefits of a service may not be obvious, the sales person needs to explain the nature of the service, its characteristics and the various benefits of the service to the potential customer.

In addition, due to the "variability" of services, the sales person needs to persuade the potential buyer that the service will meet his needs, be of high and consistent quality, and that the service provider has a strong positive reputation and longevity, thus assuring the potential customer that the company will back the service and be responsible and reliable. This is especially important in services like life and home insurance, legal and tax services, and many business services where long term relationships are important and/or the consumption of services may be thirty years later.

A key feature of personal selling in services is the continuous process of selling while the service is provided to the customer (Gronroos, 1980). The "inseparability" characteristic of services, i.e., the fact that in many services the client and the provider spend much time together as part of the process of providing the service (e.g., hair styling, consulting, financial planning, legal services, massage), leads to a situation that the provider's appearance, his behavior and the content of communication during the service delivery will strongly affect the buyer in terms of future purchases. If the appearance is appropriate (e.g., professional dress for a financial planner or consultant), if the activities are perceived as proper, if the work related communication is perceived as appropriate then, it is more likely that repeat buying will take place than if any of these was perceived as inappropriate. Thus, one sells his services (a promotional function) while one is producing

216

(or providing) the service. In addition, while providing one service (e.g., accounting or auditing) one can promote through personal selling additional services the same provider is offering (e.g., consulting, marketing or bookkeeping services).

A fourth feature of personal selling in services is the importance of developing personal trust between the seller and/or (the provider) and the client. Trust, in this case, has two elements. The first relates to the skill and competence of the service provider. When buying a service the customer needs to believe that the provider has the expertise or skill of providing the service at promised quality and timing. This relates to the variability element of services. You trust a cab company that its drivers' know-how to drive safely, and get you to your destination quickly and safely given road and traffic conditions. You trust the dry cleaners to do their best effort to clean your dress without damaging it.

The second dimension of trust in personal selling needs to convey confidentiality. This is especially important in sales of professional services like psychiatric counselling, financial planning, and medical and legal services since the professional (the seller) may be receiving sensitive and confidential information. However, this is even true in the provision of business services like office cleaning. By the time any complaint reaches a manager or the seller, the office has been reused. Thus, the evidence of a complaint based on dirty ash trays or leftover foods may have disappeared. Only mutual trust can overcome this lack of evidence.

Trade Shows and Exhibits

Trade Shows and Exhibits are not widely used to promote services due to the "intangibility" of services on the one hand, and the high cost of demonstrating a relevant service to potential customers, due to the "inseparability" of production and consumption of services, on the other hand.

However, there are service companies, especially those who provide a custom made business service like copying in four colors, or demonstrating a freight billing service using computers, or those who provide specialized training programs for overseas employees, who are using conferences, trade shows and exhibits as an important promotional tool.

Free Samples

Providing free samples to potential customers is a common promotional technique in the marketing of some products. The product characteristics which make it an attractive technique are:

1. Most customers buy the product frequently and repeatedly (toothpaste, deodorant, Diet Pepsi).
2. The product is divisible (i.e., you can give a small tube of toothpaste, bar of soap, or a 4 oz. cup of Pepsi) and the consumer could try it and gain a good idea of the product's characteristics.
3. The cost of the free sample is low (not as high as the cost of a car or TV).

While the technique is well documented in its use in products, its use in the promotion of services seems to be relatively low and it has been stated that only a few practitioners have used it (Upah, 1985). Services have used it in combination with advertising or personal selling. Examples of free samples are lawyers who provide a free session to any new client. During this session the lawyer can impress the client with his skills and professionalism, while providing the client with some legal information and services. Similarly, a chiropractor can promote his services by providing a five minute analysis of a person's bone structure at a running race, and a rug cleaning service could clean one small room or one square foot of a rug to demonstrate the service effectiveness and impress the potential customer. It is the authors' contention that as the service sector becomes more competitive and more marketing oriented the frequency of free samples in services will rapidly increase. Furthermore, we strongly believe it is a highly effective promotional tool which could provide a competitive advantage to those service organizations who will use it effectively.

Branding

Brands create an image of the service or product and as such are a method to differentiate a service from similar ones thus gaining a competitive advantage. Examples of service brands are: Disneyland, American Express, VISA and UCLA College Services, Homart installation (which is part of Sears) (Kotler, 1988). Branding is especially important for service marketing because of the variability and intangibility characteristics of services. Variability means inconsistency of services or variation in type or quality of the service provided. However, customers are trying to avoid or reduce their uncertainty and the variability. One important way to assure clients of the consistency of a service and its quality is to establish a brand name. A second benefit of branding is the development of customer's loyalty leading to repeat buying. Branding in services is not yet as common as with products. Stanton argues that service branding is difficult and complex. "However, ...in branding and standardization of quality, service industries have greater problems (than products). Branding is difficult because consistency of quality is hard to maintain and because the brand can not be physically attached to a service" (Stanton, 1985).

Public Relations

The purpose of public relations is to enhance the image of a company and develop in the public in general, and customers in particular, a positive attitude toward the company. This serves several corporate functions including marketing. An improved public image will usually enhance a firm's sales.

Since services are intangible, and have the variability factor, any additional assurances customers and potential customers can receive as to the company's prestige and reliability could reduce the customers' dissonance regarding future purchases. Thus, promoting a bank's contributions to small businesses or to a cleaner environment, impacts the potential customers' overall attitudes toward the bank and then their inclination to buy its services. In addition, a TV news review of a new bank service is free advertising of the

218

new service. Thus, public relations could be used to enhance a company's image, increase customers' trust and combat the fear of variability.

Advertising

The role of advertising in service industries is similar to its role and importance in products. However, both the content and images of service advertising may differ from those of products. Service advertising cannot "show" the service in most cases. Thus, it needs, and frequently does explain the key benefits of the service (similar to product advertising). However, because of the variability factor it needs to emphasize and strengthen the service provider's image. In particular, it elaborates on the provider's high integrity, longevity, reliability, overall image of quality and excellence of training. To do this, it often uses physical and tangible objects to represent the intangible services (George & Berry, 1981; Kotler, 1988). Examples are the Prudential rock, the Traveler's umbrella, First Chicago's building, and MacDonald's golden arches.

A key function of service advertising, in addition to informing potential customers of the nature of the service, is to portray the company brand name, strengthen its image and inform customers of any special promotions like price discounts and gifts. To balance the variability problem of services, many service advertisers incorporate information about the high standards of corporate training and work policies, which emphasize quality, convenience and service for the customers.

Another advertising content instrument to reduce perceived variability is to quote or show the high degree of satisfaction of past customers. This is also intended to increase the credibility of the message. Advertising supports branding by continuous repetition of the brand name and symbol.

Since services are perishable and inseparable, the timing of advertising is more important in services than in products. A company could increase its advertising efforts during (or just before) off season periods of slow sales and reduce its advertising efforts (or withhold it) during peak periods. This is usually done to match demand and supply and increase corporate sales during low sales periods.

Referrals and References

An important and insufficiently recognized promotional tool in enhancing one's sales is the use of referrals and references. Referrals are names of potentially new customers given to the seller by a current customer. There are several advantages to referrals. They usually include a good target market since the referral, usually a friend of the customer, has frequently similar characteristics to the current customer. Second, the customer's favorable recommendation regarding a service has high credibility to the potential customer and thus it reduces the fear of variability. The customer's implied satisfaction with the service makes the service more credible. In a way, referrals are related to personal selling since either the seller or the customer uses some personal selling.

219

References are names of past or present customers who indicated their willingness to testify about the quality of your service and their degree of satisfaction with it. They increase your message credibility, they reduce the fear of variability, they occasionally serve as a show place, showing the result of the service (e.g., house painting, architecture, gardening) and thus making it more tangible.

Many professional services (financial planning, insurance, consulting, legal services and medical services) rely heavily on references and referrals by current users. References can also be used in combination with, or in advertising.

CONCLUSIONS AND RECOMMENDATIONS

Our review of current practices in the promotion of services leads us to believe that service companies use more personal selling, advertising, referrals and references and public relations than product companies. In contrast, they use less price discounts, branding, trade shows and exhibits, as well as free samples.

Most of the promotional efforts by service companies are directed to balance the impact of perceived variability, intangibility and perishability. In addition, periodic promotional efforts are directed at improved matching of demand and supply due to the perishability and inseparability of services.

The authors suggest that those promotional tools which currently are sparsely used, can and should be more seriously considered by service industries. In particular, the authors propose the following proposals for the enhancement of service companies' promotional efforts:

1. Increase the use of free samples if the conditions listed above (see page 8 of this paper) are in effect. This makes the service (or its benefits) more tangible and reduces fears of variability.
2. Use trade shows and exhibits as a way to demonstrate your service and make it more visible, tangible and credible. It can then be combined with advertising (brochures) and personal selling. It can also be used to differentiate your service from your competitors.
3. Increase the use of branding, if possible, to reduce perceived variability. While this may be difficult for services it is a useful and underused promotional instrument.
4. Timing — use promotional techniques in general, and price discounts, advertising and personal selling in particular, during slow sales periods. This is important because of the perishability and inseparability of services.
5. Look for ways to increase the use of referrals and references. These low cost promotional techniques can be developed and refined to lead you to desired target groups, to reduce perceived variability and to make the service or its benefits more tangible.
6. Advertising content needs to focus on the service provider's reliability and prestige (to reduce fear of variability), on past users' satisfaction (more tangible), and on increasing receivers' understanding of

the nature of the service. The image of the service or service company should be conveyed by the use of something tangible (e.g., the piece of the rock, the money given out in American Express ads).

7. In advertising and personal selling emphasize personal relationships, personal contact, personal and friendly service, trust and confidence. This is especially important in people oriented services with repeat buying (banks, dry cleaning, hotels, airlines, and professional services). These elements of personal service play a much more significant role in services than in products. They need to be covered in advertising, personal selling, as well as in referrals and references.

This paper suggests three directions for future research. First, scholars and practitioners can and should conduct empirical studies on the frequency and effectiveness of the suggested promotional techniques, in spite of the inherent difficulties in conducting such studies. Second, one can choose a particular segment of the service industry like the financial service industry, legal services, business consulting, or personal counselling and examine the particular promotional techniques used in that industry and their effectiveness. This narrow focus on one industry can be of more use to practitioners since it would be more specific.

A third area for future investigation is to focus on one (or two) promotional technique in two or more service industries and compare the frequency and amount (dollars) of use and its comparative effectiveness. One could take our proposition regarding price discounts (see page 6) and subject them to an empirical test.

Obviously, much more empirical and theoretical research needs to be done on the promotion of services. Specifically, we need to focus on the measurement, use and effectiveness of the promotional techniques discussed in this paper.

REFERENCES

Barker, T. and Gimpl, M.L., "Differentiating a Service Business: Why and How", Journal of Small Business Management, April 1982, pp. 1-7.

Curry, David J., "Measuring Price and Quality Competition", Journal of Marketing, Vol. 49, Spring 1985, pp. 106-117.

George, William R., and Berry, Leonard L., "Guidelines for the Advertising of Services", Business Horizons, July/August 1981, pp. 52-56.

Goering, Patricia, "Effects of Product Trial on Consumer Expectations, Demand, and Prices", Journal of Consumer Research, Vol. 12, June 1985, pp. 74-82.

Gronroos, C., "Designing a Long Range Marketing Strategy for Services", Long Range Planning, April 1980, pp. 36-42.

Gummesson, Evert, "Toward a Theory of Professional Services Marketing", Industrial Marketing Management, April 1978.

Kotler, Philip, <u>Principles of Marketing</u>, Prentice Hall, Englewood Cliffs, N.J., 1986.

Kotler, Philip, "Managing Services", in <u>Marketing Management</u>, Sixth Edition, Prentice Hall, Englewood Cliffs, N.J., 1988, pp. 476-481.

Shostack, G. Lynn, "Breaking Free From Product Marketing", <u>Journal of Marketing</u>, April 1977, pp. 73-80.

Stanton, William J., "Marketing of Services", Chapter 44, in Britt, Steuart Henderson, and Guess, Norman F., (eds.), <u>Marketing Manager's Handbook</u>, Dartnell, Chicago, 1983, pp. 667-683.

Upah, Gregory D., "Services Marketing", in Edwin E. Bobrow and Mark David Bobrow (eds.), <u>Marketing Handbook</u>, Vol. 1, Dow Jones-Irwin, Homewood, IL, 1985, pp. 95-108.

Wheatley, John J., Chiu, John S.Y., Goldman, Arieh, "Physical Quality, Price, and Perceptions of Product Quality; Implications for Retailers", <u>Journal of Retailing</u>, Vol. 57, Summer 1981, pp. 100-113.

QUALITY CONTROL TECHNIQUES IN SERVICES MARKETING

Alfred L. Guiffrida
Canisius College

Michael J. Messina
Gannon University

Abstract

Service quality is becoming an increasing more important
concern for marketing managers and executives. Many studies
have been initiated to define service quality and to develop
conceptual models for its implementation. In this paper we
demonstrate the usefulness of Pareto analysis, Ishikawa cause
and effect (Fishbone) diagrams, and process control charts as
techniques for aiding management in the control of service
quality. Difficulties which may be encountered when using
traditionally product oriented quality control techniques in
the service marketing environment are discussed.

Introduction

Service quality is becoming an increasing important concern for
marketing managers and executives. The activities of quality
gurus such as Deming, Juran, Feigenbaum, and Crosby has
rekindled a tremendous resurgence among manufacturers that
quality is a key source of competitive advantage. Paralleling
these developments in manufacturing, there has been substantial
advancements in the literature devoted to quality in the
service sector.

Several factors account for the increased importance that is
being placed on quality in service industries. Competition
from foreign and domestic sources has intensified. Firms are
forced to continually improve the quality of the services that
they offer to stay competitive. Consumers are becoming
increasing more sophisticated and selective in their decisions
to purchase services. As services continue to make up a larger
share of the economy, consumers will have more choices when
selecting a service and a greater ability to compare the
quality of a service. The impact of service liability has
forced firms to proceed cautiously in marketing services and in
some instances forced them to exit from certain markets.

Many scholars have developed conceptual models for explaining the quality characteristics of services marketing. Considerable research has also been initiated to define service quality and to devise strategies for implementing quality in service industries. A summary of selected research studies on service quality is presented in Table 1. Based upon a review of the literature on quality in services marketing, we feel that research is needed in the development and application of techniques that can be used in controlling service quality. In Figure 1 we present a model of the service process. The service vendor is represented as an input/output submodel through which resource inputs such as manpower, capital, marketing intelligence data, and technical expertise are transformed into a marketable service. The service output is then targeted at the customer. The service quality assurance program acts as a filter and feedback mechanism throughout the macro service model. Crucial elements in the quality assurance system are sensors (quality control techniques) which identify any breakdown or erosion in the level of service quality desired by management.

Service Quality Control Techniques

Pareto Analysis

Pareto analysis involves the categorization of quality related attributes according to their frequency of occurrence. In Pareto analysis a bar chart is constructed which lists the attributes under study on the horizontal axis and their frequency of occurrence on the vertical axis. Attributes are displayed from left to right in decreasing order of magnitude. The attributes used in a Pareto analysis may be any indicators of quality that are of interest to management. A Pareto chart is illustrated in Figure 2. In this hypothetical illustration, customer complaints in airline service represent the quality attributes under study.

The Pareto concept involves the separation of the "vital few from the trivial many". The need for quality improvement in a service can be readily identified through the use of Pareto analysis. By examining the Pareto chart, management's attention is directed at the quality attributes possessing the greatest relative frequencies. Quality improvement efforts can then be concentrated on the quality attributes which are contributing the most to poor service quality.

TABLE 1
SELECTED STUDIES ON QUALITY IN SERVICES MARKETING

Conceptual Models of Service Quality

Zeithaml, Berry, and Parasuraman (1988)
Parasuraman, Zeithaml, and Berry (1985)

Defining Service Quality

Williams and Zigli (1987)
Lewis and Klein (1987)
Berry, Zeithaml, and Parasuraman (1985)
King (1985)
Lewis and Booms (1983)

Implementation Frameworks for Service Quality

Kacker (1988)
King (1987)
Butterfield (1987)
Cary et al (1987)
Haywood-Farmer et al (1985)
Shetty and Ross (1985)
Scanlon and Hagan (1983a, 1983b)
Hostage (1975)

General Discussions on Service Quality

Rosander (1985)
Fitzsimmons and Sullivan (1982)
Langevin (1977)
Juran (1975, 1974)

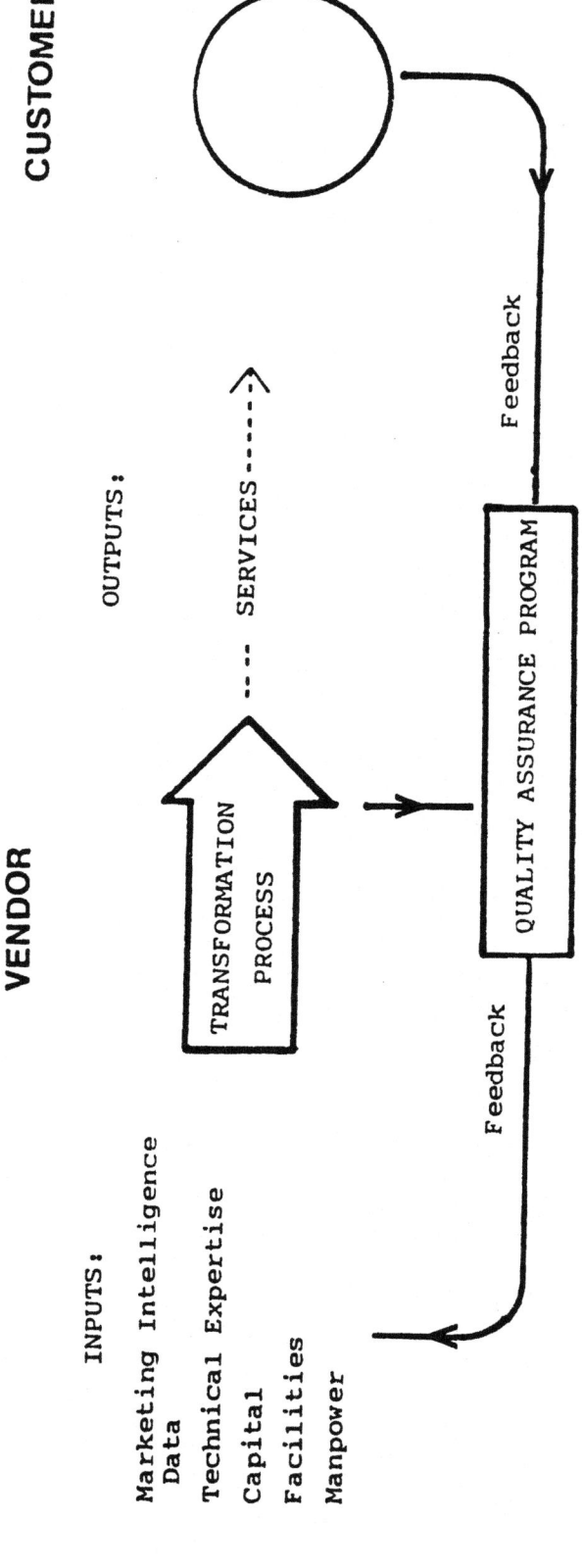

Figure 1
Service Process Model

Figure 2
Pareto Analysis

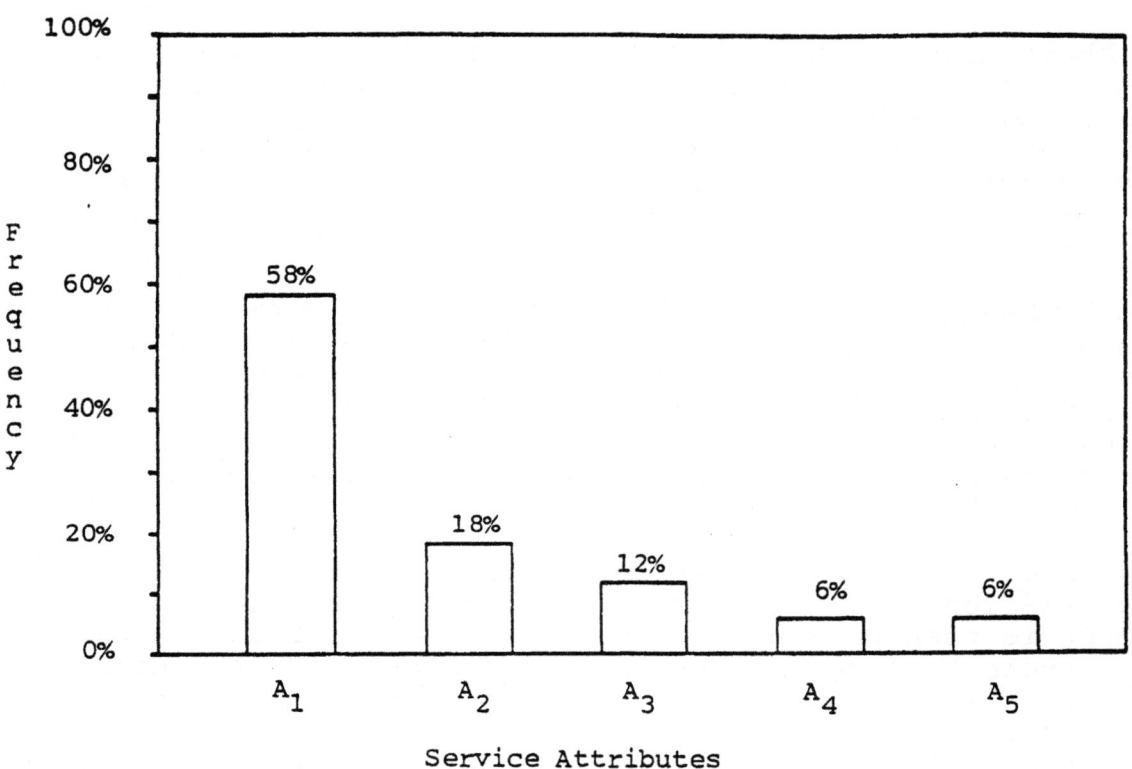

Service Attributes

Key: A_1 = Flight Delays

A_2 = Lost Baggage

A_3 = Discourteous airline personnel

A_4 = Uncomfortable seating

A_5 = Other

227

Ishikawa Diagrams

Cause and effect diagrams (also known as Ishikawa or Fishbone diagrams) represent another useful tool for controlling service quality. Ishikawa (1985) defines a process to be a collection of cause factors which must be controlled to obtain better products and efforts. Cause factors are often interlocked and dependent on one another. The cause and effect diagram can be used to systematically and scientifically examine the relationships that exist among the cause factors.

Fishbone diagrams flow backwards from the effect, e.g. the quality problem under investigation, and then branch out toward the causes. Maximum benefit is derived from using the diagrams when they are constructed by a group of individuals in a brainstorming session. The group should consist of individuals who are familiar with the process providing the service and the quality problem under study.

The Fishbone diagram in Figure 3 has been constructed to study customer complaints received in a grocery market. Based on a Pareto analysis, service delay when checking out was identified as a frequent customer complaint. The effect in this illustration is customer complaints of excessive delays when checking out. Cause factors are shown in a nested hierarchy that resembles the skeleton of a fish.

Major headings in this particular analysis include organization, equipment, workers, and layout. Each major factor is then broken down into specific cause areas which contribute to slowness in processing a customer through the checkout line in the grocery. By using the cause and effect diagram to examine this service system as a whole composed of a set of prioritized and interrelated parts, management will have a clearer understanding of the effect and will be able to more efficiently develop strategies to correct the service quality problem.

Process Control Charts

A control chart is a graphic comparison of the performance of a process to computed control limits. All processes have random variation associated with them. The goal of process control is to find the range of natural variation of the process and to ensure that the output from the process stays within this range. When a process is operating within the control limits it is said to be in a state of statistical control or "in control". If the process is operating outside the control

Figure 3
Ishikawa Cause and Effect (Fishbone) Diagram

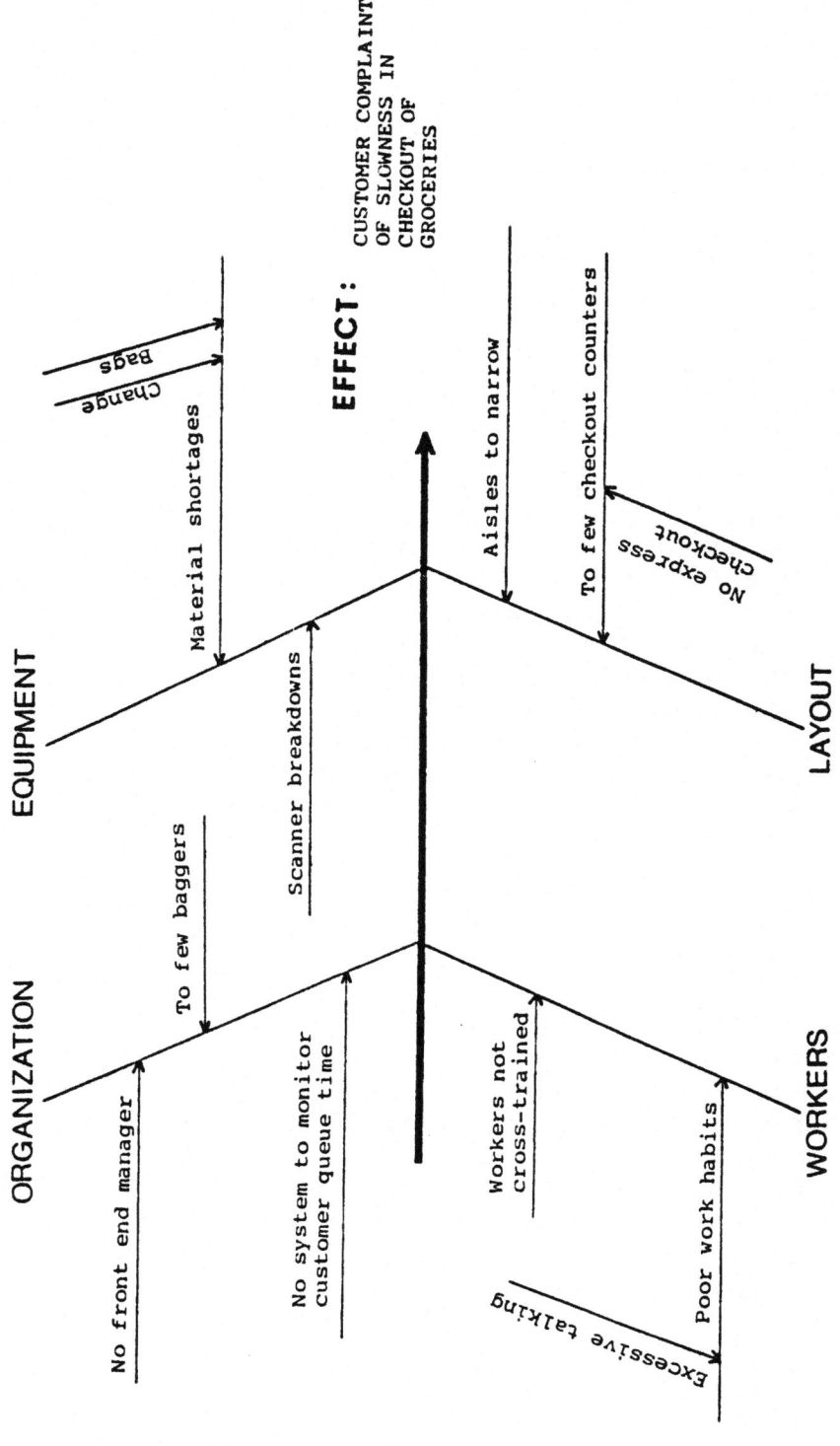

229

limits it is "out of control". The upper and lower control limits bound the natural variation that is inherent in the process. A process that is out of control is a signal to management that extraneous variation has entered into the process. Management should then study the process and determine the causes of the extraneous variation. Once identified, the assignable causes can be eliminated and the process put back into control. A process control chart is shown in Figure 4.

The control limits used may be specified by management, or statistically determined by collecting measurements from the process itself. Once the control limits are established, a small sample of observations is periodically taken from the process and used to determine if the process is operating in control or out of control.

There are several types of control charts that are applicable for controlling quality in services. Control charts may be based upon variable or attribute measures of service quality. The X-bar and R (range), or the X-bar and S (standard deviation) charts may be used in tandem for variable measures such as the length of time required to issue a replacement credit card or the average waiting time experienced by a customer in a fast food restaurant. Attribute charts such as the P (percent defective), or the C (number of defects) may be used to monitor characteristics such as the percent of complains per 1000 customers, or the number of customer complaints received per week.

Discussion and Summary

This paper has illustrated the use of Pareto analysis, cause and effect diagrams, and process control charts as techniques to assist management in controlling service quality. Limitations must be recognized in applying product oriented quality control techniques to service quality problems. Quality control techniques have been traditionally applied to manufacturing processes. The quality characteristics of manufactured products can be readily defined and measured. Services typically have more attributes than products, many of which are difficult to define and measure. As a result, service quality is difficult to define. If a high level of uncertainty exists in defining what is to be controlled, quality standards are difficult to establish and any control techniques used will be less efficient. Applications of quality control techniques in service systems have been limited

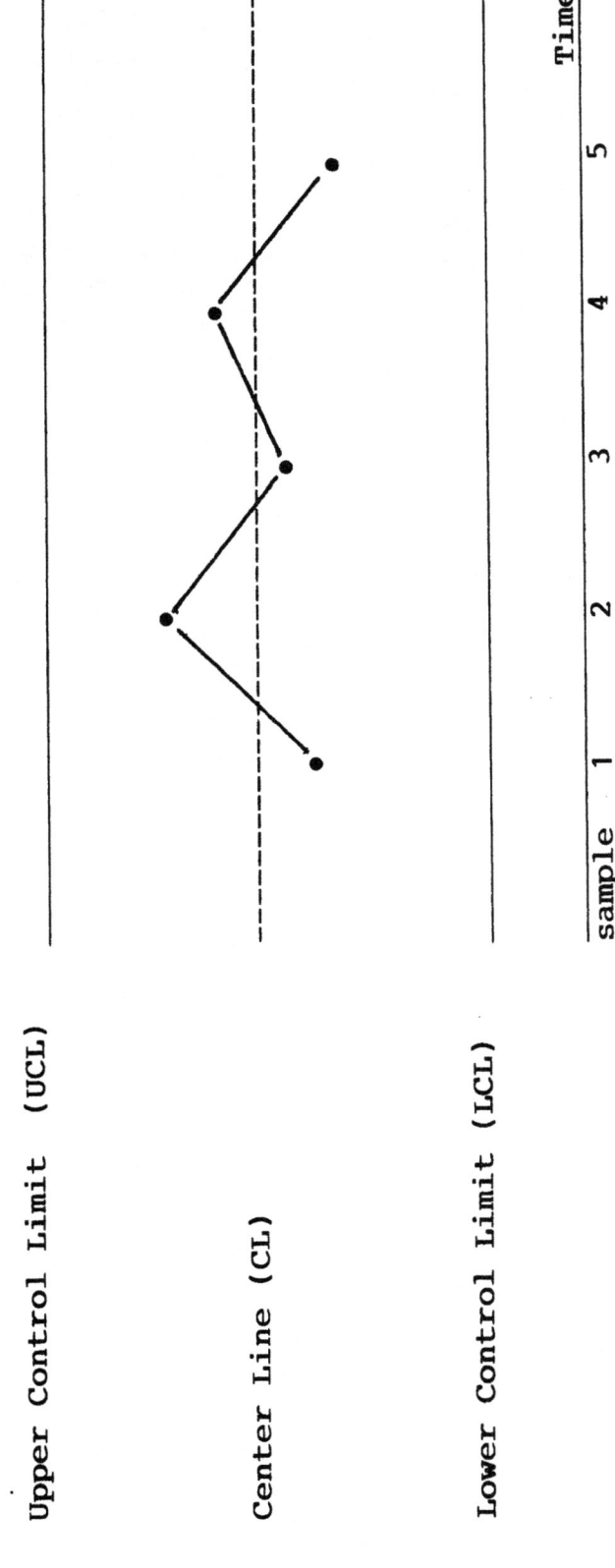

Figure 4
Process Control Chart

mainly to the technical aspects of providing service. This may
be due to the intangible characteristics of the service itself
and the difficulty in identifying the standards by which a
customer uses to evaluate quality when receiving a service.
The lack of data and formal data reporting systems in many
service environments limit the applicability of quality control
methodologies. Despite these limitations and obstacles, there
is a business value to controlling quality in the service
sector. Quality control techniques such as Pareto analysis,
cause and effect diagrams, and process control charts are
useful tools for helping managers control service quality.

References

Berry, L., Zeithaml, V. A., and Parasuraman, A. "Quality Counts in Services, Too". <u>Business Horizons</u>. 28(3), May/June 1985, 44-52.

Butterfield, R. W. "A Quality Strategy for Service Organizations". <u>Quality Progress</u>. Dec. 1987, 40-42.

Cary, M., Kay, B., Orleman, P., Robertshaw, W., Ross, G., Saunders, D., Wallace, W., and Wittenbraker, J. "The Customer Window". <u>Quality Progress</u>. June 1987, 37-42.

Fitzsimmon, J. A., and Sullivan, R. S. <u>Service Operations Management</u>. 1982, New York: McGraw-Hill, Inc., 363-386.

Haywood-Farmer, J., Alleyne, A., Duffus, B., and Downing, M. "Controlling Service Quality". <u>Business Quarterly</u>. 50(4), 1985, 62-67.

Hostage, G. M. "Quality Control in a Service Business". <u>Harvard Business Review</u>. July/August 1975, 98-106.

Ishikawa, K. <u>What Is Total Quality Control? The Japanese Way</u>. 1985, Englewood Cliffs, N.J.: Prentice-Hall, Inc.

Juran, J. M. "Quality Control of Service - the 1974 Japanese Symposium". <u>Quality Progress</u>. April 1975, 10-13.

Juran, J. M., (Editor). <u>Quality Control Handbook</u>. 1974, New York: McGraw-Hill, Third Edition, section 47.

Kacker. R.N. "Quality Planning for Service Industries". <u>Quality Progress</u>. August 1988, 39-42.

King, C. A. "A Framework For A Service Quality Assurance System". <u>Quality Progress</u>. September 1987, 27-33.

King, C. A. "Service Quality Assurance Is Different". <u>Quality Progress</u>. June 1985, 14-18.

Langevin, R. G. <u>Quality Control in the Service Industries</u>. 1977, New York: AMACOM.

Lewis, R. C., and Klein, D.M. "The Measurement Gaps In Service Quality". <u>The Services Challenge: Integrating for Competitive Advantage</u>. Proceedings Series, AMA. Chicago, 1987, 33-38.

Lewis, R. C., and Booms, B. H. "The Marketing Aspects of Service Quality". <u>Emerging Prospectives on Services Marketing</u>. Proceedings Series, AMA. Chicago, 1983, 99-104.

Parasuraman, A., Zeithaml, V. A., and Berry, L. L. "A Conceptual Model of Service Quality and Its Implication for Future Research". <u>Journal of Marketing</u>. 49(4), Fall 1985, 41-50.

Rosander, A.C. <u>Applications of Quality Control in the Service Industries</u>. 1985, New York: Marcel Dekker, Inc.

Scanlon, F., and Hagan, J. J. "Quality Management for the Service Industries - Part I". <u>Quality Progress</u>. May 1983, 18-23.

Scanlon, F., and Hagan, J. J. "Quality Management for the Service Industries - Part II". <u>Quality Progress</u>. June 1983, 30-35.

Shetty, Y. K., and Ross, J. E. "Quality and Its Management in Service Businesses". <u>Industrial Management</u>. 27(6). Nov/Dec 1985, 7-12.

Williams, R. H., and Zigli, R. M. "Ambiguity Impedes Quality in the Service Industries". <u>Quality Progress</u>. July 1987, 14-17.

Zeithaml, V. A., Berry, L. L., and Parasuraman, A. "Communication and Control Processes in the Delivery of Service Quality". <u>Journal of Marketing</u>. 52(2), April 1988, 35-48.

SOME CRITICAL DISTRIBUTION PROBLEMS IN
SERVICES MARKETING

C. P. Rao
University of Arkansas

A. Ben Oumlil
University of Dayton

Abstract

One of the more pervasive problems in services marketing today is the problem of services distribution. This paper discusses some of the critical problems of services distribution and its related issues -- people and environmental control, lack of agreement among the services marketing academicians etc. Lastly, the paper concludes with some observations of the present state of affairs and recommendations for services marketing managers.

In the past decade or so, the field of services marketing has been attracting considerable academic attention. This is consistent with the growing services orientation of the U.S. economy and the marketing challenges created by the changing environmental conditions in service industries, such as deregulation.

Basically services marketing is distinguished from product marketing by the fact that the "product" in the case of service industries is intangible, its production and consumption largely inseparable, incapable of being stored, and almost impossible to standardize. These and other differences are considered to be the main factors which distinguish services marketing from product marketing. Although in the past many academicians differed in their expositions whether services marketing required a different strategy than product marketing, for some time now there seems to be a general consensus that services marketing is significantly different from product marketing (Lewis, 1985; Booms et. al., 1981; George and Kelly, 1983; Uhl and Upah, 1983; and Langeard et. al., 1981). However, agreement that services marketing is different still leaves a "Pandora's box" of problems for the services industries, since the optimum services marketing strategies have yet to be evolved. From this perspective, one area of particular concern is the distribution of services -- how to get the service to the customer efficiently and effectively. This paper identifies some of the critical problems that arise in effective distributing services, reviewing the diverse academic points of view and suggesting some approaches.

235

The significant problems of services distribution can basically be divided into three segments: (a) lack of established channels, (b) delivery methods and their limitations, and (c) lack of agreement on the best method of distribution.

Lack of Established Channels:

The lack of established channels can be traced to at least two factors: the newness of some of the services marketing applications and some long held managerial attitudes in services industries. The services marketing revolution in the country is relatively new compared to agricultural and manufactured goods marketing, which preceded and have a long history. Many service industries are just realizing the scope and potential for a systematic application of marketing to improve their performances. Consequently, the type of marketing systems which include a distribution system, and what one can find in relation to agricultural and manufacturing sectors, are often missing in many service sectors.

Managerial attitudes have played a significant part in this lack of development of well-established channels of distribution in many service industries (Baranoff and Donnelly, Jr., 1970). In the past many service industry managers have enjoyed the luxury afforded by monopolies due to strict government regulation, especially in such service industries as banking, transportation, etc. In these industries the service managers did not have to use marketing methods, such as the development and management of channels of distribution, in order to compete -- since competition was not a problem. The fact that most services will not become obsolete has also contributed to management complacency. For example, when the nature of demand for many services is so basic and essential, and competitive pressures were minimal in the past, the net result is that there are no incentives to develop efficient marketing systems and channels of distribution as a part of such systems.

Delivery Methods and their Limitations:

At the very basic level, service industries require three methods of delivering services: those involving the physical presence of the customer in which (a) the customer must come to the service organization facility or (b) the service provider must go to the customer, or (c) those not involving the physical presence of the customer, but rather the use of intermediaries or high-tech innovations. All these types of delivery methods have their unique problems. Although some overlap exists among these delivery methods, enough distinction remains to allow a separate discussion of each of these methods. However, from the perspective of distribution, only the first two methods of service delivery -- customer-to-the-service mode and service-to-the-customer mode -- are relevant. Therefore, these two methods will be discussed.

Customer to the Service:

If all customers came to the point of service delivery, this would indeed solve a lot of problems for the service deliverer or provider. Needless to say, not all customers are willing to come to the service provider, particularly if the service provider is not conveniently located. Willingness of the customer to travel depends upon the customer's personal involvement with the service being sought. For example, patients will travel a considerable distance for the services of a medical specialist -- say for the treatment of cancer. Alternately, customers will not travel long distances for a haircut. This facet of customer behavior presents unique marketing problems for those service providers for whose services the potential customers are willing to travel considerable distances. Since the majority of these service providers are likely to be professionals, they may have to depend almost entirely on interpersonal communication networks or word-of-mouth advertising. Even though professional ethics and the law are changing to allow professionals to advertise their services, considerable evidence indicates that the public is still unfavorably disposed towards professional advertising. Under these circumstances, expanding the scope of the professional service provider's market to a broader geographic area would invariably involve taking the service to customers. This becomes necessary because of the geographic area limitations of the word-of-mouth spread process.

Service to the Customer:

In this mode of providing service, two basic methods exist: (a) direct service from one location or (b) service from many locations (branch offices or franchising). In reality neither method approaches the ideal situation of the service provider actually contacting each individual customer, as the need for service arises. With few exceptions where the service has to be provided on the premises of a customer, (e.g., plumbing and other household services), direct delivery of service by the service provider is becoming mostly extinct. A clear example of this phenomenon is doctors making house calls. Other services in this category include door-to-door delivery of milk, groceries, etc. However, door-to-door delivery of certain services may be revived in the future as American society becomes more convenience oriented, and time becomes a more scarce resource in our daily lives. Such a revival of door-to-door services has many implications for service distribution costs, organization, and efficiency on the part of the service provider. Some service providers are using the direct delivery mode as a differentiating feature in their marketing strategies. Here one may cite the example of Domino's Pizza in a highly competitive pizza business, and the changes that are taking place in the pizza distribution systems of various companies in this industry.

A more frequently used distribution approach in many services industries is to provide multiple locations of service, where the service provider can more readily go nearer to the customer and the customer can more conveniently reach the service provider. In recent years these distribution goals have been accomplished through the use of branch offices or franchising. Although at first glance this method of service delivery may seem to be the panacea, it presents one major problem -- quality control.

According to Kotler and Bloom (1984), branch offices utilize several methods of control: (a) by providing information and expertise to the branch offices, (b) by offering financial incentives to the branch offices, and (c) by utilizing legal agreements (franchising). However, even with good control measures and systems for branch offices, problems can still occur. Consider the example of a large chain of legal offices. This chain found itself in an uncompromising position when two distant branch offices were discovered to be representing opposing parties in a common legal action (Kotler and Bloom, 1984).

Franchising is fast becoming the most practiced method of distributing services and achieving the corporate goals of market expansion. According to one report, in 1981 new outlets were opening at the rate of 47 per day (Harris, 1982). However, it was also reported that many failed due to the unwillingness of the franchisees to spend sixty to eighty hours per week to make the businesses succeed. The franchise system is also plagued with the problem of franchisers often not delivering on their promises (Harris, 1982). Even though the distribution method of franchising has had some success in controlling the quality of service through the use of standardized procedures, many problems still exist.

The fast-food chain McDonald's offers an outstanding example of an effort to expand the distribution nationally and internationally, and at the same time offer consistent quality. Levitt (1974) describes in detail how McDonald's has achieved this feat of quality control by utilizing a series of finely tuned standardized procedures for doing every activity by the franchisees -- even detailed steps to be followed for producing consistent quality french fries. On the other hand, Sasser and Arbeit (1976) criticized this approach as being impractical in that while it may profit in the shortrun by using manufacturing techniques, it will also suffer the same drawbacks as manufacturing. More specifically, the authors contend that standardization of tasks will eventually contribute to job dissatisfaction and deterioration of employee performance. Since unskilled workers are usually employed in many service environments, the authors further contend that turnover will be high, and of those employees who do stay, many will be promoted and thereby removed from the area in which they are needed the most, (e.g., high customer contact positions.)

Control of People and Environment:

Since many service industries require the presence of the customer for service delivery (referred to as "inseparability" by many authors), two factors become important. These factors are first, the employee-customer relationship, and second, the environment of the service location. These twin problems arise whether the customer comes to the service or the service comes to the customer. (Examples are a customer coming to a bank to open a new checking account and an insurance salesperson coming to a customer's home to sell an insurance policy.)

When such a one-to-one relationship exists between the employee and the customer, the employee's behavior becomes crucial. Service delivered in a courteous, friendly and consistent manner becomes essential for successful

238

operation of the service organization. However, given the inadequacies of human behavior, even the most highly qualified and well-trained employees cannot produce standard, consistent and "appropriate" behavior day after day.

Proper control of the environment of the service location is also important. Kotler (1974) emphasizes the overriding importance of what he calls "atmospherics" for effective marketing. Although Kotler is not limiting the importance of "atmospherics" exclusively for services marketing, it is interesting to note that several of his examples are related to service businesses. So important is the buying environment that Kotler states: "As other marketing tools become neutralized in the competitive battle, atmospherics is likely to play a growing role in the unending search of firms for differential advantage." (1974, p.64)

How can the buying environment create problems? One would assume that through proper designing of the environment conducive for the service business, this problem would be resolved. However, two problems arise when customers come to such a carefully designed environment. These are related to the interaction of customers with each other and with the environment. Often many customers are at the service location at the same time, and frequently they must wait for the service to be provided (for example, in a barber shop). Here lies the potential trouble -- unfavorable word-of-mouth advertising can readily be spread by one dissatisfied customer. While unfavorable word-of-mouth advertising can spread at other locations, the service location simply provides a better environment for dissemination.

Moreover, customers who interact with the environment (or service location) do not always show respect for the environment and often destroy or damage the "atmospherics" intended by the service provider. For example, consider a medical specialist's office. Perhaps the specialist desires to have his/her office waiting area to be quiet, dignified and clean. If patients are loud, unkept, and messy in the waiting room, the entire image is ruined and patients who otherwise may be satisfied with the services of the medical specialist, may discontinue their patronage because of the environmental problems.

INTERMEDIARIES AND HIGH TECHNOLOGY

For those services which do not require the physical presence of customers, distribution of services is more flexible and the distribution channel can be extended through the use of intermediaries. As a matter of fact, many services do use intermediaries. Lewis (1985) provides an exhaustive list of thirty-three service industries which use intermediaries (See Appendix A). Lewis classifies these intermediaries into two categories: (a) franchisers (those requiring the physical presence of the customer, which was discussed earlier), and (b) locations that provide access (libraries for computer services, shopping malls for telephone services, etc.). He also points out that the development of tangible representations of a service will allow further use of intermediaries.

There are several potential problems associated with using intermediaries which need to be addressed in the interests of improving services marketing. First, franchising presents several problems, as discussed previously. Second, using intermediaries as an access device can cause further problems. For example, an intermediary may not provide as much access as the service user would like. For example, a computer user may need to use a computer for longer hours than is permissible in the library. It is conceivable that after a few episodes of not having access to the computer when needed, the customer will seek other alternatives. Or consider the example of an airline using a travel agency. The "danger" here lies in the fact that such an intermediary could recommend a competitor. To avoid such problems, a services marketing manager could bypass an intermediary through effective use of high-technology innovations. Through creative designing of the appropriate communications and information processing technologies, many service providers may find many opportunities to reduce their dependence on intermediaries and the attendant problems. Through these technologies service providers can reach customers directly and minimize the problems of dealing with and controlling the intermediaries in the service distribution process.

The current high-tech "revolution" has caused quite a bit of excitement and definitely caught the attention of many services marketers as a means of reaching more customers directly. However, some problems persist even with the use of the high-tech innovations.

According to Sasser and Arbeit (1976), there are three reasons why high-tech solutions may not be as successful as presumed by many writers. First, many service businesses are small and thus cannot afford truly innovative high-tech systems for reaching their clientèle directly. Second, in some service sectors high-tech methods cannot be utilized effectively as a means of channel extensions, (e.g., medical care.)

Additionally, the use of high-tech innovations can cause problems with employees and customers. Many employees feel threatened by the introduction of high tech for at least two reasons: one, it will most likely mean a change in their accustomed way of doing business, plus necessitate learning a new skill; and two, it may mean the replacement of some employees. Needless to say, no employee wants to be replaced by a machine. Even more serious is the problem of resistance to high-tech innovations by customers.

A recent study arrived at some significant conclusions regarding the use of high-tech innovations. (Langeard, Bateson, Lovelock and Eiglier, 1981). The study noted that consumers could be divided into two groups: the participators and the nonparticipators. The participators are those consumers who readily take to self-help devices. They are typically young, male, and higher educated than the average person. The nonparticipators are just the opposite. These findings are consistent with another study by Fouss (1985). This latter study, which focuses on the consumer usage of automatic teller machines, concluded that the majority of users are younger (18-34 age group). These two findings point out a potential problem, that the older segment of the population resists such innovative behavior.

Since the older segment of the population is expected to be the largest population segment in the future (Phillips and Sternthal, 1977), and the older consumers are likely to be the "nonparticipators", will this not have a limiting effect on the use of high-tech innovations?

One final note regarding the use of high-tech self-help devices concerns frustration due to mechanical failure. Frustrations caused by the mechanical failure and/or unsatisfactory service by these devices can prove to be potential problems. The services marketing managers should address these issues when they design and implement these substitutes to using intermediaries in their distribution systems. No matter what one's personal opinion might be regarding the usefulness, efficiency, and consumer acceptability of these high-tech innovations, they seem to have a pro-life rating. What remains to be seen is how helpful these innovations can be in solving the distribution problems in services marketing. It would be very beneficial for the services marketing practitioners if at least the academic experts agreed on a preferred mode of distribution.

LACK OF AGREEMENT

Perhaps practitioners could better grasp the problems of service distribution if the academicians and researchers agreed on the optimum method of solving the distribution problems in service sectors. Suggestions range from using high-quality and well-trained employees to using "hard" and "soft" technologies. Sasser, Arbeit, George, Kelly, Cook and Bessom are some of the experts who believe that well-trained, customer-contact employees is the answer to the distribution problems of service businesses. On the other hand, Levitt believes technological systems is the solution. Perhaps, the optimum method is not one method, but a combination of methods depending upon the type of service being offered, as suggested by Langeard, et. al.

CONCLUSION

As the service industry continues to grow and as competition increases, there will no doubt be a more concerted effort to solve the problems of distribution. At present, however, no concrete answers have been found. In the mean time, let us hope the following comment by a disgruntled service customer is not indicative of the state of affairs in the marketing of services in the country:

> We want you, unless we have to be creative or courteous or better than barely adequate. In that case, get lost. (Mitchell, 1984)

For the services marketing manager, this is a time of caveat venditorum. Management complacency today can deliver a fatal blow and the astute services marketing manager will prepare for tomorrow by tackling the problems of service distribution today.

APPENDIX A

Table 1

TYPES OF SERVICE BUSINESSES THAT USE
MARKETING INTERMEDIARIES

Accounting and Tax Services
Agricultural Services
Airlines
Automotive Repair & Service
Auto Wash
Auto Rental
Building Construction
Campgrounds
Catering Service
Child Day Care Centers
Coffee Services
Communication Services
Computer Services
Collection and Credit
Dance Studios
Database Services
Dry Cleaning & Laundry Services

Employment Agencies
Food Operations
Financial Services
Freight Services
Health Care Services
Hotels and Motels
Insurance Companies
Lawn Services
Legal Services
Pest Control
Printing and Duplicating
Real Estate
Tax Services
Theatres
Travel Agents
Vending Operations

REFERENCES

Anderson, W. Thomas, Jr., Eli P. Cox III and David G. Fulcher, "Bank Selection Decisions and Marketing Segmentation," _Journal of Marketing_, Vol. 40 (January 1976), pp. 40-45.

Baranoff, Seymour and James H. Donnelly, Jr., "Selecting Channels of Distribution for Services," in Buell (ed.), _Handbook of Modern Marketing_, McGraw-Hill (1970), pp. 4-43; 4-50.

Bell, Martin L., "A Matrix Approach to the Classification of Marketing Goods and Services," in Donnelly and George (eds.), _Marketing of Services_, Chicago: American Marketing Association Proceeding Series, 1981, pp. 208-212.

Bessom, Richard M., "Unique Aspects of Marketing Services," _Arizona Business_, Vol. XX, No. 9 (November 1973), pp. 8-15.

Bessom, Richard M. and Donald W. Jackson, Jr., "Service Retailing: A Strategic Marketing Approach," _Journal of Retailing_, Vol. 51, No. 2 (Summer 1975), pp. 75-84.

Booms, Bernard H. and Mary J. Bitner, "Marketing Strategies and Organization Structures for Service Firms," in Donnelly and George (eds.), _Marketing of Services_, Chicago: American Marketing Association Proceedings Series, 1981, pp. 47-51.

Chase, Richard B., "Where Does the Customer Fit Into a Service Operation?" _Harvard Business Review_, Vol. 56 (November-December 1978), pp. 137-42.

Cooke, Blaine, "Analyzing Markets for Service," in Buell (ed.), _Handbook of Modern Marketing_, McGraw-Hill (1970), pp. 2-41; 2-51.

Donnelly, James H., Jr., "Marketing Intermediaries in Channels of Distribution for Services," _Journal of Marketing_, Vol. 40 (January 1976), pp. 55-57.

Enis, Ben M. and Kenneth J. Roering, "Services Marketing: Different Products, Similar Strategy," _Marketing of Services_, American Marketing Association Proceedings Series, 1981, pp. 1-4.

Fouss, James H., "Distribution Changes for Financial Services," in Black et al. (eds.), _Services Marketing in a Changing Environment_, American Marketing Association Proceedings Series, 1985, pp. 102-106.

George, William R., "The Retailing of Services--A Challenging Future," _Journal of Retailing_, Vol. 53, No. 3 (Fall 1977), pp. 85-98.

George, William R. and Patrick Kelly, "The Promotion and Selling of Services," _Business_, (July-September 1983), pp. 14-18.

Glover, W. Gerald, R. Scott Morrison, Jr. and Alfred C. Briggs, Jr., "Making Quality Count: Boca Raton's Approach to Quality Assurance," The Cornell H.R.A. Quarterly, (May 1984), pp. 39-45.

Harris, Marlys, "Opportunities in Franchising's New Wave," Money, Vol. 11 (February 1982), pp. 76-82.

Johnson, Eugene M., "The Selling of Services," in Buell (ed.), Handbook of Modern Marketing, McGraw-Hill (1970), pp. 110-121.

King, Carol A., "Service-Oriented Quality Control," The Cornell H.R.A. Quarterly, (November 1984), pp. 92-98.

Kotler, Philip, "Atmospherics as a Marketing Tool," Journal of Retailing, Vol. 49, No. 4, (Winter 1973-74), pp. 48-64.

Kotler, Philip, Marketing for Nonprofit Organizations (2nd ed.), Prentice-Hall, Inc. (1982), pp. 319-329.

Kotler, Philip and Paul N. Bloom, Marketing Professional Services, Prentice-Hall, Inc. (1984), pp. 185-197.

Langeard, Eric, John E. G. Bateson, Christopher H. Lovelock and Pierre Eiglier, Services Marketing: New Insights from Consumers and Managers, Marketing Science Institute (August 1981).

LaTour, Stephen A. and Nancy C. Peat, An Experimental Investigation of Responses to Service Quality Inequity, Center for Consumer Research, Working Paper Series, College of BA, University of Florida.

Levitt, Theodore, "Marketing Myopia," in Enis and Cox (eds.), Marketing Classics, Allyn and Bacon, Inc. (1973), pp. 3-23.

Levitt, Theodore, "Production-Line Approach to Services," Harvard Business Review, Vol. 50 (September 1972), pp. 41-52.

Lewis, M. Christine, "Applying the Concept of Marketing Channels to Services Requires Some Modification," in Black et al. (eds.), Service Marketing in a Changing Environment, American Marketing Association Proceedings Series, 1985, pp. 98-101.

Lovelock, Christopher H., "Classifying Services to Gain Strategic Marketing Insights," Journal of Marketing, Vol. 47 (Summer 1983), pp. 9-20.

Lovelock, Christopher H. and John Quelch, "Consumer Promotions in Service Marketing," Business Horizons, Vol. 26 (May-June 1983), pp. 66-75.

Mackney, Kemsey J. and Mindy Zinn, "A Mobile Resource for Older Persons," in Cooper (ed.), Health Care Marketing, Aspen Systems Corporation (1979), p. 141.

Mitchell, Jim, "Service with a Smile? Not by a Mile," <u>Wall Street Journal</u>, (October 9, 1984), p. 1.

Nord, Walter R. and J. Paul Peter, "A Behavior Modification Perspective on Marketing," <u>Journal of Marketing</u>, Vol. 44 (Spring 1980), pp. 36-47.

Parasuraman, A., Valarie A. Zeithaml and Leonard L. Berry, <u>A Conceptual Model of Service Quality and Its Implications for Future Research</u>, Marketing Science Institute (1984).

Peter, J. Paul, James H. Donnelly, Jr. and Lawerance X. Tarpley, <u>A Preface to Marketing Management</u>, (revised edition), Business Publications, Inc. (1982), pp. 181-192.

Phillips, Lynn and Brian Sternthal, "Age Differences in Information Processing: A Perspective on the Aged Consumer," <u>Journal of Marketing Research</u>, Vol. XIV (1977), pp. 444-457.

Sasser, W. Earl and Stephen P. Arbeit, "Selling Jobs in the Service Sector," <u>Business Horizons</u>, (June 1976), pp. 61-65.

Shostack, G. Lynn, "Breaking Free from Product Marketing," <u>Journal of Marketing</u>, Vol. 41, No. 2 (April 1977), (page unknown).

Stern, Louis W. and Adel I. El-Ansary, <u>Marketing Channels</u>, Prentice-Hall, Inc. (year unknown), pp. 541-575.

Uhl, Kenneth P. and Gregory D. Upah, "The Marketing of Services: Why and How Is It Different?" (source unknown).

Upah, Gregory D., "Mass Marketing in Services Retailing: A Review and Synthesis of Major Methods," <u>Journal of Retailing</u>, Vol. 56, No. 3 (Fall 1980), pp. 59-76.

GUEST FEEDBACK AND COMPLAINT HANDLING
IN THE HOSPITALITY INDUSTRY

Tim R.V. Davis, Ph.D.   Nicholas Horney, Ph.D.
Cleveland State University   Stouffer Hotels

Abstract

A continuous flow of guest feedback is essential for improving the quality of service provided by hospitality firms. Research and writing dealing with different sources and uses of guest feedback is reviewed along with alternative methods of processing feedback and ways of integrating it with other management systems. The paper concludes with a description of the approach to managing guest feedback used by Stouffer Hotels and Resorts.

Service businesses need continual input and feedback from customers to adjust their marketing, operations, and personnel practices. This is especially true of the hospitality field. Whereas corporate management can exercise great control over the advertising and production of manufactured goods, corporate management has no such control over the marketing and production of hotel and restaurant services. The truisms that "you are only as good as your last show" and that "service is a locally manufactured item" apply in full force to the hospitality field. Corporate management can set clear procedures and standards for service delivery and create consistent impressions and expectations in the advertising but, unless the practices and standards are upheld at each hotel, the customer may well be disappointed and the prospect of repeat business will be lost. The lack of direct control over decentralized operations makes it essential for management to receive a steady stream of guest feedback to assess the customer satisfaction with hotel services.

Many service businesses rely on inadequate means of assessing and responding to consumer needs at the local level (Daltas, 1977). The dominant type of feedback used by corporate management to control local operations is usually financial (sales revenue, expenses, profit). Much of this feedback is usually delayed and after the fact. By the time higher management discovers through financial reports that one of the units is operating below par or losing business, many customers may have already been lost. Financial reports only indicate that something is wrong; they usually do not indicate what is wrong or why it is wrong. Valid, continuous guest feedback is essential to tracking customer satisfaction with hotel operations and to identify problems as they arise.

To its credit, the hotel industry was one of the first businesses to recognize the need to solicit feedback and suggestions from customers. The main sources of feedback used by hotel management include: guest comment cards, surveys, focus groups, and unsolicited letters/telephone calls from guests. Some of the main issues of concern are: What can be learned from guest feedback? What does this information reveal about customer preferences? What source of feedback is most valid and representative? How can more guests be encouraged to provide feedback? What can this feedback be used for? Should this information be processed at the local, property level or at the corporate, headquarters? How should complaints be handled? In order to answer these questions, previous writing and research will be reviewed. The paper will conclude with an examination of the crossfunctional impacts of customer feedback and a description of the approach used by Stouffer Hotels and Resorts to integrate it with other management systems.

WHAT DO GUESTS COMMENT ABOUT? WHAT CAN BE LEARNED FROM GUEST FEEDBACK?

Several studies have examined the type and quantity of feedback received from hotel guests. Cadotte and Turgeon (1988) analyzed surveys carried out by the American Hotel and Motel Association which asked member executives (mainly general managers in individual properties) to list the incidence of frequently received compliments and complaints from guests. The study did not investigate the methods used by the hotel managers to obtain guest feedback.

The rank ordering of most frequently received compliments and complaints listed in Table 1 is a summation of survey responses received from 260 lodging managers representing 280,000 rooms. On average, according to the managers, 70 percent of the feedback received from guests involved compliments and 12 percent involved complaints. As can be seen, the top 10 compliments and the top 10 complaints were quite divergent. Only quality of service and employee knowledge and service ranked high on both lists. The vagueness of these terms make it difficult to interpret exactly what is meant here. The value of the survey lies less in the precise definition of categories and more in providing general guidelines on what guests compliment or complain about. Based on their analysis of the data, Cadotte and Turgeon proposed that attributes of guest satisfaction can be classified into a fourfold typology depending on how likely a particular attribute is to elicit compliments or complaints. According to their model, attributes of guests satisfaction can be classified as "satisfiers," dissatisfiers," "criticals," and "Neutrals."

Satisfiers are those variables where unusual performance draws compliments but average performance or even the absence of the feature will probably not cause dissatisfaction or complaints. Component aspects of the physical setting such as spectacular atriums or lobbies, hanging plants, glass-encased elevators, or large open spaces fit this category. According to Cadotte and Turgeon, satisfiers are noticeable attributes that represent an opportunity for hotels to differentiate themselves from one another. Customers are receptive to higher levels of performance on these attributes as evidenced in their willingness to go out of their way to compliment the establishment. Dissatisfiers are attributes that draw complaints for low performance or the absence of the feature. Parking is an example of a dissatisfier. If guests are always able to find a space, they think nothing of it. However, if no parking spaces are available, they are quick to complain. Dissatisfiers represent the necessary or basic industry standards of service performance that equivalent hotels are expected to maintain. Other examples would be the acceptance of different types of credit cards and

247

acceptably cleaned rooms. <u>Criticals</u> are variables that are capable of producing both compliments and complaints from guests. Quality of personal service, for instance, ranked high on both lists. Others may be food quality and employee knowledge. These are factors that Cadotte and Turgeon describe as the heart of the hospitality industry on which the customer's zone of indifference may be quite narrow. From a managerial standpoint, criticals may represent both an opportunity and a threat. At the very least, management must monitor these factors closely so that, at least, minimum acceptable standards are met. <u>Neutrals</u> are attributes of hotel operations that received neither compliments not complaints in the survey. They are factors of hotel operations that guests feel indifferent about. They are either non-salient features of hotel operations or factors that can easily be brought up to guests' standards. Uniformity of the establishment's appearance and quality of advertising, may fit this category.

Table 1

COMPARATIVE RANKINGS OF HOTEL
ATTRIBUTE COMPLIMENTS AND COMPLAINTS

Attribute	Complaint Rank	Compliment Rank
Price of rooms, meals, services	1	15
Speed of service	2	11
Quality of service	3	4
Availability of parking	4	17
Employee knowledge of service	5	5
Quietness of surroundings	6	10
Availability of accommodations	7	18
Checkout time	8	23
Cleanliness of establishment	9	2
Adequacy of credit	10	21
Accuracy of bill	11	25
Helpful attitude of employees	12	1
Quantity of service	13	8
Traffic congestion in establishment	14	24
Neatness of establishment	15	3
Responsiveness to complaints	16	12
Variety of service	17	13
Overbooking	18	22
Hours of operation	19	19
Spaciousness of establishment	20	9
Management's knowledge of service	21	7
Employee appearance	22	16
Convenience of location	23	6
Quality of advertising	24	20
Uniformity of establishment appearance	25	14

(Source: Adapted from Cadotte and Turgeon, 1988, p. 48.)

Cadotte and Turgeon suggest that the satisfiers and dissatisfiers that top each list are probably the attribute areas that management needs to pay particular attention to. These may be performance areas that customers regard most seriously when making a decision to stay at a particular hotel. They are the factors that guests care most about. Dissatisfiers require minimum standards of acceptable performance to be met. The focus should be on maintaining these standards comparable to the competition without wasting resources trying to better them. In contrast, satisfiers represent an opportunity to stand out from the pack on variables that matter to guests. Spending money to improve these attributes may produce greater customer satisfaction and repeat business. Criticals must meet minimum performance levels to avoid customer complaints but also represent an opportunity to excel.

Partial support for some of Cadotte and Turgeon's ideas can be found in some earlier work done by Lewis (1983, 27-28). He investigated the types of compliments and complaints received in a 175 bed chain hotel over an 18 month period. He classified the compliments and complaints received into 1) physical environment (noise, decor, parking, view, atmosphere, ambience, accommodations, room location, etc.), 2) physical goods (food and beverage quality, climate control, temperature of pool, elevator service, cleanliness, furniture condition, pool, etc), 3) service and personnel (reservation handling, management attitude, level of service, etc.), and 4) expectations (disconfirmed expectations in relation to advertising, available facilities, packaged plan delivery, price-value, etc.). Lewis did not present raw numbers for compliments and complaints received in these areas.

The most compliments (49%) and fewest complaints (17%) were received by the hotel for aspects of the internal or external physical environment. This is consistent with the aspects of the physical environment that Cadotte and Turgeon classified as "satisfiers." An area in which a high number of compliments (31%) and complaints (40%) were received was physical goods. This may be considered comparable to Cadotte's and Turgeon's "criticals," although the types of variables listed by Lewis in this category do differ. Surprisingly, perhaps, Lewis found that services and personnel was a definite "dissatisfier." Only 9% of the compliments were received on this category but 32% of the complaints. Again there is some discrepancy here. Cadotte and Turgeon listed "quality of employee service" as a "critical." The category, "expectations," is not a specific hotel attribute but it does suggest that if the customers' expectations (through advertising or price-value assumptions) are not confirmed, they will tend to be dissatisfied. Twenty percent of the complaints could be attributed to this and only 2% of the compliments (expectations fulfilled or exceeded). Care is needed in setting service levels in the advertising and promotion that can be achieved in each property. In the hotel study by Lewis, a number of facilities (pool, sauna, dining room) that had been advertised were closed when customers wanted to use them. Apparently, operating efficiencies superceded guests' needs. This tends to invite guests criticism and dissatisfaction.

As these studies indicate, guests feedback is valuable for deciding the relative emphasis that is given to attributes in the marketing and advertising of hotels. This feedback is also helpful for pointing out what guests really care about, the features they notice, and the areas in which improvements are likely to increase guest satisfaction.

HOW VALID AND REPRESENTATIVE IS GUEST FEEDBACK?

The guest feedback discussed in the foregoing studies was obtained from surveys, unsolicited letters, and guest comment cards. In Lewis' (1983) study, 241 communications were received from guests following hotel stays during the 18 month period investigated. Twenty-nine percent of these responses were received on comment cards and 71% on unsolicited letters. Lewis does not give the total number of guests or reservations during the study period so that it is not possible to state what proportion of the guest population responded. However, these figures do give some indication of the very low rates of return of guest comment cards. If more than twice as many people took the trouble to write letters, this suggests the comment cards are filled out by a minuscule proportion of the guests. A study by Trice and Layman (1984), which will be discussed later, found that just over 1% of guests filled out comment cards. Such low rates of return, reduce the representativeness of these cards.

Lewis and Pizam (1981) have drawn attention to the questionable content validity of the commonly used guest comment card which asks a small number of vaguely defined questions. They have also suggested that mainly dissatisfied customers tend to fill them out so that these cards may provide a biased or slanted view of customers' reactions to hotel services. They contend that many of the cards currently in use can only be relied upon to give gross measures of customers satisfaction or dissatisfaction. For example, a typical five item comment card with five point scale -- evaluating 1) room condition, 2) food quality, 3) performance of the front office, 4) housekeeping, 5) food and beverage staff -- may give management some ongoing norms of performance in these areas but they certainly give no indication of what the hotel has done right or wrong if performance is rated above or below normal levels. To make them more effective, customer comment cards need to be longer and more detailed so that clearer explanations can be provided. Also, the ratio of returns has got to be increased so that a broader crossection of guests fill them out, not just complainers. This issue will be discussed further in the next section of the paper.

Another form of guest feedback is the unsolicited guest letter either complimenting or complaining about the hotel. How valid and representative is this form of feedback? In many instances, guests may prefer to write letters to explain and justify complaints or compliments. The main advantage of the complaint letter is that it is written from the customer's perception of the situation (Hudson and Ozanne, 1988). A criticism of comment cards and surveys is that the issues tend to be framed from management's point of view. Guests' letters usually describe problems and probable causes in rich detail. Because the management of many hotels insists on follow-up to investigate all customer complaints, the in depth problem solving that ensues often uncovers underlying issues that deserve attention. The main drawback with this type of guest feedback is that it is difficult to interpret, quantify, and tabulate. Again, like comment cards, it may also not be representative of the majority of hotel guests.

Lewis and Pizam (1981) emphasize surveys as the most valid approach to evaluating customer satisfaction. They suggest various steps to increase the validity and usefulness of the data collected. They recommend starting with a series of focus group sessions to determine broad areas of customer satisfaction. The next step is to have guests rate the importance of each of these factors. These factor ratings can then be regressed against an overall measure of customer satisfaction with the hotel in order to produce coefficient weights indicating the relative importance of each dimension to overall guest satisfaction. The final survey containing the significant dimensions of guest satisfaction can then be interpreted in terms of the weights assigned to them. Lewis and Pizam (1981) emphasize that customer research should be made specific to the individual property. For multi-site, chain hotels, they propose a core set of dimensions dealing with issues of common concern in all hotels and a small subset of items that deal with issues of concern in a particular type of property. For example, resort, convention, and airport properties have different customer needs. Questions need to be included to address these differences. They also recommend a series of follow-up surveys to investigate, in more depth, areas of particular concern to management.

HOW CAN MORE GUESTS BE ENCOURAGED TO PROVIDE FEEDBACK?

Given the importance of customer feedback to evaluating the quality of services, it is essential to make it easy for guests to provide their input and to actively encourage a greater volume of feedback. This is also a way to make the comment cards more representative of the guest population. Trice and Layman (1984) examined different formats of guest comment cards and different ways of distributing the cards in order to increase the return rate. Their studies were conducted at four hotels -- two Rocky Mountain resorts and two franchise operations adjacent to interstate highways in Virginia. In these hotels, the commonly used five item customer comment card was placed in each room with the stationery and room service menu. In each case, the comment card return rate was slightly above 1% and an average of 64% of these cards contained at lease one negative comment.

The investigators experimented with different numbers of questions and different ways of distributing the cards to guests. In one experiment, guests were asked at checkin to fill out the cards that were in their rooms and, in another experiment, guests were asked at checkout to fill out the cards they received at that time. In each instance, guests were told that the hotel was undergoing an evaluation and the forms would be used to improve guest services.

Compared to the previous very low response rates with no prompting, both experimental conditions produced much higher returns of the comment cards. The best rate of return was achieved when guests were asked at checkout, but those recruited at checkin returned more than 10 times the number of cards than the conventional practice of leaving the card in the room with no prompting.

Trice and Layman also tested the effects of different reward systems on improving the response rate. A one dollar tarrif reduction was offered to guests who returned the cards on checking out. In this case, 400 guests were

251

asked to help with a study of the hotel. Half the guests were offered the one dollar discount and half were offered no incentive but were just prompted on checkout. This resulted in 33.5% of the incentive group returning comment cards compared to 14% for the non-incentive group who were just prompted. This is in comparison to the total of 13 cards (1%) that were returned out of 1,128 guests who stayed at the hotel during the time the study was undertaken. These guests were neither prompted nor offered a small reward. Negative comments were found on 12% of the incentive group's cards, 25% of the non-incentive group's cards and virtually all of the 1% of the cards that were returned with no reward or prompting. These results suggest that prompting and a small financial reward may boost the rate of return and reduce the incidence of negative comments. More research is needed to determine if the greater incidence of positive comments is a reflection of a more representative group of guests or if the modest reward tended to elicit a more favorable rating.

Trice and Layman also tested alternative comment card formats that varied the specificity of the items and the number of questions asked. A ten item form and a 15 item form were added to the standard five question format. Generally, it was found that the longer forms with 10 to 15 specific items were returned in greater numbers than the short five item form with broad questions. In another part of this study, 100 guests who had not returned cards were contacted to find out the reason(s) for not responding. The two most common responses were 1) "there was nothing negative to report" (56% and 2) "no action would follow a complaint" (39%). The first, and most often provided, explanation lent support to the idea that most guests perceive the comment cards as a device for registering complaints. In all of these studies discussed here, the comment cards were returned to the individual property's front desk. No research was done comparing front desk returns with mailed returns to the hotel company's corporate offices.

The problem of countering low response rate and obtaining a representative sample are also a problem with administering surveys. Lewis and Pizam (1981) suggests doing surveys intermittently. Comment cards have become common place in hotels. Most guests ignore them. Intermittent, rather than ongoing, surveys, may be more effective. They suggest leaving them in more prominent places, such as on the guest's pillow. Like Trice and Layman, they also recommend reminders at checkout and small rewards, such as a free drink at the bar or a free continental breakfast.

Another approach that holds promise of increasing the level of guest feedback is the computerized questionnaire. Cadotte (1979) tested an electronic device that looks like a small cash register and performs like a bank, automatic teller machine except that it asks guests to give their responses to a ten item questionnaire. The test took place over a three week period in four individual properties of four major hotel chains (budget to medium price range). The push button device was placed in a visible spot close to the checkout desk in the lobby of the inns. On average, 15% of the guests used the electronic questionnaire to evaluate the service they had received -- a much higher response rate than usually achieved with comment cards. Most guests also said they preferred this type of questionnaire to comment cards. The device was hooked up to the house computer which enabled both local and corporate management to receive instantaneous feedback on performance.

Advances in electronic technology that offer guests new services may also provide a more efficient channel of guest feedback. Many hotels are experimenting with rapid checkout procedures through the TV set in each guest's room. The potential exists to build the evaluative questionnaire into the checkout procedures as a standard routine.

HOW SHOULD GUEST FEEDBACK BE PROCESSED?

If the management of a hotel tries to boost the amount of feedback from guests, then management had better be able to deal with the issues and problems that the feedback may raise. There are different schools of thought as to how this feedback is best managed. One view is that the general manager of each property is in the best position to decide on the type of feedback that needs to be solicited from guests -- in other words, each property does its own market research -- as well as decide what action should be taken in response to this feedback. The main advantage of this approach is that the general manager has maximum freedom to adapt hotel services to meet local needs. Another advantage is that complaints can be responded to immediately by local management. Information does not have to be moved up and down the line. The main disadvantage of this approach is that there may be less uniformity of action across hotels. If local management's bonus rides mainly on hitting revenue and profit targets, the temptation may be there to skimp on the level of service provided to customers in order to cut costs.

An alternative approach is for the corporate headquarters to oversee the quality of service offered at each hotel and to determine the feedback solicited at the local level and the actions to be taken in response to customer complaints. This may allow top management to stay in close touch with customer reactions at each hotel, overall market trends, and ensure that consistent action is taken in response to guests' complaints. The disadvantage of this approach is that top management may lack sufficient understanding of customer needs at the local level, and may be slow in responding to problems that may arise at each property. This approach may also compromise local management's initiative in negotiating mutually agreeable solutions to customer problems.

Understandably, the most interest in processing feedback centers on processing complaints. If complaints can be efficiently resolved, the guest may become a repeat customer. In general it is easier to settle complaints with malfunctioning products or goods than it is to resolve service complaints. What compensation should hotel guests be offered for rudeness by front desk employees, missed wakeup calls, or slow room service. Refunds and complimentary rooms can be given to guests for more serious problems, but it is often very difficult to determine appropriate levels of compensation or redress for different guests complaints and problems. A major consideration here is the effect of negative word of mouth publicity spread by dissatisfied guests. Few businesses receive as much negative word of mouth as hotels and restaurants. If each dissatisfied guest tells between 5 and 10 other people, this can significantly affect future patronage.

In Lewis' (1983) follow-up study of guests who had registered complaints with a hotel, customers were asked how likely they would be to choose this hotel again. In response to this, 50% of the guests said they probably would stay at the hotel again, 30% said they probably would not, and 20% said they were unsure. Guests were then asked to weight the main factors in their decision to return or not to return. In the case of the complainers, the substance of the complaint (i.e. the nature of the particular problem) was weighted most heavily (4.06%) followed by the level of disturbance the complaint had engendered (3.60%), the way the complaint was handled (3.00%), and the overall attitude of the hotel (2.56%). The substance of the complaint was considered the main factor by those who said they would not return, while the way the complaint was handled was considered the main factor by those who said they would return to the hotel.

Based on his research, Lewis (1983) contends that guests of middle income are more likely to use a comment card to compliment or to complain than those of high incomes. Females are more liekly to complain or compliment using the comment cards than males. Frequent users of franchise or chain hotels are likely to complain or compliment about different hotels in the chain but less likely to comment if they are repeat customers at the same hotel. Finally, those guests who have written previous compliments to the hotel are significantly more likely to complain when dissatisfied. Unfortunately, most research has shown that most dissatisfied customers do not complain to the company to which they are displeased; they just silently take their business elsewhere (Landon, 1977). Hotels need to make it easy for guests to complain, supply multiple channels for doing so, and provide fast, efficient follow-up to resolve any problems.

HOW IS GUEST FEEDBACK INTEGRATED WITH OTHER MANAGEMENT SYSTEMS?

A crucial determinant of how seriously customer feedback and complaint handling is taken is the extent to which it is woven in with top management goals and other management systems. The examination of an organization's goals, critical success factors, and information feedback, can usually reveal the level of integration.

Geller (1985) conducted a survey study of 74 executives representing 27 leading hotel companies. Included in the survey were a broad spectrum of different types of hotels. Geller examined the goals, critical success factors, and information feedback used by these executives to manage their hotel. Table 1 rank orders the goals that were common to most hotels while Table 2 lists the critical success factors (CSFs) that executives considered most crucial to the accomplishment of these goals. As can be seen, profitability or ROI was clearly the number one goal followed by growth, best management, and market share. The CSFs that the executives considered essential to the achievement of these goals were employee attitude, guest satisfaction, superior product, and location.

The number one CSF ranking given to employee attitude maybe somewhat surprising but it suggest the importance that hotel executives attach to the impressions made by employees in achieveing profit, growth and market share. The second ranked critical success factor, guest satisfaction, may have been expected to be ranked above employee attitude; however, its second place ranking may suggest an awareness on the part of the executives that employee attitude may contribute

most to guest satisfaction and, therefore, should precede it in importance.
The relatively low ranking of revenue maximization and cost containment may
also suggest the executives' awareness that pushing sales and trying to contain
costs may negatively impact guest satisfaction. In other words, if employee
attitude and guest satisfaction are considered the primary CSFs, the major
goals of sales, profit and market share will be taken care of.

<table>
<tr><td colspan="3">Table 2
GOALS MOST FREQUENTLY
MENTIONED BY RESPONDENTS</td></tr>
<tr><td>Goal</td><td>Number of
Responses</td><td>Rank</td></tr>
<tr><td>Profitability, return
  on investment</td><td>20</td><td>1</td></tr>
<tr><td>Growth</td><td>15</td><td>2</td></tr>
<tr><td>Best management (includ-
  ing image)</td><td>14</td><td>3</td></tr>
<tr><td>Greatest market share</td><td>12</td><td>4</td></tr>
<tr><td>Guest satisfaction</td><td>12</td><td>4</td></tr>
<tr><td>Shareholder wealth--value</td><td>9</td><td>5</td></tr>
<tr><td>Employee morale</td><td>9</td><td>5</td></tr>
<tr><td>Maximize cash flow</td><td>5</td><td>6</td></tr>
<tr><td>Brand loyalty</td><td>5</td><td>6</td></tr>
<tr><td>Financial stability</td><td>4</td><td>7</td></tr>
</table>

Table 2
GOALS MOST FREQUENTLY MENTIONED BY RESPONDENTS

Goal	Number of Responses	Rank
Profitability, return on investment	20	1
Growth	15	2
Best management (including image)	14	3
Greatest market share	12	4
Guest satisfaction	12	4
Shareholder wealth--value	9	5
Employee morale	9	5
Maximize cash flow	5	6
Brand loyalty	5	6
Financial stability	4	7

Table 3
CSFs MOST FREQUENTLY MENTIONED BY RESPONDENTS

CSF	Number of Responses	Rank
Employee attitude	25	1
Guest satisfaction (service)	21	2
Superior product (physical plant)	19	3
Superior location	11	4
Maximize revenue	8	5
Cost control	8	5
Increase maket share	6	6
Increase customer price-value perception	5	7
Achieve market segmentation	4	8

Table 4
MEASURES MOST COMMONLY USED BY RESPONDENTS TO MONITOR CSFs

Measure	Number of Responses	Rank
o Occupancy percentage	30	1
o Guest comment cards	29	2
o Turnover (employee)	21	3
o Inspections	18	4
o Average rate	15	5
o Rate of promotion (internal hire)	15	5
o Rate of repeat business	14	6
o Rate of return (on investment)	12	7
o Sales ($)	10	8
o Profit (or cash flow)	9	9
o Scientific sampling (of guest)	9	9
o Complaint letters	8	10
o Gross operating profit	7	11
o Outside "shoppers"	6	12
o Employee opinion surveys	6	12

(Source: Geller, 1981, pgs. 80-81.)

The final part of the survey investigated the quantitative measures or feedback
used by the executives to monitor the critical success factors. Tabe 3 lists
the measures in rank order. The top ranking measures, occupancy rate and
responses on guest comment cards, are measures of customer satisfaction as are
inspections, average room rate, rate of repeat business, guest surveys, and guest

letters. Feedback from guest mystery shoppers can assess employee attitude and those aspects of hotel operations that are visible to the customer. Employee turnover, rate of internal promotion, and employee opinion surveys are human resource measures. The remainder are financial measures dealing with revenues, profit and cash flow. Other measures mentioned, but in lower frequency, were market share, market research reports, employee grievances, and the reservations backlog.

The goals, critical success factors, and measures used by these 27 leading hotel companies are probably typical of the objectives and feedback systems used by most established hotel companies. The heavy reliance on guest comment cards as a means of measuring guest satisfaction may be considered somewhat surprising in view of their dubious validity. Similarly, given the impact of employee attitude and other aspects of hotel operations on guest satisfaction, it is surprising that a more precise system of measurement is not in place to evaluate these critical aspects of hotel services. While Geller did not examine how management used these measures, the approach seems to rely on a variety of vaguely interrelated methods as a means of tracking the critical success factors.

When a variety of feedback mechanisms are used to collect different types of information, it is essential to define what the information will be used for and how it will be integrated. The various forms of feedback discussed throughout this paper may be regarded as separate sources of information needed to support different functions. However, the uses of this information cut across all functional lines of hotel operations. Customer feedback collected from surveys or comment cards could be used for many different purposes (Figure 1). For example, customer feedback on service quality may be used as input to incorporate planning, goal setting, and marketing programs; to determine the need for corporate intervention at the local management level; to assess department performance (front desk, housekeeping, restaurant and lounge, etc.): to appraise management and employee performance; to decide on bonus pay and training needs; to revize policies, procedures, and hotel standards; and to plan future properties and facilities. Given the fact that virtually every department of a hotel at both the corporate and local level can initiate actions or programs that influence the customer, top management will either have to coordinate these activities and programs very closely or appoint a person or department who can. A good example of a department put in place to watch over the needs and interests of the customer is the Office of Guest Relations at Stouffer Hotels and Resorts.

Stouffer Hotels and Resorts Feedback and Complaint Handling System

The role of the Office of Guest Relations at Stouffer is to represent and protect the customer's interests, to collect customer feedback, process complaints, and develop incentive programs to encourage customer responsiveness. This department has developed a composite index of guest satisfaction, called the Guest Satisfaction Index (GSI), based on four approaches to evaluating service quality:

1) A guest Satisfaction Survey
2) An Operations Survey Report
3) Guest Comment Cards
4) Unsolicited guest letters and telephone calls

256

Figure 1

CROSSFUNCTIONAL USES OF CUSTOMER FEEDBACK IN HOTEL MANAGEMENT

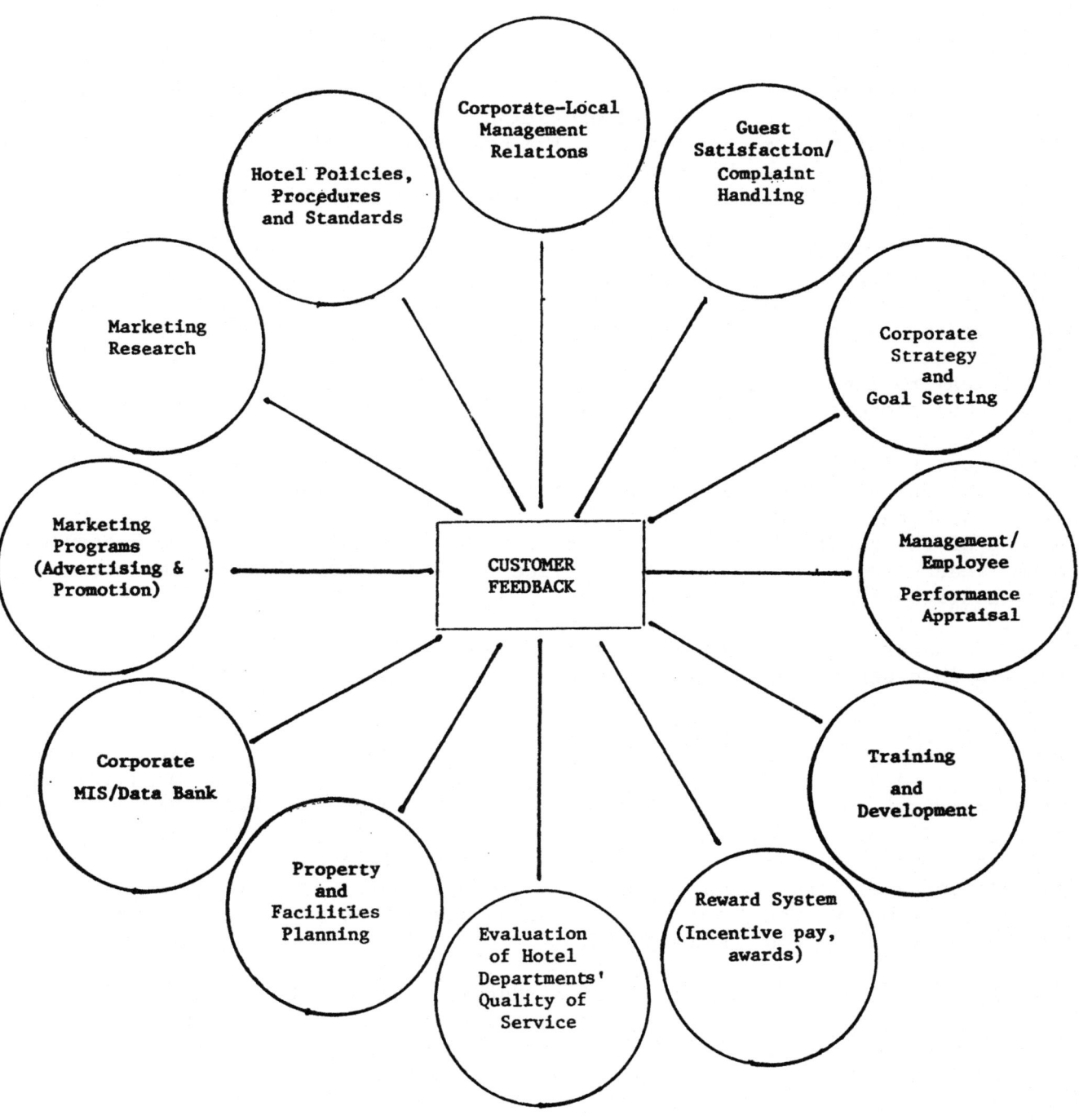

The Guest Satisfaction Survey and the Guest Comment Card request guests to give a fairly detailed evaluation of the hotel and hotel services. The comment card contains space for guests to elaborate on areas of satisfaction or dissatisfaction. It requests an overall rating of the hotel and asks whether the guest is likely to stay at the hotel again. Different versions of the Guest Satisfaction Survey and Guest Comment Card are tailored to the resort properties and the hotels. All guest comment cards are mailed to the Office of Guests Relations. The Operations Survey is a detailed study of hotel operations in each property carried out by an outside research firm once a year. The assessment covers such areas as reservations, front desk, housekeeping, room service, restaurant and bar, airport pick up, concierge, hotel courtesy, marketing, and physical plant.

Each of the four different types of feedback is given a different level of importance in the overall rating of Stouffer Hotels and Resorts. The Guest Satisfaction Survey is given the most emphasis while unsolicited guest letters and telephone calls are only given minor emphasis. Responses to each of the four components of the GSI are given numerical values and are combined to yield a numerical rating for each property. This is totalled annually to produce an overall GSI score for each hotel or resort.

Each property is also evaluated on meeting conventional sales and profit targets. The management and employees at each hotel and resort are able to win bonus awards based on their overall GSI score and on performance to profit targets. The use of the two incentive systems ensures that the management of each property do not reduce the level of customer service to meet financial and sales goals. The incentives consist of quarterly and annual recognition awards for the superior hotel and hotel employees along with executive committee bonuses. General managers in each property are encouraged to set up employee incentive programs in order to achieve sales, profit and high GSI goals.

All customer feedback from the guest satisfaction survey, the operations survey report and the guest comment cards is processed by the Office of Guest Relations at the corporate level. This information is fedback to the general managers at each property. In turn, all employees at each site are given feedback on performance. In most cases, these results are posted on large graphs in the employee lounge. Actual figures are compared with projected goals for the hotel, company averages, like property averages, and previous year averages. Interim reports are sent out regularly so that the management at each property can monitor ongoing progress toward goals.

The Office of Guest Relations at Stouffer Hotels and Resorts has also designed a problem investigation and response system for processing guest complaints and a priority system for categorizing different types of guest complaints received from unsolicited phone calls and letters, guest comment cards, and from the guest survey. This system takes much of the ambiguity out of the complaint handling process. The Office of Guest Relations oversees actions taken by each property in response to every complaint and ensures rapid follow-up and consistent action by each hotel and resort. For instance, class AA complaints are severe problems requiring immediate attention, corrective action, and a response by the general manager of the hotel. This would include claims of theft, vandalism, threatened or pending legal action. This class of complaint would also include poor employee attitude, lack of service after repeated requests, and a failure to honor a room reservation.

Different formats of letters have also been developed for responses to different forms of complaints. This takes the guess work out of how the complaint should be handled. The Office of Guest Relations keeps comprehensive records of all investigations. The department also tracks the number of guests who have registered complaints who return or do not return to Stouffer Hotels and Resorts.

CONCLUSION

The approach to managing guest relations at Stouffer is integrated with six management subsystems: 1) corporate goal setting, 2) performance reporting, 3) customer research, 4) hotel operations' research, 5) complaint processing and 6) management and employee incentives. When a separate department with high level decision making involvement is charged with representing the customer's point of view in these matters, it increases the likelihood that the customer will not be lost in the shuffle. While, theoretically, everyone who works for a hotel is supposed to serve the customer, everyday actions often fall short of this ideal. The combination of bureaucracy with hospitality, which characterizes hotels, often means that guests do not receive the service they deserve (Shamir, 1978). The managment and employees at each property are supposed to be responsive to different guests' needs but, at the same time, must comply with certain corporate policies and rules. This combination of responsive constraint or "loose-tight" structure is a frequent source of conflict between front line employees and guests, between corporate management and the local management of each property, and between different departments of each hotel which are very interdependent. The problem is further compounded by major differences in customer needs at different properties and changing demands at different times of the year. These and other complications in hotel management make it essential for both corporate and local management to keep in close touch with the customer and each other. The integration of guest feedback with goal setting, performance reporting, complaint handling, and employee incentives can help close some of the gaps in understanding between corporate and local management and build better relationships with the customer.

REFERENCES

Cadotte, E.R. "The push button questionnaire: a new tool for measuring customer satisfaction." Cornell Hotel and Restaurant Administration Quarterly, Feb., 1979, 76-79.

Cadotte, E.R. and Turgeon, N. "Key factors in guest satisfaction." Cornell Hotel and Restaurant Administration Quarterly. Feb., 1988, 45-51.

Daltas, A.J. "Protecting service markets with consumer feedback." Cornell Hotel and Restaurant Administration Quarterly, May, 1977, 73-77.

Geller, N. "Tracking the critical success factors of hotel companies." Cornell Hotel and Restaurant Administration Quarterly, February, 1985, 76-81.

Hudson, L.A. and Ozanne, J.L. "Alternative ways of seeking knowledge in consumer research." Journal of Consumer Research, 14, 1988, 508-521.

Landon, E.L. "A model of consumers' complaint behavior." In R.L. Day (Ed.) Consumer Satisfaction, Dissatisfaction and Complaining Behavior. Bloomington: Indiana University Press, 1977, 31-35.

Lewis, R.C. "When guests complain." Cornell Hotel and Restaurant Administration Quarterly. August, 1983, 23-32.

Lewis, R.C., and Pizam, A. "Guest surveys: a missed opportunity." Cornell Hotel and Restaurant Administration Quarterly. Nov., 1981, 37-44.

Shamir, B., "Between bureaucracy and hospitality -- some organizational characteristics of hotels." Journal of Management Studies, 15, 3, 1978, 285-307.

Trice, A.D. and Layman, W.H. "Improving guest surveys." Cornell Hotel and Restaurant Administration Quarterly. Nov. 1984, 10-13.

CONNECTING PRODUCTIVITY WITH QUALITY THROUGH THE DESIGN OF SERVICE DELIVERY SYSTEMS

Professor K. Michael Haywood and Professor James R. Pickworth
University of Guelph

Abstract

Management recognizes the need to improve quality, but also realizes that productivity must be raised simultaneously. However, it is accepted thinking that improvements in productivity are likely to impact adversely on quality, and vice versa. This paper addresses this dilemma by exploring the relationship between productivity and quality. After examining current thinking about productivity, the authors discuss the interdependence of productivity and quality, and then consider it in the context of service delivery systems. Using the fast food industry as an example, a model is presented to illustrate how, once marketing and production strategies have been carefully integrated, it is possible to build both productivity and quality into service delivery systems.

THE PROBLEM

Tourism and hospitality firms are under tremendous pressure to utilize resources more effectively and efficiently. Unfortunately, managers at all levels are caught on the horns of a dilemma. In their efforts to cope simultaneously with increases in both costs and customer dissatisfaction, managers are exhorted by consumer behaviorists on the one hand and hard-nosed operational advisors on the other. The behaviorists talk in terms of improving quality and value from the customers' perspective. The operational people keep hammering on the theme of increasing productivity to improve bottom-line results. Understandably, the typical manager may be confused: the proposed solutions seem diametrically opposed and neither side seems capable of reconciling the differences.

If quality and productivity problems are to be solved within a single management system there is a desperate need to reconcile the quandary in which managers are now caught. In working towards accomplishing this objective, this paper will attempt to explore the overlap evident in the approaches used to evaluate productivity and quality. Then the connection between productivity and quality will be examined in the context of service delivery systems. But, first it is necessary to understand why productivity and quality are such critical, bedrock issues in the tourism and hospitality industries today.

CHALLENGES FACING THE TOURISM/HOSPITALITY INDUSTRIES

A brief synopsis of the current challenges includes the following:

- Airline deregulation which has brought bankruptcies, employee layoffs, strikes, mergers, new entrants, wage rollbacks, and fare wars;
- Active consumerism which has promulgated federal laws to protect the travelling public from deceptive promotion, hidden charges, poor service, and impure products;
- Over building or market saturation which has resulted in both extreme and sometimes futile attempts to differentiate through repositioning and aggressive advertising in an attempt to boost unit sales;
- Changes in the structure of population which is creating a major shortage of labor in businesses that are labor intensive; and,
- Escalating wage/benefit expectations and other commodity price increases that are becoming difficult to pass on to consumers who are increasingly price/value conscious.

These challenges are further complicated by the unique set of characteristics that differentiate service industries - intangibility, inseparability of production and consumption, heterogeneity, and perishability. For example, the inability to inventory services places a premium on balancing supply and demand. This creates a problem in the management of capacity, that in turn, has a definite impact on attempts to improve productivity and quality - a topic that will be examined later in more detail.

While it has been recognized that quality is linked to both profitability and growth through the impact of quality on customers' perceived value (Buzzell and Gale, 1987), the prevailing operating climate makes it difficult to implement such improvements. The shortage of labor, for instance, places increasing pressure on managers to implore existing employees to just get the work done; quality concerns take on a secondary role. Indeed, the difficulty which some hospitality organizations have in retaining employees frequently makes training an abortive exercise. Quality improvements, when they can be made, are often thought to be expensive, and this is particularly worrisome since productivity improvements are so hard to come by (Scarfe and Krantz, 1988).

There is hope, however. Leonard and Sasser (1982) report that most efforts to improve quality result in improved productivity and vice versa, but only if management establishes a clear relationship between the two. In order to make the connection between productivity and quality, their relationship will now be clarified.

PRODUCTIVITY AND QUALITY: A MERGING OF CONCEPTS

The recession in the 1980's focused attention on the importance of productivity improvement and also stimulated consumer concern about quality. As a result, there has been considerable conceptual development of the nature of quality in service industries. The same, however, cannot be said about productivity, which, for the most part, still reflects a partial factor orientation that first needs to be challenged.

When faced with the difficulties of measuring productivity over time, many economists have tended to view a firm's productivity in terms of the relationship between labor and sales. In adopting this approach, an implicit assumption is made: any change in the labor component has no impact on output or sales. As a result, quality is treated as a constant. In the context of the service industry, it is not justifiable to assume that a change in the quality of inputs will not have an impact on the quality of outputs. But if this assumption is being made then the traditional notion of output should be challenged, particularly when applied to service industries: The concept of output goes beyond the prevailing notion of a "physical thing" to embody intangibles (Takeuchi, 1981). For example, in a hospital setting, food and its service are used as important components in helping a patient toward a speedier recovery. This raises an important question. Should the output of a restaurant, for example, be considered in terms of customers satisfied or meals produced? Since behavioral factors are so influential in determining quality levels, it can be argued that productivity in service industries should incorporate social as well as economic inputs and outputs (Katzell and Yankelovich, 1975).

Another central issue in the literature is the view that productivity has a strategic as well as a tactical focus. The industrial engineer has traditionally focused on operational efficiency; but, to be efficient is not necessarily to be effective (Mali, 1978). The demise of restaurants that selected poor locations is a clear indication that operational efficiency will not always make up for ineffective strategic decision-making. Another argument for including effectiveness in the productivity concept is that management must concern itself with how well objectives have been identified and resources deployed (Shetty and Buehler, 1985).

The way in which managers think of productivity is reflected in how they measure and seek to improve it. Many of the traditional measures used to monitor productivity, such as meals produced per hour paid, concentrate on employee productivity. This practice is understandable in labor-intensive service industries in which there is a heavy reliance on exhorting employees to work harder and smarter. Unfortunately, such programs are hard to sustain and may have a long term, dysfunctional impact on employees (Hochschild, 1983), and, in turn, on the customers served. By equating productivity with employee productivity, management may also overstate the productivity improvement arising from the introduction of labor saving equipment. Frequently, an increase in employee productivity, in the short term at least, is offset by a decline in capital productivity.

No matter how well designed the operation, poorly trained or demoralized employees will be unable to achieve optimum productivity or quality of service for that matter. In an attempt to find an answer to this problem, productivity improvement has been viewed in terms of corporate culture (Miller, 1984; Witt, 1985). Changing an organization's culture implies more than changes in its structure and processes; it means a realignment of management and employee expectations. Indeed, from a behavioral scientist's viewpoint, it could be argued that productivity improvement is a process of social change, in which the inputs are expectations and the outputs are satisfactions.

In discussing the evaluation of marketing productivity in service industries, Hempel and Laric (1976) incorporate the notion of expectations. For example, when customers enter a fast food restaurant they may expect to be served within a few minutes. If service takes considerably longer customers may be dissatisfied. It has been argued that consumer satisfaction is determined by "gaps" between expectations and performance. Any improvement in the performance of this service delivery system that will eliminate these gaps will enhance the perceived quality of service (Parasuraman et al, 1985). Consequently traditional productivity measures need to be integrated with information on customer satisfaction (Hempel and Laric, 1976). The same line of thinking is now emerging from the productivity literature with the increasing use of multi-criteria measures, which incorporate traditional productivity measures and more qualitative measures relating to quality, employee satisfaction, and so on (Sink, 1985).

Service industries have for sometime been aware of the role that customers can play as partial employees (Lovelock and Young, 1979). Self service is an obvious form of labor substitution that will boost productivity providing it has customer acceptance. From a service quality perspective, self service can provide the customer with more convenience, enhanced value, as well as an opportunity to personalize their own service experience. The realization of these productivity and quality benefits frequently depends on an "educated" customer using a delivery system that is "user friendly".

This brings us to the more familiar role that quality plays in improving productivity. Current research suggests that the strategic and tactical use of quality assurance programs can increase productivity as well as attract and satisfy customers, increase market share and build favorable images (Groocock, 1987). In goods-producing industries, Deming (1982) attributes these productivity gains to "less rework". The high cost of failure in service industries also places a premium on doing it right first time. In addition to technical quality or "what is delivered" management has to concern itself with functional quality or "how it is delivered" (Gronroos, 1982). In fact, the actual service process has the potential to be quite unproductive. For instance, a curt and poorly "trained" food server can upset many customers as well as waste time rectifying service errors. Likewise, a customer who is dissatisfied, can tie up sufficient resources to have an adverse impact on both productivity and quality. For these reasons, many service organizations recognize that they must absorb higher preventive and appraisal costs.

If quality changes can impact on productivity, the converse is also true. In manufacturing, it is evident that improvements in productivity resulting from capital investment, can lead to lower operating costs and a subsequent enhancement of customer perceived value. The myth that many service industries are not as capital intensive or as technologically oriented has been challenged by Quinn et al (1987). After studying a range of service industries, they concluded that technological and information systems will precipitate structural changes which will, over time, substantially boost both productivity and quality.

Since the marketing and production functions are integrated to a higher degree in service businesses, and have to be controlled on a multi-outlet basis across time, management needs to adopt a systems perspective. For example, in fast food the most obvious means of improving system productivity was through expansion. By centralizing such management functions such as purchasing and marketing certain economies of scale were achieved. However, as the industry saturated its market, it needed to consider alternative sources of growth. As such the "cookie cutter" approach of replicating a service delivery system nationwide has been eclipsed by the need to generate more profit from existing outlets. Consequently, service delivery systems are being refined to raise both productivity (reduce costs) and quality (increase sales). These two objectives are not mutually exclusive. Increased system efficiency enables management to process more customers when the demand exists; and, from the customers' perspective, may heighten awareness of service levels and so generate more sales by word-of-mouth advertising.

Another example will further underline the synergy to be gained from conceptually linking productivity and quality. The use of remote hotel check-in terminals at airports is a convenience to customers; it allows them to avoid long line-ups. From a management perspective, such a procedure is not viewed as another example of labor substitution, but as a strategic capital investment in an information system that will accrue long term productivity and quality benefits. Indeed, Shostack (1987) would describe this innovation as an example of how a facilitating good - an aid to or replacement for human service providers - can be used for competitive advantage. The argument, however, that automation depersonalizes and reduces the quality of the service experience, misses the essential point. Namely, if customers willingly make a trade-off based on their own preferences, then automation provides a substantial customer benefit. Management's task is to determine whether customers are amenable to such trade-offs.

Another approach to examining the relationship between productivity and quality is to note how such variables as selection, job design, and employee attitudes that are usually associated with productivity improvement, also affect quality. For example, such techniques as quality circles, productivity teams, employee involvement groups often overlap in their search to improve quality, to increase job satisfaction, or to reduce the job hassles that impede productivity. In a sense, productivity and quality share a common denominator: innovation. The research in both the productivity and quality fields strongly emphasizes the importance of harnessing "idea-power".

So far we have argued the proposition that the concepts of productivity and quality have much in common. However, the most persuasive argument for their convergence is revealed in the following more practical application of service delivery systems.

SERVICE DELIVERY SYSTEMS

Service businesses are unique in that marketing and production are integrated at the service delivery level. In fact, the design and management of a service delivery system - the process by which products/services are created and delivered simultaneously to customers (Sasser et al., 1978) - is vital to the success of service firms. A service delivery system bridges the gap between the value of the service concept to customers and the cost of providing it (Hesketh, 1987).

The key is to build productivity and quality into the delivery system from its very inception. The "blueprinting" approach has been suggested as a way of identifying specific bottlenecks in service delivery systems that create potential productivity and quality problems (Shostak, 1984). However, an understanding of the decision-making that pulls together the marketing and production strategies into a service delivery system has not been made totally clear. The following brief description of a service delivery system for a fast food operation will examine this decision-making process and illustrate, in practical terms, how both productivity and quality can be built into the system.

The value in conceptualizing a service delivery system lies in the ability to provide a structured way of analyzing the relationships between various activities within an operation. The components of a typical fast food service delivery system are shown in the model in Figure 1 (Pickworth, 1988). The design process begins with the development of a marketing strategy together with a compatible production strategy. Together these determine the basic operating characteristics of the service delivery system.

In evolving a marketing strategy, the starting point is a menu that will satisfy customer as well as management needs. Menus, however, are deceptively complex. No fast food chain, for instance, prepares their hamburgers the same way, largely because each chain has a clear marketing focus and uses its service delivery system as a means of product differentiation. Such strategies exemplify the significance of what Gronroos (1982) refers to as functional quality - the experience of the service delivery system.

In determining a marketing strategy, fast food chains have to determine the extent of customization that they want to offer. The degree of flexibility or customization to be permitted in each phase of the service delivery system has been referred to as "divergence" (Shostack, 1987). Service levels that are related to menu variety, waiting times, hours of operation need to be translated into operational performance standards. A chain can use service levels to differentiate its "product". For example, Domino's pizza has refined its delivery system to acquire a reputation for speed of service. Likewise, McDonalds emphasizes speed and standardization. In contrast, Wendy's has traded off the standardization that would have given it speed of customer throughput for a relatively high degree of customization that instead provides a higher check.

Although a chain's production strategy will reflect basic marketing strategies, decisions have to be made as to the degree of "complexity". This term is used by Shostack (1987) to indicate the number and intricacy of steps involved in the service process. For example, Burger King specifies a degree of customization which necessitates a "finish to order" inventory which, in turn, requires a holding inventory of cooked, but unfinished burgers. Other chains have adopted a "ready to serve" production strategy. Some chains have opted for a very limited menu that is fixed for all meal periods and have consequently been able to streamline their production system e.g. Kentucky Fried Chicken. However, the resulting lack of flexibility limits the creation of new market segments. Some chains, such as donut chains, have incurred considerable costs in retrofitting their delivery systems with equipment to serve additional menu offerings.

The choice of technology for a service delivery system has important implications. Burger King's continuous chain broiler requires less supervision and facilitates quality control; however, it did not provide the flexibility necessary to enter the breakfast market quickly. An egg cannot be broiled. Fast food chains, unlike independently-managed operations, tend to be technology-driven, and consequently, prior technological decisions can have a major impact on future marketing opportunities.

Much thinking also needs to go into the layout component of a service delivery system to ensure appropriate flows of materials, information, employees and customers. For example, Burger King originally used an L shaped layout with the production area on one side. This layout meant that fewer service stations could be installed compared to the straight line system of McDonald's. Consequently, during peak periods service was slower, and because McDonald's was able to process more customers, their unit sales were higher than those of comparable Burger King outlets.

The peaking of restaurant sales during meal periods suggests that seating capacity has to be balanced with demand. Yet few companies can afford to build capacity to meet peak demand - it would be highly unproductive. Consequently, determining the size or capacity of a service delivery system for a particular locality can be an extremely important decision requiring thorough demand analysis. From a productivity perspective, the issue here is one of effectiveness rather than efficiency. A excessively large outlet, although efficiently designed and managed, may be relatively unprofitable due to the absence of sufficient customer throughput. In such situations, the manager is perpetually under pressure to reduce operating costs. Consequently, both functional and technical quality may be adversely affected. However, once an outlet is built, the challenge then becomes one of capacity management involving the manipulation of demand using such techniques as off-peak pricing discounts to spread out the peaks and valleys of demand, and the manipulation of capacity using self service and part-time employees who are cross-trained (Sasser, 1978).

The production component of a fast food delivery system depends on the extensive use of specifications to minimize the costs of failure and accurate forecasting. The aim is to avoid over-staffing and over-production during slack periods while maximizing customer throughput during peak periods when the demand is there. In order to achieve this goal and maintain service standards as well, careful thought has to be given to cooking times, seat

267

turnover times and other activities that may shorten the service "critical path".

Reference has already been made of the use of "blueprints" to identify potential failure points. The problem of waiting-in-line is almost unavoidable and Maister (1985) has made various suggestions in this regard. If a customer progresses through the service process with unrealistic expectations, then it is unlikely that he/she will leave satisfied. Hence the importance of ensuring prior communication. Customers must know what to expect if the perceived or actual service is to coincide with what is expected. In the absence of advertising to communicate expectations, the external appearance of a restaurant often provides a prospective customer with an indication of service levels.

Whenever a customer and an employee interact, there is a "moment of truth". Every manager wonders - will the employee behave in a way that will reflect the firm's concern with customer satisfaction (Normann, 1984)? This component in the service delivery system highlights the importance of research into socio-technical systems which examine the impact of the work environment on employee behavior. An example of how the technical aspects of a service delivery system can affect the pattern of employee behavior will clarify this point. In some chains, each server communicates customer orders through a point-of-sale system that prints the orders out in the kitchen. However, in other operations, the customer orders are communicated verbally through a microphone system by several servers at a time. This latter approach can not only result in confusion and cause friction, but also means that the control of the production system is more diffused and less responsive to changes in demand. Consequently, management has to devote an unusually large amount of time to team-building and maintaining employee motivation.

In a sense, the service delivery system only provides latent productivity and quality of service. Whether these benefits will be realized depends on management's ability to elicit appropriate employee behaviors. The significance of the motivational orientation of employees has been stressed by Keaveney (1988), who argues that intrinsically motivated employees perform better when the service delivery system is complex. Whereas a system with low complexity will foster extrinsic motivational orientations. In short, it seems that the type of employee selected and the state of management/employee relations will be reflected in the quality of employee/customer relations.

The "consumer experience", or as it is known in the foodservice business, the "meal experience" (Campbell-Smith, 1967), is the final component of the model. This term is used to describe the combined physical and psychological impact of all the specific service experiences or encounters that occurred during the service process. Management aims to maximize the degree of satisfaction over prior expectations by ensuring that the various encounters experienced by customers as they progress through the service process are positive and attributed to the service firm (Parasuraman, 1988). The extent to which this outcome is possible depends on the socio-technical system, the predisposition of the customer at each stage of the service process, as well as on the social perceptiveness and interpersonal skills of each employee. Given the precarious nature of the consumer experience, it has been suggested that employees develop a "service repertoire", which will assist them in identifying and responding to typical consumer behaviors (Olsen and Barrington, 1987).

Monitoring service quality of consumer experiences, not to mention individual employee/customer interactions, in a multi-unit franchise chain represents a considerable challenge. To this end, Parasuraman et al's (1985) technique of identifying "gaps" between management's and consumer's expectations and perceptions of the consumer experience has been applied in the hotel industry (Lewis, 1987). Management has to strive constantly to refine the service delivery system to fill-in these gaps as well as to enhance perceived values by passing on the benefits of system productivity improvements.

In a perfectly designed service delivery system, there should be an equilibrium between supply and demand within each component of the system. For instance, customers would not have to wait, orders would be taken promptly, no bottlenecks or hassles would exist. Although this may be the goal, problems arise and a service delivery system can be expected to get out of balance periodically. The real test for any service delivery system is the responsiveness in regaining its balance when faced with excess demand and/or non-routine situations such as customer complaints and dropped trays. Despite the inevitability of operational "crises", many food service systems seem to be perpetually "out-of-sync", and are characterized by haphazard quality of service and a level of productivity that cannot be sustained unless there are spasmodic "quick fixes". The reason for this is that the significance of the service delivery concept has not been fully understood, and insufficient thought has been put into its design.

The development of a service delivery system should be the result of the careful integration of marketing and production strategies. As the basic structure of the system begins to take shape, increasing levels of detail are added to each component of the system. Take, for example, the re-birth of the "drive-thru" concept. In an attempt to provide more convenience to the customer in a hurry, the "drive-thru" enables the customer to receive food and drink within a minute of ordering without having to leave the car. The delivery system is designed with speed of service in mind: Trip wires announce the arrival of a car prior to reaching the menu board; the menu board is large enough to read from a distance of two to three car lengths so menu choice can be made in advance; a two-way speaker system allows the customer to place the order at the menu board before driving up to the window; employees wear portable headsets so the order-taker can be anywhere in the kitchen; and personnel, who hear the order on the "listen-only channel", can prepare and complete it ready for delivery to the customer at the window. As is evident from this description a prime concern in this process is to ensure there is sufficient flexibility to maintain balance in the system so that the built-in productivity and quality attributes can be fully realized.

IMPLICATIONS

The starting point for integrating productivity and quality into a service delivery system can begin with the development of either a marketing or an operations strategy. In either case, however, the fundamental and enduring nature of customer needs that must be satisfied should be considered by top management. In other words, the integration of productivity and quality usually depends on the outcome of a interactive process among functional areas.

As advocates of the marketing concept marketers can play a leading role in this integrative process. But to do this effectively marketers must have a clear understanding of service delivery systems and the technologies, perspectives and limitations of operations strategies. Unfortunately, many marketers lack this holistic view so there are barriers to effectively communicate the relationship between the concepts of productivity and quality.

In order to overcome these limitations of strategic relevance to service firms the following guidelines for future research directions are suggested:

- The development of sound, consistent conceptual and operational definitions of such key terms as productivity, quality and service delivery systems.

- The evaluation of existing and the development of new ways of measuring productivity and quality and their impact on one another.

- The examination of the impact in service businesses of the marketing strategy perspective on the production or operations strategy perspective and vice versa.

- An examination of the decision-making process used in designing service delivery systems.

Each research focus can lead to a large and diverse set of projects. Altogether, however, it suggests the boundaries of a research program that would improve our understanding of the links between productivity and quality in service organizations.

Figure 1   TYPICAL FAST FOOD SERVICE DELIVERY SYSTEM

MARKETING STRATEGY	– Customization v. speed. – Determination of service levels. – Use of product differentiation.
PRODUCTION STRATEGY	– Finish-to-order v. ready-to-serve. – Degree of on-site v. off-site production. – Level of complexity.
MENU:	– Degree of menu flexibility – Differentiating menu items.
EQUIPMENT:	– Built-in quality control. – Labour saving potential. – Technological flexibility.
LAYOUT:	– Service v. production space ratio. – Appropriate seating configuration. – Number of service stations.
CAPACITY MANAGEMENT:	– Capacity analysis to match supply with demand – Reliable forecasting methods. – Low operating costs during off-peak periods. – Built-in provisions to deal with excess demand
PRODUCTION PROCESS:	– Extensive use of specifications. – Centralized v. diffused control. – Reliable communications system. – Optimization of standard service times. – Use of self-service techniques to maximize throughput and minimize costs.
SERVICE PROCESS:	– Use of service blueprints. – Provision of features to shape customer expectations. – Procedures to minimize the adverse impact of queuing. – Intrinsic v. extrinsic monitoring of service quality.
EMPLOYEE/ CUSTOMER ENCOUNTERS:	– Effective employee scheduling. – Use of suggestive selling. – Appropriate management culture and socio-technical system to engender commitment to organize goals and facilitate motivation. – Development of service repertoire.
CONSUMER EXPERIENCE	– Matching of expectations (inputs) with satisfaction (outputs) by minimizing 'gaps' between expected and perceived service from a customer and management perspective. – Coordinating physical and psychological factors in the meal experience.

Source: Pickworth, J.R. (1988). Service Delivery Systems in the Food Service
            Industry.   International   Journal   of   Hospitality   Management.
            (Forthcoming)

271

References

Buzzell, R.D., and B.T. Gale (1987). The PIMS Principles: Linking Strategy to Performance. New York: The Free Press.

Campbell-Smith, G. (1967). Marketing of the Meal Experience: A Fundamental Approach. London: University of Surrey.

Deming, W.E. (1982). Quality, Productivity and Competitive Positions. Cambridge MA: M.I.T. Centre for Advanced Engineering Study.

Gronroos, C. (1982). Strategic Management and Marketing in the Service Sector. Melsingfers: Swedish School of Economics and Business Administration.

Groocock, J.M. (1987). The Chain of Quality: Market Dominance Through Product Superiority. New York: John Wiley and Sons.

Hempel, D.J., and M.V. Laric (1976). A Total Performance System for Evaluating Marketing Productivity in Service Industries. In W. Locander (ed.), Marketing Looks Forward, 1976 Business Proceedings. Chicago: American Marketing Association. 73-79.

Hesketh, J.L. (1987). Lessons in the Service Sector. Harvard Business Review. 65 (Mar/Apr). 118-126.

Hochschild, A. (1983). The Managed Heart: The Commercialization of Human Feeling. Berkley, California: University of California Press.

Katzell, R.A., and D. Yankelovich (1975). Work, Productivity and Job Satisfaction: An Evaluation of Policy Related Research. New York: The Psychological Corporation.

Keaveney, S.M. (1988). Adding Value to Services Through Contact Personnel. In C. Suprenant (ed.), Add Value to Your Service. 6th Annual Service Marketing Conference Proceedings. Chicago: American Marketing Association. 169-172.

Leonard, F.S., and W.E. Sasser (1982). The Incline of Quality. Harvard Business Review. 60 (Sep./Oct.) 163-171.

Lewis, R.C. (1987). The Measurement of Gaps in the Quality of Hotel Services. International Journal of Hospitality Management. 6:2 83-88.

Lovelock, C.L., and R.F. Young (1979). Look to Consumers to Increase Productivity. Harvard Business Review. (May-June) 168-178.

Maister, D.H. (1985). The Psychology of Waiting Lines. In J.A. Czepiel, M.R. Solomon, and C. Surprenant, The Service Encounter. Boston, Mass: Lexington Books. 113-123.

Mali, P. (1978). _Improving Total Productivity: MBO Strategies for Business, Government and Not-for-Profit Organizations_. New York: Wiley.

Miller, L.M. (1984). _Visions of a New Corporate Culture_. New York: William Morrow. 14.

Normann, R. (1984). _Service Management: Strategy and Leadership in Service Businesses_. New York: John Wiley and Sons.

Olsen, M.D., and Barrington, M.N. (1987). Concept of Service in the Hospitality Industry. _International Journal of Hospitality Management_. 6:3 131-138.

Parasuraman, A., V.A. Zeithaml, and L.L. Berry (1985). A Conceptual Model of Service Quality and Its Implications for Future Research. _Journal of Marketing_. 49:4. 41-50.

Parasuraman, A. (1988). An Attributional Framework for Assessing the Perceived Value of a Service. In C. Suprenant (ed.), _Add Value to Your Service. 6th Annual Service Marketing Conference Proceedings_. Chicago: American Marketing Association. 21-24.

Pickworth, J.R. (1988). Service Delivery Systems in the Food Service Industry. _International Journal of Hospitality Management_. Forthcoming.

Quinn, J.B., Baruch, J.J., and Paquette, P.C. Technology in Services. _Scientific American_. 257-6. 50-57.

Sasser, W.E., R.P. Olsen, and D.D. Wykoff (1978). _Management of Service Operations: Text, Cases and Readings_. Boston, Mass: Allyn and Bacon.

Scarfe, B.L., and M. Krantz (1988). _The Accommodation, Food and Beverage Industry in Canada_. Vancouver: The Fraser Institute.

Shostak, L. (1984). Designing Services That Deliver. _Harvard Business Review_. Jan./Feb. 33-39.

Shostak, L. (1987). Service Positioning Through Structural Change. _Journal of Marketing_. 51 (Jan.) 34-43.

Shetty, Y.K., and V.M. Buehler, (1985). _Productivity and Quality Through People_. Conn: Greenwood Press.

Sink, S. (1985). _Productivity Management: Planning, Measurement and Evaluation, Control and Improvement_. New York: Wiley.

Takeuchi, H. (1981). Productivity Measurement at the Level of the Firm. In R. Nabil and A. Dogramaci: _Productivity Analysis at the Organizational Level_. Boston, Mass.: Martinus Nijhoff Publishing. 53.

Witt, L.A. (1985). _Organizational Climate for Productivity as a Predictor of Organizational Productivity_. Ph.D. Thesis. Tulane University.

DIFFERENCES BETWEEN FIRST-TIME AND REPEAT VISITORS

Muzaffer Uysal
Clemson University

Richard Gitelson
The Pennsylvania State University

ABSTRACT

Tourism has become a vital part of most state economies. In recognition of this, most states conduct advertising and promotional campaigns to attract visitors and conduct various kinds of research to evaluate these campaigns. Although repeat visitation accounts for more than half of the discretionary trips made to many of these states, little of this research has focused on the differences between repeat and first-time visitors. This paper reports the findings from two studies that addressed behavioral differences between these two groups.

In 1988, it is predicted that tourism will represent six percent of total world exports (D'Amore, 1988). More importantly for the service industry, tourism is predicted to account for 25 percent of international trade in services, and during the past few years, tourism has been one of the world's most consistent growth industries (D'Amore, 1988).

Within the United States, approximately $256 billion was spent in 1986 by travelers on trips of at least 100 miles or involving an overnight stay (U.S. Travel Data Center, 1987). Tourism is the number one industry in a number of states (e.g. Florida and Hawaii) and is the second or third largest industry in most other states (e.g. Pennsylvania and North Carolina). According to the U.S. Travel Data Center (1987), tourism resulted in $12 billion in state tax revenues in 1986.

Recognizing this economic importance of tourism, every state maintains a travel office. According to the U.S. Travel Data Center (1988), the budget for these offices ranges from $1.2 million in Nebraska to over $20 million in Illinois and New York, with an average amount of $2.3 million being allocated for state advertising campaigns. Matching fund programs for groups cooperating on advertising programs are provided by an additional 35 states.

Nearly every state evaluates its promotional campaign, with 35 states specifically allocating money for research purposes (U.S. Travel Data Center, 1988). Most of this research has been aimed at determining the success of advertising campaigns that were aimed at stimulating inquiries for state travel information packets (Hunt and Dalton, 1983;

Woodside, 1981). Although this type of research, called "conversion studies," have come under attack[1], the data collected in these studies has occasionally been used for segmentation (Perdue, 1985).

Segmentation research can be very helpful in understanding consumer behavior and can be used "to better satisfy the specialized needs of selected groups of consumers"(Shiffman and Kanuk,1987,pg. 31). The travel market has been segmented on various forms of behavior, e.g., distance traveled (Etzel and Woodside, 1982) and degree of novelty seeking (Snepenger, 1987).

The majority of visitors to a particular state appear to be repeaters, ,i.e., having visited a specific state at least once before the present visit. For example, Howard (1985) found that 72 percent of the visitors to Oregon had previously visited the state. Perdue and Gitelson (1984) and Blazey (1985) reported that 64 percent and 65 percent of their respective samples had previously visited their destination. Thus, one potentially useful basis to segment state and local destination travel markets appears to be brand loyalty, defined here as "those visitors who return one or more times to a familiar destination" (Gitelson and Crompton,1984, pg. 201).

Although brand loyalty has been studied extensively, it has usually dealt with consumer products and has resulted in mixed findings. As Shiffman and Kanuk (1987, pg. 53) point out, brand loyalty is a useful segmentation variable, but they conclude:

> Identifying brand loyal customers and distinguishing them from those who are not brand loyal by means of socio-demographic, psychological or sociocultural characteristics is seldom easy.

Applying what is known about brand loyalty to the vacation-decision process as it applies to the selection of a destination may be inappropriate. Gitelson and Crompton (1984) point out several possible reasons why the travel decision is different than the decision to purchase other types of goods. First, the decision usually involves a high level of expense, which implies a greater degree of involvement (Engel, Kollat, and Blackwell, 1978). Second, decisions are not likely to be spontaneous or capricious due to the high psychological involvement and the limited hands-on experience that the decision maker may have with a particular destination. Finally, while most products can be touched and seen though symbolic messages before actual purchase, this is not true in the destination decision. Even where there is previous knowledge, one is unaware if the expectations one has for a previously visited place still hold true.

The primary objective of this exploratory study was to determine whether there were any significant differences between repeat and first-time visitors to destinations in North Carolina and South Carolina. The variables that were included in each study are listed in the methodology section.

METHODOLOGY

North Carolina Study

A systematic sample with a random start was taken from consumer inquiries for the 1984 North Carolina Travel Information Packet (n=2700). A self-administered questionnaire, a post-card reminder, and two follow-up questionnaires were used to collect the data. A total of 1,887 responses (69.9 percent) were received. Due to funding constraints, no attempt was made to determine the extent of nonresponse bias.

For the purposes of this study, only individuals who met the following criteria were included in the analyses: 1) they had visited North Carolina since receiving the information packet, 2) they were on vacation, 3) they were not on personal or official business, attending a convention or passing through the state, and 4) they completed the section that required them to indicate which reasons influenced their decision to travel to North Carolina. Of the 899 respondents who had visited the state since receiving the information packet, 637 respondents met the three other criteria.

The study included a section on benefits sought. Based on a review of the literature and 30 unstructured personal interviews, 28 possible reasons (benefits sought) for taking a vacation were included in the data collection instrument. Each respondent was asked to indicate how important each item was on a four-point scale which ranged from not at all important to very important. A preliminary analysis of the frequencies of the items resulted in the elimination of two reasons (seeking danger and for spiritual reasons) which were not considered important enough to this sample to warrant further study.

A factor analysis was then performed on the remaining 26 reasons to determine possible underlying factors. A Spearman rank-order inter-item correlation matrix was calculated for these items and submitted as input to a principal components factor analysis with varimax rotation. The six factors which resulted from the analysis with an eigenvalue greater than 1.0 explained 56.9 percent of the variance in the motivation scores. The items in each resulting factor with a loading of at least .50 were then considered to form a potential scale. Reliability coefficients (Cronbach Alpha) were computed for each of the potential scales. Since two of the scales had reliability coefficients of less than .60, they were excluded from further analysis.

The four scales which resulted from the factor analysis were as follows, 1) a relaxation scale (to relax, to be able to do nothing), 2) an aesthetics scale (to see interesting sights, to view scenery), 3) an excitement scale (to be entertained, to do exciting things), and 4) a social scale (to share a familiar place with others, to do something with the family. The reliability coefficients for the four scales ranged from .89 for the relaxation scale to .71 for the social scale.

Other types of variables included in the study were 1) socio-demographic, i.e., age, level of education and level of household income, 2) trip behavior, i.e., length of stay, primary section of North Carolina visited, total trip-related expenditures, type of travel party, whether friends or relatives were visited, and intention to visit the state again. A profile of the North Carolina sample is presented in TABLE 1.

South Carolina Study

Questionnaires were distributed at 10 South Carolina Welcome Centers during a seven-day period in June, 1986. The number of questionnaires was weighted based on previous traffic counts at these centers. Individuals were selected from those individuals who requested additional information from welcome-center staffs. A total of 1,500 questionnaires was distributed to individuals who were on a pleasure or vacation trip. Respondents were asked to put the completed questionnaire in a pre-addressed envelope and return it after the entire trip was over. The response rate was 26 percent. Addresses were not collected when the questionnaire was distributed, so no follow-ups could be conducted. There was no attempt to determine nonresponse bias due to the exploratory nature of the study, and the fact that the study results were not going to be generalized to the entire population of welcome center visitors.

The survey questionnaire included three sections. The first section was composed of five questions relating to information about the structure of the vacation trip. The respondents were asked which of four states (South Carolina, North Carolina, Georgia, or Florida) they visited. They were asked how many nights they spent away from home on the entire trip. Those respondents who indicated that South Carolina was their major destination were asked to complete a second section of the questionnaire concerning their stay in South Carolina. These respondents were asked the cities/locations visited, the number of nights spent in each location, types of accommodations used and future travel intentions. Additional information was collected on group size and on the overall satisfaction of respondents with their trip to South Carolina.

RESULTS

The results in TABLE 2 indicate that there were no significant differences among the socio-demographic variables between repeat and first-time visitors. This was not unexpected, considering that repeat visitors begin as first-time visitors.

The results comparing travel behavior of repeat and first-time visitors is shown in TABLE 3 for the North Carolina study and TABLE 4 for the South Carolina study. Although there were some differences between the tow samples, overall the results were consistent.

None of the three sections of North Carolina attracted more repeat visitors than would be expected, based on the Chi-square analysis. However, the South Carolina study did find some differences when destination was defined in a more specific manner, i.e., cities rather than large sections of a state. Both Charleston and Columbia were more likely to attract first-time visitors than would be reasonably expected.

The results in both studies indicated that repeat visitors spend more time at their destination than first-time visitors. Although the results were statistically significant in only two of the six destinations included in the South Carolina study, this could be more a function of sample size than the lack of any real differences, considering that repeaters spent, on the average, between one and two longer in each of the six cities where the results were not significantly different according to the Chi-square analysis. In the case of the cities where the results were statistically relevant, the additional average amount of time spent by repeaters was nearly four days.

The North Carolina study did provide some evidence that repeaters were less likely to stay in hotels or motels. The findings in both studies suggest that repeat visitors are more likely than first-time visitors to alternate forms of lodging, such as friends or relatives, rental properties, or campgrounds. This could help account for the lack of differences in trip expenditures between the two groups that was found in the North Carolina study.

Repeat visitors and first-time visitors were significantly different on one of the benefits sought scales. Repeaters score significantly higher on the social scale, which would be expected, given the nature of the questions asked.

Repeat visitors in both studies are more likely to indicate that they will return in the future. Approximately three-fourths of the repeat visitors in the South Carolina study indicated they were very likely to return to the same destination, compared with 43 percent of the first-time visitors.

DISCUSSION

The results indicate that there are some differences in travel behavior exhibited by repeat and first-time visitors. These differences have a number of implications for tourist managers, especially in the marketing efforts used to attract visitors.

For example, additional marketing efforts to attract more repeat visitors might be necessary for the cities of Columbus and Charleston, since these cities attract fewer repeat visitors than would be expected. The question is, can these cities overcome a possibly one-dimension image that is portrayed to potential visitors. Charleston is primarily known for its historical importance and beautiful homes, while Columbia is known as the state capital. Charleston has already begun to address this issue by sponsoring one the southeast's premiere cultural festivals.

The finding that additional time is spent at a destination by repeaters appears to support the conventional wisdom that tourist promoters should concentrate on extending visitor's stay at a particular destination or within a specific geographical area. However, a note of caution is in order, considering the North Carolina finding that there were no significant differences in expenditures between repeat and first-time visitors. In fact, the visitors had a slightly higher total than the repeat visitor.

Although this lack of differences in expenditures might be attributed to the choice of accommodations, it still raises questions about the marketing efforts of destinations to extent length of stay. The bottom line may be that visitors have fixed budgets for their vacations and simply spend less per day if the decision is made to stay longer.

It does appear that once an individual becomes a repeat visitor, he or she is likely to do so again. The results in the North Carolina study indicate that this is just not a function of whether the tourist has friends or relatives in the state. Also, the South Carolina study showed the importance of the getting the tourist to come the first time. Nearly 60 percent of the first-time visitors to destinations in South Carolina indicated they were at least somewhat likely to return again.

STUDY LIMITATIONS

The South Carolina study was conducted during a one-week period in June. Although the North Carolina study, which included visitors over a 12 month period, supported the South Carolina study, the time frame could make a difference in the case of cities or regions that hold major festivals at other times of the year. For example, over 70 percent of nonlocal residents attending the Central Pennsylvania Arts Festival were repeat visitors (Gitelson and Wang, 1988).

The expenditure data collected in the North Carolina study was only intended to provide rough estimates of trip-related expenses. Respondents were asked, in some cases, to report expenditures that occurred 12 months earlier. Thus, future studies which overcome this inherent weakness may show that average daily expenditure levels for repeat visitors either increase or at least remain constant at certain destinations. This type of finding would provide support for marketing efforts aimed at extending a visitor's length of stay.

Endnote

1 A task force was created by the U.S. Travel and Tourism Administration to make recommendations concerning travel related research. One of the first concerns addressed was the research efforts of state tourism offices that were aimed at evaluating promotional campaigns involving promotional material sent to inquirers. The first meeting was held April 28-29, 1988 in Rochester, New York.

TABLE 1
PROFILE OF NORTH CAROLINA SAMPLE

Socio-demographic Descriptor	Percent of total	Trip Descriptor	Percent of total
Gender of respondents(n=605)[a]		Type of Party (n=553)	
Male	56%	Couple without kids	51%
Female	44	Couple with kids	33
		Friends	16
Education (n=550)			
High School diploma		If only one section	
or less	24%	of state visited (n=405)	
College degree or		Coastal Region	45%
some college	54	Piedmont Region	19
Graduate degree or		Mountain Region	37
some grad school	21		
		Season visited state (n=617)	
Gross Family Income (n=599)		Summer	51%
Less than $15000	11%	Shoulder	36
15000 to 19999	11	Winter	12
20000 to 24999	14		
25000 to 34999	25	Length of stay in state	
35000 to 49999	24	3 days or less	19%
over 49999	17	4 to 6 days	34
		7 days or more	47
Age (n=599)			
20 to 29	18%		
30 to 39	23		
40 to 49	15		
50 to 59	26		
60 to 69	18		

[a]this variable was not included in the analysis

TABLE 2
RELATIONSHIP BETWEEN SOCIO-DEMOGRAPHICS
AND REPEAT VERSUS FIRST-TIME VISITORS - NORTH CAROLINA STUDY [a][b]

Descriptive Characteristics	Repeat visitor	First-time visitor
Age (N=599)		
20 to 29	70%	30%
30 to 39	64	36
40 to 49	64	36
50 to 59	68	32
60 to 69	69	31
	x^2=1.46	Sig.=0.83
Level of Education (N=550)		
High School or less	69%	31%
College grad or some college	67	33
Some graduate school	70	30
	x^2=0.30	Sig.= 0.86
Income		
$10,000 to 14,999	73%	27%
15000 to 19999	69	31
20000 to 24999	69	31
25000 to 25999	69	31
35000 to 49999	65	35
	x^2=1.48	Sig.= 0.91

[a] Percentages summed across rows.
[b] The results from the South Carolina study were similar to these.

TABLE 3
RELATIONSHIP BETWEEN TRAVEL BEHAVIOR VARIABLES
AND REPEAT VERSUS FIRST-TIME VISITORS [a] [b]

Descriptive Characteristics	Repeat visitor	First-time visitor		
Primary section of NC visited (n=411)				
Coastal region	44%	48%		
Piedmont region	17	21		
Mountain region	39	32		
	X^2=2.14	Sig.= 0.341		
Were Friends/relatives visited (n=622)				
yes	69%	77%		
no	31	23		
	X^2=3.92	Sig.= 0.037		
Where individual stayed (n=611)				
Hotel/motel[b]	58%	66%	X^2=3.51 Sig.= 0.049	
Friends	21%	17%	X^2=1.37 Sig.= 0.240	
Rental property	13%	10%	X^2=0.91 Sig.= 0.316	
Campgrounds	21%	16%	X^2=2.12 Sig.= 0.144	
Number of different types of lodging(n=611)				
one	76%	84%		
two	21	14		
three	3	2		
	X^2=5.33	Sig.= 0.069		
Average amount spent in NC	$466	$474	F Ratio =.077	F Prob =.781
Days spent in NC	8.3	6.4	F Ratio = 7.80	F Prob = .005
relaxation scale[c]	23.1	21.9	F Ratio = 3.78	F Prob = .052
aesthetics scale	12.4	12.4	F Ratio = .026	F Prob = .870
Excitement scale	5.3	5.4	F Ratio = .280	F Prob = .596
Social scale	4.7	2.9	F Ratio = 133.1	F Prob = .000

[a] Results from North Carolina Study

[b] Percentages represent number of repeat and first-time visitors using each type of accommodation

[c]The relaxation scale contained 9 items, the aesthetics scale 4 items, the excitement scale 3 items and the social scale had 2 items.

TABLE 4
RELATIONSHIP BETWEEN TRAVEL BEHAVIOR VARIABLES
AND REPEAT VERSUS FIRST-TIME VISITORS - SOUTH CAROLINA

Variables	Mean Scores		
	FirstTime Visitors	Repeat Visitors	Sig. Level of T test
	N=82	N=212	
Nights spent in South Carolina	x= 3.79	x= 6.53	.000
Nights spent in Myrtle Beach	x= 3.75	x= 7.11	.001
Nights spent in Charleston	x= 2.50	x= 4.06	.086
Nights spent in Hilton Head	x= 5.60	x= 7.73	.128
Nights spent in Columbia	x= 2.30	x= 4.72	.118
Nights spent in Greenville	x= 2.66	x= 4.25	.378
Enjoyment	x= 4.39	x= 4.61	.019
Party size	x= 2.18	x= 3.39	.000

Destination Cities			Chi-square	Sig. Level
Myrtle Beach				
Yes	35.4%*	38.7%	.27	NS
No	64.6	61.3		
Charleston				
Yes	34.1	14.2	14.92	**
No	65.9	85.8		
Hilton Head				
Yes	6.1	12.3	2.38	NS
No	93.9	87.7		
Columbia				
Yes	17.1	5.7	9.55	**
No	82.9	94.3		
Greenville				
Yes	3.7	8.0	1.77	NS
No	96.3	92.0		
Anticipated Visits				
Very likely	43.2	75.9	51.40	**
Somewhat likely	16.0	12.7		
Not very likely	29.6	2.8		
Don't know	11.1	8.5		

* The above percentages are based on row percentages
** prob. $\leq$ .05

References

Blazey, M.A. (1988), "The Washington Resident Travel Study: Differeces Between in-state and out-of-state vacationers", *Journal of Travel Research* 26(4):21-28.

D'Amore, L.D., (1988), "Tourism-The World's Peace Industry," *Journal of Travel Research*, 27(1):35-40.

Engel, J.E. D.T.Kollat and R.D. Blackwell, (1978) *Consumer Behavior*, Hindsdale, Illinois: Dryden Press.

Gitelson, R.J. and J. L. Crompton (1984), "Insights into the Repeat Vacation Phenomenon," *Annals of Tourism Research* 11(2), 199-215

Howard, D.R. "1986 Oregon State Welcome Center Visitor Survey", Division of Tourism, Oregon Economic Development, Salem, Oregon

Hunt, J.D. and M.J. Dalton (1983), "Comparing Mail and Telephone for conducting coupon Conversion Studies",Journal of Travel Research 21(3),16-18

Perdue, R. (1983), "Segmenting State Travel Information Inquirers by Timing of the Destination Decision and Previous Experience", *Journal of Travel Research* 21(3),6-18.

Perdue, R. and Gitelson, R. (1985), "North Carolina Welcome Center Survey Fall, 1984," report prepared for the North Carolina Division of Travel and Tourism, Department of Commerce, Raleigh, N.C. Journal of Travel Research Winter 6-16.

Shiftman, L.G. and Kanuk, L.L., (1987), *Consumer Behavior*, Third Edition, Prentice-Hall, Inc. Englewood Cliffs, N.J.

Snepenger, D. (1987), "Segmenting The Vacation Market By Novelty Seeking Role", *Journal of Travel Research* 26(2):8-14.

US Travel Data Center (1987), "The 1986-1987 Economic Review of Travel in America", USTDC:Washington, D.C.

US Travel Data Center, (1988), Survey of State Travel Offices 1987-1988, Washington, D.C. US Travel Data Center

Woodside, A.G. (1981) "Measuring the Conversion of Advertising Coupon Inquiries into Visitors", *Journal of Travel Research* 19, 38-41.

DEVELOPING PHARMACY SERVICES - A CUSTOMER DRIVEN INTERACTION AND COUNSELLING APPROACH [1]

by

Maj-Britt Hedvall & Mikael Paltschik

Swedish School of Economics and Business Administration,
Helsinki, Finland

ABSTRACT

Many traditional businesses have in the last years been facing demands of extending their core product to include considerable amounts of services. The transition from a traditional business to a service one cannot be accomplished without considering what should be conveyed to the customers and how it should be done. One example of such a business is the pharmacy.

Our study seeks to answer three questions: (1) what kind of services do different customer groups desire, (2) how can these groups be distinguished, and (3) what are the implications for pharmacy service development.

We found four different customer groups: the content pharmacist dependent customer, the independent customer, the information seeker and the discontent customer. In order to succeed in the future the pharmacies have to, when developing their service offering, take in consideration the wants of the different customer groups.

INTRODUCTION

Many traditional businesses have in the last years been facing demands of extending their core product to include considerable amounts of services. The transition from a traditional business to a service one cannot be accomplished without considering what should be conveyed to the customers and how it should be done. One example of such a business is the pharmacy.

---

1) The authors thank Christian Grönroos, Lars-Johan Lindqvist and an anonymous reviewer for their helpful comments. The authors also thank Kia Orback and Jan-Erik Ögren for helpful assistance in connection with the data gathering.

Until a few decades ago the majority of the medicines were produced in the pharmacies. Therefore, the pharmacies then emphasized mainly the production process in their task. Nowadays most medicines are produced outside the pharmacy. Therefore, their main task is now distribution. In addition the pharmacies in the Nordic countries have adopted a third task, namely that of offering advice to their customers on medicines and health-related questions. They have adopted a responsibility for their customers' medication and health behaviour. This is a new dimension which gives added value to the customers.

The medication behaviour of a consumer is a comprehensive process including the obtaining, possessing and utilization of medicines (Hedvall 1988). Pharmacies of today take part in the medication behaviour of the consumer by counselling their customers about e.g. the purchase of a suitable medicine and the proper use and storing of their medication. In addition they offer advice on different health related matters. They are trying to establish a reputation among customers as more than retail outlets for medicines. They have turned from production units into service providers.

Although the pharmacies are aiming at becoming service providers and being engage in customer counselling they are still uncertain of how to carry out the new task. The expanding roles for pharmacists have been discussed in the literature during recent years, see e.g. Adamcik et al (1986), Birenbaum, Bologh and Lesieur (1987), Chilvers (1987), Morris et al (1987a), Selaya (1988) and Sorensen (1986). According to Hedvall and Paltschik (1988) pharmacists are more critical to the services offered at pharmacies than their customers. This implies among other things that the pharmacists are uncertain of their new role as service providers. The same study also points out that customers are not totally satisfied with the quality of service offered. In order to develop the service offering in pharmacies we have to, in the first place, become aware of what kind of services different customer groups desire - a segmentation which according to the findings in Paltschik, Storbacka and Lehtinen (1987) is of crucial importance for profitability enhancement.

Service development has got attention in the literature during recent years although most of it has been quite fragmented. Some comprehensive work can fortunately be found. The gap-model proposed by Parasuraman, Zeithaml and Berry (1985) is presumably the most well-known. The ten quality determinants in the model have been beneficial in the pharmacy setting, see Hedvall & Paltschik (1988). Recently Lovelock (1988) proposed eight factors the service producer should consider when developing the customer service function. These are: (1) presence or absence of intermediaries, (2) high contact versus low contact with the customer, (3) institutional versus individual purchases, (4) duration of service delivery process, (5) capacity-constrained services, (6) frequency of use and repurchase, (7) level of service complexity, and (8) degree of risks involved. When applying these eight factors on pharmacy services we conclude that (1) pharmacies cannot use intermediaries, (2) the pharmacies have a high contact with their customers who are members of the general public which makes the service more complex to manage, (3) the service has to be delivered immediately to the customers at that point of time when they choose to come to the pharmacy, (4) the pharmacists are coming into contact with a variety of purchase patterns such as frequent users of some medication and first-time users which (7) results in a high level of complexity of the services offered, and finally, (8) that there is a high probability of service failure due to the complexity of the service offering as well as the heterogenity of the customers. In other words the pharmacy service offering is very intricate. In addition we have to keep in mind that the customer visiting a pharmacy often feels ill and distressed. The pharmacy is not a place where people come to enjoy themselves or just to spend some time and have a look around. Every customer has a specific problem - a personal one or a problem of a relative or friend - he or she wishes to solve by visiting the pharmacy. The pharmacist, the customer is coming into contact with during the short visit, is representing the whole service offering and knowledge of the pharmacy. The customer-pharmacist interaction in connection with how the routines of the pharmacy are organized constitute to core of the service offering of a pharmacy.

Lovelock (1988) also distinguishes between customer-initiated interactions and firm-initiated interactions. The interaction in the pharmacy is mainly customer-initiated while the service has to be delivered to the customers at that point of time when they choose to come to the pharmacy. Customers purchasing prescription medicines or non-prescription medicines can both choose the time when they prefer to visit the pharmacy, although the first initiator of the customer's visit to the pharmacy in connection with prescription medicines is the physician.

Another interesting aspect of the pharmacy service is how the customer participates in the production process. In most cases it is obvious that the quality of service is better if the customer can provide the pharmacists with adequate information on e.g. his or her health status. Presumably, many customers do not want to discuss such matters in public or they do not wish for some reason or another to tell a stranger about themselves. This moves the responsibility of providing accurate medication and counselling totally on the pharmacist. When developing the customer service function in pharmacies we have to identify what kind of service the customers desire. In the Nordic countries the discussion on and the development of pharmacy services is based on the assumption that all customers are in the need of counselling and happy to receive it. This assumption is in our opinion naive. We assume that different customer groups desire different kinds of services. In order to develop the service offering in the pharmacy we have to distinguish between the different customer groups and become aware of what kind of services they desire. Otherwise it will be more or less fruitless to try to achieve more efficiency from the pharmacy service delivery system.

Our study seeks to answer three questions: (1) what kind of services do different customer groups desire, (2) how can these groups be distinguished, and (3) what are the implications for pharmacy service development. We focus our interest primarily on interaction and counselling which constitute the core of the extended service concept of todays pharmacies.

DATA

The data were gathered from a questionnaire distributed to 1 000 respondents in the region of Skellefteå, northern Sweden. Twelve pharmacies in the region took part in the study. Due to time and financial constraints, convenience sampling was chosen as the most practical method for this study. Throughout one week pharmacists distributed questionnaires to customers purchasing prescription medicines. These customers were chosen as respondents because presumably their contact with the pharmacist is closer than that of non-prescription customers due to the more severe demand for medicines. They are thus in a better position to judge the quality components of the pharmacy's services. At big pharmacies, the questionnaires were distributed to all prescription customers visiting the pharmacy in the space of a specific hour each day. In small pharmacies, they were distributed to all prescription customers throughout the whole week. The customers received the questionnaire together with a stamped envelope addressed to the head office of Apoteksbolaget AB (National Corporation of Swedish Pharmacies) in Stockholm. 498 customer questionnaires were analyzed.

The questionnaire was designed on the basis of the results of 1) a qualitative study of Swedish pharmacies covering pharmacy image, customers' perception of quality components, their need of information and views on how the pharmacy of the future should be (Apoteksbolaget 1985), and 2) a quantitative study conducted among Finnish pharmacy customers (Hedvall 1985). The respondents were asked to rate their view of the pharmacy services on seven-point semantic-differential rating scales. Background questions of the respondents were also asked.

ANALYSIS

Methodology

The method of analysis is based on the utilization of factor analysis and cluster analysis on factor scores. The process has proven itself valuable in health education (Morris et al 1987b) and in service marketing, see e.g. and Paltschik, Storbacka & Lehtinen (1987). The amount of data is often considerable, while service due to its partly tangible characteristics has to be measured by several indicators. This calls for a data reduction procedure. Factor analysis can be used. If we are interested in grouping the original customer or respondent base, which can be quite heterogeneous, into more homogeneous subgroups, then cluster analysis is something to consider.

While we only had limited information of what kind of factor structure could lie behind our measurements of counselling and interaction it seemed logical to run principal components on the variable set. The choice of factor analysis is also supported by the fact that the main purpose is to reduce the data set, not *a priori* to find any underlying structure in the set. Principal components were extracted by using the usual rule of thumb of eigenvalues greater than 1. The components were varimax rotated and factor scores were computed.

Cluster analysis was carried out on the factor scores from the extracted factors. When computing distances we used cluster means calculated at every iteration. We computed several cluster solutions in order to avoid random results. We chose the one with high face validity, significant statistics and good stability of cluster membership in our runs.

Results [1]

The factor analysis resulted in eight principal components. The interpretation of solution is exhibited in table 1 [2]. Through the eight components 54.5 percent of the original variance in the variables was explained.

Table 1. The factor structure

Factor 1: CONTENTMENT
        overall satisfaction with counselling, trust in the pharmacist

Factor 2: INDEPENDENCE
        self-confidence, non-authority opinion of the pharmacist

Factor 3: INTERACTION REQUIREMENT
        requirement of discussions with the pharmacist, active verbal interaction

Factor 4: DECISION PARTICIPATION REQUIREMENT
        demand for the pharmacist's participation in the decision making concerning product choice

Factor 5: SUPERVISION AVERSION
        aversion to the pharmacist supervising the customer in matters concerning medicine and health

Factor 6: PRIVACY PROTECTION
        annoyance of questions concerning personal matters

Factor 7: NON-VERBAL INFORMATION SEEKING
        interest in written information and aversion to verbal information

Factor 8: COUNSELLING SUSCEPTIBILITY
        susceptibility to information and counselling

Factor scores for these eight factors were computed and used as an input to the cluster analysis. In table 2 we present a four cluster solution which was considered the most attractive, based on criteria presented above. Table 2 also shows the means for each factor scores in each cluster. All score means differ significantly, on a level beyond 0.001, from each other when tested by the F-statistics.

---

1) The analysis were carried out using the PC-based SYSTAT-program
2) The matrix of factor loadings can be obtained from the authors.

Table 2. Results of the cluster analysis

	Cluster1	Cluster2	Cluster3	Cluster4
Contentment	0.37	0.29	-0.23	-1.11
Independence	-0.38	1.08	-0.48	-0.20
Interaction requirement	0.08	0.13	0.27	-0.62
Decision participation requirement	0.55	-0.19	-1.24	-0.06
Supervision aversion	-0.18	0.28	0.23	-0.18
Privacy protection	-0.15	0.20	0.39	0.31
Non-verbal information seeking	-0.15	0.42	0.20	-0.43
Counselling susceptibility	0.25	-0.27	0.72	-0.86
n=	209	125	78	86

Based on the results exhibited in table 2 we name the four cluster as follows

Cluster 1: **The content pharmacist dependent customer**
Cluster 2: **The independent customer**
Cluster 3: **The information seeker**
Cluster 4: **The discontent customer**

The content pharmacist dependent customer has trust in the pharmacist and values the pharmacist's participation in decision making, is susceptible to counselling and is content with the pharmacy services.

The independent customer is self-confident, s/he knows before entering the pharmacy what s/he wishes to purchase, values non-verbal information, is asking questions if s/he feels a need for it, is content with the pharmacy services as long as the pharmacist does not interfere.

The information seeker is demanding counselling and information but wishes to protect his or her privacy, wishes particularly to make his or her own choices and is not in a great extent content with the pharmacy services.

The discontent customer is not at all happy with the pharmacies of today. S/he does not require interaction, is not interested in counselling and information, does not have trust in the pharmacist and wishes to protect his or her privacy.

Segments and background variables

In this section we investigate the four segments on specific background variables. We used the following background variables: age, sex, profession, frequency of pharmacy visits and whether the customer mainly visited the pharmacy where the questionnaire was distributed or if the patronage pattern was more disperse. The background variables were the ones available from the questionnaire.

One can assume that the degree of satisfaction and the need for more help and information will increase with increasing age. This is also the case in pharmacy services, see table 3 where the mean ages of the four customer groups are reported. The difference in means between the four groups is significant on a level beyond .001.

Table 3. Mean age

	CONTENT PHARMACIST DEPENDENT CUSTOMER	INDEPENDENT CUSTOMER	INFORMATION SEEKER	DISCONTENT CUSTOMER
	56.0	47.4	52.0	46.7

The above results were not surprising. The positive correlation between age and contentment is well in accordance with the findings in e.g. Hedvall (1985) and Hedvall & Paltschik (1988). That younger customers are more independent could also be expected.

In table 4 we report the distribution of the customers in the four groups over the two states of sex .

Table 4. Sex and customer segments

	CONTENT PHARMACIST DEPENDENT CUSTOMER	INDEPENDENT CUSTOMER	INFORMATION SEEKER	DISCONTENT CUSTOMER
Women	66.0 %	66.9%	69.2%	59.5%
Men	34.0 %	33.1%	30.8%	40.5%

Measured by the chi^2-statistics there is no significant different in the distribution of men and women in the four customer groups, and why should there be any?

When we measured profession we used three groups: people working , retired people and in the third group we have students and people doing something else, e.g. housewifes. People retired from work are a big customer group. Their capabilities are often of an other level than customers' in still an age where they are working. In table 5 we report the percentages of the three groups in the four customer segments.

Table 5. Profession and customer segments

	CONTENT PHARMACIST DEPENDENT CUSTOMER	INDEPENDENT CUSTOMER	INFORMATION SEEKER	DISCONTENT CUSTOMER
Working	52.8	69.4	52.6	61.3
Retired	45.7	24.0	36.9	28.7
Other	1.5	6.6	10.5	10.0

As the grouping on profession highly covaries with age one can assume a lower percentage of people working in segments 1 and 3. This is also the case, as is exhibited in table 5. Measured by the chi^2-statistics the difference due to profession in the four groups is significant, on a level beyond .001. This is in accordance with our expectations. Another interesting fact is the higher percentage of people studying or doing something else which is found among information seekers and discontent customers. One could suspect that housewifes are more keen on information and interaction thus expressing demand for it and dissatisfied if the service does not fulfil their requirements.

The frequency of visits to the pharmacy where the questionnaire was distributed is exhibited in table 6. The differences in the distributions are not significant measured by the chi^2-statistics.

Table 6. Frequency of visits by customer groups

	CONTENT PHARMACIST DEPENDENT CUSTOMER	INDEPENDENT CUSTOMER	INFORMATION SEEKER	DISCONTENT CUSTOMER
more often than once a month	25.7	25.7	16.9	21.1
2-12 times a year	72.2	73.5	83.1	76.3
less than once a year	2.1	0.9	0.0	2.6

Although the distribution in the whole contingency table does not express significant differences one can note the clearly lower percentage of frequent customers among the information seekers. This can be in accordance with the fact that the more seldom you patronage pharmacies, in order to have something cured, the more you need information. Very frequent customers perhaps already know what they need to know. The findings are also in accordance with the discriminating power of product familiarity which is discussed by Paltschik, Sevón and Lindqvist (1987).

Our second variable expressing patronage behaviour is the one which indicate if the customer also patronages other pharmacies than the one where the questionnaire was distributed. The results of a tabulation on this variable is exhibited in table 7.

Table 7. Spread of patronage behavior in customer segments

	CONTENT PHARMACIST DEPENDENT CUSTOMER	INDEPENDENT CUSTOMER	INFORMATION SEEKER	DISCONTENT CUSTOMER
Also other pharmacies	56.4	45.8	46.2	62.7
Only this pharmacy	43.6	54.2	53.8	37.3

The chi^2-statistics have a probability value of 0.07, indicating slight differences in the distributions. The differences are mainly due to the discontent customers where the clearly highest percentage of respondents is found who also patronage other pharmacies. This finding is logical. If a customer is unsatisfied, s/he looks for other solutions which serve the needs and wants better. There is no obvious answer to the question why the content pharmacist dependent customers also visit other pharmacies quite frequently. This question needs further investigation. Although the partial analysis of patronage behavior expressed in table 6 and table 7 cannot reflect the whole dynamics of the patronage behavior - for an excellent overview see Laaksonen (1987) - the variations in the different customer groups are well in line with expectations.

The results that we have presented on some background characteristics in the four customer groups have to a large extent been in accordance with our expectations. Nothing really surprising turned up. Thus, one can say that the results validate the outcome of our cluster analysis and thereby make the grouping of customers even more trustworthy.

IMPLICATIONS

The results are very interesting and in a way unique. We have not seen any service marketing study so far with such a heterogenity of customers in respect to their desire for interaction. In contemporary service marketing theory high interaction quality is regarded as the core of the business, see e.g. Albrecht & Zemke (1985) and Grönroos (1982). Our results imply that this is not always the case. There are customers who want to have their service provided in a very simple way without interference of a service provider, a pharmacist in this case. On the contrary, there are customers who behave like they are supposed to by the literature. Although, referring to the discussion in the introduction to our paper, customers entering a pharmacy have quite similar demands - they wish to purchase some medicine - we find them in different subgroups regarding service. These findings imply that the emphasis has to be on the service production system. It must be flexible in order to handle different customers. We need intensive interaction on one hand and very limited interaction on the other. Therefore, service production systems have to be considered from a management point of view. It is important to judge when and where interaction intensive service production is "profitable", as well as when and where the appropriate information flow can be ensured with a less demanding, more standardized service production system.

The management could benefit from adoptions of the concept of bundling, see e.g. Guiltinan (1987), when designing the service production system. Another possibility is the use of service packages (Lehtinen 1983). This discussion has been elaborated by Grönroos (1987). According to Grönroos (1987), the basic service package consists of the core service, facilitating services and supporting services. The core service of the pharmacy must be seen as securing the customer's health. This task can be carried out through development of facilitating services and supporting services. By designing these functions properly the management can secure that content pharmacist dependent customers and information seekers can have a more intensive interaction, while the independent customers can be served by a very unbundled service. For discontent customers quality improvements are called for.

REFERENCES

Adamcik, B.A., Ransford, H.E., Oppenheimer, P.R., Brown, J.F., Eagan, P.A. and Weissman, F.G. (1986): New clinical roles for pharmacists: A study of role expansion, Social Science & Medicine, Vol.23, No.11, pp.1187-1200.

Albrecht, K. and Zemke, R (1985): Instilling a service mentality: like teaching an elephant to dance, International Management, November, pp. 61-67.

Apoteksbolaget (1985): Att marknadsorientera apoteken - en framtidsstudie

Birenbaum, A., Bologh, R. and Lesieur, H. (1987): Reforms in pharmacy education and opportunity to practise clinical pharmacy, Sociology of Health and Illness, Vol. 9, No. 3, September, pp. 286-301.

Chilvers, M.R. (1987): Improving the quality of work life in the institutional pharmacy setting, Journal of Social and Administrative Pharmacy, Vol. 4, No. 2, pp. 70-76.

Grönroos, C. (1982): Strategic Management and Marketing in the Service Sector, Helsinki: Swedish School of Economics and Business Administration, Research Report No.8.

Grönroos, C. (1987): Developing the Service Offering - A Source of Competitive Advantage. Helsinki: Swedish School of Economics and Business Administration, Working Paper No. 161.

Guiltinan, J. P. (1987): The price bundling of services: A normative framework, Journal of Marketing, Vol. 51, April, pp. 74-85.

Hedvall, M.B. (1985): Apoteket som inköpsställe - en utvärdering ur konsumentens synvinkel. Finlands apotekartidning, vol. 74, pp. 398-402.

Hedvall, M.B. (1988): Consumers and self-medication. A model for the self-medication process, Helsinki: Swedish School of Economics and Business Administration, Research Report No. 16.

Hedvall, M.B. and Paltschik, M. (1988): Perceived service quality in pharmacies. In Blois, K. and Parkinson, S. (eds.): Innovative Marketing - A European Perspective, Proceedings of the XVIIth Annual Conference of the European Marketing Academy, Bradford, England, pp. 300-312.

Laaksonen, M. (1987): Retail patronage dynamics. A study of daily shopping behavior in the context of changing retail structure, Vaasa: Universitas Wasaensis, Acta Wasaensia No.22.

Lehtinen, Jarmo R. (1983): Asiakasohjautuva palvelujärjestelmä - käsitteistö ja empiirisia sovellutuksia, Tampere: Acta Universitatis Tamperensis, ser A, vol. 160.

Lovelock, C.H. (1988): Managing services. Marketing, operations and human resources, London: Prentice-Hall.

Morris, L.A., Grossman, R., Barkdoll, G., Gordon, E. and Chun, M.Y. (1987a): Information search activities among elderly prescription drug users, Journal of Health Care Marketing, Vol.7, No.2, December, pp.5-15.

Morris, L.A., Grossman, R., Barkdoll, G. and Gordon, E. (1987b): A segmentational analysis of prescription drug information seeking, Medical care, Vol. 25, No. 10, October, pp. 953-964.

Paltschik, M., Sevón, G. and Lindqvist, L.J. (1987): Consumers' and producers' basic evaluation - an investigation of objects in the field of music. Helsinki: Swedish School of Economics and Business Administration, Working Papers No. 159.

Paltschik, M., Storbacka, K. and Lehtinen O-P. (1987): Life Style Based Segmentation and Profitability. An Investigation in Retail Banking, in Suprenant, C. (ed.): Add Value to Your Service. 6th Annual Services Marketing Conference Proceedings. Chicago, American Marketing Association.

Parasuraman, A., Zeithaml, V.A. and Berry, L.L. (1985): A conceptual model of service quality and its implication for future research. Journal of Marketing, vol. 49 (Fall), pp. 41-50.

Selya, R.M. (1988): Pharmacies as alternative sources of medical care: The case of Cincinnati, Social Science & Medicine, Vol. 26, No. 4, pp. 409-416.

Sorensen, E.W. (1986): The pharmacist's professional selfperception, Journal of Social and Administrative Pharmacy, Vol. 3, No. 4, pp. 144-156.

THE INFLUENCE OF DEMOGRAPHIC CHARACTERISTICS ON CONSUMER ATTITUDES TOWARD ADVERTISING BY HOSPITALS, PHYSICIANS, AND DENTISTS

Horace E. Johns and H. Ronald Moser
Middle Tennessee State University

Abstract

Younger consumers showed a stronger preference for both hospital and dental advertising than older consumers. Lower income consumers were receptive to hospital advertising and also thought physician advertising would be useful to inform potential patients about services and specialties more than higher income consumers. Lower educated consumers were more receptive to hospital, physician, and dental advertising than were higher educated consumers. Fewer white-collar than blue-collar workers felt that hospital advertising would benefit only quacks as well as felt that it is better to deal with reputable hospitals than one that offers the lowest price.

PURPOSE OF THE STUDY

During the last several years, hospitals, physicians, and dentists have become highly competitive in marketing their services to the public. It has become common to see them advertising their services via a number of media.

The purpose of this study was to determine whether age, occupation, income, education, and sex of consumers accounted for any significant differences in their attitudes toward hospitals, physicians, and dentists who advertise. It was the intent of this study to discover information which would be useful to these health care providers in planning and improving the quality of their advertising.

PROCEDURE

Much of the initial planning of this study was based on Hite's study at the University of Arkansas.[1] Acknowledgement is given to Hite's research instrument, as well as to the instrument of Miller and Waller,[2] which served as bases for the questionnaire in the current study.

A four-part questionnaire was used to collect the data. The first section concerned demographic characteristics of the respondents. The demographic characteristics were: city of residence, occupation, age, sex, race, marital status, number of children in household, total family household income, and education.

The second section of the questionnaire included 19 statements designed to measure how favorably consumers perceived advertising by hospitals, physicians, and dentists. The respondents were asked to answer Likert-type questions in regard to their strength of agreement on a scale ranging from "strongly agree" to "strongly disagree." These 19 statements are contained in Table 1. For the purpose of illustration, the statements use only the word hospital; the questionnaire used both physicians and dentists as well.

The researchers drew a random sample of 3,000 consumers from telephone books as of July 1985 of the six metropolitan statistical areas in Tennessee: Memphis, Nashville, Clarksville, Chattanooga, Knoxville, and Tri-Cities (Bristol, Kingsport, and Johnson City). Appropriate numbers from each city were drawn according to the percentage of the population of all six urban areas. The research instrument was mailed to these consumers, and 404 usable questionnaires were finally received after two follow-ups. Data were collected during 1985 and 1986.

STATISTICAL TESTS AND FINDINGS

The data obtained from the 404 respondents via the research instrument were initially analyzed by tabulating the frequency percentages for each item on the questionnaire. Cross-tabulations were then performed between the demographic factors of age, education, income, occupation, and sex and the 19 attitudinal statements in Section II of the questionnaire. Chi square tests were then performed to detect any significant differences between the cross-tabulations. The level of significance for all statistical tests was set at the 0.05 level. This paper will deal only with the cross-tabulations and chi square tests and not the frequency percentages.

Age of Consumers and Advertising by Hospitals

The sample of 404 respondents was divided by age into two groups--younger consumers (those under 46 years of age) and older consumers (those 46 years of age and older). Tests were conducted to determine the significant differences between the attitudes of these two groups with regard to advertising by hospitals.

The results do not show a difference in the overall opinion of the respondents on any of the 19 attitude questions. A difference was found, however, in the level of agreement or disagreement on certain questions.

In response to the statement that the public would be provided useful information through advertising by hospitals, 71.2 percent of the younger respondents agreed, while only 57 percent of the older respondents agreed. Younger consumers were also more in agreement that it is proper for hospitals to advertise, with 70.4 percent in agreement as compared to 57.4 percent in agreement for older respondents. More of the younger respondents also agreed that advertising would help consumers make more intelligent choices between hospitals, although the level of disagreement to this question is very similar. Younger consumers responded with 56.8 percent agreement and 33 percent disagreement. Older consumers responded with 46.7 percent agreement and 35.4 percent disagreement.

On the negative side, both groups generally disagreed that their image of hospitals would be lower as a result of advertising. Younger consumers, however, disagreed more strongly (65 percent disagreement) than older consumers (54.4 percent disagreement). Younger consumers also disagreed more strongly with the statement that they would be suspicious of hospitals that advertise (75.7 percent compared to 61.9 percent). And once again, younger consumers (72.2 percent) showed stronger disagreement than older consumers (60.8 percent) that hospital advertising would benefit only quacks and incompetents.

Occupation of Consumers and Advertising by Hospitals

The sample was then divided into two groups by occupation—blue collar and white collar. Only two areas were found where a significant difference existed in the attitude of the two groups. Their overall opinion of these two statements was the same. The differences exist, however, in the _level_ of agreement or disagreement.

In response to the statement that hospital advertising would benefit only quacks and incompetents, white-collar workers showed stronger disagreement (68.5 to 59.0 percent) than blue-collar workers. Also, white-collar workers showed stronger agreement to the statement that it is better to deal with reputable hospitals than with one that offers the lowest price (85.9 percent compared to 74.3 percent).

Education of Consumers and Advertising by Hospitals

The sample of 404 respondents was divided into two groups based on the level of education: higher education (those with a college degree) and lower education (those with something less than a college degree).

Only one area existed where there was disagreement between the two groups on their overall opinion. More of the lower education group (45 percent) said that they would like to see more advertising by hospitals while more of the higher education group disagreed (50 percent).

Many other areas existed where there was a difference in the level of agreement or disagreement. More of the higher education group disagreed that advertising will increase the quality of hospital services in the future. Also, more of the lower education group agreed that advertising by hospitals would be a useful means of informing potential patients about services and specialties (80.1 percent compared to 69.8 percent).

In response to the statement that when hospitals advertise, prices are lowered due to more competition, 53.3 percent of the higher education group and 48.2 percent of the lower education group disagreed. Both groups agreed that advertising makes the public more aware of the qualifications of hospitals; however, those in the lower education group agreed more strongly (56.6 percent) than those in the higher education group (44 percent). Both groups also agreed that it is better to deal with reputable hospitals than with one that offers the lowest price. Those in the higher education group, however, agreed more strongly (88.4 percent) than those in the lower education group (78.3 percent).

More of the lower education group (63.3 percent) disagreed that hospital advertising would tend to lower the credibility and dignity of their services (compared with 57.7 percent for the higher education group). While the levels of disagreement (67.3 percent for the lower and 65.2 percent for the higher) that hospital advertising would benefit only quacks and incompetents is similar, the lower education group had 18.6 percent agreement and 14.1 percent undecided, whereas the higher education group had 11 percent agreement and 23.8 percent undecided.

No significant differences in consumer attitudes were found with regard to income levels and advertising by hospitals, nor with regard to sex and advertising by hospitals.

Age of Consumers and Advertising by Physicians

The results do not show a difference in the overall opinion of the respondents on any of the 19 attitude questions. A difference was found, however, in the level of agreement or disagreement on two questions.

Both groups agreed that they presently have a high image of physicians (62.1 percent of the younger respondents agreed and 62.3 percent of the older respondents agreed). Older consumers, however, expressed stronger disagreement on image than younger ones (27.2 percent compared to 19.4 percent). Younger consumers expressed stronger disagreement to the statement that advertising by physicians would benefit only quacks and incompetents (61.2 percent of the younger consumers disagreed and 19.4 percent agreed, while 55.7 percent of the older consumers disagreed and 29.9 percent agreed with this statement).

Income of Consumers and Advertising by Physicians

The sample was divided into three groups based on the level of annual household income: low ($15,000 or less), middle (between $15,001 and $45,000), and high ($45,001 or greater).

Only one area existed where there was disagreement among the groups in their overall opinion. More of the middle and high income groups disagreed that advertising would help consumers make more intelligent choices between physicians (50 percent and 43.6 percent, respectively), while more of the low income group agreed (51.6 percent).

Two other areas existed where there was a difference in the level of agreement or disagreement. A larger percentage of the middle and high income groups disagreed that advertising will increase the quality of physicians' services in the future. Also, more of the low income group agreed that advertising by physicians would be a useful means of informing potential patients about services and specialties.

Education of Consumers and Advertising by Physicians

Three areas existed where there was disagreement between the two groups in their overall opinions. In response to the statement that the public would be provided useful information through advertising by physicians, more of the lower education group agreed (54.5 percent), while more of the higher education group disagreed (44 percent). More of the lower education group also agreed (46.2 percent) and more of the higher education group disagreed (51.1 percent) that advertising would help consumers make more intelligent choices between physicians. And, once again, more of the lower education group agreed (48.9 percent) that advertising makes the public more aware of the qualifications of physicians, while more of the higher education group disagreed with this statement (53.8 percent).

Several other areas existed where there was a difference only in the level of agreement or disagreement. A larger percentage of the lower education group agreed that they would like to see more advertising by physicians. In response to the statement that advertising will increase the quality of physicians' services in the future, 62.2 percent of the higher education group disagreed, while 55.5 percent of the lower education group disagreed. More of the lower education group agreed that advertising by physicians would be a useful means of informing potential patients about services and specialties (67.9 percent compared to 55.5 percent).

Both groups did agree that they presently have a high image of physicians; however, those in the higher education group agreed more strongly (70.6 percent) than those in the lower education group (55.7 percent). Both groups agreed that it is better to deal with reputable physicians than one who offers the lowest price. Those in the higher education group, however, agreed more strongly (92.3 percent) than those in the lower education group (82.4 percent).

More of the lower education group agreed (62.4 percent) that they would use the services, if needed, of physicians who advertise (compared to 54.4 percent agreement for the higher education group). While the levels of disagreement (52.7 percent for the lower education group and 53.8 percent for the higher education group) that when physicians advertise, prices are lowered due to more competition are similar, the lower education group had 32.7 percent agreement and 14.5 percent undecided, whereas the higher education group expressed 22.5 percent agreement, and 23.6 percent were undecided.

No significant differences in consumer attitudes were found with regard to occupation and advertising by physicians, nor with regard to sex and advertising by physicians.

Age of Consumers and Advertising by Dentists

Only two areas were found where a significant difference existed in the attitudes of the two groups. Their overall opinion of these two statements was the same. A difference was found, however, in the level of agreement or disagreement on certain questions.

In response to the statement that it is proper for dentists to advertise, 59.2 percent of the younger respondents agreed, while only 45.6 percent of the older ones agreed. In response to the statement that advertising by dentists would benefit only quacks and incompetents, 65.4 percent of the younger respondents disagreed, while only 56.7 percent of the older ones disagreed.

Income of Consumers and Advertising by Dentists

Three areas existed where there was disagreement among the groups in their overall opinion. More of the low income group agreed that advertising will increase the quality of dentists' services in the future (40.3 percent), while more of the middle and high income groups disagreed (60.5 percent and 62.4 percent, respectively). More of the middle and high income groups also disagreed (49.8 percent and 48.5 percent, respectively) that they would like to see more advertising by dentists. And finally, in response to the statement that advertising would help consumers make more intelligent choices between dentists, more of the low income group agreed, more of the middle income disagreed, and opinions were mixed in the high income group.

Education of Consumers and Advertising by Dentists

Three areas existed where there was disagreement between the two groups in their overall opinions. In response to the statement that advertising would help consumers make more intelligent choices between dentists, more of the lower education group agreed (48 percent), while more of the higher education group disagreed (48.9 percent). More of the lower education group also agreed (50.2 percent) and more of the higher education group disagreed (52.7 percent) that advertising makes the public more aware of the qualifications of dentists. When asked if they would like to see more advertising by dentists, 52.2 percent of the higher education group disagreed, while the opinions of those in the lower education group were mixed (40 percent agreed and 41.8 percent disagreed).

Many other areas existed where there was a difference, not in the overall opinion, but in the level of agreement or disagreement. More of the lower education group agreed that the public would be provided useful information through advertising by dentists. More of the lower education group also agreed that it is proper for dentists to advertise (57.9 percent compared to 45.6 percent for the higher education group). Both groups generally agree that advertising by dentists would be a useful means of informing potential patients about services and specialties. Those in the lower education group, however, agree more strongly (68.8 percent) than those in the higher education group (56 percent).

When asked if they presently have a high image of dentists, 72.2 percent of the higher education group agreed compared to 58.9 percent agreement from the lower education group. In response to the statement that it is better to deal with reputable dentists than one who offers the lowest price, 91.7 percent of the higher education group agreed, while 81.4 percent of the lower group agreed.

On the negative side, both groups generally disagree that advertising will increase the quality of dentists' services in the future. Higher educated consumers, however, disagreed more strongly (62.6 percent) than lower educated consumers (52.7 percent). Those in the higher educated group also disagreed more strongly that, when dentists advertise, prices are lowered due to more competition (53.8 percent compared to 49.5 percent).

Sex of Consumers and Advertising by Dentists

The sample was divided into males and females. Only one statement showed a significant difference between the opinions of males and females. In response to the statement that the public would be provided useful information through advertising by dentists, more of the males agreed (52.2 percent) as well as disagreed (37.1 percent), while more of the females were undecided (22.8 percent).

No significant differences in consumer attitudes were found with regard to occupation and advertising by dentists.

CONCLUSIONS

The results indicate that both older and younger consumers favor hospitals advertising their professional services; however, younger consumers show a stronger preference in this regard. The results indicate that white collar workers, more than blue collar workers, do not feel that hospital advertising will benefit only quacks and incompetents. Also, fewer blue collar workers feel that it is better to deal with reputable hospitals than one that offers the lowest price. The results indicate that both lower and higher educated consumers favor advertising by hospitals; however, it appears that those consumers without a college degree are more receptive and believing toward such advertisements.

The results indicate that both older and younger consumers have a high image of physicians, with older consumers disagreeing more strongly on this point. The results indicate that low, middle, and high income consumers think advertising by physicians would be a useful means of informing potential patients about services and specialties, with low income consumers showing the strongest preference in this regard. The results indicate that lower educated consumers, or those without a college degree, are more receptive and believing toward physician advertisements than the higher educated ones.

The results indicate that both older and younger consumers favor dentists advertising their professional services; however, younger consumers show a stronger preference in this regard. The results indicate that all income segments favor advertising by dentists; however, it appears that lower income consumers are more receptive and believing toward such advertisements. The results indicate that both lower and higher educated consumers favor advertising by dentists; however, it appears that those consumers without a college degree are more receptive and believing toward such advertisements. The results indicate little difference in males' and females' opinions toward advertising by dentists; however, it appears that females are more undecided, while males have a more definite opinion.

All of the above findings perhaps could be important implications for hospitals, physicians, and dentists in planning their advertising campaigns.

Notes

[1] Robert Edward Hite, "An Empirical Analysis of Consumers' Attitudes Toward Accountants, Attorneys, and Physicians with Respect to Advertising Professional Services," (Ph.D. dissertation, University of Arkansas, 1982).

[2] John A. Miller and Robin Waller, "Health Care Advertising: Consumer vs. Physician Attitudes," Journal of Advertising, Fall 1979, pp. 20-29.

TABLE 1

CONSUMER ATTITUDE STATEMENTS*

1. The public would be provided useful information through advertising by hospitals

2. When hospitals advertise, the costs are passed on to their patients through higher prices

3. Advertising will increase the quality of hospital services in the future

4. It is proper for hospitals to advertise

5. Advertising by hospitals would be a useful means of informing potential patients about services and specialties

6. Advertising by hospitals would be more deceptive than other forms of advertising

7. It is good to deal with hospitals that offer the lowest price for routine services

8. You generally can rely more on what a friend tells you about hospitals than on advertising

9. I presently have a high image of hospitals

10. In general, my image of hospitals would be lower as a result of advertising

11. Advertising would help consumers make more intelligent choices between hospitals

12. I would be suspicious of hospitals that advertise

13. When hospitals advertise, prices are lowered due to more competition

14. I would like to see more advertising by hospitals

15. Advertising by hospitals would tend to lower the credibility and dignity of their services

16. Advertising makes the public more aware of the qualifications of hospitals

17. Advertising by hospitals would benefit only quacks and incompetents

18. It is better to deal with reputable hospitals than with one that offers the lowest price

19. I would use the services (if needed) of hospitals that advertise

---

*For purposes of illustration, the statements here use only the word <u>hospital</u>. Both <u>physicians</u> and <u>dentists</u> were included in the original questionnaire.

305

MARKETING IN HEALTH SERVICES: A REVIEW
OF RECENT TRENDS IN OBSTETRICS

Margery Steinberg, University of Hartford
Benjamin Sackmary, Buffalo State College

ABSTRACT

This paper reviews recent trends and change processes in the development
and application of marketing principles in health care, as illustrated by
the field of obstetrics. Obstetrics is a medical specialty that has
responded to both shifting consumer interests and the evolving needs of an
increasingly cost-conscious health care industry. Essential to successful
application of marketing obstetrical services has been effective internal
marketing aimed at key provider segments such as nurses, physicians and
administrators.

INTRODUCTION

In the past decade, there have been many dramatic shifts in the health care
field. These changes include: (1) the prospective payment system and DRG's;
(2) excess bed capacity; (3) growth of HMO's; (4) increased competition
among all types of health care providers; (5) deregulation that makes it
easier to build hospitals and clinics; and (6) an eroding image of
hospitals among consumers (Malhotra 1987, p. 37).

These developments have resulted in greater financial pressure on medical
organizations as well as increased concern about market share,
differentiation and positioning. Consequently, there has been a tremendous
increase in the use of marketing by health care providers. The boom in
health services marketing has seen activities ranging from efforts at
establishing national brand name recognition ("New Mayo Clinic..." 1986) to
promotional gimmicks such as hot tubs and large screen television for
patients (Hospitals Compete..." 1986).

Marketing professionals have tried to lead or at least to develop
applications for the rapidly changing field ("Health Care..." 1986). A
flood of publications have offered instruction in marketing for hospital
administrators and physicians (Coddington et al 1985; Hillestad and
Berkowitz 1984; Sheldon and Windham 1984; Kotler and Clarke 1987; Brown and
Morely 1986). In addition, there are new journals on marketing health
services and a growing professional association, the Academy of Health
Services Marketing.

Health care marketing is a dynamic area that can be used as an example of a

306

service industry that is moving from a "production orientation" to a "marketing orientation" with a focus on the needs and wants of consumers. This paper examines sources of change and the adoption of a marketing orientation in the field of obstetrics.

OBSTETRICS: CHANGING PATTERNS AND EXPECTATIONS

Obstetrical care is a leading cause of hospitalization in the United States (Hornbrook and Goldfarb 1981). National statistics indicate that 38% of all maternity patients have their first hospital experience in giving birth to their first child (Dearing et al 1987). In addition, while women comprise about 51% of the U.S. population, they occupy 70% of a hospital's beds for obstetrical as well as other health-related services (Agnew 1987, p. 9).

Women are responsible not only for decisions relating to their own care but also influence the health care decisions of their family and friends (Dearing et al 1987). Thus, servicing the health care needs of women through obstetrical services may substantially influence hospital selection and utilization rates for all medical care. OB can serve as a <u>strategic service</u> for hospitals in building long-term relationships with consumers.

Birth Rates

Needless to say, the field of obstetrics is dependent on an interrelated complex of variables. The birth rate, defined as the number of babies born per 1000 population, is sensitive to socio-economic changes as well as to innovations in method of contraception. From 1976 through 1987, birth rates among women under 25 years remained relatively stable, while birth rates among women 25 to 34 years of age increased. This reflects a pattern of delayed childbirth and is typical of women born during the most significant demographic event of the century-- the Baby Boom (Leslie and Swider 1986, p. 115).

Increased labor force participation and a desire for dual family income helps to account for the increased birth rate among older women (U. S. Bureau of Census). Other important factors that can directly influence the birth rate are: increased birth control options, greater utilization of birth control as exemplified by an abortion rate which nearly doubled between 1972 and 1983 (U. S. National Center...).

Women's Roles

Many women today are better educated and more involved in making decisions about health care (Dearing et al 1987, p. 203). They have different

307

expectations for themselves, their careers and their family responsibilities. A number of demographic changes are indicative of these shifts in female roles:

- Increased childbearing by unmarried women.
- Decisions by some women not to bear children.
- Decreasing marriage rates.
- Marriage occurring later in life.
- Increased divorce rates.
- Increased number of women in the labor force.

In obstetrics, these patterns promoted the shift from a production-oriented to a more service-oriented industry. OB is not the only service field that has undergone this transition. There are similarities between hospitals and hotels with respect to the need for a service orientation, including: (1) the use of intermediaries in the selection process (i.e., physicians); (2) the importance of physical facilities and environment; (3) the labor-intensive nature of the service delivery systems; and (4) the relatively low occupancy rates (Lovelock and Weinberg 1984, p. 579).

Fragmented Market

Women are now more heterogeneous in their decisions about selecting obstetrical services. They may vary greatly in expectations with regard to the birthing experience. For example, depending on age, education and sociocultural background, some women may prefer the traditional hospital delivery while others seek alternative birthing methods. Despite the growing number of birth options, family and friends remain the primary sources of information and influence on decision-making about health care programs and facilities (Backley and Cornell 1983, p. 29; Dearing et al 1987, p. 210).

In order to be successful in the highly volatile and competitive health care industry, providers must give careful consideration to socio-economic trends and to the changing needs of their consumers. Changes in the delivery of obstetrical services has required a significant change in attitude, orientation and action on the part of health care providers.

SERVICES AND CONSUMER SATISFACTION

Health care services, such as obstetrics, have a great deal to gain from the application of services marketing. Most definitions of services share a number of common characteristics. Services are usually described as intangible and are seen as simultaneously produced and consumed, frequently with participation on the part of the consumer. In addition, services cannot be stored, they vary considerably depending on the expertise of the provider and are often difficult for users to evaluate (Uhl and Upah 1983; Berry 1980; Carman and Langeard 1983).

For consumers, OB is a high-involvement type of service that is perceived as one that may offer financial and physical risks. Selection of a physician and a hospital for childbirth may entail extended search behavior and a lengthy decision process. The consumer may feel more helpless in the area of health care than with other types of services. There may also be considerable variation in patient satisfaction with health care services depending on the appropriateness of expectations about the treatment provided (Ross et al 1987).

This is complicated by the fact that the more important intangible obstetrical product offered by hospitals, that of a safe and healthy delivery, is evaluated most frequently on the tangible product of the environment and the personal skill and qualities of the service-deliverer.

Competition in Obstetrics

Within any community there are a finite number of babies born each year. OB program survival requires achievement of adequate market share and, due to the absolute limit on the number of customers, obstetrics is one of the most competitive fields in health care. There are other factors that also foster competition. First, there is a great deal of discretionary judgment in selection of both a doctor and a hospital. Second, there is more than enough time to permit an extensive decision process about a provider. Third, many women are interested in more than just a birth; they also want a memorable and very rewarding experience. Fourth, for hospitals, obstetrics offers a high margin service that can fill beds left empty by early discharge or by the absence of patients receiving other treatments.

Satisfaction With Obstetrical Services

There have been few studies of consumer attitudes toward obstetrical services. Much of the literature takes an applied approach with a focus on strategies for integrating marketing into obstetrical services (MacStravic 1986; Dearing et al 1987; Lee 1980; Hardy and Ekbladh 1979).

There does appear to be a general pattern of consumer satisfaction with obstetrical services. From the consumer point of view, OB service appears to be fairly homogeneous. For example, Danko and Boucher (1985) examined consumer attitudes and found little difference in patient evaluation of obstetrical services at three competitive hospitals. This may indicate the need for a positioning or an "image" building strategy for growth in market share.

The primary determinants of service satisfaction, as measured by intention of future usage of the hospital, are quality of nursing care and concern for the patient (Anderson 1982). Thus, successful hospitals must not only project a quality image, they must also deliver a quality service.

SOLVING CONSUMER PROBLEMS IN OBSTETRICS

Development of a hospital marketing strategy for obstetrical services has involved recognition of diverse consumer segments and need for a wide range of services to meet their needs. Consumers of obstetrical service can be conceptualized along a continuum ranging from a no-frills, one-day maternity stay to a full-service, single-room birth with active participation by family and friends.

As might be expected, it is at the "high-end" or full-service pole of the continuum that most of the innovative marketing activity has taken place. These marketing strategies for obstetrical service are discussed below in terms of the conventional marketing mix model.

Service/product

Fifty years ago, the new mother entered the hospital, received a dose of "twilight sleep" and awoke to find her baby already tended to in the nursery. The woman anticipated spending up to a week in the hospital whether she needed it or not. For much of this time, she was isolated from family and friends.

Clearly, expectations for obstetrical services have changed a great deal since then. Today, parents are likely to see the OB program as offering: multiple opportunities for personal growth; an emotionally satisfying birth; and increased closeness with spouse and other children. OB has become a consumer-oriented service rather than a medical procedure and, with the variety of competitive programs, women are more likely to spend time shopping for the right program or combination of features.

Obstetrical programs use a brand strategy for service differentiation. Examples of a few program names are indicative of the brand identity strategy: The Stork Club; Great Expectations Society; Cradle Club; Special Delivery; and The BirthPlace.

A second approach has been to offer a cafeteria of services, some of them gratis to the consumer. These include: 24 hour information hot-line, coupon books for newborn items, free lectures, newsletters, product demonstrations, contests, discount shopper cards, exercise classes, champagne dinners, first-aid training, loaned infant car seats, and other service differentiation efforts.

310

Distribution

There has been a major shift in the distribution of obstetrical services. In grandmother's day the service was fully decentralized and births usually took place at home. With the growth in popularity of hospital OB wards in the 1920's, births moved to these centralized locations, and by the mid-1950's, over 85% of all births took place in a hospital.

During the 1960's the process began to reverse itself with women showing less interest in an antiseptic birth environment. Some women opted for at-home births, but most preferred to have all the services of the hospital in a home-like environment. The major offerings to meet these emerging needs are: (1) the alternative birthing centers (ABC) or pleasantly furnished and comfortable "birthing room" and (2) single-room maternity care (SRM) which offers a total system of all needed services in one room. A third and more recent option is the free standing birthing center. This is a non-hospital based center for childbirth services.

Price

The majority of childbirths continue to be paid for by health insurance policies. A significant innovation is that some companies now offer incentives to employees for staying in the hospital for a briefer period of time. These "short-stay" or "one-day" maternity programs release a healthy mother and her infant within 24 hours after birth. One-day plans offer a substantial reduction in cost and tend to be used by lower income consumers or by those with limited medical insurance coverage.

Promotion

In terms of media, hospitals have made innovative use of television, radio and print advertising. Nevertheless, marketing communication programs for obstetrical services still rely heavily on the traditional mode of referral by friends and family. In addition, as with other complex personal services, the brochure is a workhorse promotional tool. A key influence over consumer selection of a maternity service is recommendation of the physician. That is, direct, face-to-face contact is still a core "selling" approach.

INTERNAL MARKETING

The consumer cannot be the only target of health care marketing efforts. Successful marketing-oriented organizations must also motivate their internal publics to be customer and service-oriented. The ability to establish a consumer-oriented organization requires substantial change in

311

both the focus and components of product and service offerings (Kotler and Clarke 1987, p. 41).

One important characteristic of health care which must be considered in the marketing of obstetrical services is that the consumer cannot evaluate what she will receive in advance of her purchase (Levitt 1981). This is particularly true if the woman is experiencing her first delivery. What she is buying when she selects a hospital is the often the promise of satisfaction. The doctors and nurses who provide obstetrical care serve as the representation of the service in the eyes of the consumer. In effect, the staff "image" becomes the key element in the perception of the service and customer satisfaction.

Resistance to Change

In service-provider organizations, such as hospitals, new procedures and services affect not only consumers, but also employees and volunteers (Lovelock and Weinberg 1984, p. 579). Unfortunately, hospitals typically will experience strong resistance to change among their service providers. A key element in successful organizational change is applying "internal marketing" to influence the understanding of and reaction of individual service-providers. These efforts at professional development can result in enhanced personal job satisfaction.

In the field of obstetrics, the recent introduction of SRM programs by many hospitals is consumer-responsive but may also cause anxiety among employees at all levels. Why inform potential patients about a new obstetrical program which does not have the support of the nurses who are supposed to be providing the new service? The likely result is lack of patient satisfaction, and perhaps even a negative hospital image due to unmet expectations. Resistance or concern about change among health care providers can be ameliorated by internal marketing. In the long run, internal marketing efforts may be even more important than those programs aimed at consumers.

The Marketing Approach

Hospital marketing has traditionally employed a pull strategy by communicating directly with potential patients and encouraging them to seek treatment at a specific hospital (Kiser and Good 1986, P. 34). This assumes that the patient plays the primary decision-making role in the hospital selection process. However, in the case of obstetrics, frequently the woman's selection of her doctor is not based on the hospital in which the doctor practices. This means that it is often the physician who "sells" the hospital to the patient.

Given the role of the doctor, marketing of hospital obstetrical services should use a push strategy with promotional efforts aim at building respect and loyalty among doctors. Such an internal marketing program can have at least two long-term, positive results. The first is the development of a marketing or consumer-oriented attitude among doctors. Second, the program can provide information that can be used by doctors in developing more effective marketing communication with patients.

Internal Marketing Program

A good internal marketing program includes marketing research, segmentation strategies and communication efforts among employees (Berry 1984, p. 271). First, it is necessary to establish a starting point; that is, to identify the knowledge base, negative attitudes and barriers to change among all internal markets. Physicians, nurses, staff and administration may all be experiencing different sources and levels of personal and professional resistance. Attitude surveys, focus groups and personal interviews can assist in the identification of effective approaches to each internal market segment.

Second, all levels of internal publics should undergo a change in the perception of their role from that of medical care provider to that of service provider. It has already been established that consumers of obstetrical services evaluate the quality of their experience in relation to the tangible service received. Thus, for example, a nurse must see her role as not only that of dispensing medication, but also that of being sensitive to the new mother's need for a friendly ear to listen to her concerns about caring for her baby (Phelan 1987, p. 48).

Third, in-service education and cross-training are also necessary to enable all personnel to deliver multiple levels of "quality patient care." In addition, on-the-job behavior is much easier to change than on-the-job attitude. Therefore, educational programs must be accompanied by demonstrated management commitment to motivating and recognizing positive and constructive behavior in relation to the programmatic changes.

Fourth, all service-providers must learn to become consumer-oriented. One effective way in which to accomplish this is by sharing consumer research and feedback with all levels of employees. For example, inviting nurses and doctors to view and discuss a patient focus group tape provides an excellent opportunity to assist service-providers in learning about consumer needs and expectations.

Adopting a marketing approach to hospital employees is important to the successful implementation of new programs. It also, however, can assist the hospital in being more competitive, not only for patients, but also for the nurses and physicians who may ultimately be the key to patients' long term hospital loyalty.

313

CONCLUSION

Implementation of marketing in obstetrics has not been easy. The process has required learning new discipline in the use of business strategy and exercising creativity in communication programs and in image building. Yet reaching the consumer is only half the effort. The organization must also identify and satisfy the needs of the providers. Adoption of a marketing orientation in health care is a multi-directional endeavor in which no segment of employees or customers should be overlooked.

REFERENCES

Agnew, Joe (1987), "Women Now Primary Market," Marketing News, (January 16), 9.

Anderson, Douglas C. (1982), "The Satisfied Consumer: Service Return Behavior in the Hospital Obstetrics Market," Journal of Health Care Marketing, 2(Fall), 25-33.

Backley, W. A. and C. M. Cornell (1983), "Closure or Expansion?: A Marketing Persepctive on Obstetrics," Health Management Forum, (Spring), 28-36.

Berry, Leonard L. (1980), "Service Marketing Is Different," Business (May), 24-29.

_____ (1983), "Relationship Marketing," in Emerging Perspectives on Services Marketing, Leonard L. Berry, G, Lynn Shostack and Gregory D. Upah, eds., Chicago: American Marketing Association, 25-28.

_____ (1984), "The Employee as Customer," Services Marketing, Christopher H. Lovelock, ed., Englewood Cliffs, NJ: Prentice-Hall, 271-278.

Brown, Stephen W. and Andrew P. Morley, Jr. (1986), Marketing Strategies for Physicians, Oradell, NJ: Medical Economics Books.

Carman, James M. and Eric Langeard (1983), "Growth Strategies for Service Firms," in Perspectives on Strategic Marketing Management, 2nd ed., Roger A. Kerin and Robert A. Peterson, eds., Boston: Allyn and Bacon, Inc., 392-405.

Coddington, Dean C., Lowell E. Palmquist and William V. Trollinger (1985), "Strategies of Survival in the Hospitla Industry," Harvard Business Review, (May-June), 129-138.

Danko, William D. and David L. Boucher (1985), "Perspectives From Users of Obstetric Services: Implications for Providers," Health Marketing and Consumer Behavior, NY: The Haworth Press, 41-48.

Dearing, Ruthie H. et al (1987), Marketing Women's Health Care, Rockville, MD: Aspen Publications.

Hardy, C. T. and Lamar Ekbladh (1979), "The Birth of a Service," Health Care Marketing: Issues and Trends, Philip D. Cooper, ed., Germantown, MD: Aspen Publications, 193-198.

"Health Care Explosion Leads to Hybrids (1986)," Advertising Age, (April 21), 6.

Hillestad, Steven G. and Eric N. Berkowitz (1984), Health Care Marketing Plans: From Strategy to Action, Homewood, IL: Dow Jones-Irwin.

Hornbrook, Mark C. and Marsha G. Goldfarb (1981), "Patterns of Obstetrical Care in Hospitals," Medical Care, (January), 55-67.

"Hospital Compete for Affluent Patients By Offering Luxury Suites and Hot Tubs (1986)," Wall Street Journal, (February 3), 23.

Kiser, G. E. and David J. Good (1986), "Factors Associated With Successful Hospital Marketing," Journal of Hospital Marketing, (Fall/Winter), 29-42.

Kotler, Philip and Roberta N. Clarke (1987), Marketing for Health Care Organizations, Englewood Cliffs, NJ: Prentice-Hall.

Lee, John M. (1980), "Marketing Ensures Success of Maternity Care Program," Hospitals, (December), 91-94.

Leslie, Linda Adams and Susan M. Swider (1986), "Changing Factors and Changing Needs in Women's Health Care," Nursing Clinics of North America, 21(March), 111-123.

Levitt, Theodore (1981), "Marketing Intangible Products and Product Intangibles," Harvard Business Review, (May-June), 94-102.

Lovelock, Christopher H. and Charles B. Weinberg (1984), Marketing for Public and Nonprofit Managers, New York: Wiley.

MacStravic, Robin S. (1986), "Relationship Marketing in Maternity Care," Journal of Hospital Marketing, 1(Fall/Winter), 115-123.

Malhotra, Naresh K. (1986), "Hospital Marketing in the Changing Health Care Environment," <u>Journal of Health Care Marketing</u>, (September), 37-48.

"New Mayo Clinic in Florida Is First Link in a Nationwide Chain to Challenge HMO's (1986), <u>Wall Street Journal</u>, (October 3), 31.

Phelan, Rose D. (1987), "Nursing: An Unrecognized Major Health Care Marketing Force for Hospitals, <u>Journal of Health Care Marketing</u>, (June), 45-49.

Ross, Caroline K. et al (1987), "The Role of Expectations in Patient Satisfaction with Medical Care," <u>Journal of Health Care Marketing</u>, (December), 16-26.

Sheldon, Alan and Susan Windham (1984), <u>Competitive Strategies for Health Care Organizations</u>, Homewood, IL: Dow Jones-Irwin.

Uhl, Kenneth P. and Gregory D. Upah (1983), "The Marketing of Services: Why and How It Is Different," in <u>Research in Marketing</u>, Vol. 6, Jagdish N. Sheth, ed., Greenwich, CT: JAI Press, 231-257.

U. S. National Center for Health Statistics, <u>Advance Data from Vital and Health Statistics</u>, No. 102.

U. S. Bureau of Census, <u>Current Population Reports</u>, P-20, N406.

MARKETING HEALTH SERVICES IN A TURBULENT ENVIRONMENT: THE ST. VINCENT MEDICAL CENTER EXPERIENCE

T.D. Schramko
St. Vincent Medical Center

M. Sami Kassem, Ph.D.
University of Toledo

Abstract

St. Vincent Medical Center of Toledo, Ohio provides a vast array of specialty services to a constantly changing market. The changes are not unique to the St. Vincent market, but are being experienced throughout the United States Health Care System. In order to address the changes noted, constant monitoring of trends and development of strategies to meet challenges are required. St. Vincent Medical Center has organized its resources to best achieve a competitive position in its market. Having a regional market presence and participating at the national level in a Health System, while also responding to indigent care delivery have positioned St. Vincent Medical Center as a leader in Northwest Ohio. Current trends and strategies are noted, as well as the organizational changes the Medical Center has experienced throughout the last decade. From joint venturing with a major local competitor, to strengthening the regional system through networking with providers in Ohio and Michigan, St. Vincent Medical Center has responded to changes through creative programs and a dynamic management.

TRENDS AND STRATEGIES

St. Vincent Medical Center is a 640 bed regional tertiary care center located in Toledo, Ohio. The trends in the health care industry experienced by providers throughout the country have also impacted the Medical Center. These trends are in the areas of:

- Indigent Care
- Payment Systems
- Technology and Information Systems
- Health Systems

Since St. Vincent Medical Center is part of a national health system, Covenant Health System of Lexington, Massachusetts, the multi-hospital system trends are most important to note. Competition in all areas of delivery will be more intense as greater emphasis is placed on reducing

317

costs and increasing quality of care. The Medical Center has noted specific trends in the metropolitan Toledo/Northwest Ohio region that will shape our strategies for the future. These trends are:

- Greater pressure by employers to reduce costs of delivery to their employees
- Significant influx of new payment systems, i.e., HMO's, PPO's,
- Increasing utilization of outpatient/ambulatory care
- Increased cooperation among providers to develop services without duplicating costs/technology

These local trends will form the basis for future business decisions as we continue to reduce our cost base while refining our product lines.

The national trends can further be expanded and analyzed in the following manner:

Indigent Care

- Cost will definitely increase
- Tax status of providers may be affected by the amount and level of care provided
- Greater numbers of individuals will be put on the indigent care rolls
- State governments will work with regions of the state to develop HMO's for the Medicaid/Welfare population to reduce the indigent care expense

Payment Systems

- Outpatient care for the Medicare patient will increase and payment for services will be expanded while inpatient care reimbursement is reduced
- Fee for service will be less the case as capitation and negotiated rate plans are promoted
- Health policy will be affected by budget considerations in the area of Medicare

Technology and Information Systems

- Costs will increase
- Technology will become available to more providers as competition increases
- Clinical patient care and the computer will be brought together for diagnosis and treatment
- Telecommunications will link educational centers with outlying regional hospital networks

318

- More hospitals will belong to systems than ever before as networks of providers are developed
- Decisions in multi-systems will be more local than from a corporate office
- Insurance products will be developed by systems for their members
- Systems will work with systems to develop linkages and shape policy

Given these trends, St. Vincent Medical Center must respond in multiple ways in order to grow in the marketplace.

The indigent care isssue is being addressed through organizing internal resources to provide more care at less cost. Working with the other hospitals in the area and presenting testimony at the state level on the issue has resulted in a changed policy for increased payment. This is an example of how the Medical Center can influence policy on a large scale. The mission of the Medical Center has always been to provide care to those who cannot afford to pay. Organizing clinics and being more efficient in the delivery of care is a way to reduce the overall expense and still fulfill the mission.

St. Vincent Medical Center, along with The Toledo Hospital, recently developed a joint venture to provide a PPO for the region we jointly serve. Through this mechanism we have established a market position wherein our services will be utilized to a greater degree, while reducing our costs and improving profitability.

Technology has always played a key role in our development. We currently are pursuing a major expansion to our surgical program and recently opened a free-standing outpatient surgery facility. In each case, the newest technology, such as lasers, will be used to advance the medical care provided. A new data processing center is also being planned, which will improve the data link with all operating departments of the hospital, as well as keep pace with new accounting and billing systems.

As stated, the Medical Center is a member of a national health systems Covenant Health System in Lexington, Massachusetts. As such, we participate in national strategies that affect our system. Developing shared services, insurance products and management services are a few results of our involvement in this national network.

PROFILE OF THE PAST AND THE PRESENT

Exhibit I describes the healthcare environment from the 1970's to approximately 1983, under a cost-based reimbursement system. The environment was very high growth oriented with little or no need to be cost effective. From 1983 to the present, and we believe well into the future, being cost effective and sensitive to pricing and controlled growth will be a necessity in order to survive. The methods for management will have greater emphasis on planning, increased awareness of competition and active participation with third party payors in designing delivery systems. We must broaden our base of operation, while also refining our product mix. We cannot be all things to all people. Networking with other providers to capitalize on strengths is more cost efficient than duplication of services for a dwindling market. Management must recognize the value of extending services beyond the boundaries of city and county and work with all providers to strengthen the system of delivery.

ST. VINCENT MEDICAL CENTER RESPONSE TO THE TRENDS

In Exhibit II, St. Vincent Medical Center has progressed from a predominately inpatient, specialty care revenue base to a multi-market facility involving both outpatient and inpatient delivery of care. From no satellite service locations in 1975, to 12 at present, and several more being planned, St. Vincent Medical Center has shifted its focus toward consumer convenience while emphasizing quality of care. The Medical Center has adjusted its costs and worked diligently with its medical staff to respond to pricing pressures and the desire of business to provide managed care plans. The Medical Center downsized its total bed complement and enhanced its outpatient capabilities. Organizing a Medicaid HMO and working closely with community leadership at both local and state levels, has helped in the indigent care area. The Medical Center completed an update to its Long Range Plan and is currently developing a Regional Health System that will form a network with selected providers in Ohio and Michigan to develop businesses that support this Long Range Plan.

St. Vincent Medical Center has responded to increased competition and pricing schemes by organizing its resources and being focused in the marketplace. Planning versus reaction to events is more the norm, as we strive to grow in this volatile climate of health care delivery.

REGIONAL PLAN

In order to meaningfully link with other providers in the region, the Medical Center established St. Vincent Corporate Services, Inc., in 1980. This wholly owned subsidiary of the Medical Center was established to work with all providers in the region in support of their respective plans and services. The mission is to provide, on a fee-for-service basis, consultations and management expertise that support the client institution. Through this mechanism the Medical Center has reached out to over 200 hospitals throughout the country and all of the hospitals in its service area. Regionalization of health services and networking with physicians is the goal of Corporate Services. Promoting the Medical Center and its specialty base by providing business management expertise is a strategy designed to respond to the national trends.

The initiation of Life Flight in 1979, the first air ambulance service in Ohio, was a direct response to the needs of the market. Since 1979, over 100 hospitals in Ohio, Michigan and Indiana have been served. The Northwest Ohio Heart Center at St. Vincent Medical Center is also regional in the effort to extend our expertise in treating all phases of cardiac problems. Centers of excellence such as cardiology, neurology, burn/plastics, trauma, ophthalmology, orthopedics and diagnostics have been organized to make better use of our resources in meeting market and community needs. The St. Vincent Medical Center Foundation has developed a resource allocation campaign targeted to financially support the program needs of our centers of excellence. Through the Foundation, capital is acquired to ensure the long-term support of needed items as we continue to plan for the future.

CONCLUSION

In 1855, when St. Vincent Medical Center was founded by the Grey Nuns of Montreal, Canada, a simple mission was evidenced. To serve the poor, needy and sick of the community regardless of the ability to pay, was the central theme of the organization. Today, over 130 years later, that spirit and mission is very much a part of the total commitment we make to the region we serve. Keeping alive a promise to care for the indigent and foster excellence in service delivery and education of professionals in all areas of health, St. Vincent Medical Center is a pro-active organization looking for opportunities and leading the way. The international market and increased research in the areas of trauma and cardiac care are potential windows of opportunity. The Medical Center intends to remain a stable organization poised for growth and well prepared for fluctuating markets and trends. Turbulence does not mean instability at the Medical Center. We look for opportunities in change and adapt to our environment rather than react. Marketing will play a key role in designing our strategies. Our programs and services will be based on need and the ability to perform.

EXHIBIT I

Health Care Industry
Economics/Market Changes

<u>Cost Based Reimbursement</u> - (1970's to 1983)

.   No need to compete on an <u>economic</u> basis

.   High growth

.   Able to create demand

.   No marketing or data base management

.   No "advertising" or creative image campaign

.   Job security assured

.   Closure or restructuring minimal to none

.   Simple organizational model

<u>Prospective Payment System</u> - (1983 to Future)

.   Fierce economic competition through pricing strategies

.   No growth - a decline in acute care stages, but an increase in outpatient or ambulatory care

.   Demand is <u>very</u> hard to create

.   Very heavy emphasis on data collection, surveys, market analysis, cost accounting

.   Virtual war in advertising and creating market niches through product development

.   No job security - workforce has been redesigned to more technical jobs with higher pay, but no guarantee of longevity

.   39 hospitals closed in 1986, 43 in 1987 and projected 60 in 1988 in the small to medium sized organization signalling the growth and survival of the Health System, rather than the free standing solo hospital

.   Complex corporate organization with a holding company and numerous subsidiaries at both the for-profit and not-for-profit level

Exhibit II

St. Vincent Medical Center
Evolution of Strategy: 1975—

YEAR	NAME	OFF CAMPUS SITES	# OF BEDS	INPATIENT/ OUTPATIENT EMPHASIS	DIVERSIFICATION FACTORS	MARKET AWARENESS/ CONSUMER ORIENTATION	MANAGED CARE PLANS
1975	St. Vincent Hospital and Medical Center	-	714	Inpatient	Intensive Care and Hi-tech	Physicians are focus	None
1979	St. Vincent Medical Center (name changed to reflect new focus)	2	742	Inpatient	Emergency Care via "Life Flight"	Physician is still major focus	One in Metro area
1980	St. Vincent Medical Center	3	742	Inpatient 95% Outpatient 5%	St. Vincent Corporate Services, Inc. was created to develop businesses that support the Medical Center and diversify organization	Physician dominant; Consumer begins to influence through employers	Zero - Plan is terminated
1982	St. Vincent Medical Center as part of Covenant Health System (National Health System created by the Grey Nuns) Continues	4	742	Inpatient 90% Outpatient 10%	Regional emphasis on Networking is established and more outpatient tech. is pursued	Emphasis on Third Party reimbursement means greater consumer awareness	Two
1986	St. Vincent Medical Center/ Covenant - Development of National Health System Continues	10	640	Inpatient 70% Outpatient 30%	Support business lines, i.e., D.M.E., Transportation, Home Health, M.O.B. Outpatient Surgery	Consumer takes lead as physicians follow managed care plans	Ten
1988	St. Vincent Medical Center/ Covenant - Joint ventures with The Toledo Hospital for Managed Care	12	640	Inpatient 65% Outpatient 35%	Directly participate in the Managed Care Market through joint venture with The Toledo Hospital	Greater identification with employers and consumers as decision makers for obtaining health services	Ten plus

FOCUS GROUP RESEARCH: A QUALITATIVE RESEARCH TOOL TO ASSESS THE STRENGTHS AND WEAKNESSES OF A CAREER PLANNING AND PLACEMENT CENTER

Raj Arora
University of Missouri-Kansas City
Richard Hartman
Bradley University

ABSTRACT

In recent years the marketing concept and marketing research techniques have been been finding greater acceptance in not-for-profit and service organizations such as hospitals and universities. This paper demonstrates the application of a qualitative research tool, viz., the focus group interview, towards identifying the salient attributes of a career planning and placement center at a mid-western university. The perceived performance of the center on these attributes is discussed.

INTRODUCTION

That marketing can be successfully applied toward the management of a university is well known. In fact various researchers have applied the knowledge of marketing discipline to identify the determinant attributes in the choice of a school (Arora 1982, Kohn 1976), and to estimate the utilities of factors affecting the selection of a graduate school (Punj 1978). The techniques used in these studies range from multiattribute attitude models to newer techniques such as logic (Punj 1978) and Linear Structural Relations Approach (Arora 1982). This study concentrates on the application of a qualitative research tool, Focus Group as an aid to understanding the salient dimensions of a specialized unit within a university, viz., The Career Planning and Placement Center (CP & PC).

The past literature on marketing of higher education institutions has focused on the variables important in the choice of a university, or the entry level variables (Gorman 1974). This is understandable since the focus by most institutions is on increasing the enrollment. Toward this end universities (and the American Assembly of Collegiate Schools of Business – see the June/August 1987, Vol. 17, No. 5 newsletter entitled, "Ten Year Effort Produces Outcome Measurement Tools,") typically focus their efforts on the input variables. These are the quality of faculty, low student faculty ratios, quality of students, curriculum, friendly atmosphere, registration related convenience issues, etc. Occasionally universities, especially private universities emphasize their high placement of graduates. This topic is the subject of the investigation in this paper.

Anecdotal evidence by discussions with enrollment managers and department chairpersons suggests that the placement of the graduates is by far, one of the most important issue amongst college students, especially the senior students. Some prospective visiting students and their parents are interested in and partially evaluate a university on the basis of the placement rate. Thus, in specific, this study focuses on determining the extent to which the existing students are satisfied with the placement center of a comprehensive university located in Illinois.

METHODOLOGY

Focus Group

Although frequently used in marketing research (Dillon et al 1987) focus group applications in marketing higher education are not very common. This method of interview is a relatively inexpensive tool for acquiring important information about the key issues. These may range from variables salient in choice of an institution, to specifics about any one program of study or a service unit such as (CP & PC). This study addresses the later issue. The basic format of a focus group is a small group (10 to 12 people) who are familiar with the issue at hand, led by a moderator in a relaxed and informal setting that is conducive to interaction and thus encourages free thoughts and discussions elaborating the key issues. Although the atmosphere appears to be informal and unstructured, it is imperative to have a "guide" for the moderator to ensure a complete and systematic coverage of the issues that are the objectives of the research.

Typically, the focus group is the first step toward generating precise information that may be quantifiable across a larger base of population. The method can be used for discovering new opportunities, discovering important needs of the target market, discovering reasons underlying the existing attitudes, etc. In order to get the maximum benefit from the focus group interview, one must set forth the questions that need to be addressed. One must also ascertain that these issues can be covered by the focus group format. These issues must then be converted into a discussion guide or the moderator's guide.

Design

Two separate focus group interviews were conducted in order to determine student's beliefs and feelings about the Career Planning and Placement Center, and also to get some confidence about the "convergent" validity of the findings. The participants were seniors in the college of business and were screened with respect to awareness of the center and having had an occasion to have used it in the past. Several steps were taken to minimize any bias that may arise due to socially desirable responses or due to the presence of a perceived "authority" figure.

For example, the moderator of the focus group interviews was also a student and no instructor or any other university administrator was present during the interviews.

Each focus group was conducted by a different moderator. The moderators seemed to meet the face validity requirements in that they were socially active in the student network, were familiar with the theory of focus group and had been exposed to professional focus groups. In addition they participated along with a group of about six students acting as research assistants in developing the moderator's guide and thus were fully familiar with the issues to be investigated prior to the interview. Each of the two focus groups lasted for one hour. The interviews were conducted in a room that was similar to the rooms used by professional research firms for such purposes. It was a carpeted room with wood paneling, a large oval table with fourteen chairs for participants. Both focus group sessions were video-taped.

Moderator's Guide

The moderator's guide contains the sequence and the issues to be explored in the interview. The outline of the topics is shown in the exhibit 1.

EXHIBIT 1

Introduction

    1. Moderator
    2. Participant Introduction (name, class standing.)

Background information

    1. Academic interests, favorite classes, career choices.

Career Planning and Placement Center

    1. Initial Reception (first experience when visiting the center, friendliness of approach by personnel, if properly attended to.)
    2. Physical Environment (location accessibility, emotions resulting from layout of offices, information display.)
    3. Referral to counselor (initial screening of academic background, career choices, geographic preferences, other determinants that may influence the referral to a specific counselor.)
    4. Other information (forms to fill out, information about recruiting firms, interviewee training.)
    5. Counselor (attitudes towards the students, advise and influence on career choice, professionalism and or perceived prejudices.)

6. Placement Opportunities (availability of preferred jobs.)
7. Image of the center (overall impressions, opinions of relevant others.)

FINDINGS

All of the focus group participants had some degree of familiarity with the Career Planning and Placement Center. For many students this familiarity began during the university freshman orientation program. Several students worked with the Center to obtain co-op positions. Other students gained insight into the activities of the Center during a one-semester hour course in Planning Employment Strategy or through discussions with their friends. Additional information about the Center was gained through reading bulletin cboard announcements and Center mailings. All of the students were currently involved in the job search process.

For many students their initial visit to the Center was an enlightening experience. They found the activities in the Center to be very fast paced and hectic. Several students indicated that Center personnel were not immediately available to help them. Although the personnel were deemed to be helpful they appeared to be overloaded with student contacts especially during the first part of the fall semester. Some students resorted to seeking help from other students using the Center's facilities.

Many students were critical of the physical facilities of the Center. The Center was located in the basement of a multi-stored building. Students believed that the space devoted to the Center library was too small and that other aspects of the physical environment could be improved. Most students felt that the physical environment of the Center was un-appealing to them (and also to prospective employers) and did not enhance the University's image.

Most students felt that Center personnel were knowledgeable and professional in their approach to students. However, several students were critical of one staff member. Students were generally satisfied with most of the services provided by the Center. Practice interviews and informative mini-guides were singled out as particularly helpful services. Several students stated they were not satisfied with critiques of their resumes.

Several students were critical of the Center library. The students felt that the library contained a significant amount of information, but the students were not shown how to use the library and screen the information. As indicated previously the space devoted to the library was deemed to be too small. Several students felt that there was an insufficient amount of information available on small firms in the geographic area surrounding the university.

The students believed that the Center's effectiveness would be enhanced if the Center could attract more national and regional "blue-chip" firms to

327

come to the university to interview business students. Many students felt that there was an insufficient number of firms recruiting students in their particular major and professional field of interest. As a result some students believed that they would have to obtain their own job after graduation.

The focus group participants made the following suggestions to improve the effectiveness of the Center:

1. Hire additional secretarial and professional personnel.
2. Relocate the Center in more desirable and spacious facilites.
3. Attract more "blue-chip" national and regional firms to come to the university to recruit business students.
4. Attract more small firms from the local area to come to the university to recruit business students.
5. Expand the service hours of the Center to accommodate the schedule of students who work part-time.
6. Expand the Center library and teach students how to use the library.
7. Encourage second semester juniors to become familiar with Center services and the job search process.

The attitudes, concerns, and recommendations of the student focus group participants were quite similar in both focus group sessions.

IMPLICATIONS

The services performed by the Career Planning and Placement Center are vital to the university's students (target market) and the appropriate image of the center is thus vital to successfully attracting the students. This paper was concerned with discovering the salient variables of the Center and the level of satisfaction derived by the users of the center.

Although the students use the services at the sophomore and junior years (for Co-operative jobs) and senior years (placement after graduation), they do become aware of the Center's existence as early as their freshman year and continue to receive information (from friends) and thus keep updating their attitudes toward the Center. Thus it is vital for the Center to develop and maintain a visible profile and not focus their efforts of information dissemination solely towards the seniors.

Some of the key areas where the Center was not meeting the expectation of the target audiences were identified. These issues are not just related to the successful outcome of finding a job, but also deal with the physical environment of the surroundings and the interpersonal relations involved in providing the services. Some of these issues may be areas which need to be addressed, while other issues may be resolved by a more accurate task of providing timely information to the students.

The appropriate image of the Center can be used to attain a comparative advantage for the university. Further research may be advisable, particularly by conducting additional focus groups of students from other disciplines across the university to compare their perceptions and experiences with those from the College of Business. Additional research is essential also to determine the stability of the students' perceptions over time. And finally, similar focus groups from the prospective employers are at least as important as those from the students. Enlightened administrators will discover that the findings of the various focus groups provide invaluable information for improving the effectiveness of the Center and for meeting the needs of the clients of the Center.

REFERENCES

Arora Raj (1982), " Validation of an S-O-R Model for Situation, Enduring and Response Components of Involvement," Journal of Marketing Research, (November), 505-516.

Dillon, W.R., T.J. Madden, and N.H. Firtle (1987), Marketing Research in a Marketing Environment, Missouri, Times Mirror/Mosby College Publishing.

Editorial (1987), "Good Focus Group Session Needs the Touch of an Artist," Marketing News, 21 (18),35.

Editorial (1987), "Focus Groups are used as Bait in Trolling for Ideas," Marketing News, 21 (18), 48.

Gorman W. (1974), " Marketing Approaches for Promoting Student Enrollment in Higher Educational Institutions," College and University, (Spring), 242-250.

Karger, Ted (1987), " Focus Groups are for Focusing and for Little Else," Marketing News, 21 (18), 52-55.

Kohn M.G., C.F. Manski, and D.S. Mundel (1976), " An Empirical Investigation of Factors Which Influence College-Going Behavior," Annals of Economic and Social Measurement, (Fall), 391-419.

Kotler, Philip (1982), Marketing For Nonprofit Organizations, New Jersey, Prentice Hall.

Punj N. Girish and Richard Staelin (1978), " The Choice Process for Graduate Business schools", Journal Of Marketing Research, (November), 588-598.

CONSUMER ARBITRATION: THE B.B.B. APPROACH

Lance A. Masters and K. Michael Clarke
California State University, San Bernardino

ABSTRACT

Services have greater potential for generating consumer unhappiness than do physical goods, yet the marketing literature is sparse on dispute resolution in this area. This paper reviews the phenomena of consumer arbitration. The authors focus on the Council of Better Business Bureaus' *Auto Line*, the largest national program of mediation/arbitration for automotive disputes, sponsored by participating automobile manufacturers, and the program's extension into non-automotive products and services. The authors review consumerism and the history of arbitration. They discuss arbitration principles and procedures, program funding, and consumer satisfaction. Criticisms of the program are addressed, as are suggestions for additional work.

INTRODUCTION

Arbitration as a means of resolving disputes has a tradition dating to Greek, Egyptian and ancient Chinese civilizations. Nevertheless, judicial decision making has recently come to dominate formal dispute resolution processes. One significant reason for this development was the emergence of a class of professional councilors with a vested interest in reserving formal mechanisms to themselves. The subsequent ascendancy over the political process exercised by legal professionals helped to entrench the institutionalized superiority of court resolution of differences to that of arbitrators.

Arbitration did not disappear but by 1925 its significance in formal dispute resolution had diminished to the extent that Congress passed the Federal Arbitration Act to eradicate the common law hostility against arbitration agreements. This hostility was particularly evident in the labor relations area where the NLRB in effect the nation's chief arbitrator found itself consistently being reversed on appeal in the courts. The Board represents the most significant challenge to judicial domination of the dispute resolution process, but its decisions are the ones most prone to legal challenge on substantive grounds.

As the numbers of litigable or arbitrable disputes increased those favoring the court system were forced to make some accommodations. Small claims courts and neighborhood courts appeared. However they have proved inadequate to deal with the flood of disputes, and are usually ineligible to deal with the price range of automotive disputes, particularly when re-purchase is sought. The emergence and development of a consumer conscious society is a significant reason for the growth of product litigation. The rise of consumerism and the significant alteration of product liability law interpretation has had a dramatic effect on the status of arbitration, all at a time when access to courts is an expensive, slow and often confusing process.

The peculiar combination of litigiousness and consumerism is helping to erode the monopoly held by the bar and to reinstate arbitration as a viable dispute resolution process. One consequence of consumerism is the demand that products and services actually perform as specified or advertised. While sellers might prefer to hide behind *caveat emptor*, this is no longer possible because of consumer protection regulations and legislation such as the California Lemon Law and increasing competition. Marketers might have accepted the domination by slow courts and sometimes even slower regulatory agencies except for the emergence of a new phenomena. Consumers began to exhibit a strong and favorable response to companies that instituted formal complaint procedures. If consumers could be satisfied by access to a fast, fair and inexpensive resolution of their problems, then companies would not necessarily lose a customer. They might retain them and gain valuable publicity. The obvious answer is arbitration.

THE AUTO LINE PROGRAM

Consumers who complain about automotive problems occasionally do not seek nor receive help at a level acceptable to them from the dealer network level nor directly from the vehicle manufacturer through the regional representatives. To meet the requirements of the Magnuson-Moss Warranty Act for provision of a formal dispute resolution procedure, some manufacturers have written the *Auto Line* program into their warranties, requiring consumers to use this process before seeking legal redress. Other manufacturers permit the use of *Auto Line* under various specified circumstances. *Auto Line* is an informal process that relies on the *United States Arbitration Act 9 USCA 1-14* for interpretation of their rules. The forum is regulated by the Federal Trade Commission, and it must handle complaints which have already been brought to the attention of the manufacturer within sixty days.

When a consumer complains through the Better Business Bureau, several principles are applied. In those circumstances where *Auto Line* has been written into the manufacturer's warranty, the manufacturer agrees to arbitrate any and all claims which do not exceed the actual cost of repairs or the product, excluding such items as taxes and insurances. Manufacturers may agree at their sole discretion and on a case-by-case basis to arbitrate incidental claims such as towing and rental car reimbursement or other consequential damage, but they are not required to arbitrate them. Punitive damages, personal injury, property damage, fraud and other criminal allegations may not currently be arbitrated in this program, and such complaints are referred to conventional legal and court process.

The Bureau has trained employees who serve as mediators between the consumer and the business. Mediation resolved 101,160 of 118,530 cases closed in 1985, or about eighty-five percent. This excludes specific components handled under a special General Motors/Federal Trade Commission Consent Order.[1] If informal efforts to resolve disputes fail, arbitration is offered. At this point a formal agreement is executed which describes the specific nature of the dispute, and defines the scope of the arbitration. A pool of volunteer and unpaid community arbitrators is maintained by the Bureau. Modified rules of the American Arbitration Association regarding selection of volunteer arbitrators are used by the B.B.B. Both the consumer and the business are provided a brief biography of a few volunteer arbitrators, and each party to the dispute is then asked to rank their preferences for the volunteer arbitrators. Generally the individual receiving the highest overlapping rating is chosen as the volunteer arbitrator. In some circumstances, a panel of three volunteer arbitrators may decide the case.

While consumers may be permitted the option of presenting their case in person, in writing or by telephone, the Bureau encourages presentation in person. In contrast, Chrysler and Ford programs do not permit in-person presentations, and all testimony must be submitted in writing to the arbitrator hired by the manufacturer. Most *Auto Line* arbitrations consist of informal (no formal rules of evidence) in-person hearings, conducted by the volunteer arbitrator. Often an inspection of the vehicle is conducted at the time of the hearing. This inspection is mandatory in the instance of a requested buy-back. Occasionally independent technical expertise is called for by the volunteer arbitrator, and the Bureau attempts to provide it. Volunteer arbitrators are usually not legally trained nor particularly knowledgeable about automotive mechanics. They gather information from the parties of the dispute to make a determination based on the facts and their sense of what is fair.

----

1. Better Business Bureau internal statistics.

Sometimes the volunteer arbitrator may facilitate a mediated dispute at the time of the hearing. Otherwise, the volunteer arbitrator will make a decision after the hearing, which will be mailed to both parties. Should the consumer accept the decision, it becomes legally binding on the manufacturer. Should the consumer reject the decision, they are free to pursue alternative remedies.

PROGRAM FUNDING

Warrantors that write an independent forum such as *Auto Line* into their warranties must provide enough funds for their effective operation, as required under federal regulations implementing the dispute forum provisions of the *Magnuson-Moss Federal Warranty Act of 1975 (16 C.F.R. 703)*. Manufacturers who participate in *Auto Line* pay its costs through direct payments to the Council of Better Business Bureaus, which then reimburses their participating offices throughout the nation for their expenses. The service is free to consumers, and receives no direct tax support.

CONSUMER SATISFACTION

Acceptance/Rejection

As previously noted, most disputes are mediated without requiring the arbitration procedure. Of those *Auto Line* complaints that were heard in arbitration from March through October, 1986, the decisions in sixty-three percent were accepted by consumers. Eleven percent were rejected, and the remaining twenty-six percent of acceptance/rejection forms were not returned, indicating a tacit rejection. Therefore the total satisfactory resolution of disputes through the combined efforts of *Auto Line* mediation and arbitration is almost ninety-five percent[2]

Statistics are not maintained on who "won" mediated complaints. During the same March to October 1986 period in arbitrated complaints, over forty-four percent of all cases result in a split decision, where the consumer was awarded some part of what was requested, such as repairs instead of repurchase. In an additional twenty-seven percent of the cases, the consumer was awarded all that was requested. In the remaining twenty-nine percent of the time, the consumer found for the company.

A 1985 consumer satisfaction exit survey with 513 respondents reported significant improvements over an earlier 1982 survey[3]. Overall satisfaction with mediation increased from seventy-eight percent to ninety percent, and over eighty-seven percent of current respondents were positive about the overall program versus only fifty-five percent in 1982. Also, ninety percent of current respondents were satisfied with volunteer arbitrator selection processes compared to eighty-two percent in the prior study. Despite an average monthly case load of over 11,000 cases in 1986 compared to about 2,000 per month in 1982, it is notable that consumers increased in satisfaction about the amount of time that was required to resolve cases, from eighty-one percent in 1982 to eighty-nine percent in 1985.

----

2. Source: C.B.B.B., 1986.

3. *Consumer Arbitrator*, (published by the C.B.B.B.) Vol.3, #1 (Summer 1986) p. 16.

TRAINING

Arbitrator Training

The Council of Better Business retains a training staff, who are sent into the field to teach prospective volunteer arbitrators in B.B.B. procedures. In 1986 over 7,000 volunteers were trained in 200 cities. Class size averages thirty to thirty-five individuals, and the national pool of B.B.B. trained volunteer arbitrators now stands at approximately 21,000[4].

The training sessions that the authors attended may or may not be typical of standard volunteer training. The single three and one-half hour sessions covered the following topics: definition and background of arbitration, the Bureau standard procedures, process and case preparation, volunteer arbitrator characteristics and functions, hearing fundamentals, and award decisions. A pre-publication draft of a written version of the training session documents important procedural detail that might not be absorbed in one session. The Bureau has proposed to provide volunteer arbitrators with copies of this proposed new manual.

No specific training is provided in reference to matters of law, such as state "lemon" laws, local statutes, F.T.C. Rule 703, or general consumer law. Likewise, no special training is provided in automotive technology or terminology. The premise of this approach is that volunteer arbitrators are to conduct hearings based on their own sense of what is fair, without special consideration of other parameters unless raised by either party of the dispute, in which case the additional information may be considered in arriving at the final decision. A March, 1986 B.B.B. fact packet reads: "They (volunteer arbitrators) are asked to apply no legal or technical standards to their decision - unless these standards seem fair to them. Instead, we recommend that they apply their own common sense of what is reasonable and fair."

B.B.B. Staff Training

The Council of Better Business Bureaus has an eight member Bureau Evaluation and Training Team who train personnel in local bureaus. Also for each of the past three years the council has sponsored annual mass training seminars in which approximately 300 *Auto Line* personnel are trained or updated on policy, procedure, supervision and other pertinent topics of interest. Four day management workshops are also staged for groups of fifteen to twenty staff personnel. Topics range from automobile mechanics to scheduling and decision-making. Like most not-for-profit organizations, bureaus may not pay wages comparable to the higher end of local salary conditions, and accordingly the staff training and development takes on additional importance. Each bureau is also subject to an annual internal audit to insure compliance with procedural and agreement requirements.

MANUFACTURER PARTICIPATION

Ten lines of automobiles are represented by *Auto Line*, including six made by General Motors (Cadillac, Buick, Oldsmobile, Pontiac, Chevrolet, and GMC light trucks up to 10,000 g.v.w.), and Nissan, Honda and Volvo. The terms of the manufacturers' voluntary exposures vary, but all participants have agreed to arbitrate covered disputes for a minimum of 36,000 miles or thirty-six months, whichever comes first. The voluntary "buy-back" agreements of a minimum of twenty-four months or 24,000 miles is substan-

----

4. Source: The Council of Better Business Bureaus.

334

tially greater than the more stringent standards of most state "lemon laws," which usually call for buy-backs only in the first twelve months or 12,000 miles. Only about three percent of all *Auto Line* disputes result in arbitration awards of repurchase or buy-back, about 4,000 in calendar 1986.

CRITICISMS OF AUTO LINE

The arbitration programs introduced under the aegis of the Magnuson-Moss Warranty Act or as a result of state legislation have come under tremendous criticism. Not withstanding the apparent success of the *Auto Line* program, serious reservations must be entertained regarding the program. The first and most critical of these is that automobile manufacturers fund the program, as required by law. However the Bureau may be perceived by consumers as an agent of the manufacturers, or biased or sympathetic towards business. It is noted that the Bureau has always been funded by businesses in an attempt by legitimate businesses to help shield consumers from illegitimate businesses. Although perfect arbitration would require that no links exist between either party and the volunteer arbitrator, such situations often do exist and even financial ties between the volunteer arbitrator and one of the parties is not totally un-usual. For example, the Office of the Arbitrator in New York is funded by city government, and in California arbitrators working under the Myers Milias Brown Act are paid by the county or city govern-ment for whom they are arbitrating cases.

A second criticism is somewhat more focused. The Better Business Bureau makes an effort to recruit or-dinary members of the community as the law requires, and in general the training suggests that volun-teer arbitrators apply common sense and fairness to disputes. This emphasis on fairness is stressed even in states where "lemon" laws give consumers statutory rights. In applying subjective criteria rather than objective law, arbitrators are often at a loss concerning appropriate judgments. This contrasts with the situation in labor relations and most other arbitration fora where the expertise and experience of the ar-bitrator is a crucial factor, particularly in contract interpretation in labor grievances. Labor contracts normally specify certain specific employee rights, and management cannot refuse to arbitrate grievances brought by the representative. Under the *Auto Line* program, manufacturers may refuse to arbitrate claims over the minimum agreement, and the program does not include actions of the manufacturers agent, the selling or servicing dealer. This has practical importance to buyers, who then do not have an arena for buy-back arbitration of additional costs such as extended warranty, tax, and license costs. Thus the manufacturers and dealers are able to limit their exposure unlike management in a labor dispute.

A third criticism suggests that programs such as *Auto Line* represent a sophisticated form of co-optation on the part of the manufacturers. Volunteer arbitrators who typically have little technical competence and who are not encouraged to consider state lemon laws unless raised by one of the parties and con-sidered fair by the volunteer arbitrator must decide cases presented by an often irate and equally inex-perienced consumer in the face of factory trained and experienced manufacturer zone representatives. These manufacturer representatives are adept at getting volunteer arbitrators to understand the manufacturer's position, for example the problems of quality control under mass production and the un-reliability of personnel at servicing dealers. In addition, the American public has been conditioned through experience to believe that mechanical faults in automobiles are a fact of life. Consumerism and the demands it implies have yet to catch up with the rhetoric of consumer spokespersons.

Finally, mention must be made of a larger picture. Programs such as *Auto Line* are in part supported by manufacturers because they supplant much more serious Federal Trade Commission consent orders for certain General Motors diesel motive cars and for certain series transmissions. Agreeing to submit such consumer complaints to a little known arbitration program, where the manufacturer can defend a cor-porate position of expired warranty on a case-by-case basis before an inexperienced and non-professional volunteer, may have more cosmetic value for the manufacturer than substantive value for consumers.

SERVICES ARBITRATIONS

The successes of *Auto Line* have spurred the growth of the generic dispute resolution device into non-automotive products and services. One of the authors has served as an arbitrator in a case of an allegedly defective slump stone wall, another in a damage caused in dry cleaning, and another in poor results of a credit rating improving service. The process was identical, and the results were satisfying to both customer and business. The service is funded by regular dues of B.B.B. business members at no additional cost to them or to the customer. Generally the amounts disputed are lower than those in automotive cases, but the motives are the same, performance of the product or service, and the mechanism is the same, arbitration. In a recent purchase of a computer system from a value added retailer, the buyer observed some new "fine print." Now the sales contract provides for binding arbitration in the event of a dispute.

SUMMARY AND CONCLUSIONS

The *Auto Line* program is very successful. It has widespread manufacturer support. When customers use the program, they are generally satisfied. One caveat remains. If consumer interests and rights continue to increase, *Auto Line* will require extensive modification. Such changes could include reducing manufacturer discretion over the scope of the arbitration, improving the training of volunteer arbitrators to include application of relevant statutes, and providing for the assessment of penalties under specified circumstances. Expansion of the non-automotive and services program is needed, as is increased awareness by consumers of its potential. Further research is needed in perceptions of consumer arbitration programs, and in ways in which such programs could be expanded and enhanced.

THE ROLE OF ATTRITION IN NON-PROFIT SUBSCRIBER SERVICE ORGANIZATIONS

ROBERT C. SORENSEN, Ph.D.
Professor of Marketing - Rider College
and President-Sorensen Marketing/Management Corporation
and
MICHAEL A. WALSH
Director of Marketing
Foster Parents Plan, Inc.

"Abstract"

Attrition/retention are key components in marketing subscription service organizations in which customers make successive payments. Critical reasons include subscriber recruitment costs, non-self-liquidating costs of initial processing and fulfillment, and attrition risk.

Major factors affecting attrition include overall membership growth, environment, service program content, systems, subscriber characteristics, conflict between subscriber expectation and experience, and marketing techniques.

Internal Rate of Return, regression analysis and subscriber satisfaction testing are useful for evaluating relevant data to implement U.S. marketing strategies for a major international child sponsorship organization with attrition problems.

THE NATURE OF SUBSCRIPTION SERVICES AND ATTRITION

Brand loyalty is essential to the marketing success of every service organization. Without repeat purchases of its offering by the same consumers, its advertising and promotion serve to activate only a single initial sale, and the life cycle of such a service plateaus as its market becomes saturated. Mail order pioneer Max Sackheim (Kobs, 1979) would admonish clients to "make customers, not sales." The distinction recognizes that businesses are not built on one-time sales but on repeat business.

If the service category must be repeatedly purchased (e.g., cable TV, magazine, or child sponsorship) by the same customer, but the individual consumer is likely to drop the service category or moves from one brand to another, brand management must work in a variety of ways to maintain that consumer's continuing brand loyalty.

Services that are sold by subscription find brand loyalty of even greater consequence than do non-subscription services. This is true for the following reasons:

1. A new subscriber is frequently more difficult to win than a "one-

shot" single item purchaser by virtue of the continued commitment over time that the new customer learns is part of the price of the service to be received.

2. A not-for-profit subscription sale cannot be self-liquidating for the marketer. The combined cost of making the sale, the beginning preparation and provision of the purchased services, and the initial processing and fulfillment procedures will usually depend on continued subscription income for recompense.

3. In addition to the continuing income generated by the renewing subscriber, the service organization has an acquisition-cost equity in that person that can be liquidated only one time. According to Rados (1981), magazines often pay three to six times more to sign up a new subscriber than a repeat subscriber, and charities often pay more on average to bring in a new donor than the initial amount donated.

For these reasons, it is vital that the newly won service subscriber be retained. Thus, marketers are compelled to invest more to keep a repeat customer than to land a new one.

Therefore, an understanding of the economics of subscriber recruitment and retention, and a focus on securing subscriber brand loyalty is critical to the marketing success of a service. This understanding does not come easy. As Douglas (1985) puts it:

> The theory of choice applies logic to the act of choosing. The rational argument is one that is not self-contradictory and likewise the rational choice. To be rational, one choice does not negate the other. Rational behavior implies some ordering of alternatives in terms of relative desirability. The logic of choice concerns non-contractual, or ordered preferences. In science, probabilities are assessments of the reliability of expectations about events. Probabilities also figure prominently in the theory of choice. The variance of the probability constitutes the risk element.

Of course, risk is also perceived by the prospective subscriber. Zeithmal (1984) argues that services can be thought to provide less sales information than goods, thus involving more perceived risk. Services inevitably are less standardized than product categories and therefore offer less certain outcomes to consumers. Moreover, most services -- and certainly the one under discussion herein -- cannot be accompanied by warranties or guarantees. The service of overseas child sponsorship cannot be "returned" inasmuch as it has already been consumed if and when dissatisfaction is realized.

338

A SITUATION ANALYSIS

Background

One subscriber not-for-profit service category is overseas child sponsorship, i.e., that offer of "foster parenthood" or other sponsorship status with respect to children and families in third world countries in return for a continuing monthly payment of a specified minimum amount. These service organizations' national marketing operations are responsible for activating and maintaining their subscriber rolls.

A leading international organization in this category is Foster Parents Plan, which currently has 80,000 Foster Parents each of whom pays at least twenty-two dollars each month. Other gift givers are not under consideration in this paper.

Alarming Trends

Recent statistical trends have suggested cause for concern:

Increasing Subscriber Discontinuances. The numbers of subscriber discontinuances (i.e., sponsors who have enrolled at some point and subsequently discontinued their contributions) have risen dramatically in the last four years and have increased 150% since 1984 (Exhibit 1).

- Rising Attrition Rate. The rate at which sponsors leave the organization (total discontinuances as a percent of the customer base) has also climbed steadily since 1961, from 16% of the total subscriber base to over 20%.

- Decreasing Subscriber Tenure. The mean subscriber lifespan has fallen steadily. Since 1981, it has shortened 26% from 7.4 to 5.4 years.

The data showed that the organization was losing substantial numbers of existing subscribers, and these sponsors were not remaining with the organization as long as they were just a few years earlier.

The Bigger Picture

Review and analysis of additional data, however, explain much of the declining statistics. The recent rapid growth in new subscribers (which resulted from increased marketing expenditures during the heavy media exposure given the African drought situation) has resulted in more subscriber discontinuances, a higher attrition rate, and shorter subscriber tenures:

- The numbers of discontinuances are positively correlated with the numbers of newly enrolled subscribers (Exhibit 2).

339

- The rate of discontinued subscribers is measured as a weighted average of the entire subscriber base. Since there exists a "shakeout period" during which certain newly recruited subscribers drop out, the organization will experience shorter average tenures and increasing weighted average attrition rates. This is due to the increasing proportion of new vs. older subscribers (Exhibit 3).

Still, growth is not a cause of attrition any more than birth is a cause of death. An understanding of the potential variables which influence attrition is necessary for the development of attrition avoidance/retention strengthening strategies.

FACTORS AFFECTING ATTRITION

As is true with for-profit organizations, subscriber brand loyalty/attrition with not-for-profit organizations is influenced by a variety of internal and external factors; some are controllable and measurable by service marketing management, some are not. Of course, one must not be unmindful of the point made by March and Simon (1958): "The organizational and social environment in which the decision maker finds himself determines what consequences he will anticipate, what ones he will ignore."

The following is the framework within which strategies, specifically marketing strategies, should be developed. It was created based on results of numerous subscriber (and ex-subscriber) research studies prepared by the Research Department and Foster Parents Plan during the past decade.

Environment. Current events, the inflation rate, recessions, peoples' economic confidence and competitive activities external uncontrollable factors which affect attrition.

Service Program. Field related factors such as quality/quantity of subscriber/recipient personal communications, progress reports on recipients and recipient field cancellations are only partially and indirectly controlled by the marketing organization.

Systems. Operational and administrative internal factors include methods of paying and quality of service to subscribers. To the extent that they involve marketing responsibilities, they are controllable but not necessarily changeable, particularly given the constraints of direct marketing and its maintenance by mail and telephone.

Subscribers. Personal circumstances, demographics and lifestyles, and expectations of individual subscribers can have a significant impact on attrition. A "flawed subscriber" is a person who is destined by virtue of certain incompatible personal characteristics -- demographic, economic or psychographic -- to lose interest in maintaining the service relationship. All other factors held constant, he or she is a person who would best never have been recruited as a subscriber.

340

<u>Conflict between subscriber expectation and experience</u>. Services and products alike frequently fail to live up to the anticipations of the customer who has purchased them. This incompatibility, sometimes known to students of consumer behavior as a variation of cognitive dissonance, is a known phenomenon, not necessarily haphazard, and is subject to both measurement and change.

<u>Marketing</u>. According to in-market tests conducted at Foster Parents Plan, the marketing and communications strategies utilized to attract new subscribers have a significant impact on subscriber attrition rates:

- The advertising message: emotional themes have more initial appeal to new subscribers than do intellectual themes, but these subscribers do not stay as long as those recruited with an intellectual message.

- The advertising medium: broadcast (television, radio) is a more cost-effective recruitment medium, but more segmented approaches result in long-term subscribers.

- The advertising offer: "loose-lead" offers (little obligation) generate more new subscribers than "tight-lead" offers (much commitment), but loose-lead subscribers tend to discontinue sooner.

- As discussed, the growth rate: the Boston Consulting Group (1988) concluded that the reason for the recent rise in the <u>number</u> of discontinuances was the growth in new subscribers.

These factors, particularly the marketing variables, influence both post-response attrition and up-front response rates. This suggests that there exists a quantitative financial tradeoff between the costs to attract and to retain subscribers. An appropriate methodology for evaluation is critical in order to understand and determine how an organization might mitigate the negative variables and influence the positive factors to reduce attrition. Only then can effective marketing and promotional decision making occur.

METHODOLOGIES FOR MEASUREMENT AND EVALUATION

<u>Expectation/Experience Compatibility Testing</u>. Albeit ex-post-facto, subscriber satisfaction and prognosis for membership duration can be tested at periodic intervals with the following factors accounted for: 1) the content and the emotions to which the subscriber perceives he/she originally responded; 2) respondent assessment of current experience in terms of differential expectations presented to him/her; 3) subsequent maintenance/termination behavior.

<u>Regression Analysis</u>. Despite the many individual factors which have been identified through internal research and testing as impacting attrition, and the limitations with these data (some are non-quantifiable and others are not available), efforts can be made to help explain and predict attrition. The regression function below has been developed to explain the variation in

and to predict discontinued subscribers:

> The annual number of discontinued customer = f (the size of the active subscriber base, U.S. personal income, inflation, sponsorship price).

Exhibit 4 illustrates the "fit" of the regression equation; the four independent variables included in the function explain 88% of the variation in discontinuances.

Regression analysis will not explain causation, however. For that we must still hypothesize. The equation and output do indicate that the size of the subscriber base (i.e., growth) is a significant variable explaining attrition. In fact, if size of customer base were the only independent variable used, it would explain fully 82% of the percent change in discontinuances. Predicting the number of annual discontinuances is important for non-profit subscriber service organizations to guide budget forecasting, staff levels and inventory control.

Internal Rate of Return (IRR). Subscriber service organizations rely overwhelmingly on advertising to perpetuate growth. Until recently, conventional wisdom for general advertising dictated that media be evaluated by the advertising cost per impression and readership studies. Direct marketing advertising historically has been evaluated with a more accountable cost-per-order methodology, according to direct response experts Nash (1982) and Kobs (1979). Rapp and Collins (1987) transcend the cost-per-order method and prescribe "the magical concept of lifetime customer value" when accounting for advertising expenditures, that is, to look beyond the cost of the initial sale, and measure the costs and returns of subscriber repeat business.

Since marketing message, offer and growth potential do (and must) differ by the source of the medium, then marketing organizations must view these media buys as investments, investments which compete with one another at the margin. Further, since the quality or long term expected value of the subscriber will also vary by medium, marketers must utilize an evaluation methodology which measures all costs and expected cash flows over the lifetime of the subscriber in the marketing investment "portfolio". The authors recommend the Internal Rate of Return (IRR) as a uniquely appropriate performance measure.

Despite criticisms which have been documented by Adelson (1965) the IRR is still widely used by financial managers to measure returns on investments, such as capital and financial assets. As defined by Weston and Brigham (1981), the IRR is the discount rate which equates the present value of expected costs with the present value of expected cash inflows. By considering the various costs of media investments with the differing expected tenure of the subscriber, marketers can determine how much to invest in a particular subscriber, and compare the marginal IRRs to arrive at an optional promotional mix.

Foster Parents Plan has utilized the IRR to transcend the myopic and oversimplified cost-per-order approach to guide media expenditure allocation. To illustrate: cost per orders from television are 50-100% less than those from the more targeted magazine and direct mail advertising. However, magazine/mail subscribers have much greater brand loyalty, making IRR levels comparable to those from television. While a cost-per-order analysis would suggest an elimination of magazine/mail advertising, the IRR approach justifies the inclusion of print and direct mail advertising in the media mix.

Service marketing strategists should also utilize the IRR to evaluate the cost effectiveness of various advertising messages and indeed various media/message combinations.

DETERRENCE OF SUBSCRIBER ATTRITION

What actions can be taken to deter subscriber termination? The following strategies are relevant to any subscriber service organization, and include:

1. <u>Focus on the Subscriber</u>. Through continued research, marketers must identify subscriber preferences and cater to them. Quality of field program and marketing service should be defined by the customers, not by management.

2. <u>Adopt Market Segmentation Approaches</u>. Subscriber service organizations' customer lists contain a variety of segments to which tailored marketing and communications programs should be directed. Further, these house lists will provide insight for external message/media segmentation opportunities. And no list of failed legitimate prospects or former sponsors or donors should be ignored for its potential usefulness in implementing another marketing strategy.

3. <u>Create Realistic Expectations</u>. Marketers must assure that external and internal promises are consistent with what is being delivered, and must continually monitor attitudes and behavior for evidence of dissonance. Personal values that can function as predictors for compatibility between expectation and experience should be identified and utilized in post experience testing.

4. <u>Identify and Absorb the Impact of Uncontrolled Intervening Variables</u>. Factors that must be reckoned with on an ongoing basis but which are subject to little if any control include sudden changes in the economy, the competition of catastrophes, and political events.

5. <u>Simplify Internal Systems</u>. Administrative procedures and operating systems should make it easy to continue and more difficult to discontinue the ongoing relationship. Rigorous testing should take place.

6.   <u>**Utilize Effective Evaluation Measures**</u>. Valid and reliable analysis which balances costs and benefits of front-end vs. post-response subscriber behavior will put attrition in perspective and foster effective marketing strategy development.

1.   Increasing Discontinuances

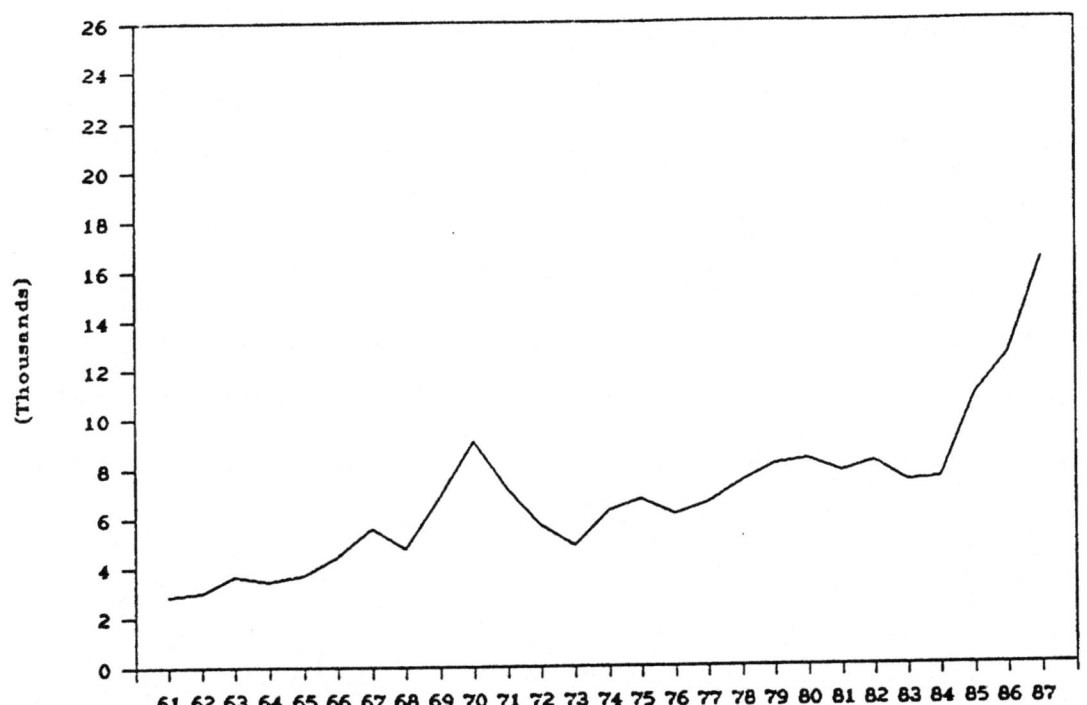

2.   Discontinuances Correlate
with New Enrollments

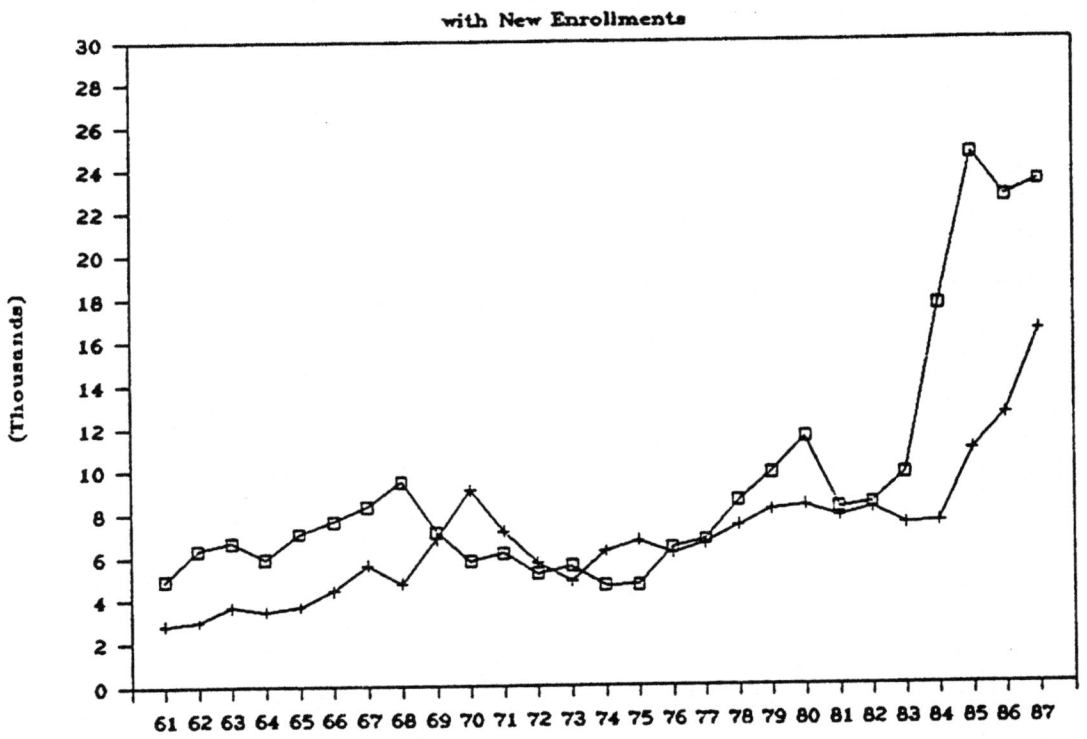

3. New Subscribers Skew Base

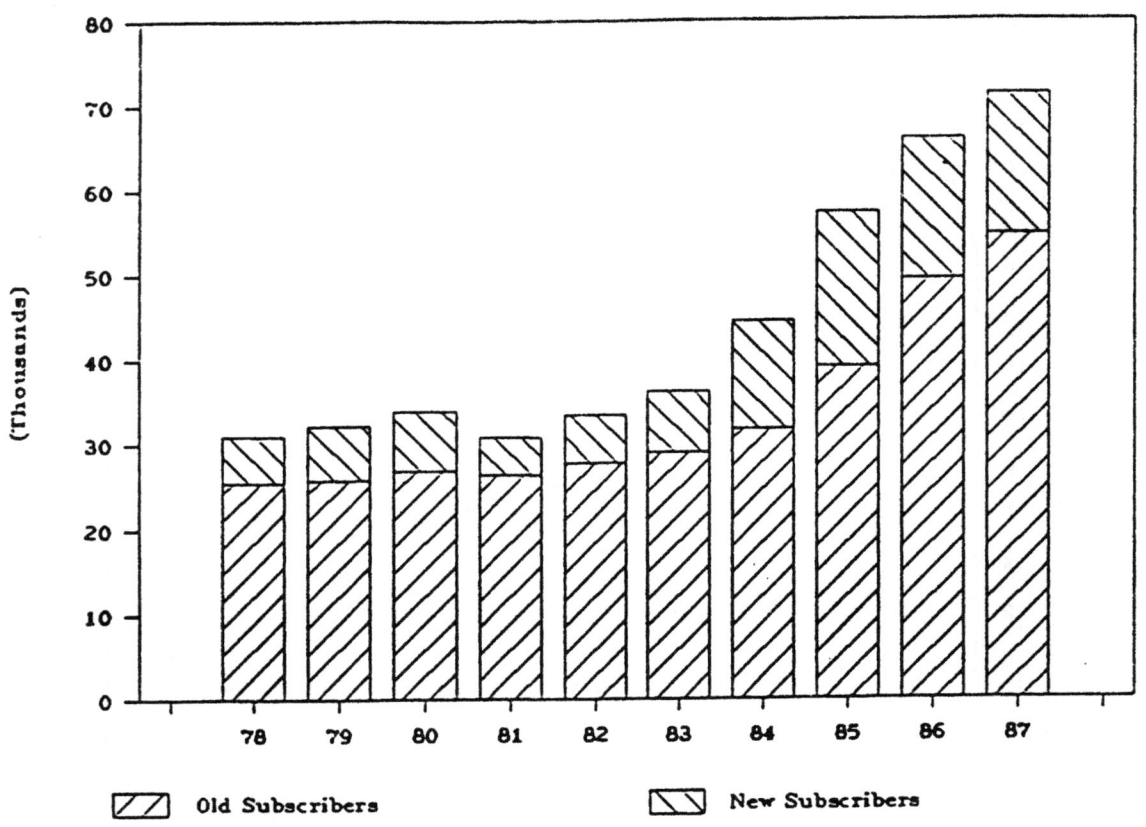

Old Subscribers   New Subscribers

4. Actual vs Predicted Discontinuances

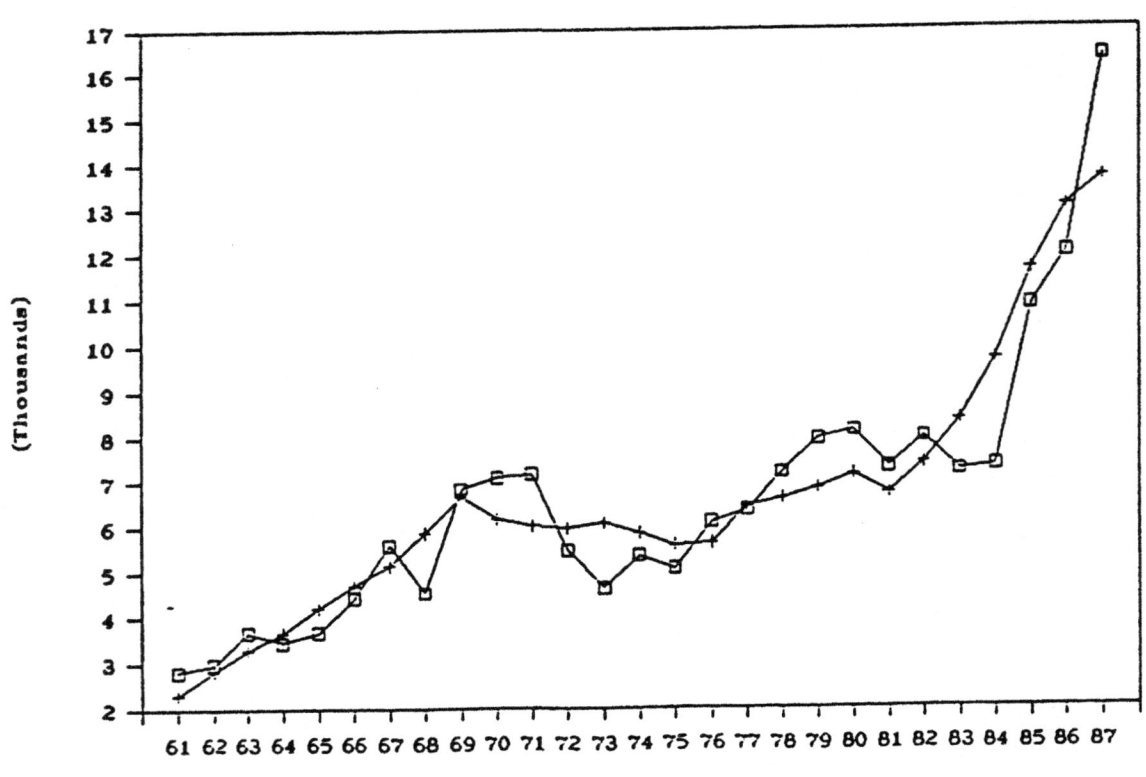

□   Actual   +   Predicted

REFERENCES

Adelson, R.L., "Capital Investment Criteria", <u>Operational Research Quarterly</u>, 16, 1, March 1965.

The Boston Consulting Group, <u>Improving Operations. A Slide Book prepared for Foster Parents Plan</u>, The Boston Consulting Group, Exchange Place, Boston, Massachusetts, March 1988.

Douglas, Mary, "Choice and Risk", <u>Risk Acceptability According to the Social Sciences</u>, Russell Sage Foundation, New York, 1985.

Kobs, Jim, "Fulfillment and Back-end Marketing", <u>Profitable Direct Marketing</u>, Crain Books, Chicago, Illinois, 1979.

March, J.G. and H.A. Simon, <u>Organizations</u>, Wiley, New York, 1958.

Nash, Edward L., "Strategic Planning", <u>Direct Marketing</u>, McGraw-Hill Book Company, New York, 1982.

Rados, David L., "Behavior", <u>Marketing for Non-Profit Organizations</u>, Auburn House Publishing Company, Boston, Massachusetts, 1981.

Rapp, Stan and Thomas L. Collins, "The Essence of the MaxiMarketing Solution", <u>MaxiMarketing</u>, McGraw-Hill Book Company, New York 1987.

Weston, J. Fred and Eugene f. Brigham, "Capital Budgeting Techniques", <u>Managerial Finance</u>, The Dryden Press, Hinsdale, Illinois, 1981.

Zeithmal, Valerie A., <u>Services Marketing</u>, Christopher H. Lovelock, Prentice Hall, Englewood Cliffs, New Jersey, 1984.

SITUATIONAL VARIABLES IN INDUSTRIAL SERVICES MARKETING: AN EXPLORATORY STUDY

Lise Heroux
State University of New York: Plattsburgh

Abstract

Industrial buyers' and sellers' behaviors in a sales encounter for services may be influenced by a variety of situational factors. This exploratory study, using a script theory framework, examines whether the service purchase process differs when dealing with (1) firms of different sizes, and (2) firms in different industries. The results suggest that, for these two context variables, no significant differences seem to exist. The industrial purchase/sale process for support services appear to be consistent across industries and firm sizes.

Belk (1975) defined situational factors as "all those factors particular to a time and place of observation which do not follow from a knowledge of personal (intra-individual) and stimulus (choice alternative) attributes, and which have a demonstrable and systematic effect on current behavior". A comprehensive and accurate prediction of behavior in the marketplace demands a situational perspective (Kakkar and Lutz, 1981).[1]

Industrial Marketing Context

In industrial marketing research, this point is clearly illustrated in a recent study by Schurr and Calder (1986) which found that, in ordinary restaurant settings, compared to fancy restaurant meetings, industrial buyers will (1) evaluate a sales representative's arguments more positively and a user's arguments more negatively, (2) judge that the user must yield to the sales representative if any disagreement arises, and (3) give a more favorable overall supplier evaluation.

Other studies have also found situational variables to influence the industrial marketing process. For example, Clopton (1984) investigated seller concession behavior, seller information, and buying firm monitoring of the buyer and found that these situational variables interact to affect the buyer's negotiation behavior and outcomes. Others (Jackson, Keith and Burdick, 1984) found that the relative influence of buying center members is constant across different buy classes, but changes across product types and procurement decision types. On a more macro level, Achrol and Stern (1988) suggest that whatever occurs in the environment of a channel is

---

[1]For a comprehensive review of the situational factors literature, the readers are referred to Kakkar and Lutz (1981).

likely to affect the degree of uncertainty experienced by its members. Their preliminary research findings indicate that the principal dimensions determining decision-making uncertainty are: diversity among consumers, dynamism, concentration, and capacity.

Service Context

Thus, industrial buyers and sellers may be influenced by a variety of situational factors. This is especially important in the case of industrial services, characterized by their intangibility, heterogeneity, inseparability and perishability, where the relationship between the buyer and the seller becomes increasingly important in the outcome of the purchase/sale process, with the absence of tangible cues.

In the service literature, a few authors (Wener, 1985; Upah and Fulton, 1985; Maister, 1985; Shostack, 1987) have discussed various situational variables influencing satisfaction with the service acquisition/consumption experience. Upah and Fulton (1985) state that marketers are often faced with the task of characterizing what consumers cannot see (the service itself) by managing aspects of the service they can see (for example, physical facilities, equipment, service providers, symbols, and so on). The objectives of "situation creation", according to these authors, are to increase the likelihood that the service encounter take place, and make that service encounter a positive and successful one for customers and service providers. The potential effects of poor environmental conditions can be considerable according to Wener (1985). If disorientation occurs with respect to understanding where facilities are and how they are to be used, the customer will perceive the situation as aversive and will possibly withdraw from the setting. Maister (1985) suggests several guidelines for practitioners to improve the waiting time experience because "the waiting-line experience in a service facility significantly affected our overall perceptions of service provided". Shostack (1987), in fact, recommended that interaction procedures, another set of tangible cues, be "blueprinted"-- that is, that every step in the interaction between customers and service providers be carefully planned in order to produce the desired outcome.

Several of the articles in the above literature review on services are qualitative and require empirical support. This study is an initial empirical attempt at describing and understanding a combined good/service purchase decision process (i.e., support service for an industrial good), which reflects the majority of purchase situations in industrial markets, using a script theory framework.

The Script Conceptualization

Abelson (1976) defined a script as "a coherent sequence of events expected by an individual, involving him either as a participant or as an observer". Schank and Abelson (1977) refined this initial definition to "a structure that describes appropriate sequences of events in a particular context". More recently, Abelson (1981) stated that "a script is a hypothesized cognitive structure that when activated organizes comprehension of event-based situations."

Scripts serve many purposes (Abelson, 1976, Schank and Abelson, 1977). First, since they are formed on the basis of repeated experience with a particular event sequence, scripts can guide one's actions and expectations during the sequence. Second, scripts are presumed to play an important role in comprehension and inference-making (Abelson, 1981; Bower, Black and Turner, 1979; Schank and Abelson, 1977). Finally, scripts play a role in attitude-formation or judgment-making, particularly about persons or social events. Thus, script theory holds that individuals repeatedly exposed to similar situations develop stereotypic action sequences for such occasions. These, in turn, guide the interpretation of information, the development of expectations, and the enactment of appropriate behavior routines.

Script theory has been successfully applied and demonstrated in consumer decision making contexts (Leigh and Rethans, 1984b) and organizational/industrial contexts (Leigh and Rethans, 1984a, 1985; Schurr and Calder, 1986). Because industrial buyer/seller interaction situations tend to be repetitive, it is reasonable to expect buyers and sellers to develop generic scripts, or stereotypic action sequences, for many of these situations which guide their respective behavior in sales interactions. Hence, scripts are potentially powerful determinants of the conduct and outcome of sales encounters. The scripts developed by industrial buyers and sellers may differ depending on the situation from which they draw their experience in the purchase/sale of industrial services. Thus, the following research question is examined in this exploratory study:

Research Question

Do industrial purchasing agents and sales representatives hold different scripts of the purchasing/sale process for services depending on (1) size of the firm, and (2) industry type?

METHODOLOGY

This exploratory, quantitative research design consisted of two phases. In Phase 1: Script Elicitation, a free elicitation (self-report) procedure developed by Bower et al. (1979) and successfully applied in other contexts (e.g., consumer decision making) was used to explore the presence of scripts for industrial buyers and sellers. Through 20 personal interviews obtained on a convenience basis in Montreal and Toronto, a script-relevant situation was described to "instantiate" (term used in the script literature to mean "trigger") the script. The respondents were then asked to provide a written list of the activities, in the appropriate sequential order, which would occur during the industrial service decision process.

In Phase 2: Script Validation, a structured questionnaire based on the script obtained in Phase 1, was sent to 250 industrial buyers and sellers in four cities (Montreal, Toronto, Vancouver, Halifax). The questionnaire consisted of two tasks, rated on a seven-point scale: (1) activity typicality (Leigh and Rethans, 1984; Smith and Houston, 1985); and (2) activity importance of each activity in the Phase 1 script to validate the commonness of the service script. A demographic profile section was also included in the instrument, including the respondent's company size and industry. Company size was determined in terms of the number of employees

(Small: 500 employees or less; Large: more than 500 employees) and the firm's annual sales volume (Small: $100 million or less; Large: greater than $100 million), while industry was classified according to the modified Standard Industrial Classification Code it best fit: (1) agriculture, forestry, mining; (2) manufacturing; (3) construction; (4) transportation, communication, utilities; (5) wholesaling, retailing; (6) finance, services.

RESULTS

Sample

Ten of the respondents interviewed in Phase 1 were purchasing agents, and ten were sales representatives in the industrial sector. They represented a variety of firm sizes and industries, and all had some experience in the purchase/sale of support services needed for industrial products. In Phase 2, 45 questionnaires were returned, a response rate of 18% from the randomized selection of respondents from the Purchasing Management Association of Canada mailing list. Two thirds of the respondents estimated their firm's annual sales volume to be $100 million or less, and one third estimated it to be more; 45% employed 500 employees or less, and 55% employed more than 500. All industries were represented.

Service Script

Since the purchase of industrial goods often involves the servicing of that good, respondents were asked to describe the decision regarding a support service acquisition. As expected, each respondent mentioned a set of common activities which presumably reflect his/her particular purchasing/selling style and experience. Since various activities ranged in frequency of mention, a group script could be defined using a frequency of mention cut-off point of 25% according to Bower, Black and Turner (1979). The script sequence was determined by each activities' most common order of occurrence (modal). The resulting support service script is presented in Table 1. A reliability measure of 95.4% was computed for coder agreement. The frequency of mention of the activities in the process may be low due to the perceived customization of the support service. All but two activities were mentioned by 25-39% of the respondents.

The script for a support service acquisition can be viewed as a series of stages, starting with the recognition of a service need by the buyer and taking the initial steps to contact sellers and ending with small talk and a possible follow-up call to assess the buyer's satisfaction with the service contract. Both buyers and sellers appear to follow the same script. Although the script for the purchase of a service resembles that of product acquisitions, some differences do appear to exist (Heroux, 1987). For example, the sales call for a product will usually consist of a discussion of the buyer's need, a brief discussion of the seller's reputation, an extensive sales presentation that includes a demonstration, and literature on the product features. In the absence of a tangible offering, the service sales call will emphasize the buyer's need, the seller's reputation, and a tangible leaflet of the service description. In the case of a service, the buyer must rely on the firm's reputation and a description of the service to make a decision. Another important difference is that product acquisition, in contrast to services, often involves the mailing of Requests for Information, Requests for Quotes or Bids by the buying firm to initiate the supplier search process. The purchase of many types of services is often less structured than the script implies. A consultant, for example, is often chosen by someone in management rather than by a purchasing agent.

To simultaneously test the hypothesis that several population means do not differ, considering all script variables together, Hotelling's Trace, a multivariate generalization of the univariate t value, was computed. Instead of computing 19 separate T-tests comparing the means of large and small firms (for example) for the 19 script activities in Table 1, Hotelling's Trace compares the means of these two groups' 19 script activities simultaneously to obtain an overall assessment of script differences.

TABLE 1

Script Elicited: Support Service Contract

Initiator	Script Activity	%
Buyer	Telephone call regarding a service need to be satisfied	*
Seller	Respond to buyer's call for service	*
Both	Establish meeting time and place	*
Buyer	Discussion of specific problem/service requirements	***
Seller	Review services offered and required	*
Seller	Promote vendor company history/reputation	*
Seller	Set up plant tour	*
Seller	Discussion of service contract benefits	*
Buyer	Discussion of service terms	*
Seller	Research department input sought to solve specific problem	*
Seller	Commitment to perform the necessary corrective action	*
Both	Review service quotation	*
Buyer	Initiate negotiation on price	**
Both	Agreement on service trial	*
Buyer	Decision to buy/not to buy the service	*
Both	Get/give the purchase order	*
Both	Exchange of parting comments	*
Seller	Leave office	*
Both	Follow-up call	*

Note:
Frequency $\geq$ 75% : ****
Frequency 50-74%: ***
Frequency 40-49%: **
Frequency 25-39%: *

Company Size

In terms of annual sales volume, no significant differences were found between large and small firms in how typical the script activities are (Hotelling's Trace: value = .61393; approx. F= .58323; sig. = .880) and how important the script activities are (Hotelling's Trace: value = .97126; approx. F = .82557; sig. = .662) in the purchase of industrial support services.

In terms of the number of employees in the firm, no significant differences were found between large and small firms in how typical the script activities are (Hotelling's Trace: value = .66204; approx. F = .75024; sig. = .739) and how important the script activities are (Hotelling's Trace: value = .97396; approx. F = .97396; sig. = .523) in the purchase process of industrial services. Given the restricted sample size, it was impossible to break the sample down further to look at very small firms. However, the very small firms that hire purchasing agents may also differ from those that do not hire a full-time purchasing agent, but rather have someone else (e.g., accountant) perform the purchasing functions. The latter would not be on the mailing list; therefore, no meaningful results would be obtained from further break-downs of the sample. This would, however, be an interesting area of research.

Industry Type

Similarly, no significant differences appear to exist in the service script followed in different industries in terms of how typical the activities are (Hotelling's Trace: value = 5.97375; approx. F = .97970; sig. = .541) and how important the activities are (Hotelling's Trace: Value = 6.08253; approx. F = .87588; sig. = .732).

DISCUSSION

The results of this exploratory study suggest that large and small firms appear to follow a similar purchase/sale process, and that this process is consistent across industries. Industrial purchasing agents and sales representatives can therefore follow the same script in the service acquisition encounter, regardless of the size of the firm with which they are dealing, or the type of industry.

It is possible that no significant differences are found with respect to these two situational variables because, in the industrial sector, both purchasing agents and sales representatives often receive some form of training, be it formal or informal (on-the-job), which guides the development of the individual's script for a service acquisition encounter. This script may even be somewhat standardized through training, across industries and sizes of firms.

From a methodological perspective, the script theory framework may not have yielded sufficiently detailed scripts from the respondents to identify real sources of differences in the scripts in larger and smaller firms, and in various industries. With the limited sample sized obtained for this exploratory study, activities mentioned by few respondents which did not become part of the final script may gain importance with a larger sample.

In contrast to recent research examining situational factors in the industrial sector, this exploratory study found no support for two situational variables (industry type and size of firm) influencing the acquisition process in the industrial sector. However, this was the first study to examine industrial support services, so that more research is needed to establish the validity of these findings. Furthermore, the service literature requires empirical support for all the qualitative articles reviewed above.

Further research is needed to examine the influence of situational variables of all kinds on the industrial service encounters. For example, do regional differences exist in the conduct of the service acquisition encounter? Do differences exist in the context of the service encounter depending on the type of service at hand (e.g. support service, financial, consulting, etc.)?

REFERENCES

Abelson, Robert P. (1981). "Psychological Status of the Script Concept", American Psychologist, vol. 36, July, p. 715-729.

Abelson, Robert P. (1976). "Script Processing in Attitude Formation and Decision Making", in Cognition and Social Behavior, J.Douglas Carroll and John Payne, eds. Hillsdale, N.J.: Lawrence Erlbaum, p. 33-45.

Achrol, Ravi S. and Lewis W. Stern (1988). "Environmental Determinants of Decision-Making Uncertainty in Marketing Channels", Journal of Marketing Research, Vol. XXV, February, p. 36-50.

Belk, Russell W. (1974). "An Exploratory Assessment of Situational Effects in Buyer Behavior", Journal of Marketing Research, Vol. XI, May, p. 156-163.

Bower, Gordon H., John B. Black and Terence J. Turner (1979). "Scripts in Memory for Texts", Cognitive Psychology, Vol. 11, April, p. 177-220.

Clopton, Stephen W. (1984). "Seller and Buying Firm Factors Affecting Industrial Buyers' Negotiation Behavior and Outcomes", Journal of Marketing Research, Vol. XXI, February, p. 39-53.

Giunipero, Larry C. and Edward F. Keiser (1988). "JIT Purchasing in a Non-Manufacturing Environment: A Case Study", Journal of Purchasing and Materials Management, Vol. 23, No. 4, p. 19-25.

Heroux, Lise (1987). "Buyer-Seller Interaction: A Script Theoretic Framework", unpublished Ph.D. dissertation, Concordia University, Montreal, Canada.

Jackson, Donald W., Jr., Janet E. Keith and Richard K Burdick (1984). "Purchasing Agents' Perceptions of Industrial Buying Center Influence. A Situational Approach." Journal of Marketing, Vol. 4, Fall, 75-83.

Kakkar, Pradeep and Richard J. Lutz (1981). "Situational Influence on Consumer Behavior: A Review", in Perspectives in Consumer Behavior, Third Edition, H. Kassarjian and T.Robertson (eds.).

Leigh, Thomas W.and Arno J.Rethans (1984). "A Script-Theoretic Analysis of Industrial Purchasing Behavior", Journal of Marketing, vol. 48, no. 4, fall, p. 22-32..

Leigh, Thomas W. and Arno Rethans (1984). "Consumer Scripts for Insurance Salesperson Behaviors in Sales Encounters", in Personal Selling: Theory, Research and Practice, Jacob Jacoby and Samuel Craig, eds. Lexington, MA.: D. C. Heath, p. 223-236.

Leigh, Thomas W. and Arno J. Rethans (1985). "User Participation and Influence in Industrial Buying", Journal of Purchasing and Materials Management, Vol. 21, No. 2, Summer, p. 7-13.

Maister, David H. (1985). "The Psychology of Waiting Lines", The Service Encounter, J. A. Czepiel, M. R. Solomon, and C. F. Surprenant (eds.). D. C. Heath and Company.

Schank, Roger C. and R. P. Abelson (1977). Scripts, Plans, Goals and Understanding, Hillsdale, N.J.: Lawrence Erlbaum.

Schurr, Paul H. and Bobby J. Calder (1986). "Psychological Effects of Restaurant Meetings on Industrial Buyers", Journal of Marketing, Vol. 50, No. 1, January, p. 87-97.

Shostack, G. Lynn (1987). "Service Positioning Through Structural Change", Journal of Marketing, Vol. 51, No. 1, January, P.34-43.

Smith, Ruthan and Michael J. Houston (1985). "A Psychometric Assessment of Measures of Scripts in Consumer Memory", Journal of Consumer Research, Vol. 12, No. 2, p. 214-224.

Upah, Gregory D. and James W. Fulton (1985). "Situation Creation in Service Marketing", The Service Encounter, J. A. Czepiel, M. R. Solomon, and C. F. Surprenant (eds.). D. C. Heath and Company.

Wener, Richard E. (1985). "The Environmental Psychology of Service Encounters", The Service Encounter, J. A. Czepiel, M. R. Solomon, and C. F. Surprenant (eds.). D. C. Heath and Company.

355

THE EFFECTS OF SIZE AND STRATEGY ON PERFORMANCE IN THE AIR EXPRESS SERVICE INDUSTRY

V. Sriram, Hofstra University
Howard Shapiro, Hofstra University

ABSTRACT

This study investigated the relationships between size and profitability and strategy and profitability in a service industry. Data was collected on asset size and performance (ROA) for the five major companies in the air express service industry. An analysis of the data indicated support for the V-shaped relationship between size and profitability. It was also found that firms pursuing one of Porter's (1980) three generic strategies outperformed those that did not. Implications for pricing and product differentiation strategies were discussed.

INTRODUCTION

Finding ways to increase profitability has always been one of the more pressing concerns of corporate executives worldwide. While cost cutting and price increases have been strategies that have been almost always successful in this quest, there are definite limits to their viability as sustainable long-term strategies.

There has been much research that has investigated the effects of size on profitability. The report of the Profit Impact of Management Strategies (PIMS) project by Buzzell et. al. (1975) seemed to provide a long-term strategic direction to improve profitability. This showed a strong, positive relationship between return on investment (ROI) and market share for the companies studied (Buzzell and Gale, 1987). In some situations they reported that a 10% increase in market share is associated with a difference of 5% in pretax ROI. The study also showed that businesses with market shares above 40% earned an average ROI three times that of those with shares under 10%. These results seemed to suggest that small companies faced a relatively low-profit future and medium sized companies needed to make costly investments in marketing and other areas in an attempt to gain market share and thereby show more favorable rates of return.

356

Large companies (ones with high market shares) were thought to be more profitable as a result of: economies of scale and the company's position on the experience curve; the company's market power and the resulting ability to demand lower prices from suppliers; the ability to command higher prices and better placement for their products as a result of brand loyalty from heavy advertising; and the quality of management of the company (Jacobson and Aaker, 1985). This perhaps explains the important role market share plays in the strategic planning of companies like Proctor & Gamble and General Electric. Kotler (1984) reports that GE has decided to withdraw from those markets where it is not at least number one or two.

Other studies seemed to indicate that a firm's goal should not be to maximize market share, but rather to attain the optimal market share. The reason was that even though the PIMS study showed a remarkable link between market share and profitability, other factors auch as antitrust suits by competitors, investigations of anticompetitive activity by the government, being targeted by consumer and public interest groups, and constant and intense marketing attacks by market challengers in their thirst for market share, tend to make it costly to be the market leader and continue the quest for additional market share. Hence, even the market leader should operate in a niche since any departure, in either direction, from this optimal share will alter the company's long-range profitability or risk (or both) in an adverse way (Bloom and Kotler, 1975).

Some other studies have found that size, and the resulting high market share, is not a necessary condition for profitability. Studies have shown that, in certain situations, some companies have been able to enjoy long-run competitive success despite low market share positions. Indeed, outstanding performance, despite nonleadership positions, has been attained in mature industries by companies that were characterized by: creative market segmentation; cost efficient research and development expenditures; controlled growth; and strong leadership (Hall, 1980). The experiences of these companies demonstrates that market leadership is not always necessary to attain the lowest cost position. They also show that the lowest cost position is not required to achieve high margins (Woo and Cooper, 1982).

A company's overall strategy is considered to be another determinant of its profitability. Porter (1980) argued that there would be a relationship between a firm's profitability and its strategy. He suggested that firms' profitability would be influenced by their choices in terms of which of three generic strategies they select in their attempt to outperform their competition. The first, overall cost leadership, emphasizes low cost relative to competitors. The second strategy,

357

differentiation, is one where the firm creates a product or service that is seen as being unique and different from competition, thus allowing it to charge higher than average prices. The third, focus, is one in which the firm concentrates on a particular group of customers, geographic areas, or product lines. Porter suggested that firms following one of these three strategies would outperform those "stuck in the middle" because the latter class of firms, by not following one of the three generic strategies, are "almost guaranteed low profitability" (Porter, 1980, p. 41).

Roach (1981) looked at the relationship between size and profitability and came to conclusions somewhat similar to Porter's (1980) in that he proposed the relationship between the two to be V-shaped i.e. small and large firms would be highly profitable but those trapped in "No Man's Land" (medium-sized firms) would not. This is because large firms achieve cost advantages and high market shares due to economies of scale. Small competitors reap high profits by developing specialized production, marketing, and distribution approaches for narrower segments of business. Medium-sized firms are too large to benefit from specialized segments and not large enough to benefit from scale economies. They are therefore "stuck in the middle". Buzzell (1984) found a similar V-shaped relationship between the vertical integration strategy and profitability (ROI) among firms in the chemical industry.

James, Planchon, Allen, Griffin, Hooper, Sharp, Whitt, and Soltys (1987) found weak empirical support for the "V-theory" in their investigation of three industries. Interestingly, they found that small companies that engaged in niching strategies had a much better growth and ROI improvement record than either the large or the medium-sized companies. In general, the large companies performed no worse than the medium-sized companies. It would appear that this evidence runs counter to the PIMS results which indicated the presence of a positive correlation between size (market share) and profitability.

This paper investigates the relationship between size, strategy, and profitability for the major firms in the air express service industry. Since service industries have received limited attention in the study of these relationships, this paper tries to determine whether the PIMS model's linear relationship or the "V-theory" more accurately describes the relationship between size and profitability in this industry. The relationship between Porter's three generic strategies and profitability is also examined.

SAMPLE AND DATA

A convenience sample of five major air express companies was examined over the five year period 1982-86. These five companies, Federal Express, UPS, Emery Air Freight, Purolator Courier, and Airborne Express, collectively account for approximately 90% of the total market share. This industry was chosen specifically to enable the investigation of size-profitability and strategy-profitability relationships in the service sector.

There are indications that this industry is in its maturity stage in the U.S., all in a relatively short time-span. Federal Express, founded in 1972, was the pioneer. Though it continues to be the market leader, it is beginning to face increasing competition from the likes of UPS which is a relative newcomer in the overnight delivery business. With an estimated 95% of U.S. cities and towns currently being served, the market is threatened with overcapacity and, as a result, has become very price-competitive. The increased availability and sophistication of facsimile and electronic mail machines poses another very serious threat to air courier services. So, in many ways, this is an industry where a shakeout may result in few survivors.
For the purpose of this study, size was determined by the value of the asset base for each company and profitability by return on assets (ROA). Strategy was defined by a subjective assessment of which of the three generic strategies these firms followed. The five-year time horizon was chosen to allow an assessment of trends rather than focus on a given point in time. The mean values over this five-year period are also provided. This is consistent with Buzzell and Gale's (1987) use of a 4-year period average to measure profitability.

RESULTS

Size and Profitability

As mentioned earlier, the increasing competition both from within the industry and from new technologies has created a great deal of price competition and, as a result, cost cutting. Since a major portion of the costs are fixed (aircraft, vans and trucks, storage and sorting centers etc.), the battle for market share is intense as companies attempt to gain economies of scale. Size is therefore expected to be a major determinant of profitability. This search for market share and size was a big reason behind Emery's 1987 acquisition of Purolator, since their combined size would allow them to be more aggressive in their pricing strategies.

As can be seen from Table 1, UPS is by far the largest in terms of total assets, with Federal Express second. This comes as no surprise because even though UPS is new to the overnight delivery business, it has been a very successful company in the door-to-door delivery of packages for many years, with an established distribution network. As a result, these size figures may be somewhat misleading because not all these assets are dedicated to the overnight delivery business.

The figures indicate that the largest company (UPS) and the smallest (Airborne) had the highest profitability in terms of return on assets. The other three showed that a decrease in size was accompanied by a decline in ROA. This data seems to provide very strong support for the V-shaped curve in that the small and large firms were much more profitable than the medium sized ones. Interestingly, taken by themselves, the three medium sized firms provide support for the PIMS finding of a linear relationship between size and profitability. The data also suggests that, with the exception of Airborne, in an industry characterized by large fixed costs, market share and size are desirable because they allow huge economies of scale which in turn enhances profitability.

TABLE 1

Size and Profitability

COMPANY	MEAN SIZE	MEAN % ROA
UPS	3376	15.44
FEDERAL EXPRESS	1485	7.42
PUROLATOR	403	6.77
EMERY	378	5.90
AIRBORNE	57	15.44

Where:

1) Mean size is mean value of assets measured in millions of dollars for the period 1982-86.
2) Mean % ROA is for the period 1982-86 except for Purolator which is for 1982-1984 and Emery which is for 1982-85.

Sources: Annual Reports, Standard & Poor's.

Strategy and Profitability

Porter (1980) argues that high relative market share and favorable access to information are characteristic of the firm pursuing the low cost strategy. Its size (it is about three times the size of Federal Express in revenues), its presence in all 50 states, its fleet of over 100 planes and its gigantic hub in Louisville, KY allows UPS to pursue the low cost strategy. This strategy has been largely responsible for the company's leap to second place in market share in the overnight delivery business and a growth in revenue in this industry from near zero to an estimated $1.3 billion annually in five years (Wall Street Journal, 1988). Federal Express has been the pioneer and innovator in the industry. With its vast array of overnight services, continuous package tracking system, money-back guarantee for delayed deliveries, PartsBank inventory management system and the like, Federal Express has undoubtedly pursued a strategy of differentiation. While it has had to cut its prices in response to price cutting by competitors, it attempts to use its reputation for dependability to differentiate itself and thereby build market share and revenue. Airborne and Purolator are companies that have employed a focus strategy. Airborne specializes in door-to-door, next-morning delivery of documents and packages, typically under 100 pounds. It also hadles larger packages, but on a non-express basis. Purolator also specializes in small package express delivery on a next-day or otherwise time-sensitive schedule. Emery provides both domestic and international cargo service of all sizes and weights. The company provides a variety of overnight, destination, and pricing alternatives for a broad range of shipments, from letters and envelopes to heavyweight cargo. Other than air freight, it is also in marine freight forwarding, customs brokerage, and shipper's risk reinsurance through its subsidiary, Blue Ribbon Insurance. All these activities seem to suggest that as an air express competitor, the company is not pursuing any one of the three generic strategies. It therefore seems that Emery is "stuck in the middle".

The summary of the strategies followed by the different companies, and their profitability is presented in Table 2. The data suggests that companies following one of the three generic strategies of low cost, differentiation, and focus, outperform the one that is "stuck in the middle". It also seems that low cost and focus strategies have been the most profitable. While Purolator did not fare quite as well depite its pursuit of a focus strategy, its acquisition by Emery in 1987 and its losses in the preceding 2 years may be an indication of other problems. It possible that both these strategies are successful because they allow them to serve their customer the best. Large firms

TABLE 2

Strategy and Profitability

COMPANY	STRATEGY	MEAN % ROA
UPS	Low Cost	15.44
FEDERAL EXPRESS	Differentiation	7.42
PUROLATOR	Focus	6.77
EMERY	Stuck-in-the-Middle	5.90
AIRBORNE	Focus	15.44

Where:

1) % ROA is for the period 1982-86 except for Purolator
   which is for 1982-84 and Emery which is for 1982-85.

Source: Annual Reports, Standard & Poor's.

pursuing the low cost strategy, with extensive distribution and
delivery networks, provide high levels of service. Companies that
focus, on the other hand, spend their resources wisely by only
pursuing a fraction of the market. The others may be losing
because they are attempting to reach large markets but their
limited resources cause them to be spread too thin. Federal
Express, for instance, continues to be the market leader in share
and reputation despite lower ROA. This may well be a temporary
artifact of its overseas expansion and the price war it is
currently waging. Once the industry stabilizes after the present
jockeying for market share, it is possible that Federal Express
will increase its ROA as a result of its share leadership and
proven differentiation.

CONCLUSIONS

The data suggests the presence of a V-shaped relationship between
size and profitability in that the smallest and the largest firms
are more profitable than the medium sized ones. However, an
analysis of the four largest firms clearly indicates the benefits
of size in an industry characterized by high fixed costs. This
implies that in their thirst for market share and economies of
scale in a maturing industry, firms will continue to cut costs
and wage potentially costly price wars. While one of the
competitors has been acquired by another, a shakeout is still
likely, with the small firms the most vulnerable.

362

The data also suggested that firms that pursued one of the three generic competitive strategies would be more profitable than those that didn't. While low cost and focus strategies were the most successful, it is possible that the differentiation strategy will also be in the long-run but is not currently, because of the turbulent nature of the industry. After the industry prices and competition stabilize, the benefits of a differentiation strategy may be more directly felt on profitability as the firms with a demonstrated superiority are able to command above-average prices. While these observations should be treated with caution as a result of the somewhat subjective determination of various companies' strategies, the results have important implications for organizational strategists.

For a small firm to survive and succeed if the industry becomes more concentrated, and indeed Airborne Express has done so up to now, the establishment of a sustainable product differentiation is crucial. If this were done, it would serve as a buffer as the larger companies used price-cutting tactics to gain share and improve profitability through scale economies. In an industry where these economies are so vital, serving a market niche with a superior product may be the only way to sustain higher-than-average prices which are necessary to maintain profitability in the absence of economies of scale. The data in this study confirms the applicability, in a service industry, of some of the findings of the research that studied the relationship between size, strategy, and profitability.

REFERENCES

Bloom, Paul N. and P. Kotler (1975), "Strategies for High Market-Share Companies," Harvard Business Review, 63 (Nov-Dec): 63-70.

Buzzell, Robert D., B.T. Gale, and Ralph B.M. Sultan (1975), "Market Share- A Key to Profitability," Harvard Business Review, 53 (Jan-Dec): 97-106.

--------- (1984) "Vertical Integration-- Does it Increase Profits in Chemicals," Chemical Strategies, Vol. 2, 20-32.

--------- and Bradley T. Gale (1987) The PIMS Principles, The Free Press, New York.

Hall, William K. (1980), "Survival Strategies in a Hostile Environment," Harvard Business Review, (Sep-Oct): 75-83.

Jacobson, Robert and D.A. Aaker (1985), "Is Market Share All That

Its Cracked Up to Be?", Journal of Marketing, 49 (Fall): 11-22.

James, William, John Planchon, Myles Allen, Howard Criffin, Ross Hooper, Joe Sharp, V.J. Whitt and Theresa Soltys (1987), "Size and Returns: An Empirical Investigation," in Robert Parsons and John Saber (eds.) 1987 proceedings of the Decision Sciences Institute, p. 459-461.

Kotler, Philip, (1984), Marketing Management: Analysis, Planning, and Control, Prentice-Hall, Englewood Cliffs, New Jersey.

Porter, Michael (1980), Competitive Strategies: Techniques for Analysing Industries and Competitors, New York, Free Press.

Roach, John D.C. (1981), "From Strategic Planning to Strategic Performance: Closing the Achievement Gap," in Outlook, New York, Booz Allen & Hamilton, p. 17-29.

Woo, Carolyn Y. and Arnold C. Cooper (1982), "The Surprising Case for Low Market-Share," Harvard Business Review, 60 (Nov-Dec): 106-113.

Wall Street Journal, January 8, 1988, p. 1.

AUTHOR INDEX

AUTHOR INDEX

(Continued)

AUTHOR INDEX

(Continued)

Printed by Printforce, the Netherlands